Auschwitz, Poland, and the
Politics of Commemoration, 1945–1979

Ohio University Press Polish and Polish-American Studies Series

Series Editor: John J. Bukowczyk

Framing the Polish Home: Postwar Cultural Constructions of Hearth, Nation, and Self, edited by Bożena Shallcross

Traitors and True Poles: Narrating a Polish-American Identity, 1880–1939, by Karen Majewski

Auschwitz, Poland, and the Politics of Commemoration, 1945–1979, by Jonathan Huener

The Exile Mission: The Polish Political Diaspora and Polish-Americans, 1939– 1956,* by Anna D. Jaroszyńska-Kirchmann

*forthcoming

Auschwitz, Poland, and the Politics of Commemoration, 1945–1979

Jonathan Huener

OHIO UNIVERSITY PRESS
ATHENS

Ohio University Press, Athens, Ohio 45701
© 2003 by Ohio University Press

Printed in the United States of America

Ohio University Press books are printed on acid-free paper ♾

11 10 09 08 07 06 05 04 03   5 4 3 2 1

Cover photograph: Birkenau, sector BII, from the tower of the camp's main gate, May 1945. APMO Nr. Neg. 21 366/3.
All photographs reproduced by courtesy of the State Museum Auschwitz-Birkenau in Oświęcim.

Library of Congress Cataloging-in-Publication Data

Huener, Jonathan.
    Auschwitz, Poland, and the politics of commemoration, 1945–1979 / Jonathan Huener.
        p. cm. — (Ohio University Press Polish and Polish-American series)
    Includes bibliographical references and index.
    ISBN 0-8214-1506-9 (cloth : alk. paper) — ISBN 0-8214-1507-7 (paper : alk. paper)
        1. Auschwitz (Concentration camp). 2. Oświęcim (Poland)—History. 3. Oświęcim (Poland)—Historiography. 4. Holocaust, Jewish (1939–1945)—Poland. 5. Holocaust memorials—Poland. 6. Memory—Political aspects—Poland. 7. Memory—Political aspects—Germany. I. Title. II. Series.

D805.5A96H84 2003
940.53'1853858—dc21

                                                                            2003051083

Publication of books in the Polish and Polish-American Studies Series has been made possible in part by the generous support of the following organizations:

Polish American Historical Association, Orchard Lake, Michigan

Stanislaus A. Blejwas Endowed Chair in Polish and Polish American Studies, Central Connecticut State University, New Britain, Connecticut

St. Mary's College, Orchard Lake, Michigan

The Polish Institute of Arts and Sciences of America, Inc., New York, New York

Additional support for this book has been provided by the following:

The Center for Holocaust Studies at the University of Vermont

University of Vermont College of Art and Sciences Dean's Fund for Faculty Development

University of Vermont Department of History Nelson Grant

Contents

List of Illustrations ix

Series Editor's Preface xi

Preface xiii

Acknowledgments xxiii

Abbreviations xxv

Guide to Pronunciation xxvii

INTRODUCTION
The Stakes and Terms of Memory at Auschwitz 1

1. Poland and Auschwitz, 1945–1947 32

2. From Liberation to Memorialization:
   The Transformation of the Auschwitz Site, 1945–1947 59

3. Auschwitz as a Cold-War Theater, 1947–1954 79

4. The Restoration of a Commemorative Idiom, 1954 and Beyond 108

5. The Internationalization of the Auschwitz Site 145

6. The Power and Limits of a Commemorative Idiom:
   John Paul II at the "Golgotha of Our Age" 185

EPILOGUE
Poland and Auschwitz in the 1980s 227

Notes 247

Bibliography 293

Index 317

Illustrations

MAPS

Map 1. Auschwitz environs, summer 1944   xxviii

Map 2. Auschwitz I Camp, 1944   6

Map 3. Auschwitz II (Birkenau) Camp, summer 1944   7

PHOTOGRAPHS

Following page 144:

1. The main gate of the base camp, Auschwitz I, spring 1945
2. The main street of Auschwitz I, looking east, spring 1945
3. Birkenau, the road between sectors BI and BII, spring 1945
4. Birkenau, human remains near Crematorium V, spring 1945
5. Birkenau, members of the Commission for the Investigation of German Crimes at Auschwitz
6. Auschwitz I, roof of Crematorium I, May 1945
7. The first exhibition at the State Museum at Auschwitz, in the cellar of Block 4 of Auschwitz I
8. A crowd gathered in Auschwitz I for the dedication ceremonies of the State Museum, 14 June 1947
9. Józef Cyrankiewicz speaking at the museum's dedication ceremonies, 14 June 1947
10. A Roman Catholic mass held in the courtyard between Blocks 10 and 11 of Auschwitz I, 14 June 1947
11. Birkenau, members of the museum's protective guard at the ruins of a crematorium, 1948
12. Birkenau, sector BIIe, former prisoners and members of the museum staff on a break from searching for evidence, 1949
13. An exhibition hall displaying prostheses, from the early 1950s
14. Suitcases on display in the museum, from a pre-1955 exhibit
15. A view of a section of the "Jewish Hall" of a pre-1955 exhibition
16. A memorial in the cellar of Block 4, Auschwitz I, from a pre-1955 exhibition
17–19. Three exhibition panels from the era of Polish Stalinism

20. Birkenau, monument to the victims of Auschwitz between the ruins of Crematoria II and III, April 1955
21. A plaster model of Gas Chamber and Crematorium II, from the 1955 exhibition
22. Women's hair on display in Block 4 of Auschwitz I, from the 1955 exhibition
23. Auschwitz I, Block 7: A reconstruction of a masonry barracks in the Birkenau Women's Camp, from the 1955 exhibition
24. A room in the "New Laundry" emphasizing international cooperation, from the 1955 exhibition
25. Participants in a motorcycle rally that included a ceremonial visit to Auschwitz and Birkenau
26. On the twentieth anniversary of the liberation, a scout and a former prisoner standing at attention next to the "Wall of Death" in the courtyard of Block 11
27. A crowd at Birkenau for the unveiling of the Monument to the Victims of Fascism, April 1967
28. The Monument to the Victims of Fascism in Birkenau, April 1967
29. Inscription at the entrance to the 1968 exhibition on the "Martyrology and Struggle of the Jews"
30. Panels from the 1968 exhibition on the "Martyrology and Struggle of the Jews"
31. The final room in the 1968 exhibit on the "Martyrology and Struggle of the Jews"
32. Pope John Paul II receiving former prisoners at the papal mass at Birkenau, 7 June 1979
33. The former *Theatergebäude* and former Carmelite Convent at Auschwitz I
34. Aerial photograph of Auschwitz I, 1996
35. Aerial photograph of Birkenau, 1996

Series Editor's Preface

BEFORE THE SECOND WORLD WAR, Poland was home to a large and thriving Jewish community. By the end of the war, the Nazis had destroyed most of the country's Jewish population while murdering large numbers of Christian Poles as well. Poland had become a different place, its population decimated, its boundaries changed. Polish "liberation," meanwhile, had left the country a Soviet satellite.

Poland's tangled prewar and wartime history complicated the twin postwar tasks of Polish reconstruction and the commemoration of the country's huge wartime losses. The epicenter of Poland's wartime catastrophe, the Nazi concentration camp complex at Auschwitz-Birkenau, where both ethnic Poles and Jews had perished, symbolized the horror of Nazism and thus became the focal point for preserving wartime memory. But commemoration proved neither an apolitical nor a neutral act. Poles would bend the memorial site at Auschwitz to the purpose of constructing postwar Polish identity and nationhood. At Auschwitz, the country also would confront what has loomed as perhaps the greatest challenge to the Poles' national project, the problem—and tragedy—of ethnic Polish-Jewish relations.

Auschwitz, Poland, and the Politics of Commemoration, 1945–1979, by University of Vermont historian Jonathan Huener, offers a balanced, nuanced treatment of this particularly difficult chapter of modern Polish history. A judicious work marked by meticulous research, disturbing descriptions, and keen analysis, Huener's study lays bare the thinking of the politicians, officials, and museum curators who planned and executed the Auschwitz memorial during the postwar period, when the site successively was transformed, contested, and reinterpreted. In its deftness, nuance, and subtlety, Jonathan Huener's book comes to us as a model scholarly work that makes an outstanding contribution to the historical literature not only in Polish studies and Jewish studies, but also in the cultural studies field.

Auschwitz, Poland, and the Politics of Commemoration, 1945–1979 is the third volume in the new Ohio University Press Polish and Polish-American Studies Series. The series revisits the historical and contemporary experience of one of America's largest European ethnic groups and the history of a European homeland that has played a disproportionately important role in twentieth-century world affairs. The series publishes innovative monographs and more general works that investigate under- or unexplored topics or themes or that offer new, critical, revisionist, or comparative perspectives in Polish and Polish-American studies. Interdisciplinary or multidisciplinary in profile, the series seeks manuscripts on Polish immigration and ethnic communities, the country of origin, and its various peoples in history, anthropology, cultural studies, political economy, current politics, and related fields.

Publication of the Ohio University Press Polish and Polish-American Studies Series marks a milestone in the maturation of the Polish studies field and stands as a fitting tribute to the scholars and organizations whose efforts have brought it to fruition. Supported by a series advisory board of accomplished Polonists and Polish-Americanists, the Polish and Polish-American Studies Series has been made possible through generous financial assistance from the Polish American Historical Association, the Polish Institute of Arts and Sciences of America, the Stanislaus A. Blejwas Endowed Chair in Polish and Polish American Studies at Central Connecticut State University, and St. Mary's College and through institutional support from Wayne State University and Ohio University Press. Publication of this particular series volume also has been aided by support from the Center for Holocaust Studies at the University of Vermont, the University of Vermont College of Arts and Sciences Dean's Fund for Faculty Development, and a University of Vermont Department of History Nelson Grant. As an ambitious new undertaking, the series meanwhile has benefited from the warm encouragement of a number of persons, including Gillian Berchowitz, M. B. B. Biskupski, the late Stanislaus A. Blejwas, Thomas Gladsky, Thaddeus Gromada, Donald Pienkos, James S. Pula, David Sanders, and Thaddeus Radzilowski. The moral and material support from all of these institutions and individuals is gratefully acknowledged.

John J. Bukowczyk

Preface

ON 30 JANUARY 1945, three days after the liberation of Auschwitz by Soviet troops, Tadeusz Chowaniec, a physician from the nearby town of Oświęcim visited the grounds of the camp complex. Shocked by the conditions in the liberated camp, he offered an account of his impressions that day, describing a landscape of burning barracks and storehouses, smoldering pyres, and scattered corpses. Reflecting on the incomprehensibility of what he saw, the physician wrote: "Humanity must see this scene, for in a few years, one will no longer believe what we witness here today. The sharpness of today's image will be blurred. What should one do to prevent this?"[1] A few hundred saw the scene in those first days after the liberation. Millions saw it in the decades to follow—in historical monographs and memoirs, on film, and, of course, at the Auschwitz site itself. Contrary to the author's fears, humanity believed what he had witnessed that day, for there were too many survivors' accounts, too many documents and post-liberation investigative reports, and too much physical evidence remaining on the Auschwitz grounds for any serious scholar or observer to doubt the sharpness of his vision or the truth of his testimony.

Since 1945 the suffering, destruction, and carnage that was Auschwitz have remained in the collective memory of Poles, Jews, and people around the world. But despite the hopes of Tadeusz Chowaniec, the image of 30 January 1945 has not been fixed. Instead, postwar images of Auschwitz and its history necessarily and inevitably have been blurred—blurred by the diverse and occasionally conflicting memories of former prisoners, blurred by the diverse and often competing narratives of postwar histories of the camp complex, blurred and even distorted by the cultural imperatives and political exigencies of postwar Polish society and politics. This is a history of those postwar images as they were manifested at the Auschwitz site during the years of the Polish People's Republic. These images—some reasonably accurate, and others distorted—I consider not only against the backdrop of the history of the camp while it was in operation, but also in the context of postwar Polish history and, not least, against the backdrop of Jewish-Polish and Polish-German relations. In short, this is a biography of post-liberation

Auschwitz. It is not limited to an administrative history of the site, a description of its memorial landscape, or a chronicle of the commemorative events that took place there. Instead, it is an analysis of the configurations and reconfigurations of memory at Auschwitz that addresses both the motivations for and, as I will emphasize, the barriers against change in the site's landscape and commemorative agenda.

My use of the term "memory" in relation to Auschwitz refers not to the memory of the individual, but to an aggregate of individual memories or, as was often the case at the Auschwitz memorial site, an officially sanctioned accounting of the past that came to have legitimate or even mythic status. As the introduction will make clear, this analysis is concerned with "collective" memory and memories as revealed by and manifested in the memorial site's landscape, exhibitions, and commemorative events. This collective memory has not arisen ex nihilo, nor have its manifestations always been disingenuous or factitious, for Auschwitz memory is necessarily based—albeit to varying degrees—in the history of the camp. Yet Auschwitz memory was constructed, maintained, and modified within a political and cultural framework, resulting in the emergence of three dominant modes of collective memory at the memorial site. First, Auschwitz was presented and groomed as a site of Polish national martyrdom. Second, the plight and struggle of the political prisoner, often styled as a socialist hero or resistance fighter, was elevated over the fate of the Jewish victim of genocide at Auschwitz. Third, the memorial site, through its exhibitions and commemorative events, was often used by the Polish state and its representatives to gain political currency and at times was even instrumentalized as a stage for political propaganda. Although durable, this framework was both bolstered and, at times, shaken by external political considerations, by the influence of prisoner groups in Poland and abroad, and even by the encroachment of historical fact.

The Auschwitz complex was a focal point for the traumatic history of wartime Poland. It was a site of Germany's most heinous crimes in occupied Poland—most prominently, the annihilation of approximately one million Jews, but also the incarceration and murder of Sinti and Roma (Gypsies), Soviet prisoners of war, Polish political prisoners, and prisoners of more than a dozen other nationalities. In this study I hope to demonstrate that Auschwitz lies not only at the intersection of monumental historical events, but also at the intersection of a variety of conflicting and competing collective memories, each with its own rituals, emphases, and interpretations of the camp's history. As these lines of memory have converged on Auschwitz throughout the postwar years, the site has functioned as an arena for public education, commemoration, and conflict. For more than fifty years, visitors to that arena have assumed the multiple roles of spectator, participant, and combatant. They have come to learn, to pray, to honor both the murdered victim and the survivor, and to demonstrate at a site that since 1947 has been institutionalized as a charge of the Polish government, bearing the name "State Museum Oświęcim-Brzezinka" or "State Museum Auschwitz-Birkenau."[2]

The State Museum that is postwar Auschwitz does not lend itself to simple definition and description, for it has always fulfilled a variety of functions. It is, of course, the site of National Socialism's largest concentration camp and extermination center, and it is therefore to be expected that for many, Auschwitz is a cemetery—the final resting place for the bones and ashes of more than a million victims. It is a site of reverence and remembrance. Yet the memorial site does not resemble a cemetery in the traditional sense. There are few grave markers, and the identity of the victims, to the extent that it is known, is preserved not in marble or granite, but in archival documents. Nor has the site received the care and protection that one might associate with a cemetery. Auschwitz II, or Birkenau, arguably the world's largest Jewish burial ground, has suffered from decades of neglect, its spacious fields marked by waist high grasses, several dozen dilapidated buildings and guard towers, and a large abstract monument at the end of a railroad spur. The *Stammlager*, or base camp, by contrast, has been maintained as a museum, research institution, and tourist center. Since 1946 it has served as the pedagogical and commemorative center of the memorial complex. Nonetheless, it is a cemetery that bears the marks of its origins. As at many cemeteries, flowers and stones are occasionally left behind by visitors to Auschwitz I and Birkenau, but they are not left at individual grave sites, for there are none. Instead, they are usually placed at the former sites of destruction—a torture cell, an execution wall, or the ruins of gas chambers and crematoria. In some cases the site of an Auschwitz victim's death can be assumed or determined, but the final resting place of a victim's remains cannot.

Postwar Auschwitz is not only a cemetery, but also, as its official name suggests, a museum. The State Museum Auschwitz-Birkenau employs tour guides and historians; it sells books and postcards; it conducts research; it attempts to conserve the artifacts of the past; and it houses extensive exhibitions for the purpose of documenting the history of the camp and educating the visiting public.

Auschwitz is also an open-air museum, for across the nearly 450-acre terrain of the base camp and Birkenau are scattered many of the structures of destruction—barracks, guard towers, administrative buildings, and even gas chambers—structures that functioned while the camp was still in operation. As a site of documentation and information, the State Museum has an important pedagogical and admonitory function. It therefore also has the power to influence the visiting public's understanding of the camp's history and the power to shape, to varying degrees, that public's memory of Auschwitz.

Not least, Auschwitz is also an arena of public commemorative ritual. For more than fifty years its monuments, structures, and open spaces have attracted pilgrims and politicians, mourners, and participants in the recurrent *manifestacja,* or government-sponsored demonstration. The Catholic devout as well as the communist activist have made Auschwitz the locus of public ritual, at times even exploiting the site by linking its history to a prevailing ideology or by evoking one commemorative message and, by extension, one memorial narrative at the expense of another. Thus in some cases, the votive and political rituals cultivated at Auschwitz in the postwar era were undertaken in an exclusionary manner, understating or even excluding the memory of nearly a million Jews killed at Auschwitz—some 90 percent of the camp's victims.

Privileging the memory of one victim group or groups is unsettling or even offensive, but it is hardly inexplicable, given the diverse lines of memory that have converged at the Auschwitz site. Memory at Auschwitz has never been fixed, for it has been subject to the vicissitudes of Polish society and politics as well as international political events. Changes in Warsaw's regimes, the waning and resurgence of anti-Semitism in postwar Poland, growing understanding of the Shoah and the Jewish past at the Auschwitz camp, and even the cold war or events in the Middle East have influenced the representation and recollection of history at Auschwitz.

All this should remind us that no single postwar image of the camp and its history can be fixed in the memory of all and that any attempt to cultivate or enforce a single memorial narrative dishonors the memory of countless victims and survivors because, simply put, it distorts Auschwitz history. Indeed, the diversity of memorial narratives of Auschwitz that have proliferated in recent years is the result of that history—a history that defies quick categorization, easy generalization, and the "master" historical narrative. With its three main camps and forty auxiliary camps scattered throughout the region, the Auschwitz complex served the SS, Reich Security Main Office (RSHA), and German industry in a variety of ways: it was a concentration camp, it provided slave labor for German industry, and it became the largest of the Nazi killing centers for European Jews. Deportees from nearly every European country were incarcerated, exploited, enslaved, and murdered at the complex, and the variety of competing and conflicting memories of Auschwitz has grown out of the diverse histories and experiences of prisoners. Moreover, historiographical traditions and commemorative practices, both in Poland and elsewhere, have produced a variety of prisoner proto-types—the patriotic Polish martyr, the conspiring and internationalist communist, or the Jewish victim of the gas chamber, to name only a few. There were, of course, prisoners such as these at Auschwitz, but no single prisoner-type or prisoner experience was representative of all Auschwitz internees.

The representation and uses of history at the Auschwitz site during the years of the Polish People's Republic are the central themes of this book. It accounts for the official—and some unofficial—historical emplotments and narratives at the State Museum, considering all the while their social and political contexts. Recognizing that all narratives are, to a greater or lesser extent, culturally and politically inflected, it does not claim to establish a fixed and finite historical standard against which all forms of commemoration at Auschwitz are measured. Nor does it propose an ideal commemorative model for the memorial site and museum. But this work does recognize a responsibility to evaluate the public manifestations of memory at Auschwitz in relation to the history of the camp. For this reason, the introduction that follows offers the reader, for the purpose of orientation, a compendium of the camp's history in addition to a theoretical and historiographical context for the work as a whole.

Chapter 1 then sets the stage for subsequent sections through a discussion of the ways early postwar Poland was acquainted with the history of the camp, examining and describing the main events and cultural currents reflecting and shaping Polish perceptions of Auschwitz in these first years of wartime commemoration. It therefore includes a discussion of the concept of "martyrology" in early postwar Poland—a cultural and ideological notion rooted in many generations of Polish history that profoundly affected both the elevation of Auschwitz in postwar memorialization and the iconographic and pedagogical goals of those responsible for the development and maintenance of the site.

The second chapter offers an account of the transformation of Auschwitz from liberated camp to museum in the years 1945–47. This includes a discussion of the challenging legal, political, and material conditions at the site, as well as the first efforts to create a museum exhibition. In addition, this chapter addresses the emergence of two distinct loci memoriae, or places of memory, at Auschwitz. The grounds of the base camp, Auschwitz I, came to serve as the maintained "museum" portion of the site, while the massive terrain of Auschwitz II, or Birkenau, the largest single site for the extermination of European Jews, suffered neglect and even plunder.

Chapter 3 focuses on the Auschwitz site in the years 1947–54. This was the most difficult period in the history of the museum, for shortly after the official dedication of the site, the ideological imperatives of Stalinism began to color and determine the site's representation of the past. Thus, it was in this period that international and domestic political considerations had their most pervasive influence on the outward appearance of the site and its exhibitions. "Hitlerites" became "fascists," the Shoah was further neglected although not actively excluded from the memorial landscape, employees and exhibitions at the museum were subjected to strict state censorship and review, while the Second World War, as well as postwar international tensions, were represented at the site as struggles between Western imperialist and Soviet-led socialist camps. Not surprisingly, this period also saw the most extreme attempts to make commemorative rituals at Auschwitz conform to prevailing political ideology, recalling and illustrating the claim of the French scholar of collective memory, Maurice Halbwachs, that institutionalized memory selects those elements of the past that best fit present needs. The years 1947–54 thus provide the most vivid illustrations of the tractability of memory at Auschwitz, as the grounds of the former camp were instrumentalized almost to the extreme of the State Museum's total effacement. Yet this uncertain period also saw the emergence of a memorial "vernacular" in defense of the site.

In the early 1950s it appeared that the State Museum at Auschwitz was dying a slow death, but changes implemented at the site beginning in the winter of 1954–55, reflecting the beginning of the post-Stalin "thaw," breathed new life into the institution. Cold-war tensions had subsided somewhat, Poland and the two German states were becoming settled in their respective blocs, and the memory work at Auschwitz had ceased to be an ideological instigator. Numerous administrative changes were undertaken at the site, the most important of which was the construction of a new exhibition. The fourth chapter therefore analyzes the reasons for these changes, locates them in the context of Polish cultural policy in the early Gomułka era, and proceeds to a detailed analysis of the 1955 exhibition (the vast majority of which is still in use), offering the reader a "visit" to the memorial site.

Although in some respects the 1955 exhibition at Auschwitz symbolized an iconographic and pedagogic return to a "Polish-national" idiom after the Stalinist internationalism of the preceding years, the changes implemented at the site paved the way for increased international involvement in the commemorative landscape and activities at Auschwitz in the second half of the 1950s and throughout the 1960s. This new "internationalization" of the site—the focus of chapter 5—reflected an increase in the museum's autonomy and added several new "plots" to the Auschwitz story, most prominently, the reinsertion of the Shoah into the iconography and vocabulary of the memorial site. Furthermore, the site's internationalization illustrated the ways in which its landscape and meaning could be influenced by events well beyond Poland's borders.

First among the new international influences at the memorial site was the activism of the newly formed International Auschwitz Committee (IAC), an organization for former prisoners of the camp from across Europe. Not only did the IAC influence the landscape and commemorative ritual at Auschwitz; it also initiated a twelve-year effort to erect a massive international monument on the grounds of Birkenau. After a lengthy artistic competition and in spite of tremendous financial barriers, the monument was dedicated in 1967. The following year—more than twenty years after the liberation—the State Museum at Auschwitz opened its first exhibition devoted to the "Martyrology and Struggle of the Jews" in Block 27 of the base camp. This exhibition, although furthering the commemorative diversity at the site, also became a topic of controversy in Poland and abroad, for it was constructed and dedicated at the same time that relations between Poles and Jews were suffering from the repercussions of the Six-Day War and the institutionalized anti-Semitism of the so-called "anti-Zionist campaign." The exhibition was often closed over the next decade, its inaccessibility a further illustration of the continuing marginalization of Jewish victims at Auschwitz and the role of its museum as a register of domestic and international political concerns.

The 1970s were a relatively tranquil decade for the State Museum at Auschwitz, but as the final chapter explains, forces were underway that would compel the memorial site to respond to an ever-growing variety of commemorative constituencies and external pressures, both domestic and foreign. These forces would converge on the occasion of Pope John Paul II's visit to Auschwitz in 1979, a turning point in the history of the memorial site. This pilgrimage, on the one hand, marked the triumph of Polish-national (and Polish-Catholic) perceptions of Auschwitz and its legacy. On the other hand, the papal visit further democratized the commemorative space at Auschwitz, legitimized it as an arena for antiestablishment protest, and, in a sense, freed the site from the ideological strictures and politicized cant of previous decades. By "liberating" the memorial site in this way, the pope's visit was the first stage in the collapse of the memorial framework erected at Auschwitz over the previous thirty-five years and also signaled the advent of controversies and debates over Auschwitz that have been characteristic of the present era.

Foremost among these debates was the highly publicized Carmelite Convent controversy, which brought the problems of contested memory at Auschwitz—along with the burdens of Polish-Jewish relations—into the international public view. Although the controversy, which is addressed briefly in the epilogue, began in the mid-1980s, it belongs thematically to the current era of what some might designate the "postcommunist" memorial site. Heated international exchanges about Jewish, Polish, or international "proprietorship" over the site, the presence of religious symbols at Auschwitz, the use of the grounds and structures of the former camp complex for more "everyday" purposes, a memorial site and museum in full view of the international media—these are phenomena that we associate with the convent controversy, but they are no less characteristic of the site in the 1990s and today. For that reason, the convent controversy is an appropriate vehicle for problematizing the proliferation of memories, competing memorial agendas, and ideological struggles that have emerged in the last decade. Recent conflicts over Auschwitz have not been sudden and spontaneous eruptions of Jewish-Catholic tension or merely a manifestation of animosity between Poles and Jews; rather, they are a reflection and registration of diverse emplotments and historical misunderstandings associated with Auschwitz memory at the site since the 1940s. Thus, the arguments set forth in this study are relevant to the most recent history of the Auschwitz site, and the conclusions suggest both the need for and a path toward further investigation in the years ahead.

Have fifty years made such a difference? Walter Benjamin observed that the dead are not safe from politics,[3] and this has certainly held true at Auschwitz, more than half a century after the killing there ceased. Pedagogy and topography, modes of commemoration and reflection at the memorial site remain matters of controversy and debate. Ultimately, the postwar history of Auschwitz reveals the futility of upholding a single commemorative interpretation of the site or seeking any redemptive perspective whatsoever in its history. Despite its efforts, the Polish government repeatedly failed to create a single and common mode of collective memory at Auschwitz. Moreover, increasing numbers of visitors, ongoing research, and new forms of commemorative practice will undoubtedly render public manifestations of Auschwitz memory yet more diverse in the years to come. Can Auschwitz, more than fifty years after its liberation, "speak for itself?" We live in an era of growing interest in the ways in which cultures and states have chosen to recall, commemorate, and distort their pasts, and the shapes and uses of memory at the State Museum at Auschwitz prompt us to reflect upon this question. The site most certainly has its own eloquence, but its meaning will undoubtedly remain subject to both our awareness of its history and the shifting contours of its memorial landscape.

Acknowledgments

THIS WORK REFLECTS THE EFFORTS and contributions of many institutions and individuals in the United States, Poland, and Germany. Research for this study has been supported by a Fulbright-Hays Grant, the Social Science Research Council Berlin Program for Advanced German and European Studies, graduate fellowships at the University of Illinois at Urbana-Champaign, the Holocaust Educational Foundation, the College of Arts and Sciences Dean's Fund for Faculty Development at the University of Vermont, a grant from the International Advisory Council at the University of Vermont, a University of Vermont Department of History Nelson Grant, and the Center for Holocaust Studies at the University of Vermont.

I am especially grateful to Peter Fritzsche of the University of Illinois at Urbana-Champaign who supervised the doctoral dissertation that was the foundation for this study. His creativity and enthusiastic support have been an inspiration to me as a historian and as a teacher. I am also indebted to many mentors and colleagues who have offered their support and critiques at various stages of this work, including Diane Koenker, Paul Schroeder, Harry Liebersohn, Charles Stewart, David Coleman, David Krugler, and Victor Libet at the University of Illinois. Patrick Hutton and Denise Youngblood, colleagues in the department of history at the University of Vermont, have also provided valuable insights on sections of the manuscript. For their advice and support I also thank Kevin Beilfuss, Stanislaus Blejwas, Bogac Ergene, Michael Eversole, Peter Hayes, Katherine Quimby Johnson, David Massell, Wolfgang Mieder, Sybil Milton, Francis R. Nicosia, James Overfield, Kathy Pence, Antony Polonsky, Brian Porter, Douglas Selvage, Sean Stilwell, and especially David Scrase, director of the Center for Holocaust Studies at the University of Vermont.

John Bukowczyk, editor of the series in which this book is published, has offered both encouragement and thoughtful critiques of the manuscript. I am also grateful to my readers from Ohio University Press, whose suggestions have improved this work in countless ways. It has been a pleasure to work with the editorial and production staffs at Ohio University Press, and I especially appreciate the enthusiasm and counsel of senior editor Gillian Berchowitz and the skills of Ricky S. Huard, an exceptional copy editor.

I am indebted to many colleagues and friends who offered their support while I was undertaking research for this study in Oświęcim, Warsaw, Kraków, and Berlin: Danuta Bielecka, Franz von Hammerstein, Hannah Lange, Annelies Piening, Faustin Plitzko, Jutta Renner, Carol Scherer, and Joanna and Adam Walaszek. There are many at the State Museum Auschwitz-Birkenau in Oświęcim who have helped bring this study to completion, especially Wacław Długoborski, Krystyna Oleksy, Teresa Świebocka, and Jerzy Wróblewski. I am also grateful for the insights and assistance of Jadwiga Badowska, Jerzy Dębski, Dorota Grela, Emeryka Iwaszko, Stanisława Iwaszko, Barbara Jarosz, Jarek Mensfelt, Piotr Setkiewicz, Kazimierz Smoleń, and Helena Śliż. Archivists, librarians, and staff at many other institutions were also tremendously helpful: Jan Adamczyk and Marek Sroka in the Slavic Library at the University of Illinois at Urbana-Champaign; the interlibrary loan staff at the University of Vermont; the librarians at the Biblioteka Jagiellońska in Kraków; and Stephen Mize and Edna Friedberg at the United States Holocaust Memorial Museum.

Finally, I thank my parents Bill and Arlene Huener for their support over the years, and especially my wife, Marilyn Lucas, for her encouragement, patience, and humor. With gratitude and love I dedicate this book to her.

Abbreviations

AAN	Archiwum Akt Nowych, Archive of New Documents, Warsaw
APMO	Archiwum Państwowego Muzeum w Oświęcimiu, Archive of the State Museum at Auschwitz
BPMO	Biblioteka Państwowego Muzeum w Oświęcimiu, Library of the State Museum at Auschwitz
CPSU	Communist Party of the Soviet Union
EZA	Evangelisches Zentral-Archiv Berlin, Central Evangelical Archive, Berlin
FIAPP	Fédération Internationale des Anciens Prisonniers Politiques, International Federation of Former Political Prisoners
IAC	International Auschwitz Committee
KdAW	Komitee der antifaschistischen Widerstandskämpfer in der Deutschen Demokratischen Republik, Committee of Antifascist Resistance Fighters of the German Democratic Republic
KL	Konzentrationslager, concentration camp
MKiSz	Ministerstwo Kultury i Sztuki, Ministry of Culture and Art, Warsaw
PMO	Państwowe Muzeum w Oświęcimiu, State Museum at Auschwitz
PPR	Polska Partia Robotnicza, Polish Workers' Party
PPS	Polska Partia Socjalistyczna, Polish Socialist Party
PZbWP	Polski Związek byłych Więźniów Politycznych, Polish Union of Former Political Prisoners
PZPR	Polska Zjednoczona Partia Robotnicza, Polish United Workers' Party
RSHA	Reichssicherheitshauptamt, Reich Security Main Office
SAPMO	Stiftung Archiv der Parteien und Massenorganizationen der ehemaligen Deutschen Demokratischen Republik im Bundesarchiv Berlin, Foundation of the Archives of the Parties and

	Mass Organizations of the Former German Democratic Republic in the Federal Archives, Berlin
SED	Sozialistische Einheitspartei Deutschlands, Socialist Unity Party of Germany
SkAPMO	Składnice Akt Państwowego Muzeum w Oświęcimiu, Document Collections of the State Museum at Auschwitz
StONO	Stowarzyszenie Opieka nad Oświęcimiem, Society for the Protection of Auschwitz
UB	Urząd Bezpieczeństwa, Security Service
VVN	Verband Verfolgter des Naziregimes, League of the Persecuted by the Nazi Regime
ZBoWiD	Związek Bojowników o Wolność i Demokrację, Union of Fighters for Freedom and Democracy

Guide to Pronunciation

THE FOLLOWING KEY provides a guide to the pronunciation of Polish words and names.

a is pronounced as in *father*

c as ts in *cats*

ch like a guttural h

cz as hard ch in *church*

g always hard, as in *get*

i as ee

j as y in *yellow*

rz like French j in *jardin*

sz as sh in *ship*

szcz as shch, enunciating both sounds, as in *fresh cheese*

u as oo in *boot*

w as v

ć as soft ch

ś as sh

ż, ź both as zh, the latter higher in pitch than the former

ó as oo in boot

ą as French *on*

ę as French *en*

ł as w

ń changes the combinations -in to -ine, -en to -ene, and -on to -oyne

The accent in Polish words always falls on the penultimate syllable.

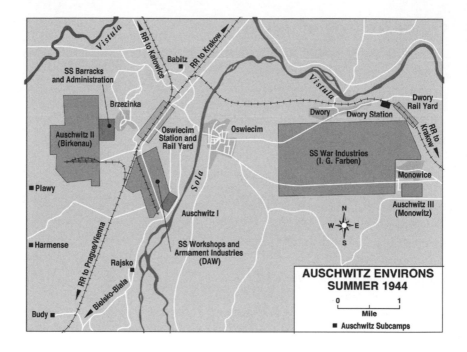

Map 1. Auschwitz environs, summer 1944.

From the U.S. Holocaust Memorial Museum's on-line Learning Center
(www.ushmm.org/learningcenter), courtesy of the U.S. Holocaust Memorial Museum, Washington, D.C.

The Stakes and Terms of Memory at Auschwitz

ALTHOUGH THERE IS A GROWING BODY of literature on the history of the Auschwitz camp, historians have paid relatively little attention to the sharply contested meanings of Auschwitz in the years since its liberation or the uses of memory there. Scholars have explored issues of collective memory, public historical consciousness, and, in more recent years, the representation of the past at monuments and memorials to National Socialist crimes,[1] but no thorough investigation of the postwar Auschwitz site has emerged from this body of literature. Moreover, those works that address postwar manifestations of memory at Auschwitz are primarily concerned with descriptions of the site's iconography, administration, or exhibitions.[2] The present work confronts these issues, and also locates the manifestations of collective memory at Auschwitz in their political, cultural, and economic contexts.

There are several possible explanations for the absence, until now, of a study such as this. First, the investigation of public memory is relatively new to the historical discipline, and only in the past fifteen to twenty years have scholars begun to examine public memory as it relates to the representation of the Holocaust, both at memorial sites and in larger social contexts. Second, given the magnitude and horror of the Auschwitz crime, as well as its "familiarity" in the postwar world, it is hardly surprising that most research has focused on the history of the camp while it was in operation.[3] Finally, most of the source material for the investigation of Auschwitz memory in Poland has become accessible only relatively recently. This is the first study of its kind to analyze the largely untapped postwar archival collections of the State Museum at Auschwitz, including its administrative documents, press archive, and collections of exhibition plans. In addition, this study includes and evaluates the perspectives and commemorative agendas introduced by organizations of former prisoners such as the International Auschwitz Committee and the Polish Union of Fighters for Freedom and Democracy, Polish governmental institutions such as the Ministry of Culture and Art and the Central Committee of the Polish United Workers' Party, and, not least, the oral interviews and written testimonies of individuals who have functioned as the stewards of memory at Auschwitz, whether former prisoners, former employees of the State Museum at Auschwitz, or government officials.

It is also worth noting that Auschwitz and its legacy in Poland have only recently been opened to renewed inquiry and debate, as the decrease in state control over scholarship and pedagogy has offered new avenues of research on the history of the Polish People's Republic and the history of the Second World War and its legacy in Poland. Scholars have, for example, begun to examine in greater detail the history of the Soviet and German occupations during World War II, Polish wartime losses under both these regimes, and the vexing issue of Jewish-Polish relations in the years 1939–45. Moreover, the recent publication of Jan T. Gross's work *Neighbors: The Destruction of the Jewish Community in Jedwabne, Poland*[4] has unleashed a storm of controversy about Polish complicity in the crimes of the Shoah and has challenged assumptions—common in Poland for decades—about Poles as an exclusively "victim" people. This victim mentality was based, of course, in the historical reality of Poland's devastating wartime losses—human, material, and psychological. But it was also cultivated, institutionalized, and mythologized in postwar Polish culture and at official memorials like the State Museum at Auschwitz. This analysis is not intended as a corrective to that process. Instead, it proposes to explain its origins and manifestations at Auschwitz, the most important site of wartime commemoration in Poland.

New scholarship and especially the growing visibility of Auschwitz in the international media have aroused greater interest in and critical investigation of Auschwitz and its place in the history of the Polish People's Republic. Perhaps now, nearly six decades after the end of World War II, this study will be all the more timely as Polish society, scholarship, and especially the staff at the Auschwitz museum attempt to focus and refocus the lens of historical hindsight. This work will clarify and interpret Polish images of Auschwitz from the liberation of the camp until the 1980s. Rather than analyzing surface images alone, this study attempts to explain the origins of and motivations for these images—all in the context of postwar Polish history, culture, and Polish-Jewish relations.

In their analyses of memory and the memory of the Holocaust, scholars Michael Steinlauf, James Young, and others have helped to break the ground for a study such as this.[5] Steinlauf, in his thoughtful and synthetic study, has effectively analyzed the origins and conflicts associated with memory of the Shoah in Poland. Pursuing a psychological perspective that is well grounded in postwar Polish history and culture, he argues that Polish responses to witnessing the Holocaust—whether repression, "psychic numbing," a "victimization competition," or even postwar anti-Semitism and anti-Jewish violence —can be situated in a social process of coming to terms with the past, the goal of which was freeing the individual Pole and Polish society from its "bondage" to the victims of Jewish genocide.[6] Auschwitz is an appropriate locus for further examination of this phenomenon, for it stands at the intersection of Poles' memories of the Shoah and memories of their own persecution under the Nazis. Moreover, as the primary site for Poland's commemoration of its wartime dead, Auschwitz and the public manifestations of memory there were inevitably infused with both patriotic zeal and political agendas. For postwar Poles, Auschwitz certainly functioned as an arena for their efforts to "master" the Shoah's tragic history in their midst, but this was not its main purpose. Auschwitz instead allowed Poles to commemorate both their own "martyrdom" within a nationalist framework and the suffering and sacrifice of others within an internationalist communist framework.

The pioneering work of James E. Young also serves as a basis for this analysis. Young has called for thorough study of camp memorials, their origins and reconfigurations throughout the years, and their role in the commemorative practices of governments and social groups. His 1993 publication *The Texture of Memory* offers an insightful description of the aesthetics and contours of Holocaust memorials and monuments, outlines some of the ways in which these memorials have become "invested" with specific and often inappropriate meanings, and issues a call for further investigation of the development of memorial sites. As Young states at the outset of this work "[W]ere we passively to remark only on the contours of these memorials, were we to leave unexplored their genesis and remain unchanged by the recollective act, it could be said that we have not remembered at all."[7] A charge of sorts to colleagues and students, Young's words should remind us of the dangers of an uncritical obsession with memorial images. Such images, whether monuments, exhibitions, or commemorative demonstrations can, of course, serve as effective vehicles of communication and commemoration, but as culturally and politically influenced representations of the past, they neither stand on their own as objects of inquiry, nor should they supersede in importance the actual events and phenomena that they are intended to evoke and recall.[8] This is especially true when confronting the history of Auschwitz and the representation of that history at the memorial site.

||

FOLLOWING THE GERMAN occupation of Poland in September 1939, the Polish town of Oświęcim, located about sixty kilometers west of Kraków, was annexed to the Reich and renamed Auschwitz. Located near the juncture of Upper Silesia, the Wartheland, and the General Government,[9] and at the confluence of the Vistula and Soła rivers, the town had a prewar population of about twelve thousand residents, more than 40 percent of whom were Jewish. Ironically, Oświęcim was a cultural center of Jewish life in interwar Poland and was regarded as model community of Jewish-Polish coexistence. The site selected for a concentration camp in 1940 lay outside the town's borders and had been a base for the Habsburg army and, later, for troops of the interwar Polish Republic.

Initially, the concentration camp at Auschwitz was intended for the internment of Polish political prisoners. With the number of inmates rapidly increasing, the prisons in the region could no longer accommodate them. In the spring of 1940 Reichsführer-SS Heinrich Himmler ordered the establishment of a concentration camp at Oświęcim and named SS Captain Rudolf Höss commandant. German authorities brought in three hundred Jewish residents of Oświęcim to ready the site, and in May 1940, ordered thirty German criminals transferred from the Sachsenhausen camp to serve as the initial elite of functionary prisoners.[10] One hundred SS men were sent to staff the camp, and on 14 June the first transport of 728 Polish inmates from the Tarnów prison arrived, marking the beginning of the camp's role as the primary and most deadly camp for Polish political prisoners, members of the underground, and Poland's intellectual, spiritual, and cultural elites.

The intelligentsia in interwar Poland included many Polish Jews, particularly in urban centers. Some were fully assimilated into the culture of Polish Gentiles, and were regarded as such. The German occupation regime, however, drew a clear distinction between Polish Jews and non-Jews, especially when it began the process of deporting Jews to ghettos in the larger cities. Throughout this analysis, the terms "Poles" and "Jews" will refer to separate groups among those persecuted by the Nazi regime. Of course, both Polish Christians (who were overwhelmingly Roman Catholic) and Polish Jews were Polish citizens. For the sake of clarity, however, this work will refer to ethnic Poles or Polish Christians as "Poles" and those defined and persecuted as Jews by the Nazis simply as "Jews." The reality of identities in wartime was, of course, much more complex and should remind us that the distinction was often artificial, even if it was observed by most Christian Poles and rigorously enforced by the Nazis on the basis of their racial ideology.

The Auschwitz camp grew steadily, and in the course of its expansion the Germans evicted and deported the local population—both Polish and Jewish—in order to establish, for economic and security reasons, an "area of interest" surrounding the camp. The resulting *Interessengebiet* of KL Auschwitz[11] covered an area of approximately forty square kilometers. On 1 March 1941 Heinrich Himmler visited the concentration camp at Auschwitz for the first time and ordered Höss : 1) to expand the base camp to accommodate 30,000 prisoners, 2) to supply the IG Farben chemical concern with the labor of 10,000 prisoners to build an industrial plant at Dwory in the near vicinity of Auschwitz, and 3) to construct a camp for 100,000 prisoners of war near the village of Brzezinka.[12] Himmler would not inform Höss of plans to use Auschwitz as a center for the "final solution of the Jewish question" until the summer, but in March—three months before the German invasion of the USSR—it was clear that Auschwitz could be used as a site for the mass incarceration and exploitation of Soviet POWs.

Expansion of the existing camp was undertaken at a rapid pace, and included the construction of housing units for the SS, administrative buildings, additional quarters for prisoners, and camp kitchens. By the end of 1941 it could house 18,000 prisoners, and by 1943 as many as 30,000 (see Map 2). Construction on the synthetic rubber and fuel oil factory at nearby Dwory, otherwise known as the *Buna-Werke,* began in April 1941. Initially, prisoners from Auschwitz were either transported by rail or walked to the factory, but in 1942 IG Farben began construction of a second camp for its workers

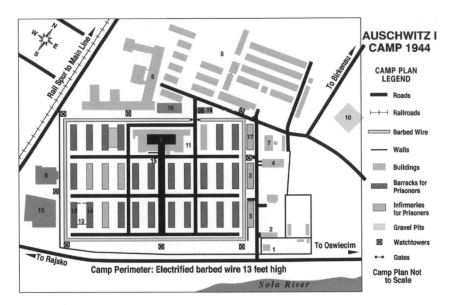

Map 2. Auschwitz I Camp, 1944. Selected features: 1. Camp commandant's house; 2. Main guard house; 3. Camp administrative offices; 4. Gestapo; 5. Reception building/prisoner registration; 6. Kitchen; 7. Gas chamber and crematorium; 8. Storage buildings and workshops; 9. Storage of confiscated belongings (Theatergebäude); 10. Gravel pit: execution site; 11. Camp orchestra site; 12. "Black Wall" (Wall of Death): execution site; 13. Block 11: punishment bunker; 14. Block 10: medical experiments; 15. Gallows; 16. Block commander's barracks; 17. SS hospital

From the U.S. Holocaust Memorial Museum's on-line Learning Center (www.ushmm.org/learningcenter), courtesy of the U.S. Holocaust Memorial Museum, Washington, D.C.

in the vacated village of Monowice (Monowitz). A subsidiary of Auschwitz, the camp was known until November 1943 as *Lager Buna.*

Meanwhile, the arrival of thousands of Soviet prisoners of war in late 1941 led to the hasty construction of an additional camp on a swampy moor near the village of Brzezinka (renamed Birkenau by the Germans), about three kilometers from the base camp. Birkenau was initially intended to hold 100,000 prisoners and was divided into various sectors and sub-camps (e.g., a women's camp established in August 1942, a Gypsy camp, or a camp for Jewish families from Theresienstadt established in February 1943), each

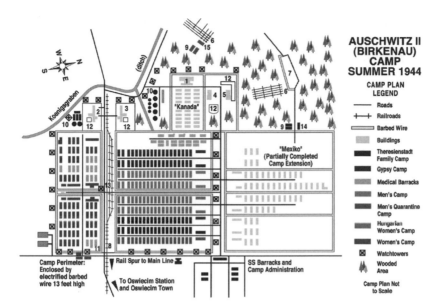

Map 3. Auschwitz II (Birkenau) Camp, summer 1944. Selected features: 1. "Sauna" (disinfection); 2. Gas chamber and crematorium #2; 3. Gas chamber and crematorium #3; 4. Gas chamber and crematorium #4; 5. Gas chamber and crematorium #5; 6. Cremation pyres; 7. Mass graves for Soviet POWs; 8. Main guard house; 9. Barracks for disrobing; 10. Sewage treatment plants; 11. Medical experiments barracks; 12. Ash pits; 13. "Rampe" (railroad platform); 14. Provisional gas chamber #1; 15. Provisional gas chamber #2

From the U.S. Holocaust Memorial Museum's on-line Learning Center (www.ushmm.org/learningcenter), courtesy of the U.S. Holocaust Memorial Museum, Washington, D.C.

separated from the next by barbed wire and guard towers. Birkenau was also marked as the largest center for the execution of the "Final Solution," for in 1941 Himmler had ordered Höss to begin developing facilities for efficient and industrialized mass murder (see Map 3).

In addition to the three main camps of the complex, forty auxiliary camps were established in the Auschwitz region between 1941 and 1944. Development of this larger network of camps was considered necessary for security reasons and helped to solve the problem of transporting prisoners from Auschwitz and its two larger subsidiaries at Monowitz and Birkenau to work sites throughout the area. The satellite camps, which housed from several dozen to several thousand prisoners, were located near industrial plants, agricultural enterprises, and mines, all of which served as part of a huge SS economic-industrial conglomerate. Thus, inmates of the nearby Harmense and Rajsko camps farmed; prisoners labored in coal mines at Jawischowitz and Janina-grube; at Chełmek they worked in a shoe factory; thousands of others were forced laborers for the coffers of German industrial concerns such as IG Farben, Siemens-Schuckert, Hermann-Göring-Werke, and Krupp.

In late 1943 a major administrative reorganization was undertaken at the Auschwitz complex. Rudolf Höss, commandant since the camp's establishment in the spring of 1940, was recalled to the Inspectorate for Concentration Camps at Oranienburg near Berlin, and was replaced by SS Lieutenant Colonel Arthur Liebehenschel. In November 1943 Liebehenschel ordered that the camp be divided into three main entities: the base camp (*Stammlager*) KL Auschwitz I, which was the original and expanded main camp and administrative headquarters of the complex; KL Auschwitz II, which comprised the camp and extermination facilities at Birkenau; and KL Auschwitz III, often simply called Monowitz, which centered on the camp adjacent to the Buna-Werke industrial plant, but included as well most auxiliary camps in the region. Auschwitz II/Birkenau was under the command of SS Major Fritz Hartjenstein, and Auschwitz III/Monowitz under SS Captain Heinrich Schwarz, both of whom were subordinate to the Liebehenschel's authority. Although this subdivision of the complex remained in effect until the liberation in January 1945, the command structure was to change again in May 1944, when SS Major Richard Baer was appointed commandant of Auschwitz. In the same month Höss returned to Auschwitz as commander of the SS garrison, this time for the purpose of coordinating the destruction of hundreds of thousands of Hungarian Jews, an effort that bore the code name "Aktion Höss," which he would supervise until late July 1944.

This brief description of the development and organizational structure of the camp conglomerate illustrates that there was not one, but numerous "Auschwitzes" of which the larger complex bearing the name Auschwitz was composed. Thus, the varied and fractured nature of the complex's topography, purpose, and command structure makes it all the more difficult to arrive at a clear definition of what the Auschwitz memorial site was, is, or should be. The number of Jews murdered at Auschwitz and the manner in which they were killed remain the most unique and striking characteristics of the camp and its history, but the experience of the Jewish deportee was not definitive. As the above account suggests, the diverse experiences of the Auschwitz survivor or victim defy convenient generalization. While one prisoner worked in the fishery of a nearby auxiliary camp, another laid railroad ties; while one prisoner never saw the Stammlager Auschwitz I, another never left it; and while many prisoners may never have seen the gas chambers and crematoria at Birkenau, the majority of Jews deported there saw nothing else.

It is therefore nearly impossible to describe in detail or even to generalize satisfactorily about the conditions under which registered prisoners[13] at Auschwitz lived, worked, and died, for those conditions varied according to each prisoner's national or "racial" status, work assignment, and, not least, location in the complex. Whether a registered prisoner lived or died at Auschwitz was often determined by whether she or he survived the first weeks or months. Generally, those prisoners accustomed to relative comfort had the most difficulty in accommodating themselves to the severity of camp life, whereas those who had already been in prisons or ghettos, or who had been prisoners of war had less difficulty adjusting to the brutality and deprivation.

Upon arrival at the camp prisoners were not only stripped of any possessions, but they were also robbed of their identities. Names, as far as the SS was concerned, became irrelevant; each prisoner was assigned a serial number that was tattooed on the left forearm or, in the case of small children, on the leg.[14] Prisoners were usually given a pair of clogs and an ill-fitting striped uniform on which was sewn a piece of cloth bearing the prisoner's number as well as a symbol designating his or her category. Jews, for example, wore a Star of David; homosexuals, a pink triangle; political prisoners, an inverted red triangle; ordinary criminals, a green triangle; and the so-called "asocial," a black triangle. Such markings made the prisoners easily identifiable to the camp guards and were immediately associated with a prisoner's status in the camp hierarchy.

Not surprisingly, the markings on a prisoner's uniform—both numbers and symbols—bore a relationship to his or her chances for survival. For instance, a German criminal with a low number had learned over the months or years many of the tricks of survival, was perhaps among the camp's prisoner elite, and may have held some supervisory position. A Jew fresh off a transport, on the other hand, even when spared death upon arrival, was usually subjected to more severe treatment and was far less likely to survive. In general, Jews and Gypsies, regardless of their country of origin, were at the bottom of the camp prisoner hierarchy and were consequently the least likely to survive. Above them were the Russian POWs, and then civilian Slavs, mostly Poles, who were considered by the Germans to be conspiratorial and inferior but who, with the exception of the Polish intelligentsia, governmental leaders, and military elite, were not marked for annihilation. Members of other European nationalities formed the next category, and at the top of the rankings were German prisoners.

The topography of the different camps at Auschwitz certainly varied, but all camps were designed to keep prisoners under strict control and at the very edge of human survival. Describing his early impressions of Auschwitz-Monowitz, Primo Levi recalled:

> [O]ur Lager is a square of about six hundred yards in length, surrounded by two fences of barbed wire, the inner one carrying a high tension current. It consists of sixty wooden huts, which are called Blocks, ten of which are in construction. In addition, there is the body of the kitchens, which are in brick; an experimental farm, run by a detachment of privileged Häftlinge [prisoners], the huts with the showers and the latrines, one for each group of six or eight Blocks. Besides these, certain Blocks are reserved for specific purposes. First of all, a group of eight, at the extreme eastern end of the camp, forms the infirmary and clinic ... Block 7 which no ordinary Häftling has ever entered, reserved for the *"Prominenz,"* that is, the aristocracy, the internees holding the highest posts; Block 47, reserved for the *Reichsdeutsche* (the Aryan Germans, "politicals" or criminals); Block 49, for the Kapos [supervisory prisoners] alone; Block 12, half of which, for use of the *Reichsdeutsche* and the Kapos, serves as a canteen, that is, a distribution centre for tobacco, insect powder and occasionally other articles; Block 37, which formed the Quartermaster's office and the Office for Work; and finally, Block 29, which always has its windows closed as it is the *Frauenblock,* the camp brothel, served by Polish Häftling girls, and reserved for the *Reichsdeutsche.*[15]

This account from one of Levi's memoirs, although descriptive only of one part of the Auschwitz complex in early 1944, suggests that although all prisoners were subjected to strict control, there were clear discrepancies in status and in the severity of their treatment at the hands of the Kapos and SS.

Because of this structure, tensions, resentment, and divisions were common, not only among prisoners of various nationalities, faiths, and Nazi-fabricated "racial" categories, but also between members of the various strata of authority. These included "ordinary" prisoners such as Levi, the Kapos in charge of work commandos, *Lagerälteste* (camp elders), the individual block supervisors, and those prisoners who enjoyed privileged and powerful work assignments, such as those occupying clerical and administrative posts. In Auschwitz I, Poles, the largest prisoner group there, held most positions of authority. In Birkenau, some official prisoner posts were held by Jews. German criminals, employed in functionary positions across the Auschwitz complex, were often the most feared. Regardless of the nationality of the functionary prisoners, differences in status added to existing rivalries, fears and resentments among inmates—a fact not lost on the SS. Moreover, the differing roles of prisoners in the camp structure and administration often blurred the dividing lines between perpetrators, bystanders, and victims at Auschwitz, placing many inmates into what Levi has called the "gray zone" of moral culpability located somewhere between the poles of good and evil, righteous and reprobate.[16]

Even if such discrepancies in status and moral culpability at Auschwitz had not existed, the camp atmosphere in general did not encourage solidarity and mutual support among the prisoners. As Yisrael Gutman writes, "In a world with all moral norms and restraints lifted and no holds barred, where congestion, severe deprivation, and nervous tension were ubiquitous, the prisoners easily succumbed to violence and rudeness. Conditions of life in the camp managed to undermine any solidarity that might be expected to arise among human beings who found themselves in identical situations. The assumption that common suffering bridges distances separating people was not borne out by camp reality."[17] Altruism and mutual aid were certainly not unknown in the camp, but Gutman's observation challenges the myth of unwavering solidarity among camp inmates, a myth—like that of the prototypic prisoner—so prevalent in the various commemorative agendas that manifested themselves at Auschwitz in the postwar years.

The conditions of which Gutman writes were intended to breed competition, further divest the prisoners of their traditional notions of human behavior and morality, and, most importantly, keep the prisoners at the edge of survival. The quarters in which ordinary prisoners lived were stifling, poorly heated in the wintertime, rife with vermin and disease, and offered no privacy. "The ordinary living blocks," Levi wrote,

> are divided into two parts. In one *Tagesraum* lives the head of the hut with his friends . . . on the walls, great sayings, proverbs and rhymes in praise of order, discipline and hygiene; in one corner, a shelf with the tools of the *Blockfrisör* (official barber), the ladles to distribute the soup, and two rubber truncheons, one solid and one hollow, to enforce discipline should the proverbs prove insufficient. The other part is the dormitory: there are only one hundred and forty-eight bunks on three levels, fitted close to each other like the cells of a beehive, and divided by three corridors so as to utilize without wastage all the space in the room up to the roof. Here all the ordinary Häftlinge live, about two hundred to two hundred and fifty per hut. Consequently there are two men in most of the bunks, which are portable planks of wood, each covered by a thin straw sack and two blankets.[18]

In comparison to huts such as these in Monowitz, the two-story heated blocks of Auschwitz I were relatively comfortable. Far worse, however, were living conditions in Birkenau, where prisoners in sector BII (the largest and most populated part of the camp) were housed in prefabricated wooden huts originally designed as stables for fifty-two horses.[19] At Birkenau they were intended to house some four hundred prisoners, but often held hundreds more.

While poor housing contributed in various ways to the death rate among inmates, the prisoners' inadequate diet, combined with work that was usually physically exhausting, made their survival even more precarious.[20] In the morning prisoners received a half-liter of ersatz coffee or tea, at midday approximately ¾ liter of thin soup averaging 350–400 calories, and for supper about 300 grams of bread with a small amount of sausage, margarine, cheese, or jam. Prisoners engaged in heavy labor were given slightly larger, yet still insufficient rations. The nutritive value of meals at Auschwitz depended on the dietary norms set for inmates of concentration camps, and these norms changed several times from 1940 to 1945. But generally, the amount and quality of food distributed at Auschwitz was far below these norms. Whereas regulations called for 1,700 calories per day for prisoners engaged in lighter work and 2,150 calories for prisoners doing heavy labor, such prisoners at Auschwitz received an average of 1,300 and 1,700 calories per day, respectively.[21] The discrepancy resulted from SS plundering of foodstuffs or the maldistribution of food by functionary prisoners, who often had the power of life and death over the inmates in their charge. Whether, for example, one's soup was served from the top or the bottom of the vat could make a tremendous difference in caloric intake.

Poor housing, inadequate diet, and physically demanding work all made the mortality rate among registered prisoners extremely high. Jewish registered prisoners, who by mid-1944 made up approximately two-thirds of all Auschwitz inmates, had an even higher mortality rate. Their treatment at the hands of the SS and functionary prisoners was generally worse than that meted out to other prisoner groups; they were frequently perceived as inferior by their fellow prisoners; and they suffered from an additional psychological burden, namely, that Jews "lived in the shadow of certainty that their relatives had perished, that their own fate was sealed, and that their incarceration in the camp was but a reprieve granted by the Germans to drain them of their strength through slave labor before sending them to their deaths."[22]

Yet those Jews who entered Auschwitz as registered prisoners were, in fact, a small minority of deportees. Although the exact number of Jewish victims will never be known, according to data compiled by Auschwitz historian Franciszek Piper, 890,000 (about 81 percent) of the Jews deported to the Auschwitz complex were not registered, but rather met their deaths immediately after arrival.[23] There is, moreover, a crucial point to be emphasized here: unlike other prisoners at Auschwitz (with the important exception of Gypsies), the overwhelming majority of Jews deported to Auschwitz were not brought there on the grounds of criminal charges, anti-Nazi conspiratorial activity, service in an enemy army, religious convictions, or "asocial" behavior. Jews were deported to Auschwitz for exploitation and extermination because they were defined and identified as Jews by Nazi racial laws. This is the critical distinction that must be made between Jews and Gypsies on the one hand and, on the other, Poles, Soviet POWs, and other prisoner groups.[24] It is also a distinction that has frequently been lost on postwar memorialists of Auschwitz.

The above description offers a picture of conditions for registered prisoners, but such a generalization should not overlook an element of Auschwitz history that sets it apart from other camps: the variety of ways in which registered prisoners lived, worked, and died there. The prisoner's experience depended on a myriad of factors. State of health upon arrival, location in the camp complex, work assignment, nationality, ability to communicate with guards, Kapos, and other prisoners, relationships with supervisors, relationships to the camp resistance movements, the length of time in the camp, the personal will to survive—these are only a few examples of the factors that could determine how, and whether, a prisoner lived or died.

Moreover, the differences in the ways prisoners experienced Auschwitz were at times shockingly crass. Some prisoners fought to stay alive by any means available; others quickly lost their will to live, became so-called *Muselmänner*,[25] and were dead within weeks of arrival. Some prisoners were well fed, although the diet of nearly all was woefully insufficient. Some prisoners enjoyed solidarity and mutual support among their peers; others were taken advantage of, abused, and left to die, friendless and alone. Some prisoners had the connections and courage to become active in covert resistance; others remained unaware of any underground conspiracy whatsoever. Treatment of Soviet POWs was infinitely worse than treatment of German criminals. One prisoner may have been in Auschwitz because of her politics, another because of her "race" as defined by Nazi ideology. At Birkenau there were soccer games and gas chambers—each within sight of the other. In short, Auschwitz, its victims, and its prisoners defy generalizations and convenient categorizations. Just as the history of the camp was multifaceted, so too have collective memories and public manifestations of those memories been diverse and at times even contradictory, to the extent that the commemoration of one prisoner or prisoner group has offended or silenced the memory of another.

Wide diversity of prisoners, complicated administrative structure, brutally harsh conditions—all are aspects of Auschwitz that render it unique among Nazi concentration camps and extermination centers. Although these characteristics are essential to our understanding of Auschwitz and are central to Polish commemorative uses of Auschwitz, the murder of nearly nine hundred thousand Jews immediately after their arrival at the camp remains the most salient and important, but not entirely definitive aspect of its history. The scale of the killing operations at Auschwitz and the manner in which they were carried out have, more than any other aspects of the camp's history, remained in the consciousness and memory of Jews and non-Jews around the world, and an awareness of the machinery of mass extermination at Auschwitz and its role in the execution of the "final solution of the Jewish question" continues to awaken both horror and interest on the part of scholars, students, and visitors to the memorial site. As the largest single killing center for European Jews, Auschwitz has appropriately emerged as a metonym for the Shoah, and its memorial grounds have become a primary destination for millions of pilgrims, both Jewish and Gentile.

Raul Hilberg has noted that the status of Auschwitz as the foremost symbol of the Shoah is based on at least three of its characteristics: first, more Jews died in Auschwitz than anywhere else; second, Auschwitz was an international killing center with victims from across the European continent; third, the killing at Auschwitz continued long after the other extermination centers of Nazi-occupied Europe had been liquidated.[26] There are other bases for the symbolic and metonymic value of Auschwitz—bases that will be addressed in the course of this study—but these three characteristics are an appropriate point of departure for a brief description of the killing operations that were undertaken at the Auschwitz complex.

Auschwitz, as the description of its early history has made clear, was not initially intended to be an extermination center for European Jews, but was a large concentration camp on annexed Polish territory. As at all concentration camps, death was omnipresent and had numerous causes. Executions by hanging or by shooting at the so-called "wall of death" adjacent to Block 11 were commonplace at the base camp and later at Birkenau, Monowitz, and the various auxiliary camps. So-called "selections"—the weeding-out of prisoners considered unfit for work—and the subsequent murder of prisoners by lethal injection or gas began in the spring of 1941. Moreover, prisoners at the Auschwitz complex were continually subjected to various forms of what could be called indirect extermination, that is, death resulting from the effects of hunger, disease, so-called "medical experiments," exhaustion, or torture.

The systematic and efficient killing of prisoners and recently arrived deportees in gas chambers was, however, a later development at Auschwitz. According to the postwar testimony of Rudolf Höss, the camp's first commandant, Himmler summoned him to Berlin in the late summer of 1941 and announced, in Höss's words, the following: "The Führer has ordered that the Jewish question be solved once and for all and that we, the SS, are to implement that order. The existing extermination centers in the East are not in a position to carry out the large actions which are anticipated. I have therefore earmarked Auschwitz for this purpose, both because of its good position as regards communications and because the area can easily be isolated and camouflaged."[27] Höss was also informed that further details of the extermination plans would be brought to Auschwitz by Adolf Eichmann, chief of the Jewish Department of the Reich Security Main Office (RSHA). Later that year Eichmann and Höss worked out many of the details of the plan, including transport and railroad arrangements and, in September, development of a suitable killing method.

When Eichmann visited Auschwitz, he acquainted Höss with the workings of gas chambers used at "euthanasia" installations and the mobile gassing vans used at various locations. Both used carbon monoxide as the poison, but neither, it was decided, would be suitable for the sort of mass extermination that was to be undertaken at Auschwitz. Instead, a preparation of hydrogen cyanide normally used as a disinfectant, fumigator, and delousing agent was chosen. The product, commercially marketed as "Zyklon-B," was readily available at the Auschwitz complex. While Höss was away, his deputy Karl Fritzsch used Zyklon-B as a killing agent for humans on a group of Soviet prisoners. When the commandant returned, he supervised the first large-scale killing in the cellar of the base camp's Block 11, where approximately six hundred Soviet prisoners of war and two hundred fifty other prisoners were gassed to death. After witnessing this second experiment, Höss became convinced that death by Zyklon-B gas would be the most efficient and appropriate means of killing Jews at Auschwitz in the future, and the mortuary of the "old crematorium" (later named Crematorium I) was converted to a gas chamber. It was first used on transports of Jewish deportees in February 1942.

The gas chamber attached to Crematorium I operated for another year, but with the advent of Nazi plans for the "final solution of the Jewish question" in late 1941, the bulk of gassing operations at Auschwitz was moved to Birkenau. Construction on the Birkenau camp had begun in October 1941, and in early 1942 the first gassings took place there in a provisional bunker known as the "little red house." A second bunker, the "little white house," began operation in June. Both of these installations were surrounded by trees. Mass graves, later to be replaced by incineration pits, were also in the near vicinity but hidden from the victims by hedges. The Jewish deportees were unloaded at a rail station two and a half kilometers from Birkenau and were then "selected" for registration and work or, in most cases, immediate death.[28] Those deemed unfit to live were then marched to the killing facilities or brought there in trucks. They were forced to undress, told that they would bathe and be deloused, instructed to remember where they had left their belongings, and then forced into the gas chamber. Once the chamber was full, the doors were sealed and SS men wearing gas masks poured the Zyklon-B pellets into slots in the side wall. The victims were usually dead within minutes. When the chamber was opened a half hour later, members of the *Sonderkommando* began their work. The Sonderkommando was a special detail of Jewish prisoners who were charged with removal of the bodies, extraction of valuables from the corpses, cremation, and cleaning of the gas chambers of blood and excrement prior to the arrival of the next group of victims.[29]

Corpses of the victims of gassings at the base camp, as well as those who had been gassed at Birkenau, were buried in pits near the Birkenau bunkers. In the summer of 1942, however, SS Colonel Paul Blobel from Eichmann's RSHA arrived at Auschwitz with orders that the corpses be removed. From September until late November 1942 a mass exhumation and incineration effort took place, as pyres of up to two thousand bodies each and, later, mass incineration pits were used to dispose of more than one hundred thousand corpses.

Work on four specially designed gas chambers and crematoria at Birkenau had begun in July 1942, but the first of the new installations there was not completed until March 1943. By June of that year four new facilities (Crematoria II, III, IV, and V) were in operation. The killing process in the new gas chambers at Birkenau was similar to that in the temporary bunkers, but it took place on a larger and more streamlined scale. At Crematorium II the process was perhaps at its most efficient. After having been selected for death, the victims were led to the entrance of the crematorium or, in the case of invalids or the weak, they were brought there in trucks. Every effort was made to delude the victims, who were told that they would bathe and be deloused. They were then led into a subterranean undressing room where they could see signs in German and in their native languages bearing the instructions "To the Baths" and "To Disinfection." Some were even given soap and towels.

As many as two thousand people could be forced into the gas chamber of Crematorium II. Once they were inside, the door was bolted and sealed, and, on the order of an SS doctor, the SS "disinfectors" opened cans of Zyklon-B and poured their contents into induction vents on the roof. In a matter of minutes—at most twenty—all inside were dead. Rudolf Höss, having witnessed the gassing process, described the effects of the sublimated poison: "It could be observed through the peephole in the door that those who were standing nearest to the induction vents were killed at once. It can be said that about one-third died straightaway. The remainder staggered about and began to scream and struggle for air. The screaming, however, soon changed to the death rattle and in a few minutes all lay still."[30]

Half an hour after the poison had been introduced, the room was ventilated and Sonderkommando prisoners began hauling the corpses to an anteroom, where they removed women's hair. They then loaded the corpses onto an elevator that brought them to the crematorium level. Prior to incineration, they removed from the bodies jewelry, gold, and other valuables. The ovens in Crematorium II could burn three corpses in each retort in about twenty minutes, depending on the size and percentage of body fat of each corpse. Ashes and partially incinerated bones were ground, dumped into nearby pits, and later deposited in nearby ponds and the Vistula River. At times ashes were also used as fertilizer at camp farms.

The total capacity of the Auschwitz and Birkenau crematoria was intended to be approximately 4,800 bodies per day. This figure was, according to a surviving member of a Birkenau Sonderkommando, at times raised to about 8,000 by increasing the number of corpses simultaneously burned in the oven retorts.[31] In the summer of 1944, after an additional railroad spur was built directly into the Birkenau camp, the cremation installations at Auschwitz-Birkenau, including additional incineration pits, could dispose of some 20,000 victims daily. That summer of 1944 also saw the largest and most systematic instance of mass genocide in history: the murder of more than 430,000 Hungarian Jews.

Himmler ordered the cessation of killing operations in the fall of 1944, but by the time Auschwitz was liberated in January 1945, it had claimed at least 1.1 million lives.[32] A breakdown of these figures comparing registered and unregistered prisoners and roughly divided according to victim group reveals the following *minimum* estimates:

1. Between 1940 and 1945 approximately 1,305,000 deportees were sent to Auschwitz, of whom 905,000 were unregistered and 400,000 were registered. At least 1.1 million deportees died, resulting in a mortality rate for the entirety of the camp's existence of approximately 84 percent.

2. Approximately 1,095,000 Jews were deported to Auschwitz, of whom 890,000 were unregistered and 205,000 were registered. Some 865,000 unregistered Jewish deportees and 95,000 registered Jewish deportees died there. In other words, approximately 88 percent of the Jews deported to Auschwitz did not survive, and 79 percent of them were killed shortly after their arrival, the overwhelming majority in gas chambers. Of the 202,000 registered prisoners who died at Auschwitz, slightly less than half were Jews.

3. Some 147,000 non-Jewish Poles were deported to Auschwitz, of whom an estimated 10,000 were unregistered and 137,000 were registered. About 64,000 of the registered prisoners and all of the unregistered prisoners died there, that is, approximately one-half of all Polish deportees.

4. Gypsies at Auschwitz had less than a one–in–ten chance of survival. Of the 23,000 Gypsies deported to Auschwitz (21,000 of whom were registered prisoners), 21,000, or 91 percent, perished.

5. There is, according to Piper's estimates, no record of any survivors among the 15,000 (12,000 registered and 3,000 unregistered) Soviet prisoners of war deported to Auschwitz.

6. Some 25,000 prisoners of other nationalities (Czechs, Russians, Belorussians, Yugoslavians, French, Ukrainians, Germans, Austrians, and others) were registered as prisoners at Auschwitz, of whom approximately 13,000 survived.

These statistics are staggering and, at the same time, disturbingly anonymous. They are an essential part of Auschwitz history, and a tremendous debt is owed to those scholars who have devoted years of research to the problem of assessing the number of deportees and number of deaths at Auschwitz and other camps. One must, however, exercise caution when using numbers such as these. They are not precise, and, more importantly, one must bear in mind that an inordinate focus on statistics can easily distract from their larger historical importance and contribute to the already disturbing anonymity of the victims and perpetrators. In short, obsession with the numbers both dishonors the Auschwitz victims and mitigates the significance of the crimes against them.

Yet these statistics have a particular relevance for an analysis of Auschwitz memory at the memorial site. The number and kind of deportees and victims outlined above provide us with an empirical measure against which we can compare the presentation of Auschwitz history at the State Museum at Auschwitz, in its exhibitions, and in the public ritual undertaken there. These numbers are, in the context of this study, important in two major ways. First, they contrast sharply with the inflated figure of 4 million Auschwitz victims—a figure cited for decades by Polish and some Israeli historians and, significantly, a figure employed virtually uncontested until the early 1990s at the Auschwitz memorial site itself.[33] Second, these statistics increase our awareness of *who* was at Auschwitz, *who* lived and died there and *how*— an awareness that is crucial to any analysis of who has been *memorialized* at Auschwitz and how. In other words, the numbers can be employed as one measure by which we can critically assess the manifestations of Auschwitz memory at the site.

Although historians have been concerned with the number of dead at Auschwitz, it is also worth noting that Auschwitz had a relatively high number of survivors in comparison to those sites (Chełmno/Kulmhof, Treblinka, Sobibór, and Bełżec) that functioned solely as extermination centers. This may come as a surprise to many who consider Auschwitz to have been the most deadly killing center, for Auschwitz was neither the first nor, in some respects, even the most terrifying of camps. It is true that more deportees, and among them more Jews, died at Auschwitz than anywhere else; but the number of deportees and specifically of Jewish deportees who were registered and subsequently used for slave labor at Auschwitz was also uniquely high. The simple fact that when Red Army troops entered the Auschwitz complex in January 1945 there were some seven thousand prisoners languishing there sets Auschwitz apart from other killing sites on Polish territory, where survival rates were shockingly low. Martin Gilbert has estimated that only three individuals survived Chełmno/Kulmhof, the first extermination center. His figures for the other killing centers are similarly bleak. Sixty-four Jews survived Sobibór, while as many as two hundred thousand were killed. At Treblinka up to seven hundred fifty thousand Jews were murdered and only between forty and seventy individuals survived. Finally, Gilbert estimates that at Bełżec, where five hundred fifty thousand perished, only two survived.[34]

If Auschwitz had, relative to other extermination centers, such a high number of survivors, it follows that many of those survivors recorded their experiences in depositions and memoirs, as well as audio and, more recently, video testimonies. There is, simply put, a wealth of information about the experiences of prisoners and the history of the Auschwitz complex. Whether

Jewish, Polish, Czech, or French, survivors have left their accounts for successive generations to read, hear, and employ in the construction of individual and collective Auschwitz memories. Initially, such accounts and testimonies added to the body of knowledge on Auschwitz and served as documentary evidence, but over the years the prisoner's account has taken on a different but no-less-meaningful function, helping to construct, maintain, and revise collective memories of Auschwitz.[35] This transformation has been evident at the State Museum at Auschwitz, where many survivors, especially Polish political prisoners, were instrumental in the site's development and in the public commemorative rituals that took place there. As a consequence, the topography and the pedagogical and political orientation of the postwar memorial site has, in many respects, reflected the memories and meaning that these survivors drew from their experiences in the camp.

|||

The preceding historical synopsis should reinforce two major points. First, the topography and features of postliberation Auschwitz can present only images of the landscape of the functioning camp complex. The memorial site is not and can not be Auschwitz, but is merely and inevitably a representation—preserved, constructed, reconstructed, or distorted—of Auschwitz as it existed in the years 1940–45. Second, the history of Auschwitz from 1940 to 1945 is far from monolithic. Some aspects of the complex's history warrant greater attention than others. Some experiences were shared by all registered prisoners. Some lessons drawn from the history of the camp are more important than others. But Auschwitz lacks a convenient master narrative, a prototypic prisoner or martyr, and it resists oversimplification and generalization.

If Auschwitz history is not monolithic, neither should any collective Auschwitz memory be monolithic. Rather, that memory should reflect the complexity of the camp's history. The memory exhibited at the Auschwitz memorial site has never been totally monolithic, as if hewn from a single stone and presented as a single narrative. Yet for more than forty years the State Museum at Auschwitz exhibited a museological, pedagogical, and commemorative orientation that, to varying degrees, simplified the camp's history, valorized certain types of deportees and their experiences over those of others, and introduced culturally and ideologically bound memorial narratives grounded in postwar Polish society and politics. Although perhaps not surprising, such a reconfiguration of the past may strike the observer as somehow unjust, for at issue here is the relationship between history and public or collective memory.[36]

The relationship between history and the memory of events that have shaped our past appears obvious. Close observation reveals, however, that the anticipated nexus between the two is always weaker than might be assumed, for the way a culture or society remembers the past seldom reflects the actual course of historical events. This point may appear obvious, but it is worth further consideration in the context of this study. Thus far, the term "history" in general and the "history" of Auschwitz in particular have been used in a conventional sense, meaning both the actual course of events at Auschwitz and these events as they have been recorded by historians and others. The former represents an objective reality that cannot be reproduced or chronicled with total accuracy; it can be approached by the scholar or student, but nonetheless remains an ideal. "History" in the latter sense refers to the chronicling and codification—in effect, the institutionalization—of the past in ways that are familiar to all of us, such as the construction of narrative texts, the development of archives, or the establishment of historical museums. The work of institutionalizing the past in postwar Poland was highly complex and subject to the demands of Polish national culture and its attendant "martyrological" traditions, as well as the ideological imperatives of the communist state. Accordingly, the construction of an Auschwitz narrative, whether the work of the scholar or the State Museum, remained inseparable from the larger collective memory of the camp.

Collective memory, far less reconstructive and organized than history, arises out of the recollections and desires of the community.[37] It is not rigid, but, as Pierre Nora writes, "remains in permanent evolution, open to the dialectic of remembering and forgetting, unconscious of its successive deformations, vulnerable to manipulation and appropriation, susceptible to being long dormant and periodically revived."[38] History as task, because of its claims to objectivity and analytical rigor, is intended to endure and present a universally valid, if not universally appreciated representation of the past. This it achieves only to a limited extent, for, as suggested above, the work of history, whether that of the scholar or that of the museum, cannot remain isolated from the forces of collective memory. Likewise, historians—some more successfully than others—can contribute to the construction of memory in a variety of ways, whether by publicizing an accurate account of the past or by distorting the past in the service of the present. Nonetheless, the "work" of history is held to a higher standard, and is therefore assumed to reflect the course of events with greater accuracy than the evolving forces of memory.

Because it constantly evolves, reflects the desires of the community, and is not subject to the strictures of the historical discipline, collective memory can also, as Jacques Le Goff has written, "overflow" or supersede history as a form of knowledge and as a public rite.[39] History is secular, whereas memory "lives on in a religious or sacred key,"[40] transcending in its formation and manifestations the structures and rules of the historian's craft. The sacral nature of memory emerges in various ways, most visibly and prominently at those spaces that Nora describes as the *lieux de mémoire,* or memory sites.[41] Such sites exist to redefine, illustrate, manifest, and embody individual and group recollections of the past. Monuments, museums, and the spaces of public ritual are all examples of common loci memoriae that function as fora of public commemoration, and it is at sites like these that memory most clearly reveals its collective, participatory, and ritualistic elements.

The State Museum at Auschwitz is one such site, but unlike many other memory sites, it exists both as the location of historical events and, simultaneously, as the arena where public commemoration of those events takes place. It is significant that postliberation Auschwitz has always had a certain tangibility. The memorial site is, of course, a smaller[42] and inevitably sanitized representation of the complex as it existed in 1945, and only the Stammlager and Birkenau remain accessible to visitors. But that they are accessible at all and have preserved many of their tangible remains (in contrast to Bełżec or Neuengamme, for example), makes them comparatively well suited to the physical objectification of memory, the synthesis and institutionalization of memorial symbols, and the use of their memorial spaces for repetitive commemorative ritual.

Manifested in symbols, exhibitions, and public demonstrations, Polish collective memory at Auschwitz has both explained history and misrepresented it; it has honored the dead and, at times, has been selective about the those whom it chooses to honor; it has shown reverent silence and has also engaged in noisy demonstration; it has been an indicator of liberalizing transformations in the cultural policy of the Polish People's Republic and has also communicated the ideological rigidity of that state. Such diversity and contradiction in the manifestations of collective memory at Auschwitz should come as no surprise. These contradictions are born of the multifaceted history of the camp complex, but they also reflect the fact that collective memory and its manifestations, as the French sociologist Maurice Halbwachs illustrated more than seventy years ago, arise from what he called the "social frameworks of memory."[43] Memories do not originate only on a purely individual basis; rather, they are constructed and maintained with the help of others. Collective frameworks are, then, the means by which the collective memory forms its images of the past, and because these frameworks are the products of present social conditions, they help to construct images of the past that are in accordance with the current cultures, identities, ideologies, and desires of the larger community.[44] In short, the past is reshaped to suit the needs of the present, its images helping to legitimize the needs of the current social order.[45]

According to Halbwachs, this presentist imperative renders collective memory unreliable as a guide to events that actually transpired. Rather than accurately reflecting the events of the past, collective memory is a composite and mutating image that inevitably deviates from historical reality because of its reliance on society's mnemonic frameworks.[46] As Halbwachs noted, "Society from time to time obligates people not just to reproduce in thought previous events of their lives, but also to touch them up, to shorten them, or to complete them so that, however convinced we are that our memories are exact, we give them a prestige that reality did not possess."[47] In short, social groups and their frameworks of memory alter or distort memory in the process of reconstructing it.[48]

The ease with which Halbwachs' social frameworks can transform memory points to the disturbing ease with which collective memory can be manipulated, both consciously and unconsciously. State, family, church, associations, and a myriad of other social groups all have the ability to direct or censor collective memory. Collective memory can be socially mandated as an institution works to create a common mode of memory by selecting those aspects of the past that appear best suited to the exigencies of the present. It is, for example, not uncommon for groups to embellish the past artificially or to abbreviate it dishonestly for the purpose of encouraging social unity in the present.[49] "One might say," Patrick Hutton has written, "that memory colonizes the past by obliging it to conform to present conceptions."[50]

"Colonization" of the past, however, exists not only in the conquest of memory, for manipulated memory is also used as an instrument of social and political power.[51] Its effectiveness as an instrument of power depends, of course, on the relative power of the social group that holds it. A state can, for example, influence the collective memory of a people's past only to the extent that it retains political power. Religious authorities can continue to shape the ways in which people perceive the origins of their spirituality only as long as their authority is maintained. A museum can influence the public's understanding of the past only insofar as the knowledge and expertise of its creators and sponsors is respected.

Polish memory of Auschwitz at the memorial site illustrates many of these characteristics of collective memory. The State Museum at Auschwitz is a *locus memoriae* that has borne the social structures of Auschwitz memory and staged its manifestations. It has done the work of the historian in attempting to represent the past accurately and objectively, and it has also shaped that past to conform to current cultural and political needs. The museum has, both by accident and by design, altered and distorted the past while attempting to reconstruct it in the tangible forms of exhibitions, monuments, and demonstrations. The site has always been selective in what it has presented to the public. As an occasional arena of cold-war propaganda, it has even functioned as an instrument of political power, at times used in vulgar fashion to condemn the western capitalist and militarist threat and celebrate the goals and achievements of Polish United Workers' Party and its mentor, the Communist Party of the Soviet Union (CPSU). Finally, the respective durability of various modes of memory at Auschwitz has been subject to the power of those individuals and institutions that have supervised the working of the State Museum. Each phase in the postwar history of Auschwitz has been marked by changes—some major, others less significant—in the memorial agenda of the museum, its staff, and those institutions of the communist state that have exercised influence or control over the site. With this in mind, it should come as no surprise that many major changes to the site have occurred within the last decade, that is, in the wake of Polish communism's fall.

Despite the applicability of Halbwachs's ideas for this study of memory at Auschwitz, it is necessary to enter a caveat: a collective Auschwitz memory and the social structures on which it is based need not be static. Rather, it has a diachronic character, subject to temporal factors beyond Poland's borders and influenced by the revisionary impulses of individuals and groups, and even by the poignancy of historical facts. Even as the collective upheavals associated with the fall of communism challenged many of the assumptions and traditions of collective Auschwitz memory in Poland, so too have the challenges of individuals, groups, and events throughout the postwar decades shaken memory's framework, causing Auschwitz memory, in a manner of speaking, to "fall out of its frame." In October 1953 former prisoners of the camp rebelled against the propagandistic memorial agenda imposed upon the Auschwitz site by Warsaw's Stalinist regime. In 1967 and 1968 members of the International Auschwitz Committee refused cooperation with the State Museum and government authorities on account of Poland's growing and officially sanctioned anti-Semitism. In 1979 Pope John Paul II visited Auschwitz. His presence, authority, and magnetism legitimized Polish vernacular notions of Auschwitz and, at the same time, transformed the memorial site into a stage for opposition to the regime. In the early 1990s a historian at the State Museum at Auschwitz rejected, on the basis of years of research, the estimate of 4 million dead at Auschwitz—an estimate that had been, until then, inviolable among Polish scholars and memorialists of Auschwitz. These examples, as the following chapters will relate, are illustrative of both the durability of collective memorial paradigms at Auschwitz and, at the same time, memory's elasticity.

The transformations of memory at Auschwitz reveal that the line between history and memory, or between the "real" and "imagined" Auschwitz, was inevitably blurred. This study remains mindful of the "real" Auschwitz as a measure of the "imagined," memorialized Auschwitz, for the distinction matters in any evaluation of the manifestations of memory at the site. At the same time, the complexity of the camp's history and the immensity of the crimes there make any precise and universally applicable standard of representation of Auschwitz history difficult to establish—and difficult to uphold. The analysis to follow will at times be critical of the cultural or ideological inflections that led to the misrepresentation of history at the memorial site, but it does not claim to set a new, neutral standard of representation. There are also suggestions at various points in the book that Auschwitz, if permitted, could "speak for itself." This is not a call for a site devoid of any interpretation or representation, nor does it imply that an Auschwitz simply left to decay would be more "real" or "meaningful" as a site of memory. In general, however, the landscape, artifacts, and survivors of Auschwitz have been the most effective pedagogical "tools" at the site, far surpassing in didactic effectiveness the ideological interpretations of many exhibitions or the politicized cant of many demonstrations.

None of this should suggest the existence of a simplistic dichotomy between "good," historically accurate "commemoration" and "bad," politically inflected "propaganda." Nor is it a call for historical relativism. Rather, this analysis recognizes the complexities of representing the past at Auschwitz and recognizes the challenges faced when approaching Auschwitz as a historian, and especially as a historian of memory. As Saul Friedländer has emphasized in confronting the "final solution": "The extermination of the Jews of Europe is as accessible to both representation and interpretation as any other historical event. But we are dealing with an event which tests our traditional conceptual and representational categories, an 'event at the limits.'"[52] Ideally, the objective historian—ever the perceptive arbiter—stands outside the subjective processes of memory, but, as Friedländer relates, "[s]ome claim to the 'truth' appears particularly imperative. It suggests, in other words, that there are limits to representation *which should not be but can easily be transgressed.* What the characteristics of such a transgression are, however, is far more intractable than our definitions have so far been able to encompass."[53] In short, there is a tension between the "real" and the "represented" Auschwitz that was and remains a source of unease for both the historian and the public memorialist. As helpful as the demarcation between the "real" and the "represented" Auschwitz may be as a heuristic device, the fact remains that Polish stewards of memory were inevitably concerned with the latter, even as they were, or claimed to be, committed to the former.

Henry Rousso has related the development and mutation of an event's collective memory to the role of these stewards—what he calls the "vectors," or "carriers" of memory and defines as "any source that proposes a deliberate reconstruction of an event for a social purpose."[54] "Official carriers" are those commemorative phenomena such as monuments and ceremonies that attempt to offer a "comprehensive, unitary representation of the event" being commemorated. "Organizational carriers" of memory are associations and organizations that join in a commemorative act for the purpose of gathering and maintaining a common mode of memory among the members of the groups. Media such as journalism, broadcasting, and literature are the "cultural carriers" of memory, providing what appear to be individualistic perceptions of the past—perceptions that are nonetheless the products of a diversity of memorial images. Finally, the "scholarly carriers" of memory are those sources, such as historians and museum curators, who attempt to reconstruct and interpret the events of the past.[55]

Since 1945 these four vectors of memory have converged on the Auschwitz site. As the following chapters will illustrate, historians and museologists have shaped the representation of the past in their publications and documentary exhibitions, and the Polish and international media have likewise left their mark on public perceptions of the site and its history. Organizational carriers such as national and international associations of former prisoners, state institutions charged with the site's care and supervision, as well as religious groups have all utilized the memorial space at Auschwitz for the purpose of forging a common mode of memory both within their own groups and beyond them. Not least, the official carriers of Auschwitz memory—the Polish government, its Ministry of Culture and Art, and the State Museum itself—have erected monuments, developed exhibitions, and choreographed ceremonies intended to instill and maintain a "comprehensive, unitary representation" of the events that took place at Auschwitz.

The interpretation, representation, and commemoration of what transpired at the Auschwitz camp was not the sole property of these four types of forces as they converged on the postwar site, for individuals and groups from within Poland and from beyond its borders have also brought their own memorial aspirations and agendas, adding to the site's landscape occasional spontaneous, unchoreographed manifestations of individual and group memory. Examples of such initiatives are Roman Catholic pilgrims or Jewish individuals and groups honoring those victims neglected in the prevailing memorial paradigms at the site. They have added controversy as well as diversity to Auschwitz.

Despite the occasional presence of diverse modes of memory, one can trace the development of a "dominant memory" (that is, what Rousso calls "a collective interpretation of the past that may even come to have official status")[56] at the State Museum and in its activities. A charge of the Polish state since its founding, the State Museum is a prime example of how memory can become institutionalized and how that institution can then utilize a prevailing mode of memory as an instrument of social and political power.

It is, of course, impossible to claim the existence of a single, dominant mode of memory at a place like Auschwitz. The camp's history has always defied generalization, the social frameworks upon which Auschwitz memory was based were diverse and at times in conflict, and the public manifestations of that memory were not static, but in flux. Nonetheless, in the period under consideration three main characteristics of collective memory emerged at the Auschwitz site. First, Poles quickly came to regard Auschwitz as a place of Polish national martyrdom. The multinational makeup of the camp's deportees and inmates was stressed at times, but by and large the particularly Polish element of sacrifice at the camp received the greatest emphasis in the site's exhibitions, iconography, and commemorative rituals. As early as 1947 Auschwitz had, in the Polish popular historical consciousness, become a camp primarily intended for the internment, exploitation, and extermination of the Polish political prisoner—a prisoner who was not a helpless victim but a resistance fighter, a hero, a *martyr* suffering and dying for some higher good, like the Polish nation, the Catholic faith, or socialism.

Second, Auschwitz was acknowledged, but usually not specified, as a place of Jewish victimization. Neither the State Museum nor the Polish government ever explicitly denied that the vast majority of victims at Auschwitz were Jews. But this fact was not emphasized; nor did it designate Auschwitz in any distinctive way. Simply put, Jews were usually included among the so-called "martyrs" of Auschwitz and regarded as citizens of Poland, the Netherlands, France, Hungary, Greece, or one of the many other countries under Nazi occupation. One has to grant that the destruction of Europe's Jews was not yet, in the first postwar years, the distinct category of historical analysis or broad, public commemoration that it is today. But the fact remains that for decades Polish postwar culture did not treat the Shoah as the salient characteristic of Auschwitz, but relegated it instead to the status of yet another example of German barbarism. Jews were to be remembered for their suffering and death, but they were neither represented as the overwhelming majority of victims at the site nor given proper emphasis in the larger memorialization undertaken there.

Third, the Polish state instrumentalized Auschwitz as a political arena. In the processes of valorizing Polish martyrdom and de-emphasizing Jewish victimization, the Soviet-imposed communist government in Poland frequently used Auschwitz as a site for the accumulation of political currency. As members of the regime and the press sought to vindicate a prevailing ideology through the recollection of Poland's tragic past, the Auschwitz memorial site, its exhibitions, and its public events served as a rallying point of sorts for the socioeconomic order, for staunchly anti-West German foreign policy, and, in the late 1940s and early 1950s, for vulgar anti-American, anti-Western propaganda. Although firmly grounded in the domestic and international political agendas of the Soviet Union and its satellites, the commemorative tone set at Auschwitz can also be viewed within the context of a postwar European anti-fascist consensus. And not surprisingly, those West European organizations that were most involved in commemorative activities at the Auschwitz site were often closely associated with the political parties of the West European left.

These are the main components of the dominant memorial framework at Auschwitz in the years of the Polish People's Republic. The foundations for this framework were laid in Poland's wartime experience and the first months after the liberation. Shifts in Poland's political landscape, the ideological imperatives of successive regimes, developments abroad, and the growing prominence of Auschwitz as a site of international commemoration would shake that framework in the 1950s, 1960s, and 1970s. By the late 1970s, domestic and international changes were under way that further internationalized and democratized the site as an arena of public commemoration. These changes, in combination with Pope John Paul II's visit to the memorial site in June 1979, initiated the collapse of Poland's framework of memory at Auschwitz, for even as the pope's words and deeds at the site legitimized the Polish-national commemorative paradigm, they also marked the beginning of its dissolution. The analysis therefore concludes with this watershed in the postwar history of the memorial site and points, in the epilogue, to some of the debates over Auschwitz since. Controversy over the Carmelite Convent, the presence of religious symbols, the uses of the grounds and structures of the former camp complex, and "proprietorship" over the memorial site—these debates were all manifestations of the framework's undoing after 1979 and coincided with the slow collapse of Poland's communist regime in the 1980s.

The transformation of the memorial site has not been rapid. Auschwitz has, since the fall of communism, ceased to be a stage for state-sponsored demonstration, and although the State Museum has embarked over the past ten years on a daunting and elusive quest to give all victim groups their rightful place in the memorialization undertaken there, vestiges of the traditional framework of memory remain. The exhibitions and commemorative rituals at the site reflect, even to the present day, many of the memorial paradigms of the 1940s, 1950s, and 1960s. In this respect, Auschwitz memory has been more durable than many expected. This study, on the other hand, emphasizes the malleability of Auschwitz memory. Just as the memory and meaning of Auschwitz are not fixed, but have remained in flux over the past fifty years, so too have the manifestations of that memory at the site been subject to shifting cultural and political currents. Emphasis on Polish martyrdom, neglect or conscious understatement of the Shoah, political exploitation of the grounds and expositions—these are controversial characteristics of the camp's postwar landscape. The remainder of this analysis will account for these characteristics, but will also account for the variations and conversions of memory at the site. By underscoring the malleability of Auschwitz in the postwar years, it emphasizes the need to extend our investigations of memorial sites beyond mere commentaries on their landscape or exhibitions, for the sources of these physical characteristics are to be found not only in the architecture of Nazi terror, but also in the postwar conditions, debates, and decisions surrounding their creation.

1 ‖ Poland and Auschwitz, 1945–1947

ON 14 JUNE 1947, some thirty thousand visitors from across Poland and abroad gathered in Oświęcim, a sleepy town of ten thousand residents on the southeastern border of Upper Silesia. It was a public event, a ceremony, and a spectacle of sorts: the occasion was the seventh anniversary of the day in 1940 when 728 Polish prisoners were brought to a former military base on the outskirts of the town, a base that would serve as a concentration camp for the next five years. But the concentration camp at Oświęcim—"Auschwitz," as the Germans called it—would become the largest death factory in all of Europe, the site where more than a million perished at the hands of the German occupiers. And so on this June day thousands gathered to remember the dead of Auschwitz, to commemorate their legacy, and to participate in the dedication of the State Museum at Oświęcim-Brzezinka.[1]

In the original camp, Auschwitz I, the day's events opened under the banners and flags of political parties, religious groups, trade unions, and organizations of former political prisoners. The ceremonies began with religious services of various faiths, followed by the speeches of visiting dignitaries and government officials. Vice-Minister of Transportation Zygmunt Balicki, general secretary of the International Federation of Former Political Prisoners, called for international solidarity among all former prisoners in the struggle against Hitlerism. Parliamentary representative Sak, speaking in the name of the Central Committee of Jews in Poland, expressed his hope for the brotherhood of all nations, while Stanisław Dybowski, the minister of culture and art in the new Polish government, announced the creation of a Polish Council for the Protection of Monuments of Struggle and Martyrdom.

Most important, however, were the words of the prime minister and leader of the Polish Socialist Party, Józef Cyrankiewicz, himself a former political prisoner in Auschwitz. The premier recalled for his audience the extent of German barbarism both on and off the battlefield during the years of the Second World War, and to his former fellow prisoners he stated: "Those of us who remain, who remember the heinous factories of death—we are, for the Polish nation, for Europe, for the entire world . . . not only a document; we must be the conscious, organized vanguard of the struggle, so that the tragedy to which we are witnesses, of which we are living documents, is never repeated." That struggle, according to the premier, included concrete goals, among them "the progress of states toward independence," "reconstruction of Poland from the ruins," and "the building of a lasting peace."[2] The only salvation for the Polish nation, he claimed, and the only way out of the abyss of terror and destruction, was for the Poles to rebuild their land from the ashes of the German invasion and to struggle for a new beginning.[3] The grounds of Auschwitz, according to the premier, would function both as a historical artifact and as an admonition to future generations. "The museum," Cyrankiewicz stated, "will be not only an eternal warning and document of unbound German bestiality, but also at the same time proof of truth about man and his fight for freedom—a document arousing intensified vigilance so that genocidal powers that bring destruction to nations will never rise again."[4] At the conclusion of his speech, the prime minister declared the museum officially open and the crowd joined in the singing of "Rota" (Pledge), a patriotic Polish anthem from the early twentieth century.

The crowd then walked the three kilometers from Auschwitz I to Birkenau, the spacious moor that had served as the massive extermination center of the Auschwitz complex. Passing through the main gate and along the railroad siding where the infamous "selection" of deportees took place, the crowd stopped between the rubble of the gas chambers and ovens of Crematoria II and III. Wreaths were laid in memory of the victims, a cross was erected atop the ruins of one of the crematoria, and the day's ceremonies were concluded with the singing, once again, of "Rota:"

> We shall not yield our forebears' land,
> Nor see our language muted.
> Our nation is Polish, and Polish our folk,
> By Piasts constituted.
> By cruel oppression we'll not be swayed!
> May God so lend us aid.

By the very last drop of blood in our veins,
Our souls will be secured,
Until in dust and ashes falls,
The stormwind sown by the Prussian lord.
Our every home will form a stockade.
May God so lend us aid.

We'll not be spat on by Teutons
Nor abandon our youth to the German!
We'll follow the call of the Golden Horn,
Under the Holy Spirit, our *Hetman.*
Our armed battalions shall lead the crusade.
May God so lend us aid.[5]

This day's ceremonies were more than a nationalist commemoration of Poland's concentration camp victims; they also provide a lens through which to view Auschwitz memory in the first years after the liberation. A new world order free of the Hitlerite menace, a museum documenting Nazi atrocities in occupied Poland, the righting of wrongs done to Poland, a vengeful patriotic anthem, and a cross erected on what is arguably the largest Jewish cemetery in the world—these are only a few examples of the public manifestations of historical consciousness at Auschwitz. The June 1947 dedicatory ceremonies were an early register of the characteristics of Auschwitz memory in the early postwar years and an early expression of the political and cultural trends that dominated the public manifestations of that memory in the decades to follow.

In this chapter I examine these trends as they contributed to the development of a collective Auschwitz memory in Poland in the first two years after the liberation. Proceeding thematically rather than chronologically, I first offer a brief discussion of the political and social context for developments at the Auschwitz site in the years 1945–47. Second, I describe and analyze events and trends in these years that communicated the history of the camp to the Polish public—events that stimulated a broad discussion of Auschwitz and its place in the history of the occupation. In the third section, I account for the development of a Polish-national commemorative idiom at Auschwitz, for by 1947 Auschwitz had become the central locus of Polish wartime martyrology. I therefore examine two formative and characteristic aspects of Auschwitz memory in the context of this idiom: the notion of "martyrdom" as applied to Auschwitz victims and the concurrent marginalization of Jewish suffering and victimization. In the course of only two years, Polish national sacrifice became the central element of Auschwitz memory, while the fate of Jews at the camp, although never explicitly denied, remained on the margins of the more comprehensive commemoration of registered Polish prisoners and those of other nationalities.

The Early Postwar Context

The Poland that rose from the ashes of the Second World War was a country much different from what any Pole would have imagined in 1939. From the arrival of Soviet troops on Polish soil in early 1944 until the communist consolidation of power in 1947, Poland was in a state of economic and demographic devastation, had a variety of parties competing for political power, and was, arguably, in a state of civil war. Already in 1943 Stalin had organized in Moscow the Union of Polish Patriots (Związek Patriotów Polskich, or ZPP), a group of exile communists led by members of the newly established Polish Workers' Party (Polska Partia Robotnicza, or PPR). In July 1944, this group formed the core of the Polish Committee of National Liberation (Polski Komitet Wyzwolenia Narodowego, or PKWN), which was installed in Lublin and hence was known as the Lublin Committee. At the Yalta Conference of February 1945, Roosevelt, Stalin, and Churchill had reached vague agreement on the formation of a "government of national unity" representing anti-Nazi and democratic forces in the reconstituted Poland. This was a clear victory for Stalin, for the basis of the new government would be the Lublin Committee. The Polish government in exile, based in London, was thus rendered inconsequential, and in January 1945 its underground military wing, the Home Army (Armia Krajowa, or AK), was officially disbanded. The PKWN reconstituted itself at the end of 1944 as the Provisional Government of the Polish Republic, which then became the Provisional Government of National Unity in June 1945. This body, claiming legitimacy on the basis of the Yalta agreements and Western recognition, was composed, in part, of PPR communists. It also included members of the London government-in-exile such the Polish People's Party (PSL) leader Stanisław Mikołajczyk, who had left London for Poland in the hope of lending this government some democratic legitimacy. Mikołajczyk would be disappointed, however, for despite nominal commitment to diversity and pluralism, the Provisional Government of National Unity was a vehicle for the steady subordination of the state to communist rule. Eventually threatened with arrest, Mikołajczyk was forced to flee Poland in late 1947.

From June 1945 until its dissolution in February 1947 the provisional government's authority rested on minimal public support. Poland had never been a bastion of leftist revolutionary politics; its proletarian classes were less developed than those in the West, and bitter memories of the 1939–41 Soviet occupation of eastern Poland remained. Indeed, for many Poles, it appeared as if the Red Army and its Moscow-trained Polish stooges had replaced the German occupier. The early months of Soviet "liberation" seemed to confirm fears of Soviet-style repression and coercion. Following the Home Army's failed Warsaw Uprising of August–October 1944, the Lublin Committee began to organize, in cooperation with the Red Army, a new police and security apparatus. Through espionage, intimidation, and terror, these organs assisted in the consolidation of communist rule. Their tactics were directed against anti-Soviet armed insurgent groups such as the right-wing National Armed Forces, against remnants of the AK known as the Freedom and Independence Movement, and against the Ukrainian Insurgent Army. The security forces and police did not, however, limit their activities to the fight against armed opposition groups. With the promulgation of a decree in January 1946, they had the freedom to punish those who had been involved in the "fascistization of political life," and six months later, they would pursue opponents of the new order on the basis of the law "On Offenses Particularly Dangerous at the Time of the Reconstruction of the State."[6]

The security forces were extensive and effective, and their power was especially evident in the weeks leading up to the parliamentary elections in January 1947. The provisional government had already shown itself capable of electoral manipulation during a July 1946 referendum, and in the January elections, the PPR-led "Democratic Bloc" garnered an 80 percent majority of the vote. The communist victory was, however, the result of falsification and intimidation at every level. A million voters were disqualified, thousands of others were arrested or beaten, workers were transported en masse to the polls—all for the purpose of consolidating PPR power while unsuccessfully attempting to give the appearance of a viable democratic process.

It is clear that the communists held the dominant position in Polish political life, but their takeover of Poland was neither a facile assumption of
power nor the imposition of authority on a population wholly opposed to
the PPR's goals for a new society. There were, to be sure, aspects of the PPR
program that appealed to various sectors of the population: for peasants, land
reform; for some intellectuals, a break from grandiose and irrational nationalist traditions; for workers, the promise of dignity and fair wages. To those
willing to support the authorities, the promised social order appeared to offer
opportunity, stability, and at least a modicum of personal freedoms, for the
regime allowed freedom of religious practice[7] and, at least in 1945 and 1946, a
relatively pluralistic press.[8]

Despite what might appear to be a straight path to Soviet-style communism in the immediate postwar period, Polish political life, as Padraic Kenney
has argued, included at least a discourse of democracy.[9] Before the onset of
Polish Stalinism in 1948–49, the language of democratic politics was not yet
vacuous, and it may come as a surprise to some that in the ceremonies and exhibitions at the Auschwitz memorial site, for example, representatives of the
new Polish state were responding to the needs of the public as articulated by
a variety of public voices. It was, as Krystyna Kersten has observed, an era of
contradictions. If installing a communist regime in Poland was, as Stalin had
claimed, akin to "saddling a cow," then it is understandable that the provisional government used force and intimidation, while in other instances it exercised restraint. As Kersten notes:

> A great majority was decidedly against the Communists, opposed the order
> established by the PPR and, at the same time, excepting the armed under-
> ground, was compelled to cooperate with the new authorities in the rebuild-
> ing of the country. In sum, that accumulation of contradictions created a very
> complex internal situation in the country. The fragmentary picture conveyed
> by the documents of that time or in memoirs gives an incomplete image, even
> a false one. The authorities attempted to win society over but, at the same
> time, burned villages and mistreated AK prisoners. The population fought
> against the authorities, even by terror, and simultaneously cooperated with
> the state. The strategy of the authorities depended on the eradication of all
> existing and potential centers of organized opposition. Society's strategy,
> which rested upon millions of individual positions, depended on the defense
> of cultural values in conditions limited by reality.[10]

The "reality" of the immediate postwar era was grim on every level and gave rise to the paradoxical situation that Kersten describes. Exacerbating the political chaos and oppression were enormous economic and social problems. Nearly 20 percent of the population was lost in the war, depriving Polish society of the energy and talent of youth crucial to the rebuilding effort. Poland's demographic upheaval was also the result of massive population movements, for the Yalta and Potsdam agreements shifted the country's borders to the west, compensating Poland for losses in the east with territory at Germany's expense. This resulted in the flight or expulsion of 3.5 million Germans from Poland. Two million Poles returning from slave labor or camps, as well as refugees expelled from formerly Polish territory annexed to the Soviet Union, replaced them.[11] Ironically, one goal of many late nineteenth- and early twentieth-century Polish nationalists became a reality: by 1947 Poland was a homogenous and overwhelmingly Roman Catholic country. The Germans and their accomplices killed nearly 3 million Polish Jews; the Soviets took the Ukrainians, Lithuanians, and Belorussians for their own; and the Poles expelled the Germans: the sum of these actions was an irreplaceable cultural loss for the postwar generation.

Population loss, economic deprivation, and political chaos had, of course, devastating psychological effects, not the least of which was a wartime legacy that appeared to be the result of defeat snatched from the jaws of victory. France and Britain had declared war against Germany in defense of Poland's independence; Poland, although defeated at home, continued to fight around the world alongside the victorious Allies, only to be abandoned to the Soviet Union as a recalcitrant member of its new postwar consortium of client states. For this, there seemed to be few clear moral explanations. The Soviet Union's tremendous wartime sacrifice resulted in the defeat of Nazism and a new superpower status. Britain and the United States could be assured that their dead had fallen in defense of freedom and democracy. Even the Germans could blame their wartime devastation on leaders who had led them astray. In Poland, none of these arguments applied or offered any consolation. Poles fought the war, opposed the Nazis on all fronts, and emerged, in a sense, victorious, but they could not reap the rewards that their honor seemed due.[12] This sense of irreparable, unjust, and, for many, inexplicable loss helps to explain the insistent and omnipresent commemoration of Poland's fallen in the early postwar years. To what end the sacrifice? The emerging culture of martyrology could ameliorate the pain of this question, if only in small measure and even if it failed to provide a satisfactory answer.

In mourning the nation's losses, Poland's commemorative culture also had to come to terms with the loss of millions of Jews on Polish lands. In the aftermath of the war, relations between Poles and their Jewish fellow citizens were strained at best. At worst, a residual and reawakened anti-Semitism resulted in pogroms and murder, and it stands as one of the tragic ironies of the Polish situation that anti-Semitism would take this form in the country that suffered most under Nazi regime.

Of the few Jews remaining in Poland or returning after the war,[13] a sizable percentage attempted to reorganize themselves as a legitimate national minority with religious, educational, and cultural institutions. Many of these Jews, believing they would be secure under a socialist or communist government, were even optimistic about the future.[14] Conditions in Poland, however, were not as accommodating as they had perhaps anticipated, for a wave of attacks against Jews swept across the country in the years 1945–47. In 1945 alone, 355 Jews were killed in Poland, and in the July 1946 Kielce pogrom, 41 Jews were killed and 59 wounded.[15] By summer 1947 nearly 1,500 Jews had died as the result of violent attacks, although it is unclear what percentage of them were murdered because they were Jews.[16] Not surprisingly, many surviving Jews emigrated to western Europe, the United States, or Palestine.

Part—but only part—of the explanation for the violence lies in a history of anti-Semitism in Polish culture and society that reached its apex in the years just prior to the war. In the words of one contemporary commentator, the national tradition of anti-Semitism "continues in Poland as a residual attitude, as a habit, and as a reflex."[17] Moreover, the prevailing stereotype of the *żydo-komuna,* or Jewish-inspired communist conspiracy, fueled anti-Semitism and incited violence. In Poland, as in most other European countries, many associated the communist movement with Jewish conspiracy. In addition, popular perceptions alleged that Jews had enthusiastically welcomed and served in the administration of the Soviet occupation of eastern Poland in 1939,[18] suggesting not only pro-communist sympathies, but also a traitorous anti-Polish attitude. Because of these assumptions and stereotypes, many in early postwar Poland identified Jews with the unpopular Soviet-installed provisional government and especially its security forces.[19] As Władysław Bartoszewski, a member of the wartime Council for Aid to the Jews, or "Żegota," explained:

After the Second World War, the stereotype of the communist Jew—advanced by the pre-war parties and right-wing political groups, and also to a certain extent by Church circles—was unexpectedly and spectacularly reinforced by the public activity of those Jewish communists who played an important role in the security and propaganda apparatus, at a time when the majority of Polish society was inclined to see this activity as pursued in the direct interests of the USSR. There was a dangerous, and morally absolutely unacceptable tendency to blame the Jews in Poland *en masse* for the complete suppression of human rights by the new authorities and for the misfortune of the nation which felt it had lost its independence, despite nominally winning the war against Germany as one of the Allies. It should be added that similar generalisations regarding members of the security apparatus who were *not* Jewish were notable for their absence.[20]

To immediately link a helpless Jew to the communist takeover in Poland was, of course, absurd, but many supported this view with the common assumption that a disproportionately large percentage of the new governmental elite in Warsaw was of Jewish origin, as were many prewar Polish communists and socialists.[21] In the words of Michael Steinlauf, the notion of the żydo-komuna was "[t]he product of labyrinthine interaction between systems of myth and stereotype on one hand and historical experience on the other."[22]

There were also more immediate and material causes for renewed discrimination against Jews. According to several scholars, the reclamation of former Jewish property was central to the problem.[23] After the war thousands of Jews returned to their homes from refuge in the Soviet Union or from the camps. Much of their property and even many of their synagogues had been appropriated by Gentile Poles who assumed that they would never return. In his journalistic memoir, S. L. Shneiderman rather melodramatically described the dilemma faced when Jews began to return from the camps and abroad:

They were now returning to look for what was left of their homes or their relatives. But when a Polish peddler hands a Jew a loaf of bread or a bowl of soup, he wonders whence this Jew has come. He was persuaded that he would never again see a Jew. Many of these street peddlers have furnished their homes with the belongings of murdered Jews; some are living in Jewish apartments; others have inherited the workshops of Jewish tailors or shoemakers. Looking at the returning Jews, they wonder whether among their number there is not some relative of the Jews whose goods they had appropriated. In the smaller towns, where the inhabitants do not feel the hand of authority as directly as do those who live in the capital, such newly returned Jews have often been murdered.[24]

Postwar anti-Semitism was also rooted in a factor unique to the Polish situation: unlike the situation in other countries under German rule, where anti-Semitism was generally identified with fascist quisling governments, anti-Semitism in Poland was not wholly discredited by the experience of the occupation. Writing in the journal *Odrodzenie,* Kazimierz Wyka observed in 1945:

> Why has the anti-Semitism of the educated classes, although at present it has no real basis, become tied with reaction in so many cases? Reaction alone cannot explain this. The core of the problem is elsewhere: it lies in the fact that Poland had no Quisling. Please do not imagine that I am trying to be paradoxical. Nevertheless, the tragic paradox of the present situation is that Poland is now the only country in Europe where anti-Semitism is still a factor and is inspiring murders. Ours is the country where the Jews were most thoroughly exterminated and where the resistance against the Germans during the occupation was the strongest, and yet it is here that Hitlerism has left its cuckoo egg. . . . If Polish anti-Semitism had comprised itself as collaborationist, it would later have been destroyed or at least unmasked. But since it never had a Quisling character, it retained its position and is still considered a mark of patriotism.[25]

Wyka's argument is perhaps a bit simplistic, but it remains worthy of consideration as one of many reasons for the persistence of anti-Semitism in these years. There were certainly collaborators in occupied Poland, but there was no collaborationist government executing Nazi policy toward Jews. This factor is not decisive in explaining the presence of anti-Semitism in early postwar Poland, but it does invite one to speculate on the forms Polish anti-Semitism might have taken had it been identified with a discredited quisling regime.

Regardless, it is clear that in the first postwar years Poles were able to evade a thorough confrontation with the problem of anti-Semitism. Wartime devastation, reconstruction, demographic upheaval, and political conflict allowed for and even encouraged a retreat from the "Jewish question." It also encouraged Poles to face the challenge of coming to terms with their "own" losses in the Second World War and turn to the cultivation of a Polish-national martyrological idiom—an idiom that came to center on the history and commemoration of Auschwitz. As Poles learned more about the camp, its place in the German occupation, and the crimes perpetrated there, Auschwitz quickly emerged as the most compelling symbol of Polish martyrdom.

Auschwitz in the Public View

Any consideration of Auschwitz and its place in Poland's early postwar commemorative culture must come to terms with the presentation of the camp's history to the Polish public, for the ways of conveying that history—the postwar vectors of Auschwitz memory—helped to define its meaning in the years to come. The nature of the crimes, the identity of both perpetrators and victims, and the significance of the crimes for postwar Poland were all issues open to public discussion as governmental institutions, the press, and former prisoners related the history of the camp to the public at large. Auschwitz was well known to the Polish population even during the occupation, as word of the brutal conditions in the camp spread via the channels of underground resistance[26] and reports of prisoners who had been released.[27] Even if Auschwitz had a certain symbolic status prior to the liberation, in the first months after the war its history and meaning were far from clear, as the Polish public was confronted with an array of inconsistent evidence and speculative reports on the crimes committed there.

The attempt to ascertain the number of victims at Auschwitz and other camps illustrates the confusion. On the day of Germany's unconditional surrender a Red Army publication announced that 4 million had died at Auschwitz, a figure based on the findings of the Soviet investigative commission that had begun its work after liberating the camp.[28] In late summer 1945 the Warsaw daily *Życie Warszawy*, citing a report by the French occupation authorities in Germany, claimed that a total of 26 million died in German camps during the war, with 12,000–14,000 murdered daily in Dachau alone[29]—a fanciful figure because Dachau did not function as an extermination center. A year later, the British prosecuting attorney at the Nürnberg Trials set the total number of dead in camps across Europe at 12 million.[30] In May 1945 a report in *Życie Warszawy* stated that 5 million had been murdered in Auschwitz,[31] and in January 1946 a Nürnberg witness claimed that 4 million Jews alone had perished in Auschwitz.[32] A month later a report in *Gazeta Ludowa*, based on the estimates of the American Joint Distribution Committee for the Aid of Jews, stated that a total of 4.4 million Jews from across Europe had been murdered in all the camps.[33] The lack of consensus undoubtedly confused many Poles, but reports such as these left no doubt that the German atrocities at Auschwitz were of an unimaginable magnitude.

Sensational as reports on the number of victims at Nazi camps may have been, they were only part of the wave of "publicity" after the liberation in January 1945. In the following weeks reports and survivor testimonies appeared in the press and in book form,[34] while the Soviet forensic commission began its highly publicized investigations at the Auschwitz site on 4 February.[35] The work of this group was augmented by the investigations of other organizations, each with its own research agenda. The Polish Institute of National Remembrance, committed to gathering information on German crimes "lest the heroics of the Red Army be lost,"[36] was the initiative of the newly formed Ministry of Education. The Central Committee of Jews in Poland[37] formed a subsidiary Jewish Historical Documentary Commission to study the fate of Jews in the camps and to determine their countries of origin.[38] In addition, local courts across Poland collected evidence related to German crimes.

For most Poles, however, the main source for information about Auschwitz was the Central Commission for the Investigation of German Crimes in Poland (Główna Komisja Badania Zbrodni Niemieckich w Polsce), an institution called into force by the provisional government in early 1945.[39] The commission was the main agency for the collection and analysis of evidence related to Nazi crimes on Polish territory, both in camps and at large. The Central Commission also had several subsidiary groups, most notably the Kraków-based Commission for the Investigation of German Crimes at Auschwitz. This subsidiary commission issued the first report on crimes at Auschwitz, and its findings hit the press on the same day as news of the German surrender. The report not only included descriptions of the gassing and crematory processes, but based on research of killing capacity, interviews with survivors, and the testimony of the former commandant Rudolf Höss, it also estimated that 4 million citizens of Poland, the Soviet Union, France, Yugoslavia, and other nations had been murdered at Auschwitz.[40]

The estimate of 4 million dead was, as noted in the introduction, inviolable for Polish and many Israeli scholars, and for decades it remained inscribed in a variety contexts at the Auschwitz site. At the same time, according to the Auschwitz historian Andrzej Strzelecki, the figure took on a symbolic value that hindered further attempts to assess accurately the number of dead.[41] Although this was certainly the case, the number, while inaccurate and based on insufficient research, should not be regarded as a conscious attempt in 1945 to inflate the number of dead for the "polonization," "dejudaization," or "internationalization" of Auschwitz and its memory. There is simply not sufficient evidence from these early years to support the claim of conscious manipulation of the figures.

It is also worth noting in this context that just as the number of 4 million Auschwitz victims was for decades considered immutable, so too was the figure of 6 million Polish citizens (3 million "Poles" and 3 million "Polish Jews") killed during World War II. The number was set already in January 1947 and has remained a constant in postwar Polish scholarship and discourse. While the number of Polish Jews killed is still believed to be around 3 million, recent research has reduced the number of ethnic Poles killed and also has accounted for losses among members of other minorities who were citizens of the interwar Polish Republic.[42]

Inflated figures such as these can, of course, invite a simplistic and undifferentiated representation of wartime history, whether at Auschwitz or in general. This was especially the case with regard to the figure of 4 million dead at Auschwitz; Polish literature on the subject insufficiently demonstrated or even tended to minimize the Jewish tragedy at the camp.[43] Eager to portray themselves and their country as having suffered the most under German occupation and seeing in the horrific extent of crimes at Auschwitz a clear illustration of the German security threat in the early postwar years, Poles were not inclined to offer conservative estimates of the number of victims at Auschwitz. Nor were they inclined to designate Jews as a separate category of victim that had suffered differently than other victim groups. Instead, Jews were generally included simply as citizens of their countries of origin. Thus, just as the number of Polish citizens who died in the war was typically set at approximately 6 million, the fact that half were Jews was often neglected. Similarly, the number of Auschwitz dead was taken to be approximately 4 million, but the precise number of Jewish dead or the proportion of

Jews among those dead often remained unspecified, leading to the erroneous assumption that the Nazis subjected Polish Jews, Polish Gentiles, and other prisoners to equal treatment.

The research of the Central Commission and its Auschwitz branch proceeded slowly. The results of its research were provisional and the numerical estimates of victims certainly inaccurate, but in 1946 the group published a more comprehensive preliminary account of its findings. Entitled *German Crimes in Poland,* the volume is significant for a number of reasons. First, it classified German camps in Poland into four groups: *Umsiedlungslager* (resettlement camps), *Arbeitslager* (labor camps), *Vernichtungslager* (extermination camps) and *Konzentrationslager* (concentration camps). According to the report, only four extermination camps existed in Poland: Chełmno, Bełżec, Sobibór, and Treblinka, and the latter three were used exclusively for the extermination of Jews and Gypsies. Auschwitz-Birkenau, Stutthof, and Maidanek were classified as Konzentrationslager with extermination facilities attached.[44] Moreover, the Auschwitz complex was a special case, for it consisted of forty sub-camps and three major camps. The Auschwitz complex thus served as concentration camp, forced labor camp, and extermination center combined. This cast doubt upon the prevailing belief that Auschwitz was the largest and most "efficient" extermination camp in Nazi-occupied Europe, and made it all the more difficult to categorize Auschwitz and to arrive at a fixed and accurate understanding of *what* kind of camp it was, *who* its victims were, and *how* the camp was to be remembered and memorialized. Moreover, the report's classification of Auschwitz as a concentration camp with auxiliary extermination facilities may have strengthened the perception among many Poles that it was a camp primarily intended for Polish political prisoners and Soviet POWs. The commission's report was brief, vague, and left many questions unanswered. But it was the first published exposition of the Auschwitz crime which, unlike memoirs and newspaper accounts, relied on legal testimony and documentary evidence. As such, the report lent the ongoing investigation of Nazi crimes a degree of verifiable authenticity and, most importantly, offered the public a glimpse into the nature and extent of the horror of the camp.

Like the research and reports of organizations like the Central Commission, trials of Nazi criminals in Poland and Germany were also an effective source of information about Auschwitz and helped to shape its meaning in the early postwar period. The British trial of Joseph Kramer, Höss's adjutant and later commandant of Birkenau, was held in the north German town of Lüneburg, far from Poland. The Polish press nonetheless covered the trial, and it provided a certain amount of information about the life and death of prisoners in the camp.[45] Likewise, the proceedings of the International High Tribunal at Nürnberg received extensive press coverage. The report of the Central Commission for the Investigation of German Crimes in Poland may have been the most authoritative source of information on crimes at Auschwitz, but Nürnberg, a sensational event of international proportions, received far greater attention in the Polish press than did the Commission's findings. Thus, shocking headlines such as "Auschwitz: A Fate Worse than Death," witnesses' descriptions of children burned alive, and the testimony of Rudolf Höss, in which he confessed to supervising the murder of 3 million deportees at Auschwitz,[46] would remain fixed in Polish memory for decades.

Höss's own trial, held in Warsaw in the spring of 1947, was one of the greatest media events in early postwar Poland, and probably more than any other event focused the public's attention on Auschwitz. As the commandant responsible for the construction and early expansion of the Auschwitz complex, Höss was regarded as the personification of Nazi bestiality in occupied Poland. At Nürnberg, the former commandant had been exceptionally forthcoming and frank about his own role at Auschwitz and, for many Poles, took on the role of the prime executor of Hitlerite enslavement and extermination policy. It was only fitting, then, that he be extradited to Poland, tried, and executed in the country where he committed the worst of his crimes. Moreover, Poland saw itself as bearing a special responsibility to the rest of the world: the nation was the arbiter of judgment not only on Höss, but on the system he represented and had helped to create. As Tadeusz Cyprian, one of Höss's prosecutors, wrote in March 1947: "[T]he court that strips bare the motives of their [the Nazis'] actions with the merciless and cold approach of a surgeon, which penetrates the entire structure of the system in which they were raised or they themselves created—such a court fulfills the postulate of historical justice, for the court itself writes the history of the crime."[47] Indeed, the Höss trial was both a chronicle and interpretation of Auschwitz crimes, and the proceedings assumed spectacular proportions. Throughout March of 1947, full-page newspaper reports of the trial proceedings were the order of the day, reports that bombarded the reader with sensational headlines such as

"Rudolf Höss—Murderer of 4 Million—Stands before the Polish Court," "Testimonial Proof of the Crimes of Rudolf Höss—Freezing to Death of POWs," "Fields Fertilized With Human Ash—Entire Transports Perished in the Crematoria in Five Hours," or "2,850,000 Gassed in Auschwitz."[48]

The Höss trial, extensive media coverage, and reports of the government's forensic commission were the primary means of conveying the Auschwitz story to the Polish public in the first years after the liberation. They informed, interpreted, and directed Poland's attention to Auschwitz as the salient example of German wartime brutality. There remained, however, room for further definition of the significance of Auschwitz in postwar Poland. Nationalist traditions, the pull of political expediency, and the development of a Polish "martyrological consciousness" would place Auschwitz at the center of the country's commemoration of the occupation.

Toward a Martyrological Idiom

Władysław T. Bartoszewski has succinctly described why Poles and Jews have often been at odds over the meaning of Auschwitz. For Jews, the camp has become synonymous with the Shoah, a metonym for the extermination process that reached its horrifying conclusion there. It is therefore a locus of Jewish historical identity around the world. "In the collective memory of the Poles," however, "Auschwitz is primarily the camp set up to destroy the most prominent elements of the Polish nation."[49] Bartoszewski's insight points to the core of the Polish-Jewish debate over Auschwitz: the extent to which it is a memorial to the Nazi extermination of European Jews and the extent to which it is a memorial to Polish political prisoners. More importantly, it points to a Polish perception of Auschwitz that grew in the first years after the liberation—the perception that Auschwitz was to be remembered primarily as a place of Polish national suffering and sacrifice.

The reasons why Auschwitz became such an important element of Polish postwar identity are clear: Auschwitz I initially interned Polish political prisoners and Soviet prisoners of war, and the complex was certainly the largest single execution site for the prewar Polish intelligentsia, civic leaders, those who resisted the Nazi occupation, and tens of thousands of ordinary Poles. Yet Auschwitz was also an international camp that incarcerated inmates from

every European country. The Polish press and Polish authorities readily acknowledged this in the first years after the war, and there were clear attempts,
both in the press and in early plans for the Auschwitz museum, to make the
former camp a locus of international remembrance. But despite references in
speeches and official documents to the diversity of victims, the public discourse surrounding the camp and its memory increasingly emphasized the
memorialization of a specifically Polish martyrdom at the hands of German
invaders. Auschwitz, wrote one columnist just prior to the dedication of the
State Museum, was "the mass grave of the greatest sons of the fatherland."[50]

The term "martyrdom," a constituent element of Poland's postwar commemorative vocabulary, is a useful indicator of Polish considerations of
Auschwitz and the place of the camp in the country's culture. "Martyrs,"
"martyrdom," and "martyrology" were consistently used to describe Auschwitz victims, their fate, and their memory. Designating the victims of Nazi
persecution "martyrs" was not a practice unique to Poland, but was common
in other cultures in the early postwar years. For Poles, however, the specifically Polish and Christian overtones in these terms—natural to their traditional Roman Catholic discourse—were obvious, and lent the Auschwitz
inmate a quality of virtue and sacrifice for a higher good, such as patriotism
or socialism. Polish prisoners or "martyrs" at Auschwitz were not simply
suffering, but suffering and dying because of their Catholic faith, their political convictions, or their love of the fatherland. There were, of course, tens of
thousands of Poles condemned to Auschwitz who were neither soldiers, resistance fighters, members of the intelligentsia, nor in any way a threat to the
Nazi occupation regime. In the broad outlines of the Polish commemorative
mantra, however, they, too, were included in the heroic martyrs' narrative
simply *by virtue of being Polish.* Jews and Gypsies, representing the overwhelming majority of victims at Auschwitz, were generally not dying in the
service of any higher belief or cause, but were victims of genocide. Thus, to
designate the Auschwitz victim as a "martyr" was, depending on one's perspective, either broadly inclusive, or ahistorically exclusive. In any case, to
designate all Polish and non-Polish victims as "martyrs" was to keep Auschwitz in a conventional trope of nineteenth-century romantic nationalism and
to undermine the historical uniqueness of the camp and the diversity of experience there.

The origins of Poland's martyrological culture are found in nineteenth-century Polish nationalist thought. After Poland's partitions (1772, 1793, and 1795) by Prussia, Russia, and Austria, it disappeared from the map of Europe, living on as a nation only in the minds of its patriots. In the course of and following the 1830 November Uprising, there emerged in Poland what Brian Porter has labeled a "rhetorical framework" that "gave Polish intellectuals a vocabulary with which to talk about their nation as they tried to cope with the failure of 1830." "The struggle for Poland," Porter argues, "already joined with the welfare of humanity, was further justified through use of a heterodox religious terminology: the quest for independence became a divine imperative and Poland became the 'Christ of Nations.'"[51] Thus, nationally minded philosophers and poets, many in exile, successfully cultivated and propagated a mystical doctrine of Polish sacrifice and messianism. This approach to and justification of the Polish national cause motivated Polish patriots through much of the nineteenth century and was effectively harnessed in the twentieth during the crisis of World War II and the years immediately thereafter. God may not have prevented Poland's defeat, but there was a divine purpose in her demise: a Christlike historical mission to redeem the nations of Europe through suffering and example. Once resurrected, the Polish nation-state would be a beacon of tolerance, freedom, and political morality.[52] In the words of Adam Mickiewicz, Poland's most revered romantic poet: "For the Polish Nation did not die. Its body lieth in the grave, but its spirit has descended into the abyss, that is into the private lives of people who suffer slavery in their country . . . But on the third day the soul shall return again to the body, and the Nation shall arise, and free all the peoples of Europe from slavery."[53] For many in Poland's wartime generation, this messianic vision of the nation's destiny became an inspirational myth, and the German occupation provided the perfect example of righteous suffering—whether at the front in 1939, in the Warsaw Uprising of 1944, or in Auschwitz—at the hands of a foreign invader.

In the years between 1939 and 1945 Poland lost nearly 20 percent of its prewar citizens (more than half of whom were Jews who perished in the Shoah), and 2 million were sent to the Reich for labor. Between September 1939 and February 1940, more than two hundred thousand Poles were forcibly expelled from the annexed Warthegau region, and in the first months of the occupation more than fifty thousand Poles were killed. There were, to be sure, Poles who collaborated with the Nazi regime—with its bureaucracy, military, and agencies of terror and destruction—and the regime certainly inspired collaborationist behavior on an individual basis. The German occupiers were not, however, interested in establishing a collaborationist government, as in France, or a collaborationist administration, as in the Netherlands. Instead, they colonized and enslaved the Polish lands, decimating the country's infrastructure and human resources. More than 38 percent of physicians, 28 percent of university and college professors, 56 percent of lawyers, and 27 percent of Catholic priests did not survive the occupation.[54]

Despite this destruction, the Germans met fierce resistance. Poland had the most extensive underground network and army in Nazi-occupied Europe, and the Germans did not hesitate to use collective reprisals in retaliation for acts of resistance. For good reason, Poles have commemorated and mourned these tragic years in the history of their country, years that seemed to confirm the romantic perception of Poland as the eternal victim of injustice and exploitation. Likewise, the efforts of underground resistance movements were evidence of a redemptive tradition of Polish sacrifice for a higher good.

Poland's responsibility to the world did not end, however, in 1945, for it also had a postwar mission: to investigate and prosecute Germany's crimes, to cultivate and maintain the memory of the occupation, and to be a beacon of warning, alerting other nations to the dangers of Hitlerite fascism and racism. Auschwitz and its history had, in this respect, a tremendous commemorative value, and were symbolic of the suffering of Poles and their responsibility to future generations. In the words of the Polish premier Cyrankiewicz on the occasion of the State Museum's dedication:

> One of the concrete manifestations of that battle [against the danger of a new Auschwitz] will be the museum that we open today in Oświęcim, not for reminiscences but as a warning and demonstration to the entire world that the tragedy of millions murdered in the concentration camps must not vanish into thin air with the smoke of crematoria chimneys. For all those who survived this great tragedy, may the museum in Oświęcim become the great battle cry "Never again Auschwitz!"[55]

Recognizing the importance of commemorating the occupation on a variety of levels, the provisional government had established, even prior to the German capitulation, a "Department of Museums and Monuments of Polish Martyrology" within the Ministry of Culture and Art.[56] As the state authority responsible for the creation and maintenance of sites of commemoration, the department developed and publicized the terms by which Polish national martyrdom was to be understood. Registered in various contexts, these terms colored the discussions surrounding the genesis of the State Museum at Auschwitz as well as early exhibits at the memorial site.

One of the department's early position papers pointed to two problematic, even contradictory currents in Polish memory of the war years. "On the one hand," it stated, "the war experience was so strong and so deep a violation of Polish society that for many people it remained the dominant element of postwar life." At the same time, by contrast, there was "a weariness of the tragic theme in society and a desire to retreat from it in the hope for a life free and undisturbed by the horror." Given such symptoms of war-weariness and psychological retreat, the department deemed it necessary to "regulate the resurrection of the past against the background of the new current and . . . clarify the methods of commemoration of the history of the Poles in the years 1939–1945." These methods were to take two separate, yet parallel, paths: the erection of artistic monuments and shrines of commemoration (a grass roots initiative that had begun during the war) and the documentation of history, primarily through the organization and administration of museums of Polish martyrology such as the one in Oświęcim. Noting the impossibility of commemorating each individual wartime tragedy ("because given the range of German crimes we would have to create out of Poland a land of cemeteries"), the position paper maintained that documentary commemoration in the form of museums, and artistic commemoration in the form of monuments should be limited to the actual sites of mass crimes.[57]

Although public remembrance of wartime suffering may have come naturally to Poles, it is instructive that this document urged caution and restraint. Commemoration of suffering and sacrifice may have been a reflex response for some; others, however, may have experienced a certain aversion to the memory of the occupation in the hope of returning, as one publicist stated already in March 1945, to a "psychological balance."[58] It was therefore incumbent on custodians of memory not only to cultivate, but also to limit and direct Poland's commemoration of the war years.

The document's reference to the need to "regulate the resurrection of the past against the background of the new current" refers to the need to bring Poland's postwar commemorative culture into line with the regime's current political goals. Martyrology, the paper made clear, was concerned not only with death, but also with life, or, more specifically, with the emancipation of those suffering among the living. An awareness of the victory gained, and commemoration with a view to the future would lead Poland on the path of progress and social emancipation. "Poland," the document stated succinctly, "will not be the land of the martyred dead. Poland will be the land of the living."[59]

The new Polish state was clear in delineating a mode of remembrance that would accommodate both national commemorative traditions and the political exigencies of the present. Polish wartime martyrdom and its commemoration, the position paper stated, incorporated two elements: the criminal acts of the Germans and, conversely, the Poles' suffering and struggle, which were not in vain and did not result in the defeat of the Polish nation. Martyrdom, this document noted, grew out of the "contact and interaction of the Hitlerite psyche with the Polish psyche." "The German psyche," it stated,

> was established on unusually fertile soil from which arose the new German religion: Hitlerite racism. . . . And thus in the years of occupation the Germanic "master race" declared war on the Polish "slave race," the purpose of which was the extermination of our nation. Yet, the nation of the "enslaved" began to defend itself, answering aggression with aggression. The nation of the "enslaved," unable to reconcile itself to the yoke of bondage, thus called itself to battle. The "master race," unable to tolerate opposition, further tightened the noose of terror. In the course of the years the struggle became increasingly obstinate, and the implacable consequences of its growth were, first of all, the consequence of the new German religion: murder of several million people; the second consequence was the psychic posture of the Poles: the fight for freedom at the cost of one's own blood.[60]

Racist German brutality and heroic Polish virtue were common to the Polish understanding of the wartime experience, and these nationalistic and dualistic categories proposed a politically useful and culturally accessible way of recalling the past. They offered Poles an identity based in common suffering, left room for the sacrificial and messianic traditions in Polish commemorative culture, and at the same time provided a model of national solidarity that could be projected onto the challenges of reconstructing the Polish state and building socialism. Not least, they provided a clear justification for Poland's expansion westward at the expense of a depraved and vanquished

Germany. In sum, it was possible to cultivate this notion of martyrdom by combining both national tradition and current political goals.

Despite its appeal and effectiveness, this Polish-national martyrological paradigm was limiting, because in the years to follow, it was difficult to reconcile with the element of Auschwitz history that would define the site in the collective memory of most of the world: the Shoah. Although the mass extermination of Jews was not denied in the public presentation of Auschwitz in the early postwar years, Jewish genocide was seldom upheld as a unique phenomenon. Instead, the paradigm either marginalized the mass murder of Jews or, as was often the case, implied that Poles had shared in that fate, not only as the first victims of Nazi aggression and occupation, but also as certain victims of Nazi extermination policy in the future. Nazi policy in Poland was the basis for this perception, especially during the first two years of the occupation. Jews remained in Poland, but the Nazis deported Poles by the hundreds of thousands to Germany for slave labor; Jews had their own governmental institutions or councils, subject as they were to the Nazis, but Poles had no political or cultural representation; Jews were clearly the victims of Nazi violence and murder, but Poles were also randomly and systematically rounded up, incarcerated, and tortured as political prisoners.[61]

Polish historians and publicists also pointed to evidence suggesting that Poles, in the course of time, would have been marked for extermination as well. Citing a stenograph of a November 1942 speech by Himmler, representatives of a district commission for the Investigation of German Crimes in Poland concluded at a June 1946 meeting that the Nazi invaders had, in fact, planned for the mass extermination of Poles. The expulsion of Polish peasants from the Zamość region in late 1942 and early 1943, their report stated, was only a preliminary step leading to the goal of mass extermination for the purpose of providing more *Lebensraum* (living space) for the German people.[62] Describing the goals of Nazi ideology, the 1946 report of the Central Commission for the Investigation of German Crimes in Poland stated: "It aimed at the wholesale exploitation of the forces of the conquered nations for the benefit of Germany, and afterwards at their extirpation. The Jews were to be completely extirpated before the end of the war; the Poles were intended to do slave labor for the Germans before sharing their fate."[63] Similarly, the report concluded that "the camps in Poland were one of the principal instruments for achieving the criminal aims of Himmler, Greiser and Frank: the complete extermination of the Poles after a short period of exploitation."[64]

Prime Minister Józef Cyrankiewicz echoed this theme in his testimony at the Höss trial. According to the Polish premier, the German invaders had undertaken "an unmerciful, nihilistic plan to exterminate nations, especially Slavic nations, and first and foremost the Polish nation, which was to follow the *praeludium* of eradicating the Jewish nation."[65] And at the April 1945 ceremonies commemorating the second anniversary of the Warsaw Ghetto Uprising, Minister of Education Skrzeszewski reminded his audience that "not only Jews had to pass through the death factories, but also a great number of our nation and other nations. The unleashing through Hitlerism of anti-Semitism and the consequent eradication of 3,200,000 Jews in Poland had in view only the invitation to further victims and beyond that the liquidation of those easily determined victims: we and the Jews."[66] Or, in the words of one publicist, "The Germans prepared for Jews and Poles a common fate on Polish soil. The differences consisted only in time." This is why, according to the author, Jews and Poles were brothers in blood and defense in "struggle for your freedom and ours."[67]

There was some validity to speculations and fears that the Nazis had been planning to annihilate the Poles. On 1 May 1942, Artur Greiser, Gauleiter of the Wartheland, proposed the "special treatment" of thirty-five thousand tubercular Poles. In December of that year, Dr. Wilhelm Hagen, from Warsaw's Nazi administration, claimed in a letter to Hitler that there were secret discussions about the extermination of one-third of some two hundred thousand Poles to be resettled in the General Government, the central region of occupied Poland under the authority of Hans Frank.[68] Raul Hilberg, although in no way equating the genocide of Jews with the treatment of other victim groups, has nonetheless noted that "[t]he Germans . . . did not draw the line with the destruction of Jewry. They attacked still other victims, some of whom were thought to be like Jews, some of whom were quite unlike Jews, and some of whom were Germans. The Nazi destruction process was, in short, not aimed at institutions; it was targeted at people. The Jews were only the first victims of the German bureaucracy; they were only the first caught in its path."[69] Polish fears of becoming the "next victims" were real, and there is evidence to suggest that even if the course of events during the occupation did not appear to justify these fears, leading Nazis did consider the possibility of undertaking mass killings of Poles.[70] At Auschwitz approximately ten thousand unregistered Polish deportees were murdered, and one hundred thirty-seven thousand registered Poles were subjected to enslavement, torture, starvation, and mass execution. Moreover, Poles had only a 50 percent chance of survival at Auschwitz.

The validity of this claim notwithstanding, the fact remains that Poles were never subjected to a systematic and comprehensive policy of genocide, and to equate the German treatment of Poles with the treatment of Jews was an oversimplification and distortion of the historical record. Nonetheless, the notion of Jews and Poles subjected to a common fate—whether under the occupation as a whole or in the Auschwitz camp—remained an enduring myth that could, in subsequent decades, be politically exploited in a variety of ways, especially during the so-called "anti-Zionist" campaign of the late 1960s.[71]

In the immediate postwar years, however, it was the designation of the occupation as characteristically *German* that offered the most political capital in the context of the Polish martyrological paradigm. The reader will recall references to the "Hitlerite" and "German" psyche in the position paper of the Department of Museums and Monuments of Polish Martyrology. It was the "German religion" of "Hitlerite racism" and the Polish response to it that was at the source of Polish martyrdom and its commemoration. Likewise, Auschwitz was a distinctively German crime, and not a "war crime" or crime of ideology. In the early postwar period, the Polish press was filled with the vague terms "Hitlerite" and "Hitlerism." Government officials or Polish journalists much less frequently used the terms "fascist" or "National Socialist" to describe the invaders. There were fascists and Nazi sympathizers in Poland prior to and during the war, and to label the SS and occupation authorities as such would blur the all-important national distinctions between German and Pole. To put it another way, a crime motivated by ideology rather than by nationality was more difficult to label as specifically German. Moreover, to label the Germans as "National Socialists" would perhaps tarnish the popular appeal of patriotic sentiment and "socialism"—two themes that the early postwar government was eager to cultivate among the Polish population. Finally, to designate Auschwitz and other death factories in Poland as "war crimes" would undermine the specific and singularly Polish element of these camps and would place their horrors within the larger context of European conflict. It is therefore hardly surprising that the Polish press and representatives of the new regime presented the Auschwitz crime as uniquely German, as a crime typical of that nation, and as a crime inflicted by evil personified upon the martyr-country.

Emphasizing the German menace was one way for Poles to articulate their common suffering and common cause, and this served the political exigencies of the fledgling Warsaw government. The threat was not a temporary, exceptional phenomenon, but an ever-present danger in a long historical continuum of Teutonic aggression toward the Slavs and, more specifically, of German aggression toward the Poles. This was, for example, the theme of a 1946 Warsaw exhibition on German crimes, the purpose of which was "to show that the Hitlerite crimes in Poland do not constitute an abstract episode in German history, but are a culminating point—the crowning of eternal German annexationism in the East."[72] By recalling German crimes and emphasizing the continuing German threat, the regime was able to posit national identity, national unity, and nationalist fears against a common enemy in the service of its larger political goals, such as international recognition of the Oder-Neisse Line as Poland's western frontier or the highly symbolic prosecution of Nazi criminals. As the nation that had suffered the most under the Germans, Poland had not only a right, but also a responsibility to annex German territory, to punish German criminals, and to inform the world of the horrors of Auschwitz and other camps. The moral duty was clear. As one Polish publicist wrote in May 1945:

> The Polish press has written and continues to write much and often about Auschwitz. But it is all still too little, even for the development of the most superficial view of the immensity of German atrocities. It is necessary to write about Auschwitz again and again. It is necessary to write just now as we have arrived at the day of judgement for the perpetrators of those inhuman crimes. It is necessary to write lest the crimes fall into the shadow of oblivion, so that a false sense of compassion does not become the cause of impunity or easy treatment of the criminals. It is necessary to write in order to rouse the conscience and eradicate the indifference and dullness that has overcome the world after six years of war. We must avenge these crimes— those 4 million innocent victims of Auschwitz call for it.[73]

Writing and rewriting meant italicizing Polish suffering, underscoring Nazi atrocities, and even deleting references to Jewish mass death while emphasizing throughout the call to bear witness to and avenge German crimes. Revenge could take many forms: territorial "reclamation," reparations, or the expulsion of Germans from Silesia, Pomerania, and East Prussia. Such were the early postwar goals of Warsaw's policy toward a defeated Germany, and Poles had little patience for German cries of postwar injustices inflicted upon them or for voices in Britain and the United States that were sympathetic to the Germans' plight or calling for Germany's rehabilitation. It was Auschwitz, more than any other wartime site of destruction, that pointed to the naïveté, danger, and insult of a conciliatory policy toward Germany. As an editorial columnist wrote on the occasion of the Auschwitz museum's dedication in 1947:

> We are a nation that has suffered the greatest wrongdoing at the hands of the followers of the [German] system. We are not repeating the Auschwitz story in order to spread an unnecessary and harmful self-pity. We are reiterating this doubtless truth because we are a state that is sentenced for all time to be the neighbor of Germans—the nation that invented and carried out "genocide." That is why we, above all else, should be alert to what transpires beyond our western border. And we, above all, have to remind other nations that what was *yesterday* our lot could befall other nations *tomorrow*.[74]

Auschwitz memory was to be a catalyst for anti-German attitudes and policy, a pillar of support for a consistent policy on the Oder-Neisse issue, and a general caution to the rest of the world. This admonitory role was an appropriate complement to the symbolic role of Auschwitz as the "golgotha" of the "Christ among nations," for a martyrological idiom that emphasized the suffering and sacrifice of the Polish nation also gave that nation a unique responsibility, or even mission, to the rest of the world.

As inspiring and politically serviceable as this narrative may have been, it left little room for historical specificity and nuance of interpretation. It emphasized, in the first place, the Nazi goal of enslaving the Poles and destroying their state and nation. Auschwitz was, of course, the most memorable and visible symbol of this, and it represented for many Poles their own exterminationist fate, or at least what would have become so had the Nazis had the opportunity to follow through with their plans. Second, the narrative emphasized the sacrificial suffering of the Polish nation and, at the same time, the resistance and resolve of the prisoners. Neither element of the story could easily accommodate the unregistered deportee, Jewish or otherwise; both offered postwar Polish society a locus of common identity and the postwar Polish state a degree of much-needed legitimacy. As Jonathan Webber has noted, "in the post-war Polish construction of the symbolic meaning of Auschwitz, to identify Jews as the principal victims would have been to clutter, if not to obfuscate, the cultural and political message; it was an inconvenient irrelevance best left to one side."[75] Webber's insight is accurate, especially when applied to the early postwar development of the Auschwitz site and museum, for a Polish-national martyrological idiom required the concurrent marginalization or assimilation of other victim groups. It would be convenient to claim aggressive anti-Semitism as the main author of this narrative, or to dismiss it as the product of communist machinations at the state level. Anti-Semitism *was* a tragic and obvious problem in postwar Poland, and a new communist regime *was* consolidating its power in the years 1945–47. But neither of these influences was decisive on its own. One also has to allow for the possibility that the stewards of Auschwitz memory in these early years were drawing upon broader, non-ethnic, and assimilationist notions of "Pole" and "victim"—notions that eschewed Nazi racial categorizations even as they inappropriately blurred the historical distinctions so important to the process of accurate memorialization. In short, the Polish-national martyrological narrative was more complex than is apparent at first glance, and designating the Auschwitz site and museum as its principal illustration was a natural stage in the process of constructing a viable framework of memory in the postwar era.

2 ⫼ From Liberation to Memorialization

The Transformation of the Auschwitz Site, 1945–1947

To MANY POLES in 1945, the need to preserve the Auschwitz site as a memorial to those who had suffered and perished there was obvious. The topography and structures of the Auschwitz complex were well suited to the Polish-national martyrological narrative emerging in the early postwar years. Representing the apex of German racism, it was a center of Polish suffering and heroic Polish resistance. As the site of the largest mass crime in history, it could provide both documentary commemoration in the form of a museum, and artistic commemoration in the form of monuments and memorials. Moreover, the site's tangibility, artifacts, and open spaces made it an appropriate location for the institutionalization of memorial symbols and rituals.

The first initiatives for creating a memorial site at Auschwitz arose among prisoners in the camp while it was still in operation. As Kazimierz Smoleń, a former prisoner and subsequent director of the State Museum recalls:

> We did not know if we would survive, but one did speak of a memorial site. . . . some kind of institution, a monument, or something of that sort. . . . These were not, of course, open meetings or anything like that. One simply could not speak openly of such things or discuss such things. . . . we only knew that it would be impossible for mankind to forget the crimes that were committed in Auschwitz. Certainly the idea of somehow creating a *sacrum* out of this place existed already in the camp. One just did not know what form it would take.[1]

Prisoners could not be certain of their fate while still behind the wires of the camp, but after the liberation, they were, not surprisingly, at the forefront of the effort to establish a "sacred space" at Auschwitz.

Such an initiative was not a simple matter. On the one hand, the testimonies and memoirs of former prisoners, press accounts, and the sheer number of visitors reveal a public preoccupation with Auschwitz and tremendous support for transforming the site into a memorial and museum. On the other hand, conditions at Auschwitz were chaotic in the first months after the war: state institutions and organizations competed for control and use of the grounds, the structures of the camp were steadily falling into ruin, and there was a lack of consensus over the topographic and spatial definitions of the memorial site. The transformation of the site into memorial and museum was therefore a difficult process, lasting more than two years. This chapter describes that process, accounting for the challenges facing those responsible for the preservation of Auschwitz and the public documentation of its history. The result of their efforts—the State Museum dedicated in June 1947— was provisional and open to revision in the future; yet its exhibitions and uses of commemorative space at Auschwitz illustrated the martyrological narrative employed in these early postwar years and set the tone for subsequent uses of the site in the decades to follow.

The Liberated Site

Conditions at Auschwitz in the first weeks and months after the liberation were hardly conducive to transforming the site into a memorial and museum. The sick and dying required medical attention, bodies of the dead had to be buried or cremated, and surviving prisoners needed food and clothing. Assuming the dual role of liberator and occupier, the Red Army was initially responsible for supervising these activities and also helped to protect the site from looters and to maintain order—certainly a difficult task given the expanse of the terrain, which covered more than 450 acres. Already on 1 May 1945 a decision of Poland's provisional government had placed "those parts of the concentration camp in Oświęcim that were connected to the immediate destruction of millions of people" (practically speaking, this meant the grounds of Auschwitz I and Birkenau) under the administration of the Ministry of Culture and Art, which from that point on had responsibility for protecting the site and creating a concept for a future museum.[2] This decision, however, did not prevent further desecration (or, to use the common Polish term, *pro-*

fanacja) of the grounds; after the Soviet Army vacated the Birkenau site, a group of former prisoners found it necessary to request that the grounds receive the protection of the Ministry of National Defense.[3]

In the first months after the liberation, Auschwitz also functioned as a prisoner-of-war camp and internment center for so-called *Volksdeutsche*.[4] Although few details are known about the operation of these Soviet and, later, Polish camps, recent research indicates that from March or April 1945 until autumn of that year prisoners were interned at Auschwitz I, and until spring 1946 on the grounds of Birkenau.[5] Several accounts discuss the living and working conditions of the Germans in these camps. One witness, a nurse with the Polish Red Cross, described how in May 1945 several thousand German POWs were brought to the camp and housed in Auschwitz I,[6] while a brief diary of a German prisoner chronicles the grim conditions in the POW camp from his arrival in June 1945 until shortly before his death from illness and malnutrition less than a month later.[7] The POWs and Volksdeutsche worked in various capacities: exhuming corpses, clearing the grounds, dismantling equipment in the factories of the complex (including the Buna-Werke at Monowitz), and dismantling wooden barracks for shipment from Birkenau.[8] In addition, a number of prisoners were occupied with structural repairs to buildings, and even helped with the construction of some of the museum's early exhibitions.[9]

Ironically, the presence of Germans at Auschwitz aided efforts to secure and preserve the site. Not only were they an inexpensive source of labor, but the POWs and Volksdeutsche also required military supervision, which in turn reduced the threat of grave robbers and plunderers. The internment of Germans on the grounds of Auschwitz, a practical measure undertaken with perhaps a touch of vengeful justice, illustrated the complexities of transforming the site from camp to memorial. Even if the provisional government had, in early May 1945, set aside the grounds for preservation, the presence of Soviet and Polish military authorities made clear that the site was, at least for the time being, to fulfill a variety of functions.

The first concrete legislative initiative for the protection and memorialization of Auschwitz came from a former Birkenau prisoner and delegate to the National Homeland Council, Alfred Fiderkiewicz, on 31 December 1945. Fiderkiewicz's recommendation called for the establishment in Oświęcim and Brzezinka of a site commemorating Polish and international martyrdom.

A government commission for culture and art approved the recommendation unanimously on 1 February 1946[10] and named Tadeusz Wąsowicz, a former prisoner, director of the site.[11] Several weeks later, the provisional government's Council of Ministers provided a rough and ambitious blueprint for the future of the site: the Ministry of Culture would organize a museum, with Blocks 10 and 11 of the Stammlager preserved as "mausolea." In addition, one block would serve as a hostel for visitors, one block would be set aside for the research of German crimes, and one block was to house a so-called "Peoples' University" for postsecondary vocational education. Furthermore, these provisional plans set aside twenty blocks in Birkenau for exhibits dedicated to various nationalities and to the history of other camps. Finally, the blueprint called for the erection of a monument near the Birkenau gas chambers and crematoria as a symbol of international martyrdom.[12] It is significant that in these early plans so much attention and space appeared to be devoted to the "international" character of the future museum and memorial. In the months and years ahead, however, practical concerns, lack of funds, and an awareness of the centrality of Auschwitz in Poland's emerging commemorative culture de-emphasized the international element at the memorial site.

By April 1946, a group of former prisoners had assumed de facto control of the grounds. The socialist leader Józef Cyrankiewicz, serving then as head of the Polish Union of Former Political Prisoners (Polski Związek byłych Więźniów Politycznych, or PZbWP), requested from the minister of defense that employees of the Ministry of Culture and Art take control of the Auschwitz site from the Polish regiment stationed there. Although the Polish Army was still holding German POWs at Auschwitz, the military force protecting the site was, according to Cyrankiewicz, no longer needed. These duties, he (mistakenly) believed, could be fulfilled by former prisoners employed as guards. Moreover, the number of visitors to Auschwitz required that the memorial site be staffed by former prisoners familiar with the camp's history and competent as tour guides.[13] It was, then, more than fifteen months after the liberation that the staff of the memorial site began its work. Their reports and correspondence suggest that their highest priorities were to salvage the ruins of the camp, protect remaining evidence, and maintain control over—to use Cyrankiewicz's words—the "wild conditions"[14] then prevailing on the camp grounds.

Conservation was certainly the most important and most difficult task facing the cadre of workers at Auschwitz.[15] The structures of Auschwitz I were relatively intact, and Birkenau, if considerably more dilapidated, nonetheless showed clear traces of the camp and the extermination process there. Reports indicate that in addition to the masonry barracks, guard towers, ruins of crematoria, and other durable structures, many of Birkenau's wooden barracks were still standing. Investigators also located mugs, bowls, and plates near the site of Birkenau's massive storehouses; personal effects and money of Jews on the railway platform or "ramp"; singed prayer books near Crematorium V; and at the entrance to Crematorium II, numbered changing-room tags used to deceive prisoners entering the gas chamber.[16]

Clearly, conditions at the site in the immediate postwar years were difficult on a variety of levels, yet visitors today are often critical of the small number of original structures remaining there, especially in Birkenau. The lack of original "evidence" perhaps cannot be excused entirely; it can, however, be explained in part by the inability of the museum staff, despite their efforts, to prevent decay and destruction on the grounds. In short, the site was undergoing a process of steady ruin, and it was all but impossible to maintain the grounds in a state resembling that of January 1945. One need only consider the sheer size of the grounds, the disastrous material conditions in war-torn Poland, the lack of funds for preservation work, and the inability—despite the presence of armed guards—to protect Birkenau from looters.

The necessity of creating a protective guard to keep people *out* of Auschwitz is a particularly disturbing aspect of the memorial site's early history. Immediately after the liberation, looters (or "hyenas," as the Polish press referred to them) began seeking riches at the camp. These were frequently individuals from the local population who salvaged goods from the grounds or made a practice of sifting through ash pits in search of valuables, especially gold. There were a number of arrests, and even an incident in which a former prisoner serving as a guard shot and wounded an intruder.[17] The presence of looters at Auschwitz was alarming and was widely condemned in the Polish press as, in the words of one commentator, "the profaning of a holy place of martyrdom of seventeen European nations, and especially the Polish nation."[18] It was also a cause for alarm among Polish ex-prisoners, who justifiably feared that reports of such plundering would find their way into the foreign press and portray Poland in a negative light.[19]

Although the Ministry of Culture appeared committed to securing the borders of the camp through the formation of a protective guard, it was unfortunately resigned to the hopelessness of preserving everything on the grounds. As Wincenty Hein, an early associate of the museum staff, noted in a report on the early history of the memorial site, "The entire strength of the museum was directed to the rescue and conservation of that which remained. . . . It is necessary to remember that between the liberation of the camp and the arrival of the first crew of workers for the museum there was a period in which the process of destruction . . . was very intensive. That process was, historically in a way, a conditioned response of society, which had no concept of certain values."[20] The "process" to which Hein was referring included both the natural decay of structures on the grounds and the dismantling and removal of materials by the local population—a "society" more concerned, in war's immediate aftermath, with the raw materials of daily existence than with the historical and commemorative value of their plundered goods. For example, of the hundreds of wooden barracks in Birkenau, only a fraction remained when the museum opened two years later.[21] Hein's report also touched on the legal issue of property rights to the grounds of the liberated camp:

> The question of ownership rights on the terrain of the former Auschwitz camp seems simple on the surface level. The law for the protection of Monuments of Martyrdom of the Polish Nation and Other Nations [1947] established a legal situation by which the grounds became the property of the state—that is to say, the question of ownership was solved by the law. But in practice it was necessary to wait about four years for clear orders regarding the borders of the State Museum at Auschwitz. In the meantime, a strange situation developed: the grounds belonged to the museum, yet the lack of a suitable number of guards made it impossible to surround the grounds with effective protection. . . . The local populace either lost out, returned to the sites of their former homes (which is of course understandable), or dismantled existing camp barracks in order to take them away and set them up elsewhere (which is certainly less understandable).[22]

To the Polish government, to former prisoners working at the site, and to the Polish public at large, Auschwitz *was* a "sacred space"; yet the size, character, and remaining "evidence" of what had transpired there was subject to legal, political, and, not least, financial limitations. The Birkenau barracks, for example, were not always the victims of plunder. Eighteen of them were sold to members of the local population in July 1946, with each barracks divided among five villagers.[23] Later in the year, the town of Dąbrowa Tarnowska obtained a number of barracks to be used for housing construction and the building of a local market,[24] while in 1947 barracks from the site were shipped to various localities throughout Poland.[25] The dismantling of artifacts such as these reveals the perceived, or perhaps genuine, inability of the Polish state to preserve and protect much of what was left of the Auschwitz camp complex, and also illustrates even more graphically what appear today as rather reckless, if practical, measures taken by the local population in a period of extreme material want.

Preservation work at Auschwitz was also hindered by the presence at the site of a branch of the Office for the Liquidation of German Property (*Urząd Likwidacyjny*).[26] Using the buildings of the *Lagererweiterung*,[27] this government agency was responsible for the storage and distribution of German property remaining after the liberation and was, in the words of site guard Adam Złobnicki, "not known for its excessive honesty."[28] Złobnicki and another early employee of the museum, although not allowed regular access to the warehouses of the extension camp, witnessed the enormous quantities of goods confiscated from prisoners, first by the SS and subsequently by Polish authorities—goods that included items such as suitcases, baskets, furniture, blankets, shoes, underwear, and Jewish ritual vestments.[29] Precise documentation of the destinations of these goods is not available, but reports suggest that the Liquidation Office was responsible for the loss of much of the remaining property confiscated from Jews deported to Auschwitz. There was even an unconfirmed suspicion that the office had shipped a large amount of human hair found after the liberation to an upholstery factory in Silesia.[30]

It is clear, in any case, that confiscated property and artifacts found in the camp complex were not properly stored, catalogued, or, for that matter, exhibited at the Auschwitz Museum. Krystyna Szymańska, a member of the Kraków Commision for the Investigation of German Crimes at Auschwitz, recalled her surprise at the disappearance of so many items in the course of only two years: "A long time after concluding our trips to Oświęcim . . . I participated in the opening ceremonies of the State Museum at Auschwitz. In the newly opened exhibition were shown artifacts like documentary photographs, striped uniforms from the camp, women's hair, and dentures. I was shocked at the time, even horrified, at how few things remained at the place in comparison to the amount that I had seen in 1945."[31] Not surprisingly, the Liquidation Office saw former prisoners at Auschwitz—that is, those charged with preserving and protecting what remained on the grounds—as a threat to its activities. In addition, the office had control over the financial management of the grounds until the museum was provided with its own budget from the Ministry of Culture in 1947.[32]

The lack of funds for the Auschwitz site was a chronic problem throughout the postwar decades and was especially acute in the first two years after the liberation, resulting in a state of affairs that was, according to one journalist, a national embarrassment. "One must therefore fear," he wrote in 1946, "that in the future, should the subsidies continue to arrive in the current modest sums, visitors could get the impression that the Polish government and Polish society do not give enough attention to national historical sites that bring glory not only to our martyrdom, but to our heroism as well."[33] Subsidies for the museum were initially informal; when the money ran out, director Tadeusz Wąsowicz would simply return to Warsaw and request more.[34] By 1947 the site was allotted a monthly subsidy of 500,000 zlotys.[35] The sum was woefully inadequate, and it is worth noting that for decades the Ministry of Culture remained the site's only source of funding. The museum may have received a consistent, if inadequate, influx of funds, but its financial dependence on central authority allowed Warsaw to shape more effectively the landscape of the site.[36]

Not surprisingly, there was a variety of proposals and methods for financing the museum from within: requests for donations, sale of materials, admission fees for visitors, and economic utilization of the grounds, to name only a few. One proposal suggested the near-total economic exploitation of the terrain of the camp complex, using the industrial and agricultural infrastructure left behind by the Germans. This maximalist plan called for the museum to manage five hundred hectares of land, which would have included such diverse enterprises as the vegetable gardens and fisheries of nearby auxiliary camps.[37] This plan never materialized, but members of the museum staff were nonetheless industrious in their use of the grounds. They grew potatoes in sector BIIA of the Birkenau site, bred and stabled horses in two blocks of Auschwitz I, kept chickens in the guardhouse adjacent to the commandant's villa, and grazed sheep in Birkenau.[38]

Was economic utilization of the Auschwitz site inappropriate, or were

workers at the site to be commended for their resourcefulness in a time of extreme material want? It was certainly impossible to maintain the grounds of
the entire Auschwitz-Birkenau-Monowitz complex, not to mention the
grounds of the auxiliary camps in the area, in their January 1945 state. Far too
much had been confiscated by Soviet and Polish authorities, stolen by looters, and ruined by the elements. Moreover, there is no indication that the museum or its staff reaped any profit from such undertakings; rather, they likely
saw such small-scale efforts as aiding in the work of the museum and easing
their day-to-day financial and material needs. Like the issue of the Birkenau
barracks, however, the exploitation of the Auschwitz site, as necessary as it
may have seemed at the time, points to the larger problem of the status of the
former camp. On the one hand, the Polish government had, already in January 1946, designated Auschwitz and Birkenau (but not Monowitz) as memorial sites—sites too important to neglect totally or to exploit simply for
agricultural or industrial purposes. On the other hand, despite repeated emphasis on the significance of the grounds as a locus of national heroism and
martyrdom, the Polish state was either unable or unwilling to provide the site
with suitable protection from looters, a satisfactory budget, and an adequate
work force.

Workers at the memorial site were recruited from the ranks of former
prisoners, and their story is a particularly interesting aspect of the early history of the museum. Their presence at the Auschwitz site was, to some extent,
an expression of the solidarity they had felt as prisoners. It was also a mark of
their commitment to preserving the memory of their experiences and carrying
that memory into postwar society at large. As one visitor to the site com-
mented in spring 1947, "We look with astonishment toward those people who
dared to remain here for good—the director of the museum Wąsowicz, the
custodian Targosz, and the administrative director Podziemski. Often the art-
ist Brandhuber travels here from Kraków. He even has his guest room. They
cannot separate themselves from Auschwitz."[39]

Whether Wąsowicz and his staff were psychologically unable to "separate themselves from Auschwitz" is not clear, but former inmates housed in
the base camp undoubtedly experienced disturbing reactions to their envi-
ronment. Despite the challenging circumstances, former employees have recalled the early years at the museum with nostalgia. Wages were low, and
they often worked long hours seven days a week, but there was also a high

level of enthusiasm, cooperation, and collegiality among members of the cadre. As Tadeusz Szymański has recalled:

> Everything was important. Everything was urgent. Rescue everything that needed to be rescued. The days were filled with work. . . . But to us it seemed so little, for we had nothing to compare it to. Each did what he could in spite of insufficient time and strength, for even the everyday necessities of life cost more than a little time and energy. No one complained of the low pay or the lack of provisions. There was something more important than the trifles of day-to-day existence, and the "collective" understood this perfectly, thanks to Baca [Wąsowicz] and his close associates.[40]

The museum administration also provided educational programs for the workers, many of whom had not had the opportunity to obtain a high-school diploma prior to the war. Employees were also offered lectures for the purpose of training them as guides, for even those working as guards were required to accompany visitors around the site.[41] As odd as it may sound, it appears that workers at the memorial site were doing their best to establish some degree of order and normalcy in their lives at the former camp. From the perspective of more than fifty years, at a time when the contours and future of the memorial site are often the locus of international controversy, this may seem peculiar. The staff at the site, however, was composed primarily of survivors who were willing to return to their nightmares and to participate in the documentation and preservation of Auschwitz. Perhaps the museum cadre was, in a way, experiencing the contradictory currents in Poland's collective war-memory discussed in the previous chapter. The war years, and specifically the time spent in Auschwitz, were undoubtedly a defining element in the lives of those working at the memorial site, but it is hardly surprising that they needed to escape from their memories into the mundane aspects of everyday life. The efforts of these workers to slow the process of destruction at the site also represented a process—although at times a seemingly irreverent one—of coming to terms with their own Auschwitz past, reflecting both the need to remember and commemorate the camp's dead and the need to retreat from the painful memories of the war and occupation. Perhaps such self-examination was beyond the ken of many of these former prisoners at that time. Faced with collapsing buildings, looters, and disastrous material circumstances, they were understandably most concerned with the practical matters of documentation and preservation of artifacts. In this they enjoyed some success, to the extent that they were able to slow the steady ruin of the former complex in the face of tremendous practical limitations. Most importantly, their work laid the groundwork for the museum's early exhibitions.

The State Museum at Auschwitz

When former prisoners began planning the first large-scale public exhibit at the Auschwitz site, they faced a task without pattern or precedent.[42] As the former prisoner Kazimierz Smoleń related, "Of course it was very difficult to organize anything because . . . we unfortunately (and thank God!) had no model, since there was, at that time, no such museum. . . . And a 'museum' was, historically speaking, not even the right concept. . . . at least that which one normally understands by the concept 'museum.' This was anti-culture and not culture."[43] Using more direct language, Wincenty Hein described the confusion and lack of direction in the early stages of planning the museum's exhibits. "After all," he stated, "not one of us had a precise idea how to shape the activities of the newly opened institution."[44]

Prior to the museum's official opening in June 1947, the only public exhibits at the site were in Blocks 11 and 4a[45] of the base camp. Organized already in the summer of 1945,[46] this brief visitor's route was rather devotional in character.[47] It included a visit to the "Block of Death" (Block 11) and displayed, in the basement of Block 4, artifacts testifying to the extermination process.[48] A visitor to the site in November 1946 captured the votive images of this memorial:

> We proceed further, recalling the many who prematurely left this world, murdered by the German executioners. So we enter Block 4a. The entrance is gloomy in the deeply subdued reflections of red lights. We enter the room and are turned to stone. The basement of the block mirrors the entire magnitude of the crimes committed in Auschwitz. In numerous alcoves are revealed the symbols of various strata of society that here found their deaths. Thus, a peasant's coat next to a mountaineer's costume; liturgical vestments of all faiths. In another niche children's slippers speak for themselves, and next to them the hair of murdered women induces a shudder of horror. For

a long time we are unable to depart from this Sanctuary of Martyrology—
we are moved to the depths of our emotions.[49]

Surrounded by barbed wire, the displays in the basement of Block 4 simply
presented "evidence" in the form of items plundered from deportees to
Auschwitz: clothing, prostheses, shoes, and human hair. Lacking explanatory inscriptions, the exhibit was intended to evoke a devotional mood—a
mood accented by the presence of an illuminated cross at the end of the hall.
An obvious appeal to Christian religiosity and the sensibilities of Polish national and, therefore, Roman Catholic martyrdom, the cross and these reliquary objects also testified to the circumscribed Polish character of the
exhibit. Subject neither to the antireligious constraints of subsequent regimes
nor to an international and therefore "ecumenical" commemorative agenda,
the creators of this temporary exhibit were making use of the objects and referents available to them: artifacts of destruction and symbols of virtuous
sacrifice. There is no evidence that the early creators of this exhibit were consciously using the cross to shroud or supersede the story of Jewish suffering
at Auschwitz, but it was hardly a neutral symbol. Depending on the point of
view of the visitor to the exhibition, a cross could be understood as a mark of
death, mourning, sacrifice, redemption, or victory. Perhaps it was a mild expression of resistance to the regime, which, although not yet communist, was
clearly leftist and supported by the Soviets. In any case, it is clear that this
early exhibition in Block 4 was constructed and viewed within a Roman
Catholic cultural idiom that contributed to the perception of the early "museum" as a site of Polish national martyrdom.

The reliquary atmosphere of this exhibit may have been effective in
evoking an emotional or votive response, but the artifacts and symbols in
Block 4, in and of themselves, had limited didactic value. Consequently,
planners of the State Museum were intent on representing Auschwitz history
in a more vivid and explanatory manner. This required, in the first place,
significant restoration work at the site and, second, extensive planning for the
new exhibition.

Restoration work began in the early months of 1947. Prisoner Blocks 15
and 16 were renovated, the confinement cells *(Stehzellen)* in the cellar of Block
11 were restored to their prior condition, and the chimney and Zyklon-B
chutes of Crematorium I were reconstructed.[50] It is significant that the Minis-

try of Culture undertook this restoration work on the grounds of Auschwitz I at the same time that the Birkenau site was being plundered and its barracks dismantled. There were, of course, practical reasons for locating the "museum" portion of the site (i.e., its exhibition space) in the base camp: the structures of Auschwitz I were more or less intact, it covered a smaller and more manageable area in comparison to the expanse of Birkenau, it was closer to the center of Oświęcim, and the staff's administrative offices and many of the workers' apartments were located there. Yet the decision to locate the exhibition only on the grounds of Auschwitz I also reflected the emphasis on the experience of the Polish political prisoner and on the base camp as the primary locus of Polish national martyrdom.

For the purpose of planning the new exhibition, the Ministry of Culture and Art convened, in December 1946, a conference that brought to Oświęcim some thirty participants—scholars, journalists, artists, representatives of the Central Commission for the Investigation of German Crimes in Poland, the Jewish Historical Institute, and the PZbWP. The wide diversity of participants at the meeting reflected broad interest in the museum project. Moreover, it showed that the Auschwitz memorial site and museum were, at this early stage, very much a public project open to a diversity of influences and commemorative agendas, and not solely the result of calculated state directives. In fact, throughout 1946 and 1947, the PZbWP and its press organ *Wolni Ludzie* had led a public conversation on the future of the site. More than any other organization, the PZbWP—with its membership[51] drawn from the ranks of former prisoners—endeavored to invest the site with a Polish-national commemorative emphasis. Its populist appeals, in combination with its close proximity to centers of power in Warsaw,[52] helped to make the PZbWP a visible and effective champion of the museum's cause.

The protocol of the conference indicates that several sections of the large exhibition were already complete in December 1946. Plans for additional exhibition blocks were ambitious, utilizing nearly all the available space in the base camp. Block 15, as the entrance to the museum, was to provide a general history of German-Polish relations. Blocks 16, 17, and 18 would outline the duties and composition of the SS at Auschwitz, life and work inside the camp, and slave labor outside the camp confines, respectively. Blocks 1–3, 12–14, and 22–24 were set aside for the exhibitions of other nations whose citizens had perished in Auschwitz, while Blocks 19–21 and

25–27 would house artifacts and documents depicting the history of other major camps.[53]

These exhibits were to give a thorough presentation of German aggression throughout history, especially during the recent occupation, highlighting the prisoners' experiences in Auschwitz I. Moreover, in setting aside nine blocks for "national" exhibitions, the conference's recommendations foresaw the participation of various countries in the further development of the site. This goal, however, remained merely a hypothetical abstraction until the first national exhibits were opened in the late 1950s and 1960s. It is possible, at this early stage in the site's development, that other countries and their organizations of former prisoners were less than forthcoming with plans for the "international" development of the museum. It also appears, however, that the museum and its supervising ministry in Warsaw did not place the international element of Auschwitz history or the international makeup of deportees to the camp—both Jews and non-Jews—at the forefront of their efforts. In April 1947 the Ministry of Culture and Art commissioned the former prisoner Wincenty Hein with the task of developing a "foreign office" at the museum to coordinate cooperation in the development of additional exhibitions. Hein, however, was prevented from traveling to the international congress of the Fédération Internationale des Anciens Prisonniers Politiques (FIAPP) in Paris later that month. Delegates to the congress passed a resolution calling for cooperation with the State Museum at Auschwitz in the construction of various national exhibits,[54] but plans for an "international office" at the State Museum never materialized.[55] A more extensive "internationalization" of the site's exhibits would certainly have been appropriate at this early stage, but this important aspect of the camp's history remained limited to official pronouncements and the information provided by museum guides.

Although there appeared to be general consensus over plans for the base camp, the future of the Birkenau site was a more difficult and controversial issue for the participants in the December 1946 conference. As Alfred Woycicki, author of the conference's protocol, stated:

> Far more difficult is the issue of the Birkenau camp, which will receive further elaboration and analysis. Today, in its raw state from January 1945, it makes a nightmarish impression and shocks one to the depths—particularly the women's camp. The human imagination is not in a state to compre-

hend the fact that tens of thousands of women from all of Europe were forced to live in such monstrous imbrutement and degradation, sentenced to extermination by the "master race." It is necessary to give the most serious consideration to this problem and its solution.

The grounds of the destroyed crematoria and the ditches in which corpses were burned are also among the most difficult issues. The entirety of those grounds permeated with human remains must be secured and commemorated in a manner worthy of the majesty of a martyr's death. May the voice of society be decisive in this matter.[56]

Lacking the self-explanatory structures of the base camp, the topography of the Birkenau site was capable of evoking an emotional reaction on the part of the visitor, but appeared to have limited didactic value because of its "raw state." It is also significant that the protocol singled out the former women's camp as the most disturbing element at Birkenau. Many, if not all of the masonry barracks in the *Frauenkonzentrationslager* were still standing, unlike the hundreds of wooden barracks that had already been torn down in the other sectors of Birkenau. Perhaps the women's camp was, like the blocks of the base camp, a more accessible locus of memory. Poles had survived it, and many associated it with the writings of prisoners such as Krystyna Żywulska, Zofia Kossak, and Seweryna Szmaglewska who, shortly after the liberation, had published accounts of their experiences there.[57] It is clear, in any case, that the conferees were at a loss as to what to make of the site. Birkenau, of course, had changed significantly in the course of less than two years and was certainly not, as the protocol claimed, in the same condition in which it had been in January 1945.[58] The most notorious of all Nazi killing centers, in effect, had lost much of its iconographic and pedagogical value precisely because it had not, as Woycicki had stated, been "secured and commemorated in a manner worthy of the majesty of a martyr's death."

The plans set out at the December 1946 conference, ambitious as they were, met with revision in the following months, for the exhibition opened in June 1947 had a simplified structure, and was limited to Blocks 4–6 and 8–11.[59] Although museum documents do not allow a block-by-block analysis, they do reveal an important characteristic of the exhibition: its separation of the camp's history into two periods. To quote Professor Ludwik Rajewski, director of the Department of Museums and Monuments of Polish Martyrology, the first phase in the history of Auschwitz was "the period of the biological destruction of the Poles, and especially the Polish intelligentsia," while the second marked the "period of the biological ruin of the Jews, [when] . . . conditions and life in the camp were easier, but the victims were in the millions, eight times as many as in the first period."[60] Rajewski's periodization was appropriate to the extent that it testified to the lack of uniformity in the experiences of prisoners in the camp over time. In addition, it helped to distinguish, if only in small measure, between the treatment of non-Jewish registered prisoners and unregistered Jewish deportees. Yet such a periodization was also simplistic and misleading, for in its reference to the "biological destruction of the Poles" it attributed to non-Jewish Poles a smaller number of victims, but a comparable level of suffering in the camp—the implication being that Jews were left to languish in the camp, resulting in millions of deaths, and that non-Jewish Poles were also the victims of systematic genocide.

The available evidence suggests that the fate of the Jews at Auschwitz—as a category of historical representation—was neglected at the museum even in its earliest phase of development, and a comparison of planning documents for the exhibition illustrates this claim. The first version of a set of guidelines entitled "Principles for the Planning of the Museum in the Former Concentration Camp Auschwitz" proposes treatment of the Shoah in the following manner:

> From 1942 (summer) until the fall of 1944 was the period of biological annihilation of Jews. With respect to life in the camp, this period was undoubtedly easier, but with respect to the number of victims, the numbers were much higher. They were transported from all countries of Europe, and if they were not immediately needed they were one hundred percent annihilated. This period was undoubtedly more horrific, as it has to do with the extermination of millions, and if one were concerned only with numerical comparison, this was an eightfold increase.

The document continues:

> [W]e must discuss the most important issue in the Auschwitz camp, that is, the Jewish question. The State Museum at Auschwitz will contact the Central Jewish Commission in Łódź and request their cooperation. Because Jews had, under the circumstances, suffered the greatest loss, they should provide materials for the purpose of depicting the magnitude of their de-

struction, as well as the possible methods of that destruction. . . . In all statistical data the number of Jewish victims must be given. . . . Jews are to be divided into groups according to the states from which they came. The proportion of Jewish artifacts depends on the contributions of the Central Jewish Commission, but should not give the impression that Auschwitz is a place of exclusively Jewish torment.[61]

Although subscribing to Rajewski's periodization, the "planning principles" quoted here are clear and accurate in their brief description of the Jewish fate at Auschwitz; they leave no room for doubt that the greatest number of victims at the camp were Jews; and they designate the Jews' destruction as "the most important issue in the Auschwitz camp." But a revision of the guidelines from the files of the Polish Union of Former Political Prisoners radically abbreviates the "Jewish question" at the museum, stating only: "The issue of the extermination of the Jews demands special treatment. In agreement with the Central Jewish Historical Commission, Jewish victims must be designated, to the extent possible, as citizens of particular states."[62] The final and publicized version of this document appeared in the PZbWP organ *Wolni Ludzie* on 15 June 1947, the day after the museum's opening ceremonies, and its discussion of how the extermination of the Jews would be treated in the exhibitions was identical to that of the abbreviated second version.[63]

Given the PZbWP's proximity to power in Warsaw, it is possible that this revision, subsuming rather than highlighting the crimes against Jews at Auschwitz, reflected the wishes of the regime and the political exigencies of the period. Although available documents and exhibition photographs do not allow us to measure with absolute precision the treatment of the Jewish genocide in the museum's new exhibition, it appears that the Shoah, as an object of historical research or as a phenomenon standing alone among the criminal policies of National Socialism, remained at the margins. As late as April 1947, there had been plans to place Blocks 4 and 11 at the disposal of the Central Committee of Jews in Poland, reflecting at least the goal of developing a Jewish exhibition at the site;[64] but at the museum's opening, the only space marked for the commemoration of Jewish victims was a single room in Block 4.[65] The museum's director and staff had certainly expressed the intent to address in some fashion the extermination of Jews at Auschwitz, but the issue remained on the periphery as simply one more example of German barbarism. The State Museum at Auschwitz, it must be emphasized, never denied or effaced the Jewish genocide from its exhibitions. It did, however, marginalize this history or subsume it within the broader treatment of the "Extermination of Millions," as the title of the exhibit in Block 4 suggested. Jews were to be remembered for their suffering and death at Auschwitz, but that suffering and death was neither given unique emphasis, nor adequately set apart from the dominant Polish-national martyrological idiom cultivated at the site.

Kazimierz Smoleń and former minister of culture Lucjan Motyka—both early associates of the museum—have suggested that political considerations were instrumental in this abbreviation of the historical record.[66] Not only would an accurate representation of Jewish suffering and death at Auschwitz overshadow the martyrdom of Gentile Poles, it could also stimulate existing anticommunist and anti-Jewish sentiment in this period of political instability and anti-Jewish violence, undermining the credibility of the museum and the state that supported it.[67] In other words, Poles visiting or reading about a museum and memorial site giving the Shoah its proper emphasis might feel that their monument to national martyrdom had somehow been appropriated by Jews, and an emphasis on and valorization of Jewish victims at the camp could alienate the visiting public and undermine the regime's effort to uphold Auschwitz as a site of Polish martyrdom.

The failure to identify Jewish victims as such was inappropriate and misleading. Often ascribed simply and exclusively to anti-Semitic traditions in Poland, this practice was, in reality, more complex than is frequently assumed. Although it may have reflected an ahistorical and politically expedient concern over the Polish public's identification of the postwar Auschwitz site with a perceived żydokomuna and an unpopular government in Warsaw, the museum's planners were, in fact, subscribing to standard methods of identifying victims and the losses suffered by various nations during the war. And there is an additional irony: those responsible for the planning of the Auschwitz site wished to avoid accusations of racism that might arise, were they to designate victims specifically as Jews. On this point, Lucjan Motyka explains:

> There is a further problem in the portrayal of the museum. In 1947, when the museum was organized . . . in Germany and in Poland and in other camps one considered how many citizens of those countries perished, and one did not speak of Jews, Poles—only 6 million citizens of Poland. At that time there was no Jewish state, and in the discussions then, we did not want

to subscribe to Rosenberg's principles[68] that a man or citizen of a given country is counted only on a racial basis. . . . So the use of Hitlerite principles—that he was a Jew because his grandfather was a Jew—seemed to us to be an acceptance of Rosenberg's racial laws.[69]

At stake here are a number of issues crucial to the future of the Auschwitz Museum and Polish perceptions of Auschwitz history in the postwar era: the relative emphasis of one victim group over another, the breadth of "martyrdom" as a commemorative mantra, the extent to which Jews should be designated as the largest victim group at Auschwitz, and, finally, whether or not it was appropriate for the custodians of Auschwitz memory to use, in their public representation of the camp's history, categories employed by the perpetrators of the Auschwitz crime. Motyka's statements illustrate the complex and sensitive issues faced when attempting to designate and categorize Auschwitz victims. They are not intended as an exculpation for the understated presentation of the Shoah at the memorial site, but they are descriptive of the dilemmas faced by the museum's planners and point to the inability or unwillingness to confront the Jewish issue at the memorial site. This failure was not simply and exclusively a manifestation of anti-Semitism or the result of malicious design, but appears to have been the product of a studied ignorance, a collective memory of a Polish Auschwitz, and a degree of political control that would intensify in the years to come.

By the time of the opening ceremonies of the State Museum in June 1947, the Auschwitz site had undergone a remarkable transformation. In the course of only two and a half years, a site of carnage and destruction had become the central locus of institutionalized public memory, martyrology, and wartime history in early postwar Poland. Poles flocked by the thousands to the commemorative arena at Auschwitz. Whether on All Saints' Day, on the anniversary of the first transport of Polish "politicals" to the camp, or on other occasions, one hundred thousand visitors converged on Auschwitz in 1946, and one hundred seventy thousand in 1947. The historical exhibitions at the museum—as well as the failure to maintain and develop the Birkenau site— reflected the currents of Auschwitz memory in Poland as they developed in the early postwar years. Polish national martyrdom and the perpetual German threat were the outstanding features of official Auschwitz memory and its physical manifestations, while the extermination of Jews at Auschwitz would remain, for decades to come, a fact acknowledged but inadequately expressed at the memorial site. In effect, Poland had retained the more complete landscape of the concentration camp in which Poles had languished and where many had met a brutal death, but had abbreviated the extermination camp in which European Jews had perished.

In 1948 a British publicist, after a visit to Auschwitz, reflected on his experience there:

> To know evil is to enter into it, to become it in some sort; and there is no knowledge of good without knowledge of evil. The realisation of the evil of Birkenau sets one at the core of the moral struggle of our world, in a flash of absolutes. And this difficult moment is, after all, what one came here to meet . . . one feels that there is a moral difference between the nations for whom Birkenau or its like is a simple fact, confronted, set aside, unforgotten, and those who have never known or discovered it. . . . How soon the green comes, and the plough goes over.[70]

Whether the author knew it or not, he had hit upon a central problem of Auschwitz memory in Poland. Auschwitz was unforgotten, and the construction of the camp's commemorative framework was far from complete, but by 1947 notions of Polish martyrdom and the marginalization of the Shoah had become cultural and ideological fixtures of its memory. Poland had, in fact, simplified Auschwitz and routinized its meaning, setting it aside for the next generation to exploit, or perhaps to efface, from Poland's memorial landscape.

3 ⫼ Auschwitz as a Cold-War Theater, 1947–1954

> The struggle for a lasting peace in all the world at the side of the
> Great Soviet Union with the standard-bearer of peace, Com-
> rade Stalin at the fore—this is the guarantee that sites of torment
> in the form of Auschwitz and Birkenau will never rise again!
>
> An anonymous inscription in the guest book
> of the State Museum at Auschwitz, 11 January 1951

IN APRIL 1949 the local leadership of the Polish United Workers' Party
(Polska Zjednoczona Partia Robotnicza (PZPR) organized a rally in
Oświęcim under the slogan "Never Again War   Never Again Concentration Camps." On what was called this "Great Day of Auschwitz," participants came from the town of Oświęcim and the surrounding region to
demonstrate, in the words of one journalist, "for the idea of peace" as they
"passionately protested against any attempted Anglo-Saxon instigation."
The crowd offered its enthusiastic support for the party, for the decisions of
its constitutive congress in December of the previous year, and for its resolve to stand firm as an ally of the Soviet Union. Speeches by delegates
from youth organizations, local government representatives, and officials
from the Auschwitz Museum were strident and agitative in tone. The local
PZPR representative, for example, lashed out against "Anglo-American
politics, planned from above in order for the Germans to rebuild after the
war, so that they might, together with the Germans, reach for the treasures
of the East."[1] After condemning the 1944 Allied bombing of the chemical
works at Auschwitz-Monowitz as an attempt to cripple the future of Polish
industry, he went on to strike a more optimistic tone, invoking "[t]he crea-
tive power of the Polish farmer and worker," which would "lead our nation

to a better tomorrow, to the building of socialism and in the struggle for world peace."

The high point of the event was the speech of Jan Chlebowski, a former prisoner and party activist. As one press account stated, "the old Auschwitz prisoner and member of the underground resistance movement illustrated in the most artistic manner the dark night of the fascist-Hitlerite occupation." Former Auschwitz prisoners were, Chlebowski claimed, especially justified in raising their voices against current Western, anti-Soviet policies. Applying a historical lesson to the present danger, he pointed out that "just as Anglo-American capital armed the Hitlerite hordes, so today it arms the murderers and mercenaries of Chiang Kai-Shek and Dutch imperialists."

Under the influence of Polish Stalinism and increasing Cold War tension, memory work at Auschwitz became a blunt instrument of Polish domestic and foreign policy. As this April gathering illustrates, the memorial site could function as a political aesthetic for a variety of notions: support for the communist government, solidarity with the USSR, historical revisionism, or vigilance toward a Western security threat. Neither a symbol of Polish suffering and martyrdom in the past nor a metonym for the Shoah, the Auschwitz commemorated at this April 1949 event pointed to an activist future, spurring support for the upcoming struggle between the Soviet bloc and the capitalist, imperialist powers of the West. "Auschwitz," as Chlebowski concluded, "is a synonym for the revolutionary struggle in defense of peace."

The State Museum at Auschwitz opened in 1947 with an established Polish-national commemorative framework, but subsequent changes in Poland's political landscape and concomitant demands for increased state control over the site radically altered its exhibitions and public function. Instrumentalization of the site was not new, for earlier uses of Auschwitz also had reflected the regime's political goals. During the years of Stalinist rule, however, ideological rhetoric and choreographed commemorative ritual became the norm, and Auschwitz served the regime as a political weapon. This chapter examines the political exploitation of the memorial site in the years 1947–54, a period in which state control over the Auschwitz grounds was comprehensive and manipulation of the past there was remarkably transparent.

Shifts in the State Museum's agenda had begun already in late 1947, as the Ministry of Culture worked to invest the site's exhibits with a more positive tone, emphasizing the prisoners' valor and ultimate victory over their martyrdom at the camp. Thereafter state control over the site increased dramatically, and in 1950 authorities ordered a total reconstruction of the Auschwitz exhibition to bring it in line with the ideological rigors of Stalinism's cultural revolution. For the next four years, socialist heroism, not tragedy, was the order of the day, and the "fascist" and "imperialist" motivations of the United States and its allies supplanted the German menace as Poland's greatest threat. Likewise, official public gatherings at Auschwitz, whether ceremonies on the anniversary of the liberation or mass political demonstrations, appeared awash in a sea of hyperbolic cold-war rhetoric.

Before embarking on an analysis of these years, however, it is necessary to enter a caveat. The era of Polish Stalinism at Auschwitz was certainly an era of politicization and crass instrumentalization, but this should not imply that other periods in the site's history were devoid of political agendas. The late 1940s and 1950s may provide the most glaring examples of political instrumentalization at Auschwitz, but this analysis—although highly critical of the abuses of the site and its history that took place during these years— also recognizes that even in the absence of overt pressure, commemorative strategies remain culturally and politically inflected. This makes it all the more difficult, or even impossible, to define or juxtapose evil, manipulative "propaganda" and objective, appropriate "commemoration," for to do so would suggest a false dichotomy. At the same time, the need to condemn vulgar abuses of history and memory remains, as does the need to recognize the work of more objective memorialists. All this is, in the end, illustrative of the tension referred to in the introduction—the tension between the "represented" Auschwitz and "real" Auschwitz that remains so unsettling to both the memorialist and the historian.

That tension manifested itself in the late 1940s and early 1950s in paradoxical ways, for the use of Auschwitz as a political medium diminished, rather than elevated, its importance as a locus of wartime memory. Despite the site's role as a center for the commemoration of Poland's suffering and heroism under the German occupation, as early as 1948 there were also calls for abbreviating and even removing Auschwitz from the landscape of People's Poland, thus putting the grounds to more economically productive use. Such calls were renewed in 1953, suggesting that by then Auschwitz and its symbolism were neither appreciated by the state as a site of homage and mourning nor considered necessary for the regime's current political agenda. Total effacement of Auschwitz would, of course, have made Auschwitz "functional" to the extreme, and would likewise have been the ultimate testimony to the malleability of memory there. On the other hand, the historical voice of the camp could not remain totally mute, for the nationalist vernacular of Polish martyrology periodically reasserted itself and eventually made possible the resuscitation of the State Museum in the mid-1950s.

The Context of Polish Stalinism

Transformations at Auschwitz corresponded to changes in Poland's political landscape under the growing influence of Stalinism. If in 1947 the Polish Workers' Party had exercised its dominance over Polish politics through manipulation of the January elections, in the course of the next two years it firmly established hegemony over the country's political, economic, and, not least, cultural affairs. Bordering Germany in the west and the Soviet Union in the east, Poland had a precarious but crucial geopolitical importance among the client states in the Soviet sphere. Consolidation of communist rule in Poland was therefore inseparable from events abroad. The division of Europe and strains in relations between the United States and Soviet Union were becoming more evident in 1947 and 1948, as American opposition to communism became official policy with the announcement of the Truman Doctrine in the spring of 1947. In the summer of that year Poland followed the Soviet Union's lead in rejecting Marshall Plan aid, and in September the Communist Party of the Soviet Union and its client parties established the Cominform as a forum for the ideological homogenization of the Soviet Bloc. In March of the following year, Britain, France, and the Benelux states signed a treaty of mutual assistance; the Soviet Union imposed a blockade on the western sectors of Berlin; and Tito's Yugoslavia, straying from the Stalinist model, incurred the condemnation of East European communist governments for its "nationalist deviation" from the party line.

Meanwhile, Poland's communists struggled with the imposition of control over a nationally minded and fractious population. The PPR's general secretary, Władysław Gomułka, was a tough and uncompromising politician convinced of the need for a strong alliance with the Soviet Union. At the same time, however, he advocated a "Polish road" to socialism that would allow Poland a modicum of independence. For Gomułka, socialism in Poland would challenge, but also recognize, the country's unique political and cultural characteristics, such as the powerful role of nationalist sentiment and the peasantry's opposition to collectivization. For several years Stalin had been willing to tolerate Gomułka and his brand of socialism, but by 1948 the USSR was in a position to assert its authority and oust the Polish leader. Whereas in 1945 Stalin desperately had needed Gomułka and his "homeland" comrades, by 1948 the Soviet Union had won the war, tested the atomic bomb, embroiled itself in the first Berlin Crisis, and grown intent on maintaining unquestioned leadership among its client governments. Gomułka's days were numbered. He was deprived of his party posts at a Central Committee plenary meeting in August and September 1948, and in January 1949 he removed himself from the government. His fall, along with the forced merger of the PPR with the Polish Socialist Party in December 1948, cleared the path to the establishment of communist rule along the Soviet model.

Although Poland maintained its reputation as an ungrateful and undisciplined subordinate, Soviet presence and influence in the late 1940s and early 1950s was evident in ways both subtle and obvious: tens of thousands of Red Army troops were stationed in Poland; a personality cult surrounding the Polish president, Bolesław Bierut, was clearly imitative of the Stalin-worship in the Soviet Union; Konstanty Rokossovsky, a Soviet marshal of Polish origin, was appointed vice-premier, minister of defense, and a member of the PZPR's politburo; and the new constitution enacted in 1952 was modeled after that of the Soviet Union. Not least, ubiquitous demonstrations and commemorative events, such as those held at the former Auschwitz camp, made a slavish ritual of paying homage to the valor of the Soviet liberator and to Stalin's firm guidance on the path to socialism.[2]

Stalinism— whether in the Polish, Hungarian, East German, or Soviet context—is most often identified with terror and political oppression, and, lest the label be applied too loosely, it is worth noting that enforced political conformity and terror, although certainly characteristic of this period in postwar Polish history, never reached the extremes of other Soviet client states. Unlike Rudolf Slánsky and László Rajk in Czechoslovakia and Hungary, respectively, Władysław Gomułka never stood trial, and Poland never experienced the use of show trials against those of its leaders regarded as ideologically unfaithful or politically dispensable. Recalcitrant Polish peasants were collectivized against their will, but were not deported. Nonetheless, in the conformist, paranoid, and security-obsessed atmosphere, especially after 1948, the use of torture became more common, the network of labor camps grew, and the activities and powers of the Ministry of Public Security expanded exponentially. Whereas in 1949 the ministry had employed more than twenty thousand agents and informers, by 1954 that number had nearly quadrupled.[3]

While the state suppressed political opposition, it also implemented in draconian fashion the economic transformations outlined for the Six-Year Plan (1950–55), waging a broad attack against the remnants of a market economy, investing enormous capital in heavy industry, and, beginning in 1950, embarking on a drive to collectivize Polish agriculture. In the cultural sphere, artists, academics, and writers with suspect backgrounds (such as links to the Home Army, relatives abroad, or emigration during the occupations of the Second World War) were silenced or even imprisoned. Those favored or merely tolerated by the regime were required to comply with its educational priorities, academic guidelines, or, in the realm of theater, literature, and the visual arts, the aesthetic conventions of Socialist Realism.

Stalinist ideology held that intensified class struggle was a necessary characteristic of the preliminary and intermediate phases of the socialist transformation. This resulted in the rapid and often brutal political streamlining of the country's social and cultural institutions. Conforming to this line, the newly formed PZPR assumed an increasingly active role in setting the ideological priorities and administrative structure of all public museums. Hence, the vocabulary of commemoration at Auschwitz became part of the class struggle.

The State Museum at Auschwitz was in a unique position to further the government's agenda as it strengthened its hold on the site. Like the former Pawiak prison in Warsaw or Maidanek near Lublin, it was a novel "museum" that had no prewar model on which to base its exhibits and public role. Yet the Auschwitz Museum also offered the Ministry of Culture and Art an opportunity; its exhibitions and public landscape, in comparison to those of many other museums under the ministry's control, were easily adaptable to the prevailing ideological needs of the regime. This would require, however, closer supervision and tighter regulation of the site, and so, only weeks after the State Museum's official opening in June 1947, the ministry issued a series of guidelines for the site and imposed a rigorous cycle of censorship for the exhibits.[4] Censorship would ensure that plans for the museum were subject to the scrutiny of experts and government authorities, and it also severely encumbered the ability of the museum and its historical commission to implement their own agenda at the site. This was, of course, in the interest of the Polish state, which sought to assert its control over the landscape and uses of the grounds. At this site of "enormous propagandistic and educational significance,"[5] the past could serve the present in a variety of complementary ways.

In the first year after the museum's official opening, its staff continued the efforts to conclude the construction and modification of the site according to the initial plans formulated by the Ministry of Culture in 1947. The ministry's agenda for the site, publicized in the press,[6] spurred a lively public discussion on the goals of the museum and the extent to which Auschwitz should function as a memorial to Polish suffering or, conversely, as a memorial to wartime heroism and victory. Wincenty Hein, chairman of the newly appointed historical commission and always an articulate voice of the museum administration, argued in an August 1947 article the necessity of moving beyond conventional devotional reverence at Auschwitz to a recognition of "political realism" that would make the most of the site's educational potential. "Is it possible today," he questioned, "to erect here a museum that must limit itself exclusively to the role of a site of suffering and martyrdom?" If Auschwitz were to illuminate the realities of the German occupation, it should also, according to Hein, be an "instrument of foreign policy" alerting the visitor to contemporary threats posed by German rehabilitation. Moreover, he argued, traditional notions of martyrology carried with them a potential danger, namely, "that too glaring a definition of martyrology and loss be considered a symptom of weakness and a lack of political realism." Poles should learn from Auschwitz and use it as tool of current foreign policy, but they should also remain vigilant lest the site become a symbol of weakness and political naïveté vis-à-vis the German threat—an image potentially damaging to the country's consciousness and historical identity. "If the task of the museum," Hein wrote, "is to evoke among visitors a wave of horror, sorrow, and empathy, should it not evoke, as well, the feeling of the indestructible power of the Polish nation?"[7] Auschwitz, in other words, might remain a monument to Poland's martyrs, but it should also serve as a symbol of strength and, in the words of another commentator, a "sign of the victory of the Polish spirit that not even the most sophisticated forms of torture nor the fires of the crematoria could strangle."[8]

Vice-Minister of Culture Zygmunt Balicki took up this theme as well when, in March 1948, he warned the Council for the Protection of Monuments of Struggle and Martyrdom against the "cultivation of suffering" in its work at Auschwitz and elsewhere, noting that "not only suffering, but struggle was the central moment of international unity in the war, the consequence of which was total victory over fascism. It is precisely that moment of struggle which should be dominant in the work of the Council and its commemoration should be one of its primary tasks."[9] Implementing this goal at Poland's most important commemorative site, the council, along with the museum's historical commission, issued in April 1948 a new set of guiding principles for the further development of the Auschwitz grounds.[10] Although this agenda for the museum remained within a Polish-national framework, it also presaged an emphasis on international antifascism in the museum's exhibitions and the exploitation of the site as a rallying point for political activism.

"Oświęcim Zaorać"

Debates in the year following the dedication of the State Museum indicated a high level of public and governmental engagement in the affairs of the memorial site and suggested as well that the future of Auschwitz, if in some respects undefined, was nonetheless guaranteed. But for some, prevailing notions of Polish martyrdom at the camp or even calls for an emphasis on Polish struggle and heroism were both ideologically suspect and highly impractical in the developing economy and forward-looking culture of the new, socialist Poland. In June 1948 an article severely criticizing the State Museum appeared in the journal *Odrodzenie* (Renaissance), beginning a heated controversy over the future of the site and spurring an initiative aiming at closing the museum.[11] Jerzy Putrament, a leading literary figure and the author of the article, had served as editor of *Dziennik Polski*, was secretary general of the Union of Polish Writers and a member of the Polish Workers' Party, and in the years ahead would sit on the Central Committee of the PZPR.[12]

Putrament's irreverent discussion of the current state of the museum, in the form of a chronicle of his visit there, was characterized by sarcasm; he mocked the museum and the work of its staff at every turn. Critical of the tours given at the site, Putrament ridiculed the former prisoners responsible for accompanying visitors: "The guides in Auschwitz are youthful, polite, agreeable. But they are guides. In the course of the few years that the 'State Museum' has functioned, they have taught themselves to memorize a few hundred facts necessary to show around a tour group.... In a word, the former prisoners have already become professionals, and that is a rather horrible thing."[13] Not only did Putrament regard the museum guides as incompetent; he even went so far as to question the need for such "unproductive" individuals at all in a developing socialist society: "I look at these sunburned peasants [the guides] and think: What a horrible profession you have chosen for yourselves! Instead of working, building, developing, day in and day out they lead dozens of tours, mumble their commentary, the repetitiveness of which nearly detracts from the horror of its content—if only they had something to build—like a crematorium."[14] The author's most scathing commentary was reserved for an indictment of what he regarded as an unwarranted sensationalism at the site. Deriding the pedagogical orientation of the museum and not missing an opportunity to express his contempt of the United States, Putrament offered a hyperbolic prediction for the future of the grounds:

> I can imagine perfectly the sort of American tour by Cook: "Do you know the largest extermination center in the world?" "Encounter hell!" Such tours would be divided into normal, tourist, and "special." The special tours, for a suitable extra charge, would include the following: transport to the camp in boxcars (the last ten km) with 120 people in each car, a cattle drive with truncheons carried out by specially uniformed SS men (Authentic! Just in from the Denazification Commission!), undressing, entering the chamber just like going to the gas ... [and] all those returning would be entitled to a handful of ashes. For an additional charge one could have a number tattooed on the forearm.
>
> We are far from America, that's for sure. But it appears that the Auschwitz museum is aimed in no other direction.[15]

Putrament's comments are extraordinary for a number of reasons. Their tone was without precedent in previously published analyses of the museum. Moreover, the author failed to propose any constructive remedies at all for what he considered the incompetence of the guides or the carnivalesque atmosphere at Auschwitz, as if the museum's cause were hopeless. Finally, in light of the author's proximity to centers of power in the regime, it is unimaginable that in mid-1948 such a provocative, glib, and controversial article could be published without the sanction of the censors or the press section of the PPR's Central Committee. At face value it appears illogical that the Polish Workers' Party and the Warsaw government, as guarantors and administrators of the State Museum at Auschwitz, would stand aside as an authoritative voice, supposedly representative of their interests, issued a caustic attack on the central site of Polish wartime commemoration.

Kazimierz Smoleń, a member of the Auschwitz Museum's historical commission at that time, has suggested that Putrament was writing on behalf of the party and voicing the party's plans for the Auschwitz grounds. The Polish government, he concludes, was contemplating the closure of the site and using the respected and ideologically allied author as its mouthpiece.[16] By 1948 it was clear that the State Museum at Auschwitz could serve as an effective political instrument, but according to Putrament, its grounds and facilities could better serve the production quotas and economic restructuring of the Three-Year Plan.

Three months later, another scathingly critical article appeared from the pen of the well-known journalist and author Kazimierz Koźniewski.[17] Although it lacked Putrament's sarcasm and irony, Koźniewski's article, entitled "A Delicate Problem," criticized the Auschwitz site not for its sensationalism, but for its representation of history, which, in the author's estimation, was so far removed from the reality of the camp that it made impossible any realistic appreciation of its former horror. "Unfortunately," he began,

> the "Auschwitz Museum" does not offer even an approximate truth about the Auschwitz camp. It depends on a paradoxical situation: either one wishes to maintain the external arrangement of the camp—then it is necessary to conserve it and ultimately eliminate its horror—or . . . the horror in the blocks not restored will last a year or two, but will in the end diminish due to the effects of time. Personally, I convinced myself not long ago that the original walls do not provide the essence of the camp system but, despite the efforts of the museum's creators, actually distort the reality of Auschwitz.[18]

For Koźniewski, the distortion lay in the pristine and tourist-oriented atmosphere of the grounds. Disturbed by the manicured paths, flower beds, and fresh paint, he was unsure of the response that the site was to evoke. "I am baffled," the author stated, "as I wonder whether the pleasant, grassy, low hillock that is supposed to be the crematorium looked as innocuous back then—is it possible that my imagination is deficient, or that I am so insensitive?" "Everything," he continued, "glistens of order and smells of cleanliness. German inscriptions—everywhere here—are reconstructed clearly, exactly, and they sound . . . gentle, for 'uncover your head,' 'keep quiet,' and numerous similar orders find themselves, after all, in dozens of schools, cloisters, and normal prisons around the world; they aren't anything cruel at all."[19] The Auschwitz that Koźniewski experienced during his visit was, he believed, a sanitized memorial incapable of impressing upon the visitor anything resembling the horror of the camp. While his conclusions may have been exaggerated, they brought to light for the first time in the public arena a dilemma faced by the museum since its foundation: Can a preserved or even reconstructed Auschwitz effectively represent history? Can an "authentic" Auschwitz left in its "original" state (and therefore left to deteriorate) do the same, and with what effect on the visitor? Moreover, the article effectively highlights a broader issue that remains contentious to the present day: the aestheticization of the memorial site. Is the maintenance of portions of Auschwitz or construction of exhibitions synonymous with its aestheticization (and distancing from the reality of the camp), or would deterioration of the site likewise distance the visitor from the horror? What images are embedded in a reconstructed Auschwitz, or in a decaying Auschwitz? Koźniewski's conclusion was that a "museum" at the site did more harm than good. "It is a contradiction," he stated, "that cannot be reconciled. Despite its apparent authenticity, Auschwitz transformed into a museum belies the truth of Auschwitz. It falsifies the truth. . . . and fewer and fewer people will believe in the truth about Auschwitz, in that system that looks like a museum. Instead, the museum dissipates even the horror of legend. And therein lies its danger."[20] For the author, then, the presence of maintained buildings, exhibits, and guided tours at Auschwitz could only diminish the reality of the prisoner's experience—a position clearly opposed to the plans for documentation, exhibition, and commemoration that the museum's planners had been at such pains to develop. Speculating on the future of the site, Koźniewski ended his article with a wistful prognosis: "And who knows whether after a time the remains of Birkenau will be scattered in the wind, whether few people will personally remember the horror then, whether it will be necessary to restrict entrance to the museum to historians and even to demolish the blocks of Auschwitz, to plow the grounds under, sow crops—and to establish there a symbolic cemetery where families may honor their dead."[21] Koźniewski's call for the establishment of a simple cemetery, when considered in conjunction with Putrament's article, supports the theory that the government was considering closing or at least abbreviating the memorial site. In fact, the "plowing-under of Auschwitz" (in Polish, "Oświęcim zaorać") became the catchphrase in late 1948 for what was regarded as a movement to close the museum and put its grounds to more "productive" use.

The "Oświęcim zaorać" initiative had its origins in the state apparatus, or at least had the state's approval. According to Kazimierz Smoleń, the former director of the museum, there were two reasons behind the initiative. First, he has argued that some governmental leaders viewed the museum and Auschwitz/Birkenau memorial site as a waste of valuable soil and capital that could be used in a more productive, economically profitable manner. This was the thrust of Putrament's article. Second, Smoleń has speculated that the initiative to shut the site down was related to vivid Polish memories of Stalinist terror during and after the war: to document the crimes of Germans and to commemorate their victims would revive the memory of Soviet crimes and invite comparisons that the Warsaw regime was eager to avoid.[22] An Auschwitz site documenting German atrocities was, according to former Minister of Culture Lucjan Motyka, "at the same time an indictment of Soviet camps, only we were not able to utter a single word about Soviet camps."[23] Soviet labor camps, forced deportations of Poles to the East, and the Katyn Massacre[24] had not been erased from the Polish collective memory of the years 1939–45; nor were Poles unaware of the repression, terror, and political incarcerations of their own postwar regime. Hence, too vivid a depiction of Nazi crimes would blur the all-important distinctions between German and Russian, Hitlerite and Soviet, fascist and communist, perpetrator and liberator.

It remains difficult to determine precise motives for the "Oświęcim zaorać" initiative, but there exists little doubt that it was guided from above.[25] Putrament's and Koźniewski's unprecedented criticisms of the museum clearly received the sanction of the Office of Press Control. Moreover, Putrament's well-known party activism and his subsequent membership in the PZPR's Central Committee support the theory that the party either was using the respected author and journalist as a mouthpiece or was willing to entertain his radical commentary on the status of the Auschwitz site in order to measure public response to it. In all likelihood, the PPR was sending up a trial balloon of sorts, using the voices of these writers to test public reaction to the prospect of closing the site or reducing the size and scope of its exhibitions and activities.

This was, however, a step for which the Polish public was not yet prepared, for Putrament's and Koźniewski's proposals elicited a vocal response. Koźniewski's article alone, in the words of Wincenty Hein, "caused an uproar in society,"[26] and in autumn 1948 numerous articles, editorials, and unsolicited letters in support of the museum and its mission appeared in the Polish press. While some were critical of developments at Auschwitz,[27] the majority advocated the preservation of the site and ardently defended the museum and its staff.[28] For example, in a response to Koźniewski's call for greater "realism" at Auschwitz, one of the museum's conservators asked, "Are we therefore required today, when the museum is to be a document, to scrape up the walls, riddle the doors with holes, and smash the windows? Is it necessary to send high voltage through the wires? Who among the visitors will want to be convinced of that?"[29] Likewise, the Ministry of Culture and Art issued its own rebuttal to proposals for closing the site: "This was precisely the aim of the Hitlerite creators of the camp—to hide from the world those crimes to which their fascist organization led. On the contrary, an independent and democratic Poland desires to guarantee peaceful rest to the remains of the fighters for freedom and to create an objective, documentary picture of that fascism which threatens humanity."[30]

If, in fact, party or government officials were testing public reactions to the possible "plowing-under" of Auschwitz, then they could only have been discouraged by the public outcry against such a possibility. Not only did proposals to liquidate the museum meet with opposition in the press, but the growing number of visitors also made clear that Auschwitz remained a site of national and international homage and pilgrimage. According to statistics of the State Museum and the Ministry of Culture and Art, more than 100,000 visited the museum between January and September 1948, with more than 10,000 from abroad. On All Saints' Day—perennially one of the most frequented commemorative occasions—3,500 pilgrims paid homage to the Auschwitz dead,[31] and in 1949 some 250,000 visited the site.[32]

The "Oświęcim zaorać" initiative remains a peculiar chapter in the history of postwar Auschwitz. It testified to the regime's ambivalence toward the site and, at the same time, to the regime's commitment to exploiting it. Plowing under the grounds in the service of the Polish economy or closing it in an attempt to divert the public's association of its images with Soviet oppression would be tantamount to the site's total instrumentalization. It was clear, however, that memory at Auschwitz could not be manipulated to the extreme of its effacement. The site and its memory were not mute, for continued support, expressed both in the press and in the number of visitors there, testified to its enduring importance in postwar Polish consciousness. Dissuaded by the defenders of the memorial site and recognizing its potential political value, the Polish United Workers' Party subsequently rejected initiatives to close the museum and elected instead to assert its role in cultural politics and to intervene directly in the reconfiguration of memory there.

From National Martyrdom to "The Struggle for Peace"

In early 1949 the party resuscitated and intensified calls for a greater emphasis on resistance at Auschwitz and focused its attention on a new exhibit in Block 21. The final exhibit on the visitor's route, Block 21 was to address the theme of "Struggle and Victory" at Auschwitz. Earlier plans for the museum had called for an exhibition of the same name to focus on the underground resistance in the camp, but new plans for Block 21 demanded a more inclusive, internationalist, and politically relevant depiction of the theme of wartime resistance.

Tadeusz Hołuj, a former Auschwitz prisoner and, according to a memorandum submitted to the Propaganda Department of the PZPR Central Committee, the only member of the museum's historical commission who "strives to maintain a Marxist stance," penned the blueprints for the exhibition.[33] As the final exhibit on the visitor's route of Auschwitz I, the block, according to Hołuj, was to "have the most powerful and choice pedagogical accent, the final inference for the visitor—an optimistic inference with a clear political resonance." This final accent was to emphasize to the visitor that "despite great suffering, horrible physical and psychological conditions, despite terror and mass extermination, the camp fought and, in the end, conquered."

And Hołuj firmly placed this victorious fight at Auschwitz in the hands of the "international forces of progress, with communists at the fore."[34]

The revised plans for Block 21 signaled a further transition in the vocabulary and interpretation of Auschwitz. In the public memory of years past, "Auschwitz" as a historical concept had been considered essentially the property of the Germans, a manifestation of their culture and war aims, and a locus of Polish suffering and death. Now, however, not only the Auschwitz site, but also the Auschwitz idea, had become the domain of Polish *and* international communist resistance. This, in effect, marked an expropriation of Auschwitz, transforming it from a site of suffering and death into a synonym for Europe's international struggle with the fascist occupant. Official pronouncements and public events at the memorial site had frequently designated Auschwitz as a site of international martyrdom, but plans to emphasize the international aspect of the camp's history had been directed primarily toward the future construction of various national exhibitions. Block 21, however, signaled the emergence of a new commemorative tone intended to extol internationalism specifically in relation to the camp's clandestine resistance organizations and leftist resistance groups across occupied Europe. Internationalization of the site in this manner was not only inspiring; it could also provide, in its depiction of the international antifascist struggle, a model for militant antifascist activism in the early days of the cold war. As Tadeusz Hołuj reported at an April 1949 planning conference in Oświęcim (called by the Ministry of Culture for the purpose of coordinating and controlling the museum's work), it was essential to strike a powerful, optimistic tone in the museum's final exhibit, showing "that the camp had fought and won the battle. Auschwitz was not only martyrology, but struggle as well." The communist leadership of the resistance was, moreover, part of an international movement, "a fragment of the general fight against fascism."[35]

The April conference also focused on fascism and how to depict it at the Auschwitz site, particularly in the context of the exhibition in Block 4, "Extermination of Millions." Until then, "Hitlerite" had been the generally preferred term to describe the Nazi invaders; this designation, however, was nearly absent from the April conference's protocol. It had, in fact, been superseded by "fascist"—a less nationally bound, more inclusive designation that could now also be associated with Warsaw's current ideological enemies: the West's capitalist and militarist forces that utilized and rehabilitated Nazi criminals in the service of their imperialist agenda. Poland's commemorative lexicon had theretofore portrayed the Nazis first as Germans, then as fascists, and third, as uniquely cruel and depraved. But at the April 1949 conference, Vice-Minister of Culture Balicki stressed on several occasions the need to expand treatment of fascism beyond its German variation to include Italian, Greek, Spanish, and even Polish forms. In short, a specifically German "Hitlerism" was no longer the prime international threat; rather, "fascism" in any of its forms threatened the progressive camp of "people's democracies." Moreover, according to Hołuj it was necessary to cast the victims of fascism in a broader light. The annihilation of the Gypsies, for example, demonstrated that "the Germans could apply the methods of destruction to every national group without being governed by any criteria," the implication here being that total annihilation, whether at Auschwitz or in general, was not directed at clearly defined and targeted victim groups, such as the Gypsies and Jews, but was instead directed toward a variety of nationalities, such as the Poles, Russians, and other Slavs.[36]

Plans for the renovation of Block 15, the first to be viewed at the State Museum, reinforced these themes. Originally intended to illustrate issues of Polish-German relations, this block was now "devoted to the investigation of world fascism."[37] Its analysis would be "developed in accordance with a Marxist approach" and would refer to the speeches of Stalin. In addition, the exhibit would illustrate the origins of genocide (embedded in the roots of fascist ideology) and the "inevitability of Auschwitz-type crimes resulting from the imperialist-capitalist phase." Finally, Block 15 avoided anti-German bias and cited instead the progressive forces of the nineteenth and twentieth centuries in Germany, culminating in that country's successor to its prewar Communist Party, the Socialist Unity Party.[38]

These shifts in official commemoration of Auschwitz and interpretation of its history were both a reflection of and response to developments abroad. The emergence and cultivation of an international "antifascist consensus" in the Soviet Bloc and among Western European communist parties was perhaps a general motivation for the shift in emphasis at the Auschwitz site. "Hitlerites" had become "fascists," as the prospect of a rehabilitated united Germany appeared far less likely than a West German state integrated into an "imperialist" camp in opposition to the goals and policies of the "people's democracies." The end of the Berlin Blockade and formation of the Federal Republic of Germany in May 1949 pointed to the emergence of the German Democratic Republic, an ideologically conformist ally that would be established in October of that year. In other words, the traditional emphasis on the organic characteristics of the German nation was clearly superseded by 1949. Moreover, the signing of the North Atlantic Treaty in April 1949 made the East-West division in Europe all the more apparent and likewise made the need for the countries in the Soviet sphere to close ranks and defend their gains against any Western ideological and military threat all the more urgent.

"Closing ranks" at Auschwitz required not only transformation of the commemorative vocabulary at the site, but also comprehensive control over its activities and personnel. This reflected the steady advancement of Stalinism in 1949, which culminated in November with the purging of "rightist-nationalist deviation" from the party's Central Committee (including the dismissal of Gomułka from that body) and the forced appointment of the Soviet Marshal Konstanty Rokossovsky as minister of national defense and commander-in-chief of the Polish Army. Increasing party control over the museum should have come as no surprise, for ideological homogenization of the Auschwitz site required a corresponding administrative and ideological consolidation. Correspondence and documents from that year reveal that the Ministry of Culture and Art no longer served as the museum's final authority. Instead, exhibition blueprints were sent to the PZPR Central Committee and even to Prime Minister Cyrankiewicz for approval.[39] Moreover, by late in the year there was serious concern in party circles about the museum staff and the direction of its work. A lengthy report submitted to the Central Committee's Propaganda Department recommended that the PZPR assume a still-more-active role in the activities of the museum. This would include the Central Committee's scrutiny of proposals for exhibits and ratification of each name commemorated at the site, whether a hero of the resistance or a victim of the Nazi terror. Finally, the museum was enjoined to "avoid accents evoking nationalist inferences ('eternal German aggression'), inferences that only Jews were subjected to mass extermination, and macabre inferences."[40]

The concern that the museum placed inappropriate emphasis on Jewish victimization at the site hardly seems justified, given the marginal attention to the Shoah in the museum's early years. The perceived danger was this: to uphold the extermination of the Jews as a central element of the Auschwitz story could detract from the combative themes of international antifascism that the party was intent on cultivating at the site. There were, of course, Jews involved in resistance efforts at Auschwitz, most notably in the Sonderkommando revolt of October 1944, but the process of industrialized mass murder that doomed the vast majority of Jewish deportees did not easily lend itself to the image of conspiratorial, cohesive, and, above all, politically progressive opposition to the fascists. At the same time, Stalin was undertaking what Jakub Berman, one of the pillars of Poland's communist regime at the time, referred to as a "programmatic struggle with cosmopolitanism"[41] that continued until Stalin's death in 1953. Under this guise, official anti-Semitism, although not as obvious and publicized in Poland as in neighboring countries, resulted in the purging of high-level government officials and, beginning in 1949, became evident in the PZPR's propaganda.[42] In the context of this anti-Semitic campaign, the Jewish deportee had as little place in Stalinism's image of the Auschwitz past as in the Polish-national memorial paradigm fostered only a few years earlier.

The regime further enhanced its control over the Auschwitz Museum through its deployment of the Union of Fighters for Freedom and Democracy (Związek Bojowników o Wolność i Demokrację, or ZBoWiD), founded in September 1949 on the tenth anniversary of the German invasion of Poland. The union was successor to eleven different organizations for veterans, prisoners of the Nazi regime, and resistance fighters and, like its most important predecessor, the PZbWP, was close to centers of power in the capital. Part of a general streamlining of social institutions in this period, ZBoWiD helped to ensure party control over the activities of veterans and former prisoners and to curb nationalist and potentially oppositional tendencies among them. It also exerted a powerful influence on the character of the museum and coordinated hundreds of demonstrations and events at Auschwitz and other memorial sites.[43] Such demonstrations and commemorative events provide a tableau of commemorative ritual at Auschwitz throughout the decades and, in these years of party control over the site, reveal Warsaw's effective use of ZBoWiD's ranks as the ideological "shock troops" of Poland's Stalinist commemorative culture.

One such demonstration took place in April 1950 as part of the ZBoWiD-sponsored "Week of International Solidarity of Fighters for Freedom, Peace, and Democracy." The week of demonstrations was part of the government's "peace campaign" in the wake of the Stockholm Appeal calling for the abolition of nuclear weapons. At the Auschwitz site, the ceremonies drew more than thirty thousand participants, including resistance fighters, former prisoners, participants in the 1944 Warsaw uprising, and representatives from France and Spain. Gathered on the fields of Birkenau, the crowd sang the Polish national anthem and heard speeches by foreign guests, ZBoWiD functionaries, and government representatives, including an address from the Vice-Premier Antoni Korzycki. "On the grounds of Auschwitz," he stated,

> it was not only the wild beast representing capitalist imperialism in all its hideousness that revealed itself. In the face of horror and common danger there arose here as well the friendship among nations—and that is why it is no accident that on this day, the fifth anniversary of the liberation of anti-fascist fighters around the world we hold here, on the fields of Birkenau, a commemorative ceremony. On this day we demonstrate . . . against the criminal preparations of the imperialist powers for a new world war, for new crimes, and for new factories of death.[44]

Korzycki supplemented his condemnation of the West with a homage "to the nations of the Soviet Union that under the genius leadership of Generalissimo Joseph Stalin liberated our country, as they did other occupied countries, from the inevitable extermination for which the fascist criminals were preparing us."[45] Led by the USSR, the "camp of peace," Korzycki claimed, had enjoyed successes in the victorious struggles of the People's Republic of China and German Democratic Republic.

Echoing the themes of the vice-premier's speech, participants in the rally also put forth a resolution calling for solidarity with all those dedicated to world peace and for continuing the fight against imperialist industrialists. Finally, the resolution called upon ZBoWiD to approach the Fédération Internationale des Anciens Prisonniers Politiques with the demand that the organization uncover among its ranks any supporters of Titoist Yugoslavia.[46] The blunt rhetoric of this event speaks for itself, for amid the hyperbolic vocabulary is a rhetoric of political sanitation that bore little relationship to the reality of the Auschwitz camp and experience of its prisoners.

Two months later ZBoWiD deployed its forces at Auschwitz in a very different manner. Attempting to undermine the authority of Roman Catholicism in Polish culture, the regime had undertaken various efforts toward the formation of a fifth column in the Church. One effort was the establishment of a regime-friendly opposition within the Church, the "Patriot Priests." Never particularly popular among the rank-and-file clergy and never seriously weakening the Church's authority, the "Patriot Priests" nonetheless had a visible presence in the early 1950s.[47] In September 1949 ZBoWiD formed a partner organization to the "Patriot Priests" known as the "Priests' Commission," open to Roman Catholic clergy who were former prisoners or war veterans. The Priests' Commission was intended to infiltrate the clergy through the use of agents, to serve as a forum for clerical activism in the service of Church-state cooperation, and to rally Roman Catholic support for Poland's foreign policy.[48] In addition, the Priests' Commission was to "protect and cultivate memories of the struggle for liberation of the nation and society."[49] This final aim is perhaps most significant, for it was precisely the goal of exploiting the memory of the occupation that brought the Priests' Commission to Auschwitz in June of 1950.

A pilgrimage of sorts, the visit of the Priests' Commission to Auschwitz was organized, as one news account stated, "to pay homage to the murdered priests and the millions of victims of the war."[50] "The ceremonies," the report continued, "were transformed into a spontaneous, passionate demonstration of 470 priests . . . for peace, for close cooperation of the Catholic clergy with the government of People's Poland and the entire Polish population in the effort to maintain and bolster peace."[51] The priests celebrated mass in one of the prisoners' blocks of Auschwitz I, read a congratulatory letter from Premier Józef Cyrankiewicz, and recited prayers for the Polish president Bolesław Bierut. After mass, the ceremony moved outdoors, where the participants laid wreaths bearing inscriptions such as "Our patriotism empowers us in work for People's Poland" in the execution courtyard of Block 11.[52] The event concluded with the singing of the national anthem. Inspired by the day's events, a former Auschwitz prisoner offered a passionate interpretation of the larger significance of the ceremonies:

> [E]very word, every declaration, and every signature given in this place of torment is sanctified by the martyr's blood of millions of innocent people—these must resound deeper [here] than just anywhere. And every voice of protest and judgment sent from here to the addresses of the enemies of peace, the powers resurrecting new crimes of mass destruction—in this case atomic genocide—every voice must, with the echo of thousands, break

forth from the barracks of Auschwitz and resound throughout the country and throughout the entire world.[53]

The presence of priests was nothing new to the Auschwitz site. Catholic masses were common on various commemorative occasions throughout the year, and Polish clergy and their parishioners frequented the site to pay homage and to pray for the souls of the camp's victims. What is striking about these June 1950 ceremonies is that an institution of the Communist state—a traditional adversary of Polish Catholicism—was responsible for the event and succeeded in bringing so many priests to Oświęcim in the name of patriotism, cooperation with the regime, and protest against the threat posed by the capitalist West. Although it may not have succeeded in garnering public support for the government or effectively infiltrating the ranks of the clergy, ZBoWiD had upstaged traditional, nationally bound Catholic commemorative ritual. The Priests' Commission never received the sanction of the Polish Episcopate; nor can it be considered a particularly popular and influential organization.[54] Nonetheless, ZBoWiD was effective in creating a unique and unprecedented public display of official commemorative rhetoric and clerical solidarity with the fledgling communist regime.

ZBoWiD's efforts to shape the politics and culture of memory at Auschwitz were not limited, however, to the staging of public events. As an arm of the state, the union also succeeded in enforcing ideological control over the site and its staff. In June 1950 a four-member commission undertook an inspection of the Auschwitz grounds. The ZBoWiD representative, Henryk Matysiak, then submitted to the PZPR's Central Committee a highly critical report recommending several strategies for bringing the museum into line with the party's current domestic and foreign policy goals. References to the recent visit of a Soviet delegation to Auschwitz suggest that the delegation's response may have been the impetus for the ZBoWiD inspection in the first place. The report referred to a succession of "un-Marxist" errors in the museum's plans, claiming, for example, that "nationalism shows through in nearly all artifacts, inscriptions, and exhibition panels. The German nation [is] represented as the eternal enemy of the Slavs and the Hitlerite administrative apparatus (SS, Gestapo, NSDAP, etc.) as the elite and executive agents of that annexationist, cannibalistic nation."[55]

Such criticisms reveal a continuing concern over the representation of history in national terms and, more specifically, a concern that Nazi expansion-ism and war crimes were represented as specifically German phenomena and not simply as manifestations of fascism and imperialism. Complaints about such "nationalist inferences" at the museum were, by then, nothing new, but apparently the Polish-national and anti-German tone of some of the exhibits had still not been sufficiently muted. By 1950 any presentation of inherently "German" crimes or an unchanging "German" character would have been the source of political embarrassment. Nine months after the establishment of a Soviet-sponsored German "people's democracy" on Poland's western frontier—a German state that, not insignificantly, recognized Poland's post-war borders—Warsaw could hardly wish for the Auschwitz visitor to leave the site with the impression that the German people and nation were neces-sarily anti-Polish. The enemy of the Polish state and Polish people was not an inveterately aggressive and anti-Slav German nation, but the "fascist" and "imperialist" camp led by the United States, Britain, and the Federal Repub-lic of Germany.

Reacting to these and other "errors," the commission recommended that a large portion of the exhibition be removed and that renovations to the mu-seum follow an ideological line emphasizing the "unmasking of Hitlerite fas-cism as one form of international fascism inspired and financed by Anglo-Saxon imperialists." In addition, the commission stipulated that the site's ex-hibitions should highlight the collaboration of the international bourgeoisie with fascism, as well as the solidarity and resistance of the international working classes in the camps and among partisan groups. The recommenda-tions also included the demand that the museum emphasize presentist for-eign policy concerns by noting "attempts by Anglo-Saxon imperialists to revive fascism" and "the role of the USSR in the worldwide front for the de-fense of peace." Finally, the commission issued a call for the replacement of the "reactionary" and "clerical" museum director, Tadeusz Wąsowicz, with a politically reliable successor capable of supervising the necessary changes at the site.[56]

The commission's recommendations characterized the radical change in pedagogical priorities at the Auschwitz site. Outdated emphases on Polish national martyrdom or Polish struggle and heroism were abandoned, and if closure of the site constituted a political risk, it was still possible, in this era of intensified class struggle, to exploit Auschwitz as an ideological battlefield and tool of the party. Simply masking problematic elements of the Auschwitz Museum would not suffice. Rather, "un-Marxist" errors of interpretation, to use Matysiak's language, had to be "liquidated."

The PZPR Central Committee therefore called for a new "verification commission"[57] for the museum. It ordered a rapid and thorough revamping of the site's exhibitions, and the result was the most ideologically laden and exploitative interpretation of the camp's history and meaning to date. According to the minutes from the commission's first meeting, "The purpose of the museum in Oświęcim is the unmasking of the essence of international imperialism, the most glaring form of which was Hitlerite fascism and its continuation, the Anglo-American imperialism of today."[58] To this end, the commission gave special attention to Block 4 ("Extermination of Millions"), Block 15 ("The Sources of Genocide"—now the third theme for the block), and Block 21 ("Struggle and Victory"). In addition, Blocks 5–11, 1, 17, and 19–21 were slated for renovation. The PZPR also issued an order that all work at the site be completed by 6 November (the eve of the anniversary of the Bolshevik Revolution), necessitating the closure of the museum for three weeks.[59]

As a result of these demands, the renovations were undertaken in a hasty manner. Protocols of meetings at the site register complaints that the museum did not have the necessary materials or manpower available to carry out the recommended changes and that work was complicated and delayed by a requirement that changes be verified by the PZPR Regional Committee in Kraków.[60] Undertaken at a Stakhanovite pace, the renovations in October and November 1950 required the full participation of the entire museum staff, including even the security guards. Remarkably, the party orders were, for the most part, fulfilled.

In Block 4, devoted to the extermination process at Auschwitz, ideological imperatives overshadowed historical documentation. Photographs of freed "criminals from IG Farben" with the text "American imperialists release the manufacturers of Zyklon" replaced diagrams depicting the toxic effects of the poisonous gas.[61] In the museum's account of the Sonderkommando revolt of October 1944, the explanatory text indicating the nationalities of some of the insurgents ("seven Jews and two Poles") was removed. Moreover, revisions to the block emphasized the struggle of German communists and antifascists from around Europe, and red flags on a map indicated the sites of revolts in concentration camps throughout German-occupied Europe.[62] The exhibit undoubtedly left a misleading impression: American "imperialists" were the successors and postwar patrons of German criminals, and concentration camps were not simply sites of senseless suffering and death, but arenas of antifascist struggle and victory for the progressive and internationalist resistance forces. The perceived contemporary relevance of genocide at Auschwitz had replaced historical documentation; but lacking in political relevance was the issue of Jewish genocide at Auschwitz. Already in the summer of 1950 the so-called "Jewish Hall" in Block 4 was likewise dismantled through an agreement with the communist-dominated and subservient Central Committee of Jews in Poland.[63] Moreover, the verification commission demanded that the "Jewish issue" not be "isolated," lest the visitor get the impression "that Auschwitz was a site of almost exclusively Jewish execution." On the contrary, the exhibit was to "reveal that the enemy of Jews was, at the same time, the enemy of Poles and others."[64]

Block 15, the first to be viewed on the visitors' route, now housed a new exhibit on "The Sources of Genocide," for according to prevailing ideology, the origins of genocide were in international imperialism, currently under the leadership of American and British capitalists.[65] Hence, the exhibition showed the atrocities of British and American imperialism, such as the establishment of concentration camps during the Boer War. The exhibit was intended to treat the issue of racial persecution and genocide in such a manner as to suggest that the Nazis had simply perfected the methods of their Anglo-American predecessors. In addition, quotations from Stalin as well as texts illustrating "Anglo-Saxon monopolies cooperating in the Hitlerite crimes" and the "collusion of IG Farben and Standard Oil" helped set the tone of the exhibit. The purpose of Nazi anti-Semitism, according to the new exhibition, was to distract the masses from the machinations of their true class enemies. And finally, striking an empowering chord, a flame replaced the gallows as a symbol of the underground resistance.[66] The exhibition was insidious on a number of levels. Not only did it relativize Nazi crimes in general and the Shoah in particular, but it held the British and Americans partially responsible for the crime of genocide during World War II.

Changes to Block 21, "The Struggle for Peace," were also stridently ideological and presentist in their political message.[67] Billed by the minister of culture and art as "the logical accent in the representation of the facts of Hitlerite barbarism,"[68] Block 21 included, for example, analyses of the destruction and terror of imperialists, with the destruction of Hiroshima upheld as the salient example. In addition, the exhibition alerted the visitor to the existence of concentration camps in Greece, Spain, and Titoist Yugoslavia; it lauded the successes of the Six-Year Plan in Poland and the Third Five-Year Plan in the USSR; and it highlighted the anticolonial struggles in Asia. It also aimed a salvo of condemnation against current imperialist injustices, most prominently the war in Korea. This was perhaps most vividly depicted by the image of an American soldier in Korea, wading through a sea of blood while carrying a flag bearing the dollar sign.[69]

Not surprisingly, Block 21 presented problems for the museum staff. Not only could it be a cause for embarrassment should visitors from the West see it, but the museum was unable to keep the block's exhibitions current with international developments and shifts in cold war politics and therefore closed it in 1951. The irony is striking to the present-day observer: Auschwitz should have both an eternal significance and contemporary relevance, but bound as the site was to the political needs and ideological imperatives of Stalinist Poland, its exhibitions could not possibly remain germane to current events around the world. The PZPR and ZBoWiD had, in effect, domesticated Auschwitz and tamed its horror, as both the documentation of the camp's history and the commemorative culture of the early postwar years were subdued by the crass ideological indoctrination of the cold war.

The public uses of Auschwitz in these years effectively illustrate the tractability of memory at the memorial site. It was as if the authors of these official memorial agendas could, with apparent ease, shape the site's landscape, memorial inscriptions, and commemorative vocabulary in accordance with the regime's needs. What they failed to recognize was that the manipulation of history for the purpose of ideological conformity could only cheapen and delimit the site's rhetoric and iconography. This would become clearer in the years ahead, for political and ideological imperatives are subject to change: peace returned to the Korean peninsula, cold-war tensions subsided, Stalin died, and, as a result, many of the contrived memorial images at the site quickly lost their relevance. It is not surprising, then, that one contemporary observer referred to the Stalinist years as a period when the State Museum at Auschwitz appeared to be "dying a slow death."[70]

Such was the pull of Stalinist cultural policy in the early 1950s. The ideological imperatives and pedagogical priorities set by the PZPR continued to define the site, and although the staff continued to make minor changes, museum protocols suggest that it undertook no significant renovation of the blocks until 1955.[71] Against this backdrop of uncertainty, the State Museum at Auschwitz struggled through the chaotic period before the its revitalization in the mid-1950s. Financial difficulties, dismissal and resignation of employees,[72] and the museum staff's apparent impotence vis-à-vis party authority were evidence of the disastrous state of affairs at the site during these years. So chaotic were conditions at the grounds that by the end of 1953 Paweł Hoffman, director of the PZPR Central Committee's Department of Culture, lamented in a letter to Prime Minister Cyrankiewicz that "Auschwitz has slipped out of our hands."[73] What Hoffman failed to realize, however, was that the firm, yet exploitative hand of party control had led to the disastrous state of affairs that he hoped to remedy.

The Auschwitz Museum was a high priority for Hoffman and Cyrankiewicz, but in 1953 and 1954 there were renewed calls for closing the site and putting it to more productive use. These included, for example, proposals to maintain at the memorial site only a single row of prisoners' blocks in the base camp and to use the remainder as housing for the local Oświęcim population, to locate a circus company on the grounds, and even to use the camp's kitchen as a hog barn. "It is just fortunate," recalled Wincenty Hein some years later, "that someone in the ministry . . . expressed the absurdity of that idea to the minister, using as an argument the question of whether it would be possible to lead a foreign delegation through a herd of swine." "It is my sense," Hein concluded, "that at the time certain governmental circles openly intended to liquidate the museum [while] the role of Wiernik[74] as director was one of preparation for a liquidation in a painless manner."[75] Plans for this "assisted suicide" of the site were a clear indicator that it no longer had the commemorative or didactic importance it had enjoyed in 1947, or even in 1951. Distorted in the early years of the decade by Stalinist rhetoric and then subjected once again to the threat of liquidation, the memorial site appeared an irrelevant victim of political exploitation. It was as if the site had no voice of its own, and no longer mattered.

Fortunately, the fate of the memorial site was not entirely in the hands of Warsaw's ministerial bureaucrats and political ideologues. Despite contrivances of the party and ZBoWiD, overly didactic exhibits, and threats to the museum's very existence, the Polish public continued to frequent the site, thereby sustaining its role as a locus of individual homage, prayer, and commemoration. This represented the reassertion of a Polish commemorative vernacular over the jargon of Stalinism—a vernacular expressed in the gestures of everyday visitors to the site, and also in a peculiar incident at Auschwitz in the fall of 1953.

In October of that year a group of several dozen former Auschwitz prisoners, including Tadeusz Hołuj, Kazimierz Smoleń, and Franciszek Targosz (curator at the museum and organizer of the event)[76] gathered for an unofficial and what state authorities would later designate "illegal"[77] conference held at the site, ostensibly for the purpose of collecting information and materials concerning life in the camp. The meeting resulted in an explosive situation, with repercussions at the highest levels of government. As a PZPR Central Committee report on the gathering related,

> The participants in the meeting . . . among them members of the Party, had breakfast with imported vodka and, in a semi-intoxicated state, wandered around the blocks. In one of the blocks a small group from the meeting accosted a Soviet guest by attempting to remove his cap in order "to force them [the Soviets] to express honor for the place in which they found themselves." Unnamed participants in the meeting likewise accosted a group from the GDR, screaming that they could not bear to hear the German language spoken. The case is being attended to by the Voivodship Party Security Service in Kraków.[78]

Other descriptions of the event are less dramatic, but still testify to the political significance of what occurred that day at Auschwitz. According to Wincenty Hein's more sympathetic and balanced account,

> [T]here was a Soviet delegation there whose members were not behaving in a fitting manner (they left their hats on and were smoking cigarettes). I do not recall the exact course of the incident; I know only that someone from the delegation had his hat ripped off. The fracas developed into a political matter. It was necessary to offer some kind of satisfaction, hence, Targosz had to leave. I do not know if Targosz was the one to remove the hat (I am inclined to think he could do it) or someone else, for instance, the guide."[79]

Similarly, a museum guide's deposition describes the anti-German outbursts of one of the participants. "When I returned from Birkenau," he wrote, with a foreign delegation from the GDR . . . an individual unknown to me approached us, stating that he was not hearing the Polish language, but only German, here at the site where he sat imprisoned for four years. When he hears the German language he has the impression that he is in the camp for the second time, that the political situation had not changed. It is necessary, however, to change it, so that the German language is not heard in this place.[80]

Although it is not clear which of these reports best describes its character, the incident had tremendous consequences for the museum. Perceived as a further illustration of the loss of control over activities at the site, it caused an uproar in the Ministry of Culture and Art and among the party leadership. As a result, the ministry and the Security Service undertook an investigation that required written depositions from members of the museum staff and eventually led to the dismissal of Francziszek Targosz—allegedly the organizer of the meeting—who was sacrificed to satisfy the Soviets.

What is most striking about the event, however, is that it occurred at all. Party documents do not point to its purpose, and participation in an unauthorized, "underground," and potentially subversive gathering such as this was certainly dangerous for all concerned. Yet one can understand the appeal of a meeting, conference, or even social gathering of onetime comrades from the camp. The Auschwitz they commemorated was not an aestheticized stage of socialist internationalism and solidarity with the Soviet Union, but a site of horror, suffering, and German crimes—a site that demanded reverence. Perhaps these men were, in a way, staging their own "unofficial" commemorative event, free from the PZPR's ideological cant and ZBoWiD choreography. In effect, this October affair foreshadowed, in an admittedly indecorous and ultimately dangerous manner, the "reclaiming" of Auschwitz from the ideological strictures of the previous years. It may not have been possible to change, as the rebellious former prisoner demanded, the "political situation" in Poland, but the incident certainly sent, as a Central Committee memorandum stated, an "alarm signal"[81] to the party regarding the situation in Oświęcim.

It would take more than a year, however, for an official "reclamation" of the site to begin. Anticipating the "thaw" associated with process of destalinization in Poland, the PZPR and Ministry of Culture once again attempted to set a new agenda for the State Museum at Auschwitz and in 1954 initiated a thorough renovation of the site, providing it with a new director, a radically increased budget, an improved comprehensive exhibition, and, most importantly, an unprecedented degree of stability. According to Kazimierz Smoleń, who was appointed director of the museum in 1955, the new structure and exhibitions of the memorial site were, in fact, a realization of the plans for the museum developed by former prisoners in 1947.[82] Poland had begun to turn from the Stalinist rhetoric of the past, to restore a national idiom to the site, and to reclaim Auschwitz for itself.

4 ⫶ The Restoration of a Commemorative Idiom, 1954 and Beyond

> It was, finally, understood that Auschwitz does not require any "framing."
>
> Tadeusz Hołuj, "Sprawa wiecznej pamięci,"
> Życie Literackie, 30 October 1955

IN THE FIRST HALF of the 1950s the future of the State Museum at Auschwitz was uncertain at best. The demands of Stalinism against the backdrop of cold-war entrenchment had resulted in the crude instrumentalization of Auschwitz and its memory, had undermined the historical accuracy and social relevance of its ideologically laden exhibitions, and had even called into question the need for any memorial site at all. Auschwitz and its museum may have been "dying a slow death," but beginning in the winter of 1954–55 changes implemented at the site—reflecting the advent of destalinization in Poland—breathed new life into the institution. Cold-war tensions had subsided somewhat, Poland and the two German states had settled in their respective blocs, and Auschwitz had ceased to be a propagandistic instigator.

In late 1954 the Ministry of Culture and Art placed the Auschwitz Museum once again in the hands of an experienced cadre of Polish political prisoners who were then responsible for developing a new "permanent" exhibition. Although this exhibition reflected, on the one hand, the PZPR's continuing influence and even control over the culture and politics of memory at Auschwitz, it was also the product of a renewed effort to emphasize objectivity and documentation in the presentation of Auschwitz history. To be sure, the pull of political expediency was still evident at the site, for the new exhibition, despite the sentiment expressed in the epigraph above, did fit within an ideologically based framework of memory. Yet the new exhibits and commemorative tone at Auschwitz eschewed the glaring politicization of recent years and recognized the authorial voice of the site's history and landscape. In many respects, the changes implemented at Auschwitz in 1955 represented a return to the commemorative agenda of 1947 and gave renewed emphasis to the themes of Polish national martyrdom and heroism.

There are three main reasons for the major changes undertaken at the Auschwitz site beginning in 1954. Observance of the tenth anniversary of the liberation, to be held in April 1955, provided the immediate impetus. As organizations of former prisoners abroad initiated plans for the anniversary, it became clear to Polish authorities that this would be an international event drawing participants from across the continent. Faced with the potential embarrassment of appearing in the eyes of an international public as an incompetent steward of the site, the Polish state initiated a thorough renovation of the Auschwitz grounds and exhibitions. Only a few years before, the site had been politically exploited to such a degree that in the opinion of some, it was no longer needed. Yet international initiatives to hold a mass commemorative event there in 1955 emphasized that even if the Polish state could do without Auschwitz, the international community could not. The second and proximate cause for the changes at the Auschwitz site was related to the first. After years of insufficient funding, intentional neglect, administrative chaos, and political exploitation at the site, it became clear to the Ministry of Culture and Art and ZBoWiD that the museum and grounds were desperately in need of renovation and improvement. The Polish state had finally become aware of the limits to the site's instrumentalization and had recognized that Auschwitz could and must exist independently of its current ideological serviceability. Third, the changes at Auschwitz occurred within the context of a general relaxation of cultural politics in early post-Stalinist Poland. It is significant, however, that the restructuring of the site began in 1954. Changes at Auschwitz were therefore not simply a response to the "thaw"; they occurred in the initial stages of destalinization and foreshadowed greater and broader changes in Polish cultural policy in 1955 and 1956. Auschwitz had retreated from the front lines of the cold war, and although it had functioned for some years as a site for the revision of collective memory and historical interpretation, it was now at the forefront of the post-Stalinist transition in Polish cultural politics. A Polish-national commemorative idiom was prefigured in the original plans for the museum, maintained in the Polish public's continuing pilgrimages to the site, and voiced again in the outbursts of former prisoners in 1953; beginning in 1954, the relaxation of state control over Poland's cultural institutions and the advent of Gomułka's "national communism" in 1956 helped to restore this idiom, but in modified form.

This chapter accounts for that restoration. I begin by contextualizing the changes in memory politics at Auschwitz and then move to an analysis of the government initiatives for renovating and resuscitating the State Museum at Auschwitz. I then turn to a closer examination of the site in the year 1955, describing how it was used in the April 1955 anniversary ceremonies and, more importantly, how it appeared to the visitor in that year. This "walk" through the memorial grounds offers a rather detailed description of the most accessible and important carrier of memory at the memorial site: the extensive new exhibition, the majority of which is still in use today. Moreover, this survey of the grounds, structures, exhibits, and empty spaces at Auschwitz should give the reader a sense of the broader political and cultural framework of memory at the site. Even if the stewards of memory at Auschwitz in the 1950s believed that the site required no "framing," the representation of history there remained subject to the influence, and nuance, of political authority.

The "Thaw" at Auschwitz

Observers have generally identified the "thaw" in Polish politics and culture with the "Polish October" of 1956 and Władysław Gomułka's return to leadership of the Polish United Workers' Party. The relaxation of the Stalinist grip in Poland began, however, somewhat earlier. Stalin's death in March 1953 seemed to have no immediate and visible effects on the state's control over public life; on the contrary, repression of the Roman Catholic Church increased, and there was no obvious curbing of police terror or the extensive powers of the Security Service (Urząd Bezpieczeństwa, or UB).[1] In January 1955, however, at the Third Plenary Meeting of the PZPR Central Committee, President Bolesław Bierut offered an explicit criticism of the UB, noting numerous "mistakes" resulting from "the tendency to widen the field of activity of the security forces, from attempts to extend their function, or from their interference in various aspects of state and social activity under conditions which did not justify such interference."[2] An unprecedented self-indictment such as this meant, in the words of one analyst, that "'official circles' began to admit tacitly what the rest of the country already knew: that the security service had for years been abusing its authority, employing illegal and sadistic methods of interrogation, creating for itself a privileged position, a state within a state."[3] The public revelations of Colonel Józef Światło, vice-director of the notorious Tenth Department of the Ministry of Public Security,[4] in conjunction with other actions curbing the power of the UB, spurred a popular movement in Polish society for greater democracy and openness in government and cultural policy. Although only one aspect of the general loosening of state control, the shake-up in the security apparatus had monumental effects across Polish society. As Jan B. De Weydenthal has observed:

> To the degree that this development signaled a general weakening of the coercive pattern of rule, it prompted a revival of public interest and more active involvement in politics. The process, marked by an almost incessant chain of literary and press discussions and re examinations, created an ideological background for the rapidly expanding political ferment. It led to a proliferation of ideas on ways to promote social and economic change, to increase popular participation in public affairs and, finally, to enlarge personal and cultural freedom of expression.[5]

As journalists, academics, and students became increasingly outspoken in their calls for reform, censorship was relaxed, and a burgeoning cultural boldness began to penetrate a host of institutions under the supervision of the Ministry of Culture and Art, among them the State Museum at Auschwitz.

A causal nexus between the shift in cultural politics and the changes implemented at Auschwitz is perhaps not obvious, but events unfolding during the early "thaw" do provide a context for understanding the transformations initiated at the site in 1954 and 1955. The State Museum, like other public institutions in Poland, was subject to the state's pervasive control. The Security Service was certainly no stranger to the Auschwitz site,[6] and the character of the exhibitions there was subject to strict ideological censorship. Commenting on Poland's cultural policy, Stefan Żółkiewski, a member of the PZPR Central Committee, wrote in June 1955 that "[t]he biggest mistake of the Party had been that it had directed the ideological-political development of culture through 'naive' and 'vulgar' commands."[7] Such was the case at Auschwitz in the first half of the 1950s, when the memorial site had become, as Tadeusz Hołuj recalled, "a peddler's booth of cheap anti-imperialist propaganda."[8]

Tendentiousness and hyperbole were not entirely absent from the museum after the "thaw," but political expediency no longer defined its exhibitions or shrouded the presentation of the camp's history. Changes at the site and the renewed priority of Auschwitz in Polish commemorative politics were not only a response to a wave of public activism and boldness in this phase of destalinization, but were also an early marker of both a greater cultural openness and a renegotiation of the terms and stakes of public memory. Specifically, the changes represented a shift from the vulgar politicization of the early 1950s to a renewed reliance on documents and artifacts in commemorating Auschwitz. Moreover, the mid-decade transition also marked a renegotiation of authority to interpret and present that history, as the Ministry of Culture and party granted members of the museum staff a hitherto unknown level of autonomy in the execution of their plans.

The first initiatives to resuscitate the Auschwitz site came in the fall of 1954, when the Ministry of Culture and Art ordered an estimate of probable costs for renovation and reconstruction.[9] A new International Auschwitz Committee[10] of former prisoners had already begun plans for an international event to commemorate the tenth anniversary of the liberation in April 1955,[11] and it was incumbent on the Polish authorities to prepare the site for the occasion. The event promised to be the largest single commemorative rally since the opening of the museum in June 1947. Auschwitz and Poland would draw international attention, and the overtly tendentious elements of the exhibition would undoubtedly prompt criticism from abroad. Thus, renovation and reconstruction of buildings, as well as the development of a new exhibition, were a manifestation of Warsaw's desire to appear as a good steward of the site. In light of the upcoming anniversary, good stewardship meant maintaining or improving the physical integrity of the grounds and eliminating glaringly propagandistic elements of the exhibits. Moreover, to enhance the site's international profile and lend it a more significant official status, the Central Committee of the PZPR ordered that Auschwitz be transformed into Poland's central commemorative museum and research center for issues relating to German camps.[12] Stalin's death may have broken the ideological lock on the site, but the tenth anniversary of the liberation and extensive ceremonies accompanying it forced the site open to an international public.

Concurrent with proposals for the physical restoration of buildings at the site, the PZPR and Ministry of Culture and Art initiated plans for yet another comprehensive exhibition in late 1954.[13] This exhibition would, in fact, live up to its designation as "permanent," for most of it is still in use today. The circumstances surrounding the massive six-thousand-square-foot exhibit are illustrative of the broader shift in cultural politics in these years. Kazimierz Smoleń has recalled the stealth and haste of initial plans for renovation.[14] Employed as a legal advisor to the Economic Planning Commission in Warsaw, he was summoned in late 1954 to appear at the PZPR Central Committee's Department for the History of the Party. Not being a party member, Smoleń was understandably confused by these orders; his confusion only mounted, when, arriving at the Department's offices, he found himself in the company of Tadeusz Hołuj and Stanisław Kłodziński, two associates of the State Museum, as well as Dr. Jan Sehn from the Central Commission for the Investigation of German Crimes in Poland.[15] The composition of this group is significant: Hołuj, Kłodziński, and Smoleń were former prisoners, all had been active as members of the museum's defunct historical commission, and all had long been involved in the affairs of the Auschwitz site. It appeared—and was, in fact, the case—that the ideological grip on the museum was loosening and that its future was being placed the hands of an "old guard" of former prisoners.

Unaware of the task that awaited them, Smoleń and his colleagues were received by the head of the Department for the History of the Party and ordered to undertake the total and immediate reconstruction of the current exhibition. Smoleń has noted that his minor position outside the party apparatus made it difficult for him to understand the real significance of what was happening at Auschwitz and in Poland at large. He has stated, nonetheless, that "in that office one sensed something—a new era. As we say, a spring wind had entered into politics." More specifically, it was becoming obvious in party circles, to use Smoleń's own words, "that you just can't go that far with Auschwitz"[16]—in other words, that the Polish authorities had reached the limits of the site's instrumentalization.

In short, the memorial site was to undergo a sudden and remarkable change both in its appearance and in the official role it was to fulfill. Propagandistic exhibits that really no longer "needed" Auschwitz as their stage were to be replaced by a historical representation "depicted in the simplest, most transparent, and most documented manner";[17] a dying institution was to be transformed into the central site of Polish wartime commemoration; a dilapidated site was allotted several million zlotys for its restoration and re-construction. These measures perhaps appear as nothing more than instru-mentalization in different form, but unlike the site's transformations in years past, the transformation of the mid-1950s occurred under conditions of growing political and cultural openness and would, most importantly, bring the landscape of the site and its exhibits closer to the historical reality of Auschwitz and the experiences of its victims.

By 17 April 1955, the date set for the international commemoration of the tenth anniversary of the liberation, the new Auschwitz exhibition was com-plete.[18] A marker of many of the changes that had characterized the general transformation of Auschwitz in the mid-1950s, the anniversary ceremonies represented the reassertion of a more accessible historical narrative at the site. Moreover, the overwhelming public response to the April ceremonies dem-onstrated that the site, transformed or not, still functioned as a central *locus memoriae* for Poles and for a growing number of visitors from abroad. The newly established International Auschwitz Committee, as well as other na-tional associations of former prisoners, had worked to publicize the anniver-sary ceremonies[19] and, for the purpose of garnering international support, even had proposed a patronage committee made up of notables from various countries to sponsor the event. With the support of well-known politicians, scholars, and authors, the anniversary was to attract international media at-tention and to ensure "that men and women the world over will become con-scious of the extent of the Auschwitz crimes and convince them of the necessity that they never be repeated."[20] The extent to which the patronage committee achieved this lofty goal is not clear, but its presence points to a growing international preoccupation with the Auschwitz site as a physical reminder of the camp experience and as the premier arena for its representa-tion and memorialization.

The scale of the April 17 event was also an indicator of the enduring significance of Auschwitz. Estimates of the number of participants ran as high as one hundred fifty thousand,[21] with hundreds of foreign delegates—former prisoners, resistance fighters, families of the dead—arriving from seventeen European countries.[22] It was, without a doubt, the largest event ever held in Oświęcim, and the site of the former camp could hardly accommodate the swell of participants. Describing the atmosphere of the day's proceedings, a member of a German delegation reported: "The Sunday . . . will remain unforgettable for me. Already at day's dawn thousands upon thousands, ranks upon ranks of the Polish people made their way to Auschwitz. An endless army of national pilgrims. Chartered trains, buses, and trucks brought a hundred thousand people to the consecration of the memorial at this site of bestiality and horror."[23] And in the words of another participant, "Here unfolded on 17 April a powerful demonstration of representatives of seventeen European countries—former Auschwitz prisoners, the loved ones of the victims of Hitlerite terror, together with more than 100,000 citizens of Poland."[24] Public commemorations and rallies were nothing new to the Auschwitz site, even during the difficult years of the early 1950s, but never before had so many from Poland and abroad made the journey there.

Just as the number of participants testified to the enduring importance of Auschwitz as a site of memory and mourning, the content of the anniversary ceremonies reflected both a relaxation of ideological control over the Auschwitz site and an important turn in its commemorative vocabulary. As in the past, the day's activities had been organized well in advance and were subject to PZPR approval.[25] They were not, in the strict sense of the word, spontaneous, but the scope of the event and international participation in its planning made any rigid choreography or strident political exploitation impossible. The program for the day included the traditional laying of wreaths at the Wall of Death adjacent to Block 11, opportunity for visitors to view the new exhibition, and a march in Birkenau to the ruins of the crematoria where the mass rally was to take place.[26] Birkenau was undoubtedly the only open space on the memorial grounds that could accommodate such a crowd, but it remains nonetheless significant that, unlike most commemorative occasions in the past, the grounds of the extermination center, and not those of Auschwitz I, were the stage for the main event.

The speeches of the day marked a retreat from the commemorative agenda and vocabulary of recent years. The keynote speaker was not a Polish government official, but Marie Normand, head of the French Auschwitz Committee. Speaking on behalf of all the foreign delegations, her words recalled the valor, internationalism, and spiritual leadership of the resistance movement in the camp. Organized resistance at Auschwitz had been a common rhetorical theme on such occasions, and Normand's adulatory description of the resistance movement's role at the camp (for example, "Thanks to the activity of the resistance movement, the certainty of the victory of the people over Nazi barbarism remained alive in the hearts of prisoners.")[27] was reminiscent of varnished and hyperbolic narratives of years past. But absent from her address were what by then had become routine references to the Western imperialist threat and the oft-repeated claims that the foreign policy of the United States and its allies was genocidal Nazi expansionism in different garb. Lacking as well was the frequently invoked leadership role of communists and socialists in the resistance movement. Rather, Normand invoked the legacy of the resistance with the injunction that "peace-loving peoples, irrespective of political, social, and religious views" unite against the possibility of such a tragedy repeating itself. Internationalism was the order of the day, but no longer an internationalism limited to those with socialist convictions and willing to subject themselves to Soviet leadership. Finally, Normand concluded with a warning: the threat of a new Auschwitz lay, above all, in permitting the "cadres of former murderers to regroup" and placing weapons in the hands "of those responsible for these crimes."[28] This was an obvious condemnation of the Federal Republic of Germany's rearmament and integration into the NATO alliance, but it is significant that Normand made neither a specific reference to the West Germans nor an overt condemnation of their American sponsors.

Józef Cyrankiewicz, a fixture at such occasions, likewise focused his address on the meaning and legacy of Auschwitz. "Never again Auschwitz!"—the slogan resounding throughout the address—was not only an effective rhetorical device, but also a vehicle for explanation. "Never again Auschwitz!" stated the premier,

> This means . . . never to be defenseless . . . to struggle relentlessly against the militaristic instigators attempting to threaten the nations with the hydrogen bomb despite the obvious fact that they have no monopoly on it . . . to stand together with the entire camp of socialism and peace . . . for the Polish nation and its government to firmly and faithfully lead in the spirit of the Polish *raison d'état*. . . to guard as the apple of one's eye and daily confirm the alliance and friendship with the Soviet Union, with the great Chinese, with all people's democracies . . . to strengthen daily the unshakable unity of the nation under the leadership of the Party of the working class, under the banner of the National Front . . . to build strength and security for the future of our beloved Fatherland.[29]

Cyrankiewicz was, like Normand, evoking the horrors of the past in order to awaken vigilance in the present, for his exhortations were clearly intended to rally support for the Warsaw regime. The themes resounding in the Premier's speech were certainly not new, but like Normand, Cyrankiewicz refrained from explicit condemnations of American foreign policy and avoided the simplistic association of Anglo-American "imperialists" with German fascists. Moreover, Cyrankiewicz's patriotic appeals to the "Polish *raison d'état*" and "beloved Fatherland" marked a reinsertion of dormant Polish-national themes into the official commemorative vocabulary at the memorial site.

Commemoration of Poland's martyrs would not, however, dominate the day's events. Instead, the most solemn and ceremonial moment was a testimony to the multinational composition of the Auschwitz dead. With drumrolls in the background, members of each foreign delegation ascended the site designated for a new monument and deposited ashes they had brought from camps across Europe. The ashes were then entombed in a sarcophagus-shaped vault near the Birkenau crematoria.[30] As one witness recalled,

> Around the Monument of the Fallen in Birkenau, at the site of mass murders of men, women, the aged, children, infants—was a sea of bared heads. To the accompaniment of drums, there flowed into the great urn the ashes of the champions of a conquered, martyred, but fighting Europe: ashes of Soviet partisans and British prisoners of war, of the martyrs of Oradour and Lidice, of Germans who in the time of the greatest outbreak of Hitlerite fascism sacrificed their lives in order to give testimony to the fact that there is another German nation—not only that one of which Hitler spoke.[31]

Through this liturgical act, unity in life and unity in struggle was transcended by unity in death, blurring all distinctions of nationality, creed, or race. The solemnity of the moment also elevated the symbolic importance of the memorial site, for just as prisoners had been brought to Auschwitz from nearly every European country, so too were the ashes from the camps in their homelands brought to the grounds of Europe's largest death factory ten years after its liberation. This commemorative gesture demonstrated, if nothing else, that Auschwitz, despite the propagandistic exploitation and physical neglect of years past, had remained indispensable as a locus of international wartime remembrance.

A Visit to the Memorial Site

What was the Auschwitz of 1955? What images confronted the visitor, and what images were effaced or missing? To what extent was the visitor compelled to rely on documentation, explanatory descriptions, or guides? Commenting on his visit to Auschwitz in 1956, Hermann Pörzgen, an editor for the *Frankfurter allgemeine Zeitung,* noted that "[o]ne does not need a tour, one does not need the Polish inscriptions that provide explanations. The objects here cannot be misunderstood. They are mute witnesses against which there can be no objections."[32] Perhaps explanatory inscriptions, a tour guide, and the like would have been a distraction for Pörzgen. Certainly somewhat familiar with the history of the camp, he was likely making these claims in order to magnify the dramatic effect of his article, but further reflection puts them into question. Some visitors needed tours and some did not. For some, the inscriptions were an aid to understanding; for others, they were perhaps irrelevant or misleading. The point here is that commemorative objects *can* be interpreted in a variety of ways, or even misunderstood. Any walk through the memorial grounds at Auschwitz is colored not only by the appearance of the site, but also by the knowledge, expectations, experiences, or even prejudice that a visitor brings. This premise makes it nearly impossible to analyze in this context the ways in which tourists, pilgrims, and members of official delegations reacted to Auschwitz and the images conveyed there. The following description, however, can acquaint the reader with the salient features of the Auschwitz site, its grounds and structures, its artifacts and ruins, and especially its new exhibition opened in 1955.

Perhaps the characteristic that most distinguishes the State Museum at Auschwitz from other memorial sites is its immense size. As one participant in the April 1955 ceremonies recorded, "I myself was imprisoned in Auschwitz and had many horrible experiences there—but to form an accurate image of the unimaginably massive extent of the horrible crimes of the Hitlerite henchmen—this I could do only ten years later, upon seeing once again kilometer upon kilometer of the grounds of organized mass murder."[33] A 1956 report stated that the total area of the State Museum at Auschwitz, composed of the somewhat abbreviated terrain of Auschwitz I and Birkenau, encompassed more than 450 acres. On the memorial grounds were one hundred (out of four hundred original) buildings and structures, thirty guard towers, and approximately one hundred kilometers of barbed wire.[34] These statistics applied only to the confines of Auschwitz I and Birkenau; Monowitz was not included as part of the memorial site, nor were the grounds of the numerous satellite camps scattered throughout the region.

Birkenau may have been more impressive to the visitor in terms of size, but the physical, pedagogical, and ideological center of the memorial site remained Auschwitz I, and only a minority of enterprising visitors went beyond its borders. Proximity to the center of Oświęcim, availability of exhibition space, and not least its primary function as a concentration camp for Polish political prisoners—these were the main factors that made the Stammlager the most appropriate location for a "museum" in the traditional sense. With the exception of the buildings of the Lagererweiterung, the grounds of Auschwitz I were and remain to this day ordered, well-kept, and more or less as they appeared in 1942,[35] with thirty-one masonry buildings, several wooden structures, a gas chamber and crematorium, the commandant's villa, and the so-called *Aufnahmegebäude,* a large building for the reception of prisoners completed in 1944.[36]

In 1955 the entrance to Auschwitz I was not at the camp's internal gate marked with the famous inscription "Arbeit macht frei." Rather, the museum entrance was at the north end of the camp, near Crematorium I. The visitor was most likely expecting an immediate confrontation with suffering and horror, but instead encountered at the museum entrance a stylized heroic image of the liberation of Auschwitz. Hermann Pörzgen recorded his first impressions this way:

> [I]n the waiting room there is order and cleanliness. A fresco showing the liberation of the site by Russian troops. There stands . . . a broad-shouldered hero and he is joyfully embraced by a haggard prisoner in striped zebra clothing. His comrade lifts, in a brotherly fashion, a little dwarf with dark eyes, shaven head, and clothed as well in a prisoner's uniform. In the background: blue sky, the menacing barbed wire, and liberated prisoners. Polish children are now gathered in front of this picture and hear from their teacher how this relates to Auschwitz.[37]

Leaving the reception hall of the museum, the visitor passed through an entrance traversing two rows of barbed-wire fencing, with guard towers looming to the right and left, and then entered one of the two main "streets" of the camp, flanked on either side by two-story brown masonry buildings. To this day, many visitors to Auschwitz I are impressed (or perhaps even disappointed) by the ordered and peaceful impression the site evokes. The brick prisoners' blocks, clearly demarcated paths, trees and shrubs—all these "artifacts" create an impression of regimen, tranquility, and permanence. During most of its wartime existence, Auschwitz I did appear ordered and groomed. If critics in the late 1940s had decried and even ridiculed the manicured and ordered appearance of Auschwitz I, such criticisms still echo today, when the poplars lining the main *Lagerstraße* have grown to a majestic height and the brick prisoners' blocks are subject to frequent restoration work. Whether one considers the external appearance of the former base camp an appropriate representation or not, the fact remains that it conveys a sense of peaceful order. As a French visitor observed in early 1955, "Although in Birkenau the barracks remind one of miserable stables, we found here [in Auschwitz I] real buildings, two-storyed, made of stone and brick. It reminds one, if one looks away from the surrounding barbed wire, more of a workers' community or hospital than a center for the systematic organization of extermination."[38] The bucolic appearance of postliberation Auschwitz I was and remains a significant feature of the memorial site, and it raises many of the same questions voiced during the 1948 controversy over the site's future: Would the totally uninformed visitor deduce, on the sole basis of the external appearance of Auschwitz I, that it was place of torture, disease, starvation, and murder? If so, what would the visitor learn and with what images in mind would he or she leave the site?

That these questions are posed at all suggests that the memorial site may not, on its own, speak clearly enough, and this ambivalence points to the importance and function of the new 1955 exhibition. Commenting on the new character of the site, one journalist stated: "The reorganization was decided upon the correct basis that the historic preserve in Auschwitz and Birkenau must stand as the most essential, main part of the museum. On the other hand, the museum exhibition should be only an explanation, a concluding statement on that which the historic preserve cannot express—a clear systematized documentation of the crimes committed by Hitlerism."[39] In other words, Auschwitz and its history were to be given the opportunity to speak for themselves, and this was nothing less than a broader conceptualization of the "museum." Rather than relying on contrived and overly interpretive exhibits to relate the history and contemporary meaning of Auschwitz, the new exhibition intended, through ambitious use of documentary sources, to complement visible evidence on the grounds. The operative assumption was that barbed wire and barracks, gallows and execution walls, crematoria and ash pits would more effectively convey the lessons of Auschwitz than the megaphone of Stalinist didacticism. The new exhibition's purpose was to develop and amplify the themes already embedded in the physical reality of Auschwitz; it was to complement, not usurp, the existing character of the memorial site. In the succinct words of Tadeusz Hołuj: "It was, finally, understood that Auschwitz does not require any 'framing.'"[40] In other words, a less interpretive, less ideological Auschwitz could be a more effective pedagogical tool and also create more poignancy for the themes reemerging at the post-1954 site.

Block 15: "Introduction"

In this the new exhibition may have succeeded, but an extensive interpretive framework nevertheless remained. Upon entering Block 15, the first museum halls offered a broad context for the Auschwitz camp in the ideology and goals of the Third Reich. According to its creators, the exhibition's main overarching theme was the danger not of American, but of German imperialism. The exhibition planning documents, or *scenariusz*, stated: "Through the memorialization of the martyrdom of millions and the documentation of the crimes of Hitlerism, the Auschwitz museum shall awaken the sensitivity to and struggle against attempts to revive German militarism and imperialism. This primary purpose of the Auschwitz Museum should likewise be accented strongly in the entire exhibition."[41] The year 1955 was a crucial one in East-West relations: Stalin was dead; a Korean armistice was in place; the Soviet Union concluded with its allies the Warsaw Pact, worked toward a reconciliation with Yugoslavia, proposed normalization of relations with the Federal Republic of Germany, and initiated a foreign policy line later known as "peaceful coexistence" with the United States and its allies. With this relaxation in cold-war tensions, the salvos against American imperialism were, at least at Auschwitz, now directed against the Federal Republic, its rearmament, and its military integration into NATO, which was formalized in May 1955.

The displays in Block 15—the museum's introduction—were thus intended to awaken the visitor to forms of German imperialism across Europe before and during the war. The blocks that followed—4, 5, 6, 7, and 11—depicted in detail how German imperialism was manifested at the Auschwitz camp complex, and the concluding section of the exhibition addressed examples of West German imperialism since 1945. Block 15 would thus serve as the first of two extensively documented, yet clearly interpretive "bookends" for the exhibition as a whole.

"What led to the establishment of the Auschwitz camp?" This was the general question that Block 15 was to answer, and the exhibition's basic response invoked an explanation of the "sources of Hitlerism and German imperialism." Solidly grounded in a Marxist materialist interpretation of the rise of Nazism, the displays and documents outlined the influence of monopoly capitalism, Nazi terror, and militarism in accounting for Hitler's rise to power. They also gave special attention to the forms and effects of "racial persecution—the first step towards genocide," as one of the explanatory inscriptions read. The exhibition's treatment of this theme—by detailing the terms of the Nürnberg Laws and the plunder and violence of the so-called *Kristallnacht* in 1938—made clear that Jews were the primary victims of German racism in the 1930s. The exhibition also emphasized that Nazi racial policy was not limited to anti-Jewish measures, but extended as well to the Slavs, as documented in quotations from Hitler ("[T]he German nation has the right to reign over Europe and transform it into the German Reich of the German nation.") and Himmler ("[W]e must destroy 30 million Slavs in order to rule the East ..."). Hitlerite racism and militarism thus led to a policy of aggression throughout central Europe, and culminated in the 1939 invasion of Poland.

The issue of the Nazi campaign against Poland provides an interesting illustration of the tensions between party censors and the former prisoners at the site. Although the exhibition's planners, in comparison to workers at the site in the early 1950s, were relatively free to set their own agenda, the PZPR and Ministry of Culture had nonetheless installed a special commission to review all changes to the museum.[42] The controversy in this case revolved around the ideologically laden problem of when to date the outbreak of the Second World War. Smoleń and Hołuj had, appropriately, set the beginning of the war at 1 September 1939, but the Warsaw inspectors insisted on designating the German invasion of the Soviet Union in June 1941 as the outbreak of the true "world" war. To do otherwise would indict the USSR as a coaggressor in the 1939 invasion of Poland. After a week's debate, however, members of the review commission finally acquiesced to the original plans. On more than one occasion museum workers were forced to defend the more rigorous documentary orientation of the exhibition against the censorship and even proposed distortions of the party[43]—a reminder that despite a nascent movement for cultural and political openness, the structures and traditions of party control over the site persisted.

With this point clarified, the exhibit then turned to the documentation of Hitlerite crimes in Poland: crimes of the German army against civilians and prisoners of war, forced resettlement, street roundups, destruction of cultural artifacts, and the extermination of Polish Jews. In describing this final element, Block 15 provided new illustrations of the liquidation of the Warsaw Ghetto, destruction of synagogues, and extermination actions in East Galicia —altogether resulting in the deaths of 434,329 Jews. The specific reference to Jewish persecution and death at this point in the exhibition was new, and perhaps suggested to the visitor that the singularities of the treatment of Jews at Auschwitz would be appropriately addressed later. The final display in Block 15 was a large map showing the extensive network of concentration and extermination camps in German-occupied Europe. Auschwitz, the blueprints indicated, "was only the beginning of a massive and planned extermination of European nations." "Of the 10 million imprisoned in concentration camps," the generic final inscription read, "4 million were put to death in Auschwitz."

Block 4: "The Extermination of Millions"

After this introduction to the larger issues of German imperialism and Hitlerite crimes, the visitor to the Auschwitz base camp then proceeded to Block 4, the section of the museum that was, in the words of the exhibition's plans, to tell the story of "[t]hose 4 million nameless and unnumbered victims of Hitlerism," who "came from all over Europe." The annihilation of Jews was the most remarkable and unique element in the history of Auschwitz, yet the appearance of the former base camp gave little indication of the mass extermination for which the complex was so renowned. Entering the memorial grounds, the visitor passed by the small Crematorium I, which could easily be mistaken for a storage magazine (it had indeed served this purpose at one time) or protective bunker. Where were the gas chambers, the ash pits, the infamous selection ramp? These traces of German atrocities were in Birkenau, three kilometers away.

Auschwitz I did not function primarily as an extermination center, and mass extermination on the scale of Birkenau was not part of that site's history.

In the absence of such tangible "evidence" of mass murder, the museum staff attempted, first, to document the extermination process in the context of the exhibition at Auschwitz I and, second, to create a locus memoriae at the base camp, apart from the locus historiae of Birkenau. The museum could claim success in the former endeavor; in the latter, it failed. The base camp never effectively symbolized the extermination facilities of Birkenau, but remained instead the site for commemorating primarily, if not exclusively, the registered prisoner, the Soviet POW, and the resistance fighter.

Documentary portrayal of the extermination process in the base camp's exhibition was yet another point of contention between the museum staff and the Warsaw review commission. The controversy revolved around the extermination of Jews at Auschwitz and the placement of the theme "Extermination of Millions"—regarded as a particularly "Jewish" theme—at the beginning of the visitor's route.[44] According to the review commission, to begin the exhibition with a documentation of the extermination process would place too prominent an emphasis on Jewish genocide at Auschwitz, thereby diminishing the fate of the Polish political prisoner. In the end, former prisoners prevailed in upholding their original plans to stress "genocide" as the salient feature of Auschwitz, albeit in an understated and unspecified manner. Tadeusz Hołuj in particular is to be credited with defending this priority, for his reputation as an author of some renown, his convincing argumentation, and, not least, his party membership allowed him to present a persuasive and convincing case to those members of the commission opposed to the plans.[45]

In spite of this small victory, the portrayal of the Shoah in the exhibition and at the site as a whole remained subject to the enforced understatement that had characterized the Auschwitz site in years past. Annihilation of Jews at Auschwitz certainly received greater attention in the 1955 exhibition, yet the elimination of references to the fate of Jews and the desire to emphasize the history of registered prisoners in the presentation of the camp's history betrayed a continuity with the past. To be sure, the party had permitted a greater degree of independence at the site, and the former prisoners had been successful in debating and defending a number of contentious elements of the exhibition. Early signs of the "thaw" such as these should not be ignored, but there was little doubt that control over the memorial was firmly in the hands of the PZPR. It was simply a question of how much ideological and interpretive freedom the party was willing to grant to the museum staff.

Block 4 undoubtedly presented some of most disturbing images of the entire exhibition. Stark and unadorned, the first exhibition room confronted the visitor with a huge photographic enlargement of heaped corpses and a quotation from the sentences handed down at Nürnberg, accenting the number "4,000,000." The room was otherwise barren, save for a clear glass urn filled with ashes from Birkenau. Through the complementary images of incomprehensible numbers, photographed corpses, and encased ashes, this scene was to evoke reactions of both horror and funereal reverence.

The remainder of the block was devoted to the explanation and documentation of the extermination process at Auschwitz. The epigraph "The Hitlerites murdered more than 3.5 million immediately after arrival in Auschwitz" dominated the second hall, which emphasized the centrality of the Auschwitz complex in Nazi extermination policy. A map of Europe showed arrows from various countries leading to the camp. All roads, as it were, led to Auschwitz, depicted here as the graveyard of Europe, the final destination of nameless victims from across the continent. But who were these victims, and why were they deported to Auschwitz? The answer may not have been immediately clear, for the exhibit's planners emphasized first and foremost the diversity of victims, especially in terms of national origin. "Gathered here for extermination," a memorial inscription in Hall III read, "were infants, children, youths, the aged, women, men, people of various faiths, political orientations, and social origins." On one side of the hall stood flags, arranged alphabetically in Polish (and hence not according to numbers deported or killed) showing the nationalities or citizenships of the victims: Americans, Austrians, Belgians, Bulgarians, Czechoslovakians, Dutch, Egyptians, English, French, Germans, Greeks, Gypsies, Hungarians, Italians, Jews, Norwegians, Poles, Rumanians, Russians, Spaniards, Swiss, Turks, Yugoslavians. On the other side of the room was an assortment of photographs, documents, and inscriptions characterizing both the national and social origins of the victims—this in order to emphasize, as the exhibition plans stated, the "randomness" or "role of chance" *(przypadkowość)* in the selection process. The intent here was to stress that victims of extermination "were murdered not only for concrete activities, but above all simply for their ancestry, their 'race.'"

Emphasis on the diverse origins of deportees was appropriate, for it was suggestive of the variety of prisoner experience in the camp. Moreover, the accent on racial persecution, as opposed to political persecution, indicated a departure from the hitherto prevailing and exaggerated image of the Auschwitz deportee as resistance fighter and political prisoner. It is, however, also worth noting how the exhibit could have been misconstrued. The vast majority of Auschwitz victims were murdered, of course, because of the Nazis' racial-ideological definitions of their ancestry, but the exhibit did not yet give any indication that the ancestry most frequently in question was Jewish and not, for example, Polish or Russian or Czech. Moreover, the deportation of Jews to Auschwitz was hardly a random process, but a latter stage in a broad policy of identification, discrimination, ghettoization, exploitation, and, finally, extermination.

The exhibit appears to have implied that the overwhelming majority of victims at Auschwitz were Jews, for Jews were listed first in the sequence of "categories" of victims in this hall. "Here was realized the program of total extermination of the Jews," read the display, which included documentation in the form of confiscated Jewish liturgical vestments and quotations from Rudolf Höss's testimonies and memoirs. Subsequent epigraphs and documents further emphasized the diversity of victims: "Here took place the mass murder of Soviet prisoners of war"; "Here thousands of Gypsies were murdered"; "Here perished thousands of clergy and people of various faiths"; "Here people of various social classes and professions were murdered"; "Here were murdered the healthy and the infirm, invalids, and those incapable of work"; "Here were murdered infants, babies, and small children." Although certainly effective at impressing upon the visitor the breadth and magnitude of the killing process, the exhibit could also have led to the erroneous conclusion that Jews and Soviet POWs, priests and the disabled, physicians and children were summarily led from the transport wagons to the gas chambers, while failing to emphasize that it was ultimately Jewish ancestry and not profession, age, or ability to work that was most often the criterion for immediate death at Auschwitz. In short, to portray Jewish victims as simply one of many national and social groups "randomly" murdered at the Auschwitz complex failed to underscore the uniqueness of the Jewish experience and Jewish tragedy there.

The remainder of Block 4 was devoted to the process and mechanics of extermination, that is, the steps in the path of destruction from the roundups in ghettos and villages, to the transports to Auschwitz, to arrival and "selection," to the gas chambers and crematoria. Extermination did not end, however, in the crematoria of Birkenau, for the process was continued in the economic exploitation of the victims at Auschwitz. The organized confiscation of victims' property was therefore represented as the final stage of exploitation and destruction, exemplified by the epigraph "People to the gas—spoils to the storehouse." Not only were the victims' clothing, valuables, and personal effects confiscated; economic exploitation took on a yet-more-grisly rigor in the extraction of victims' gold fillings, the use of women's hair (mounds of which were displayed in a large glass-enclosed case) for the production of fabric, and the use of human bones and ashes as fertilizer.

Finally, Block 4 illustrated the actual killing process, depicted in some detail with the help of a large model of a Birkenau crematorium. The actual Crematorium II, in ruins and located three kilometers away, was seldom on the visitor's agenda. For most visitors, then, the detail and plasticity of the model were a substitute for the visit to Birkenau. In effect, the new exhibition transported an important aspect of the "Birkenau experience" to an exhibition hall in Auschwitz I, substituted one memory site for another, and reinforced the prevailing emphasis on the base camp as the primary and most significant site of reverence and recollection at the Auschwitz complex.

Block 5: "Evidence of Mass Extermination"

The reconstruction of Birkenau's main gate, selection ramp, and crematoria —images familiar to many through memoirs, photographs, and film—would have been a practical impossibility at Auschwitz I. Visitors intent on viewing these ruins were forced to trek the three kilometers to the Birkenau site, and only a minority did so. It was, however, possible to transport a small part of "Canada," the massive storehouses of goods plundered from the victims of extermination, to Block 5 of the base camp. These personal effects were on display in the third stage of the exhibition as further "evidence" of mass murder, and complemented the previous block's descriptions of plunder and exploitation. The huge cases of Block 5 contained, as the exhibition's documents stated, "the only physical proof" of mass extermination. The exhibit's planners therefore eschewed written documentation in favor of simple epigraphs, each indicating that on display were objects recovered at the site after the liberation. Suitcases inscribed with the names and dates of birth of their owners, men's, women's, and children's clothing, Jewish liturgical vestments, dishes, spectacles, corsets, cookware, toiletry articles, shoes, prostheses—

hundreds upon hundreds of these items lay in glass cases, some more than fifty feet in length. Personal items such as these, perhaps more than any other element of the exhibition, challenged the anonymity of the "4 million" innocent victims. Each suitcase displayed, with vivid human proximity, the name, date of birth, and address of its owner—all hastily inscribed just prior to deportation. The clothing and shoes, although dusty and worn, were perhaps not all that different from what the visitor in 1955 was wearing. The hundreds of shaving brushes, spectacles, and toothbrushes, although now encased in glass, were not really the stuff of museums, but everyday utilitarian objects known to all visitors.

These items may have succeeded in bringing the visitor "closer" to the experience of the deportee, but was this type of exhibit an effective pedagogical tool or, as one might be tempted to claim, a voyeuristic display of the relics of the dead? Referring to such objects as "evidence" of mass extermination, the creators of the exhibit were undoubtedly attempting to assuage any doubts as to the reality or magnitude of the crimes. Beyond that, however, these displays added a certain reliquary "shock value" to the exhibition by personalizing the otherwise anonymous victim. This was particularly true of the mounds of human hair, first displayed in Block 4 as one aspect of the extermination process and later moved to Block 5 as "proof" of the crime.[46] Whether the block's museological emphasis on "artifactuality" as opposed to "factuality" was appropriate or not, it provided further testimony to the crimes committed at Auschwitz and, significantly, lent the victims of mass extermination a degree of identity and individuality that would otherwise have been lost in the incomprehensibility of statistics and documents.

Blocks 6 and 7: "The Life and Work of the Prisoner" and "Living Conditions"

Having shown the fate of the unregistered deportee, the exhibition then turned, in Blocks 6 and 7, to a depiction of life and death in the camp complex. These blocks were to present the camp as a more traditional work/labor site and to illustrate the experience of the registered prisoner, summarized by the epigraph in the first hall of Block 6: "We were some 400,000 numbered slaves dying of hunger, murderous work, and as the result of torture, terror, and horrible living conditions." Memoirs, letters, and the accounts of family members likely made this portion of the exhibition especially accessible to the Polish visitor, who was already inclined to regard the base camp as the primary site of Polish wartime martyrdom and the last stop for the registered political prisoner.

Planning documents relate the authors' concern over the difficulty of this section. Not only were a wide variety of historical themes—camp organization, the work day, health and hygiene, and so on—evident in this portion of the exhibition, but the museum staff also faced the problem of how to show the plight and personality of the registered prisoner as an individual. They decided to rely heavily on artistic representation in this portion of the exhibition. "This is not an artistic exhibition," the design plan stated, "yet the drawings and sculptures of former prisoners or persons using evidentiary material must be a *document* on a par with the testimonies [of former prisoners]. . . . How to reveal the murderous work, beatings, and hunger, if not through artistic elements?" To rely on artists' renditions of the camp experience was, perhaps, to open the door to criticism of the exhibition's adherence to accuracy, but given the lack of suitable photographs and the limited appeal of written text as evidence, artistic representations were deemed an effective and necessary medium.

The displays in Block 6 were divided into six related topics: arrival, life and work in the camp, hunger, the plight of mothers, and treatment of children. The registered prisoner's experience upon arrival at Auschwitz set him or her apart from the deportee led directly to the gas chambers of Birkenau. Although spared immediate loss of life, the registered prisoner experienced an immediate loss of dignity and identity. "Man becomes a number," read the epigraph of one display explaining the tattooing process. In addition, the exhibit emphasized that registered prisoners—and especially Poles brought to the camp in its early days—were quarantined (described as "the first step to extermination") and frequently subjected to beatings and exhausting physical exercise known as "gymnastics."

The paintings of Władysław Siwek and Jerzy Brandhuber, two former prisoners, illustrated these themes. Siwek's paintings have been praised for their jarring images and photographic realism. His renditions of life in the camp, while not necessarily inaccurate representations of his memories, offered stylized images of the haggard prisoner and ruthless SS guard, frequently represented as a grinning sadist showing no mercy to those under his charge. Without challenging the veracity or effectiveness of his work, it is

worth noting that Siwek's portrayal of German sadism fit the newly resuscitated martyr-and-persecutor schema of Polish commemorative images at the
museum.

Presentation of "A Day in the Life" of an Auschwitz prisoner also made
use of artistic images, supplementing the exhibit with the drawings of the former prisoner Mieczysław Kościelniak. Morning roll call, exhausting work, the
role of common criminals as functionaries and Kapos, isolation from the outside world, torture—all of these aspects of camp life were represented in
Block 6. The exploitation of the prisoners as slave laborers was worthy of an
entire hall of its own. Beginning with "Arbeit macht frei," the cynical epigraph that greeted prisoners at the gate of Auschwitz I, the exhibit introduced forms of prisoner exploitation: digging gravel, mining coal, meat
processing, baking, arms production, agricultural labor, and, not least, the
construction and expansion of all three main Auschwitz camps. Block 6 also
emphasized the huge profits reaped by Germany's large corporations through
the exploitation of Auschwitz labor. Although the politically laden references of years past to German "monopoly capitalists" were absent, the exhibition listed some twenty-five industrial enterprises affiliated with the
Auschwitz camp, including Siemens, the Deutsche Reichsbahn, and, most
notably, the chemical concern IG Farben-Industrie. IG Farben was well
known in this context because one of its subsidiaries, the Deutsche Gesell-
schaft für Schädlingsbekämpfung, was the manufacturer of Zyklon-B. In addition, the concern also built, with cheaply brokered Auschwitz labor, the
huge factory for the production of synthetic fuel and rubber at Monowitz.
The exhibition emphasized the magnitude and human cost of this project: between April 1941 and November 1942, Auschwitz prisoners in the service of
IG Farben had moved 1,434,000 cubic meters of earth, built 75,000 square
meters of road surface, and laid 20,000 meters of railroad tracks.

While Block 6 described forced labor and other murderous cruelties of
camp life, Block 7 replicated the deathly housing conditions at the camp.
The museum staff constructed, in eight different halls, eight life-sized diora-
mas: the room in which members of the first transport in 1940 were housed;
a prisoners' block in 1940, both at night and during the day; a room in
Auschwitz I in 1944; a reconstructed section of a Birkenau barrack. In addition, the second floor of Block 7 housed an extensive exhibit on sanitary
conditions, disease, hospital services, and criminal medical "experiments."

These reconstructions of prisoners' living conditions represented the only attempt at the Auschwitz site to create a "true-to-life" rendering of the camp experience. Obviously, the exhibits required some interpretation and imagination on the part of the visitor, but they were undoubtedly effective in conveying the variety of conditions at Auschwitz. These reconstructions, in combination with displays in Block 6, testified to the important fact that there had been no single "Auschwitz experience." There was, instead, more than one Auschwitz, and more than one way to live, to work, to die, or to survive. Two complementary themes therefore emerged from this section of the museum: first, the experience of the registered prisoner as distinct from that of the unregistered deportee murdered upon arrival and, second, the brutal conditions of the registered prisoners that were, in effect, also a form of "extermination." Blocks 6 and 7 presented the hunger, bone-crushing labor, sanitary conditions, torture, and daily routine of the prisoner not simply as stations on the way to death, but as calculated methods of extermination. This was not immediate extermination in the gas chambers of Birkenau, as represented in Block 4, but an extermination *process* that provided the Germans with inexpensive labor along the way. In the exhibition's vocabulary, "extermination," a terminus usually associated with the fate of the Jews, was rendered synonymous with the registered prisoner's suffering and death by starvation, disease, or exhaustion. The final goal appeared the same; it was the pace and means of achieving that goal that differed.

Block 11: "Extermination and Struggle"

The sixth block on the visitor's route had an especially high priority for the exhibition's architects. Nearly one-third of the exhibition's design documents were devoted to "Extermination and Struggle" at Auschwitz, and Block 11 was the perfect location to address this theme. As the so-called Block of Death, it was the place at Auschwitz I where, more than anywhere else, prisoners were tortured, patriots were executed, and resistance fighters died for a righteous cause. It was also the main destination for Polish pilgrims who laid wreaths, recited prayers, celebrated masses, mourned comrades, and, perhaps, found hope and solace in the remains of despair and destruction. If Auschwitz I was the pre-eminent commemorative site of Polish national martyrdom, Block 11 was its votive sanctuary, a place of reverence and devotion, but also a place of suffering, drama, sacrifice, and even sainthood.

Block 11 was at the intersection of numerous commemorative currents at Auschwitz, for this building and its adjacent execution yard represented the confluence of Catholic martyrology, patriotic resistance against the oppressor, socialist heroism, and international solidarity—memorial themes articulated at the site in 1947, suppressed to varying degrees during Poland's Stalinist years, and revived after 1954. Because the Block of Death served so many different functions throughout the camp's history, it could easily fulfill this important role. The seat of the Auschwitz I penal company, "quarantine" housing for new arrivals, a detention center for the Katowice Gestapo, a summary court for Silesian resistance fighters, a torture chamber, interrogation cell, execution site—these were its functions, and all these aspects of its history were dramatically reconstructed in Block 11 as museum.

First to be viewed was the cellar, the site of the first gassings at Auschwitz in late summer 1941 and renowned for the so-called "bunkers," or standing cells for the punishment and torture of prisoners. Explanatory inscriptions related that a night in the bunker frequently resulted in death by suffocation or starvation, and one of the cells had a section cut away so that the visitor could see the square meter space into which as many as four prisoners were confined at a time. Of special significance was cell number six where Maksymilian Kolbe, the Franciscan friar who gave his life for another prisoner, had been confined. Kolbe was eventually beatified in 1971 and canonized in 1982, but honoring his self-sacrifice, suffering, and death had been part of Auschwitz commemorative ritual since the early postwar years. Kolbe did not die in the bunker, but was killed by phenol injection after failing to succumb to food deprivation. His cell, nonetheless, had become one of the most important memorial sites for Catholic pilgrims from Poland and abroad. In 1950 the party's verification commission for the Auschwitz Museum had ordered that all wreaths and candles left at Kolbe's cell be removed,[47] but the planners of the 1955 exhibition, setting aside the anticlericalism of years past, were willing to recognize the cultural significance and public appeal of the priest's memory.[48]

The ground floor of Block 11 was divided into several rooms, each reconstructed to reflect its purpose at one stage or another of the camp's history. Visitors could view, in effect, the prisoners' path to execution: the block scribe's chamber *(Schreibstube)* and summary courtroom, the room that had served as a prisoners' cell in 1944–45, and the disrobing rooms for men and women about to be shot in the courtyard outside. These two rooms displayed prison garb and civilian clothing strewn about the floor, hair cutting machines, and even a thick pencil for writing the condemned's number on his or her flesh.

The upper floor of Block 11 offered no reconstructed rooms or artifacts, but contained an exhibit devoted to two main themes: methods of punishment, torture, and execution at Auschwitz, and resistance in the camp. As the exhibit related, prisoners could be punished for the most minor breach of camp rules, or simply for the purpose of terrorizing other inmates. Punishment could take countless forms: whippings, hard labor, or standing for days on end, to name only a few. There also seemed to be no limits to the sadistic methods employed for the extraction of information or confessions: food deprivation in the bunkers, hanging by the wrists, and beatings were only some of the brutal techniques.

Execution, as the ultimate form of punishment, was usually done in a timely and efficient manner, either by hanging or, as was usually the case, by a bullet to the back of the head. Although such executions could be carried out for even the most minor offense or for no apparent reason at all, the exhibition lent the death sentence a postmortem significance by elevating the prisoner-martyr to heroic stature. "For the terrorization of the camp and society throughout the country . . . ," an explanatory text stated, "thousands of prisoners and civilians were executed here as a result of prewar patriotic activities, battle with the occupant, and retaliatory actions of the underground resistance." In other words, these prisoners had not died in vain, for their deaths contributed to a patriotic political narrative. For further emphasis, the exhibition's authors provided examples and documentation of the SS's summary "justice" at the site. The following represent only a few illustrative epigraphs: "Fact: The execution of 168 prisoners-artists, Kraków intelligentsia, and officers taken hostage in retaliation for a purported attempt on an SS officer's life"; "Fact: The SS summary court sentenced to death nearly all civilians arrested by the Kattowitz Gestapo, some 3,000 . . ."; "Fact: Fifty activists of the camp underground resistance hanged for an escape attempt."

With these grim statistics in mind, the visitor proceeded to the concluding section of Block 11: the rooms devoted to the struggle against the Auschwitz imperium. "In the fight against extermination, terror, and deprivation the prisoners allied themselves, and as anti-fascists, created first a Polish, and later an international resistance movement." This introductory inscription reflected conventional Polish perceptions of "resistance," both within the camps and beyond: the fight against the Germans was highly organized, led by anti-fascists with patriotic Poles at the forefront, and later assumed an international character under Polish leadership. The exhibition's creators did, nonetheless, account for some of the diverse forms that resistance could take at Auschwitz. At its most basic level, resistance could be in the form of "self-help" and solidarity among prisoners. This included theft, group readings, secret religious services, pastoral counseling, or even artistic work and the composition of music. The remainder of the exhibit, however, addressed more dangerous and confrontational forms of resistance, including sabotage at work, smuggling of materials and information to and from the outside world ("To the camp: the conspiratorial press, medicine, food, weapons, means of escape. From the camp: conspiratorial materials, situation reports, documents on SS crimes, escapees."), aiding prisoners in their attempts to escape, uncovering and "liquidating" the network of SS informants ("Enclosed behind the wires, the anti-fascists fought for a front of solidarity against the helpers of the terror apparatus—the spies and functionaries.") and, finally, armed revolt against the SS.

The exhibition also emphasized the activities of the Camp Military Council, a conspiratorial group headed by incarcerated army officers, and included among the displayed documents an excerpt of their manifesto. "The Camp Military Council," it read,

> regards that the liberation of the camp, in whole or in part, from the perspective of the international significance of Auschwitz as one of the most gloomy symbols of German Hitlerism. The Camp Military Council does not wish that the liberation of Auschwitz be treated exclusively as an action in aid of the prisoners. The Camp Military Council believes that the Auschwitz camp is, from a military point of view, a massive reservoir of human strength.

This is a text embedded with optimism. In the eyes of its authors, the liberation of Auschwitz was not simply a moral or humanitarian imperative, but because of the reserve of manpower in the camp, was a military goal. Written from the perspective of the organized, activist political prisoner, it does not seem to take into account the haggard, terrorized, competitive, or apathetic condition of most Auschwitz inmates. It assumes instead the will and ability to resist. The document also reflects traditional Polish perceptions of an organized armed resistance, and was perhaps intended to offer an optimistic and forward-looking tone to the concluding section of the exhibition. After becoming acquainted with forms of torture, punishment, and execution in Block 11, the Auschwitz pilgrim or tourist could end his or her visit there on a more positive note. Suffering and death, the exhibition emphasized, was only a part of the Auschwitz story, for out of this abyss of horror grew solidarity, mutual aid, the resolve to survive, and the will to continue fighting oppression and injustice both within the wires of the camp and in the world beyond.

From the terror and subjugation of the past to the struggle for justice in the present—this was to be the legacy of the Auschwitz resistance. To underscore these values and to encourage personal identification with the fighting prisoner, the exhibition included a gallery of heroes and heroines of the resistance, complete with brief biographies. Among the dozens listed were familiar names such as Józef Cyrankiewicz, the French communist leader Danielle Casanova, the Polish socialist youth leader Kostek Jagiełło, the Austrian communist Heinz Dürrmeyer, and Tadeusz Wąsowicz, former director of the State Museum at Auschwitz. Most of these heroes were Poles identified with the prewar communist or socialist parties. That the exhibit included resistance fighters not affiliated with the political left, such as Wąsowicz, was an indicator of the broader and more inclusive commemorative tone of the exhibition.

The visit to Block 11 concluded with a viewing of the sand-strewn courtyard and infamous Wall of Death, the execution site for thousands of prisoners of differing nationalities, social backgrounds, religious faiths, and political orientations. This was the premier location at Auschwitz for pilgrims and dignitaries to light candles, offer prayers, lay wreaths, and reflect on the legacy of those who had sacrificed their lives there for a higher good. The rather politicized narrative of the exhibitions in Block 11 may have upheld the memory of the organized Polish underground, and undoubtedly these prisoners and conspirators were the intended objects of the visitor's homage in the courtyard outside. Yet just as the courtyard and execution wall had united a diversity of victims in death, so too did the site function as a magnet for diverse commemorative ritual in the postwar era, illustrating and bridging what might be called the disparity between "intended" and "real" use of this memory site. Catholics and communists, Poles and Germans, soldiers and civilians—all could meet here and pay their respects to the Auschwitz martyr. Ultimately, however, the

Wall of Death and Auschwitz I as a whole were intended as a memorial to triumph—triumph over the Hitlerite German, the fascist, the occupant, the oppressor. Auschwitz I was not to be remembered as the site of nameless and quiet death, the camp where the typhus-infected, emaciated prisoner died in his bunk. Here died the hero.

The "New Laundry": Expansion of the Auschwitz Camp and Epilogue

The last building on the visitor's route at Auschwitz I was the wooden structure known in camp terminology as the "New Laundry." This exhibit included two concluding themes: the spatial development of the Auschwitz complex and what the design plan described as an "epilogue" to the camp's history. The visitor entered a large hall dominated by a horizontally displayed plaster model depicting the expanse of the Auschwitz and Birkenau camps in 1945. In addition, documents and texts chronicled the history of the camps' expansion, from the establishment of Auschwitz I in 1940 to the development of satellite camps in the surrounding region. In effect, these displays provided both a fitting conclusion to a visit to the base camp and a topographical introduction for a visit to Birkenau. Even if the compact, pristine, and well-maintained grounds of Auschwitz I bore little similarity to the expansive desolation of Birkenau, the map could give the visitor at least a scaled impression of the extermination camp, whether that visitor was planning to walk the three kilometers to Birkenau or not.

The exhibition's epilogue was, save for the introductory section in Block 15, the only portion of the visitor's route that did not deal exclusively with the history of the camp. Rather, it was devoted to themes like the liberation from German occupation, allied victory, and contemporary problems of peace and security in Europe. It is worth recalling that in 1952 there had been an entire block of Auschwitz I ("The Struggle for Peace") devoted to the postwar East-West conflict. By contrast, in 1955 six wall panels in the New Laundry conveyed the story of allied harmony in the victory over Nazism and in laying the groundwork for a fragile postwar European peace. When compared to the slogans of 1952, the epigraphs of the new exhibition were indeed remarkable: "The common struggle of the nations as well as the smashing of Hitlerism by the Soviet Army, in unity with the allied armies, put an end to genocide"; "The unity of nations brought victory"; "The resolutions of the Potsdam Agreement are realized."

Equally remarkable, and illustrative of the new political tone, was the shift in responsibility for international instability. The Auschwitz Museum of the early 1950s had portrayed the United States and its allies as heirs to the imperialist and genocidal legacy of German fascism; in 1955, the Federal Republic of Germany was the new danger and bore the onus of responsibility for an uneasy postwar European peace. West Germany had rearmed, permitted the establishment of Nazi veterans' organizations, and was letting convicted war criminals run free. By contrast, the German Democratic Republic was a model people's democracy striving for peace, stability, and progress in Europe. Written in five languages, "Never Again Auschwitz" was the closing epigraph of the exhibition. As in Józef Cyrankiewicz's April 1955 speech, these words were a warning, an injunction, and a rallying cry in the effort toward peace in Europe. The specter of Auschwitz was still alive—not in the United States, Great Britain, Korea, or Indochina, but in West Germany. Although treatment of these issues certainly reflected current foreign policy priorities of the Warsaw government, gone were the crude, generalized anti-Western propaganda of the early 1950s. Rather, the new exhibition focused on the narrower and, for an era of "peaceful coexistence," altogether safer West German target. Just as the April 1955 commemorative ceremonies had reflected the beginnings of a thaw and a retreat from the vulgar anti-Western rhetoric of the past, so too did the new exhibition offer a less confrontational interpretation and politicization of the Auschwitz legacy in current international affairs.

Birkenau

Planners of the new exhibition in 1955 were at pains to base their work on documentary evidence and to maintain the site, as their design plan stated, "in a crude and severe manner, as close as possible to a historic preserve with the predominance of museal elements [i.e., tangible artifacts] over exhibition elements." To a greater extent than ever before, the landscape and artifacts of Auschwitz were given the opportunity to educate, testify, and commemorate on their own. Yet as the above description has made clear, the 1955 exhibition at the base camp did, in fact, provide a narrative framework for understanding and commemorating the camp's history. Birkenau, by contrast, offered nothing of the sort. There were simply no "exhibition elements" at all—only ruins. Although parts of the base camp's exhibits, most

138 I Auschwitz, Poland, and the Politics of Commemoration

notably Block 4, emphasized some of the salient elements of Birkenau's history, the site of Nazi Germany's largest extermination center conspicuously lacked any interpretive framework or explanatory inscriptions. Rather, images of desolation, disrepair, and neglect dominated the site.

What, then, was to see at Birkenau? And what was the tourist, perhaps uninitiated by the exhibition in Auschwitz I, to learn? The words of a Swiss journalist, although written some ten years later, effectively convey the mood of the site. Auschwitz I, with its tourists, souvenir stands, and snack bars was a "carnival of sensationalism," but "Birkenau," the visitor recalled,

> is much different. Here there is little left standing: the main guard tower with the tunnel-like entrance for the tracks, the infamous "ramp" of the railroad siding, where the tens of thousands of arriving prisoners were "selected" for work or extermination . . . a few of the countless, horribly primitive barracks designed by the camp's planners for "52 horses or 744 prisoners." . . . In Birkenau, unlike in the Auschwitz camp, reigns an unearthly calm. Only rarely do tourists come here, although this branch camp covering an area of 170 hectares is only about three kilometers from the base camp. A lonely guard under the main gate's arch is the only living soul in a world of death. . . . Between the ruins—a horrifying and, at the same time, comforting symbolism—grass grows in abundance; it grows on the blood-drenched soil of the "ramp," stands meter-high in a bizarre forest of chimneys from the barracks, springs from the iron jaws of the overturned crematory ovens and spreads itself like a soft carpet over the upturned clods of what once were mass graves. Where the tracks of the "ramp" end stands a simple stone monument; not far from it, in the brackish water of the ponds where the ashes of the dead were once strewn, is the reflection of the birches that gave this site its name.[49]

As the author indicates, a visit to Birkenau first offered a view of the railroad siding passing through the main guard tower. Like many of the structures of the base camp, this red brick guard tower evoked solidity, but it was one of the relatively few structures remaining on the grounds. Once inside the camp confines, a walk along the railroad tracks brought the visitor to the so-called "ramp" for the "selection" of arriving Jews. To the left was Sector BI with the remains of some thirty low masonry buildings, some of them open to the curious visitor. Dirt, crumbling mortar, damp walls painted with German exhortations to the prisoners—these barracks of the former

Women's Camp, despite having been subjected to the elements over the previous ten years, remained much as they had looked in 1945.

To the right of the railroad bed stretched Sector BII, the city of low wooden huts that was divided into separate camps by miles of barbed wire. Only a tiny fraction of the more than three hundred wooden barracks had survived postwar looting and demolition, and all that remained of the others were chimneys. The scene was not unlike that of a town destroyed by fire or a petrified forest rising from the swampy ground. A look into the remaining barracks evoked conditions yet more squalid than in the former women's camp. The huts were, in fact, horse stables: approximately four hundred square meters of floor space, drafty, dark, damp, lacking any sanitary facilities, with three-tiered bunks to accommodate hundreds of prisoners at a time. Adjacent was a camp latrine, a similar wooden barracks with fifty-eight holes cut into a slab of concrete over a drainage ditch.

Clearly, this was the site of a giant prison camp, but a camp run by whom? For whom? The answer would not have been obvious to the uninformed visitor who, returning to the railroad siding, could continue to its end. There lay the rubble of two structures that at some point in the past had been demolished with explosives. All that remained were the foundations, what appeared to be cellars, and the concrete and steel of collapsed walls and ceilings. At the end of the tracks stood a rectangular block bearing the inscription "Oświęcim, 1940–1945." This was the unimpressive sarcophagus-like monument, erected for the April 1955 ceremony commemorating the liberation and containing ashes from camps across Europe.

It was a site with little inscription or explanation, and it was a site full of contradictions. Here at the end of the rail line, between the ruins of Crematoria II and III, was where hundreds of thousands of Jews had met their deaths, where tens of thousands had gathered for the April 1955 ceremonies, where dignitaries and guests from across the continent had paid their respects. It was also a site where cows grazed in the distance, where children played, where unused blocks of granite intended for a monument lay scattered, and where only a minority of visitors to Auschwitz ventured.[50]

This is where most visits to Birkenau ended. The more ambitious visitor could explore more of the site's vast acreage—the field where the storehouses of "Canada" had once stood, the large disinfection facility known as the "Sauna," the massive tanks for the conversion of human waste to methane gas, the pond amid the birches, or the sites of ash pits and crematory pyres. All of this was accessible, but there was no "visitors' route," no exhibition, no photographic display, no documentation. In short, Birkenau resembled a wasteland or a cemetery far more than it resembled the "museum" of which it was a part. Auschwitz I accommodated hundreds of visitors every day, while the fields of Birkenau seemed desolate. Auschwitz I and its structures had been preserved and repaired, more or less, while Birkenau suffered from continual neglect. Auschwitz I gave a sense of permanence, while Birkenau appeared to be transient and slowly disappearing into its landscape. Auschwitz I was the site of resistance, martyrdom, and final victory, while Birkenau remained the site of death on such a scale that it still challenges human comprehension. Auschwitz I was filled with interpretation and exhortation, while Birkenau offered little explanation at all for what had transpired there. Auschwitz I was authorial and vocal, while Birkenau, lacking any sort of narrative context, remained subdued, or even silent.

This "silence" at Birkenau may suggest an unwillingness or even inability to approach and understand the past. For reasons both practical and political, the Polish state had always emphasized the history, exhibitions, and legacy of Auschwitz I over the ruins of Birkenau. But, paradoxically, many visitors have since found the quiet, unvarnished, unheroic voice of Birkenau more effective in articulating the past. Although the lack of explanation and interpretation at Birkenau allowed for continued ignorance, or even distortion of its history, the site was permitted to speak for itself. Unable to compete with the narrative drone of Auschwitz I, the voice of silence remained, for many, far more articulate.

Although the renegotiation of the stakes and terms of memory at Auschwitz was most evident in the new 1955 exhibition, these physical changes to the site were only initial steps in the processes of stabilization and internationalization that continued well into the 1960s. The new exhibition and the site's increasing visibility spurred a spirited and remarkably open public discussion over the future of Auschwitz. The growing journalistic freedom of the era allowed Tadeusz Hołuj, one of the main architects of the new exhibition (and author of parts of the old), to offer a scathing attack on the mismanagement and propagandistic exploitation of the site over the previous ten years. "Millions have gone into the maintenance of the museum," Hołuj stated, yet much was "wasted through shoddy and improvised work, the lack of long-range planning, and incompetence." In short, as Hołuj claimed, the site had become nothing more than "a peddler's booth of cheap anti-imperialist propaganda,"[51] and only with long-range planning and adequate financial and governmental patronage could it be expected to retain its historical significance.

Echoing Hołuj's criticisms, others rallied to the museum's cause with equal vigor. The former prisoner Czesław Ostańkowicz recalled his embarrassment over the state of the grounds as he escorted a French visitor through the base camp and Birkenau. "How to explain," he asked,

> [t]hat with the funds collected by former prisoners there was organized not a competition for a monument for your children, but a horrible "anti-imperialist" exhibition? . . . How to explain to you that 180,000 zlotys collected from the widows of our camp comrades were taken for that evil purpose?. . . . [I]t does not appear that you find yourself on the site of the greatest camp of the fascist Reich, although close by stand exhibition halls. They are closed to visitors because . . . there is the threat of collapse. There is, moreover, the threat that the authorities responsible for the state of Auschwitz will be greatly discredited; first and foremost the Ministry of Culture and Art (pre-October), ZBoWiD (pre-October), and still many other instances from those gloomy years.[52]

The comments of Hołuj, Ostańkowicz, and others were not limited to complaints over past mismanagement and neglect, but included as well demands for the future—demands for the final regulation of the site's borders, demands for an on-site archive of Auschwitz-related documents at the museum, and demands for an increase in both public and private funding for its activities.[53] By late 1956 there was, according to one departmental director in the Ministry of Culture and Art, a veritable "wave of indignation in society regarding the neglect in the area of memorialization of sites of struggle and execution" and a public outcry for renewed attention to their upkeep.[54]

There were also clarion calls from within the museum administration for improvements to the Auschwitz memorial grounds. Replacing the incompetent and politically compromised Stefan Wiernik, in October 1955 Kazimierz Smoleń had assumed the directorship of the site, a position the former prisoner would hold until 1990. Already in his first year, Smoleń issued numerous requests to Warsaw for both material and moral support for the site. In June 1956, for example, the new director petitioned the Ministry of Culture and Art to send funding requests for the museum directly to the highest echelons of party and government power: Prime Minister Józef Cyrankiewicz and the PZPR Central Committee.[55] Most significant, however, was the director's annual report submitted to the ministry at the end of that year. Critical of the politically motivated mismanagement and neglect of the site over the previous ten years, Smoleń listed a number of grievances and in unprecedented fashion made several bold demands. Essential to the continued scholarly work of memorial site was an extensive archive at the site, he argued. According to the director, it had been impossible to develop such an archive because countless documents had been confiscated by the Soviets or remained in the hands of other Polish institutions, such as the Central Commission for the Investigation of German Crimes in Poland and Warsaw's Jewish Historical Institute. The new director also called for the reactivation of the museum's historical commission, a productive advisory body to the museum staff and Ministry of Culture in the late 1940s that had been disbanded in the Stalinist years. Also on Smoleń's agenda were the construction of a permanent exhibition in Birkenau, production of a film about Auschwitz, development of the museum's international contacts with other commemorative sites and organizations, and construction, finally, of a suitable monument in Birkenau.[56]

It was an ambitious agenda, to be sure, but the most serious task facing the site in 1956 was conservation of its buildings. "The matter looks worse than catastrophic," Smoleń claimed in his report, noting that dozens of structures would soon collapse if work was not undertaken soon. "Fortunately there have been no accidents," he continued, "[b]ut this is no reason to relax. How was it possible to allow for such a state of things? Who bears the responsibility for such matters?"[57] In posing questions like these the director was not only emphasizing the urgency of the situation, but also encouraging the Ministry of Culture and Art to hold accountable those individuals and institutions who were to blame for the errors of the past.

The public outcry in support of the museum and the efforts of the new director were not in vain, for in the months and years to follow renovations and improvements continued, albeit at a slower than ideal pace. A crucial step in this direction was a meeting of Smoleń, Jan Sehn, Stanisław Kłodziński, and the journalist Mieczysław Kieta with Prime Minister Cyrankiewicz. The group of former prisoners petitioned the premier for the transfer of documents relating to the history of the camp to the Auschwitz Museum. Cyrankiewicz personally intervened in this matter and the transfer was completed in

1957.[58] The premier also approved, at long last, the allocation of fifty to sixty million zlotys to compensate members of the local community whose land had been confiscated by the Germans and had become, in turn, part of the museum grounds.

Two years later, in preparation for the fifteenth anniversary of the liberation, the premier approved additional funds for publication of the museum's new historical journal *Zeszyty Oświęcimskie* (Auschwitz Notebooks), for stipends for museum employees to undertake research abroad, for the production of a documentary film on the history of Auschwitz, and for subsidies for the work of the International Auschwitz Committee.[59] In addition, the government addressed the continuing problem of preservation. Although the restoration and reconstruction work of successive years was, as always, inadequate, there is nonetheless a record of thirty million zlotys allocated for the upkeep of the site's structures between 1961 and 1965.[60]

Smoleń's accomplishments in the early years of his directorship should not be underestimated. By the mid-1960s, the memorial site had developed into a stable, multifunctional institution dedicated not only to the memorialization of Auschwitz victims, but also to scholarship and public education. A library, research archive, staff of historians, scholarly journal, dozens of guides—all contributed to the growing profile of the museum in Poland and abroad.[61] Moreover, the number of visitors to Auschwitz grew steadily, from 178,000 in 1956 to nearly 540,000 in 1968, 108,000 of whom were visitors from abroad.[62] Most importantly, what had been, as late as 1954, an irresponsibly neglected site used as a stage for cold-war politics had finally earned the financial and moral commitment of the Polish state. Public activism, pressure from abroad, calls from within the museum administration, and the relaxation of control over Poland's cultural institutions at mid-decade all contributed to the revival of postwar Auschwitz as a center of public commemoration and education. The advent of "national communism" under Władysław Gomułka had allowed for the resuscitation and elaboration of the commemorative agenda intended for the museum in 1947, and with the museum administration once again in the hands of former political prisoners, a Polish interpretive framework was again in place. Although sturdy, this framework was not rigid, for in the years ahead it would bend to the growing stresses of Polish domestic politics and the diverse needs of an increasingly international constituency.

1. The main gate of the base camp Auschwitz I, spring 1945. APMO, Nr. neg. 21 334/90

2. The main street of Auschwitz I, looking east, spring 1945. APMO, Nr. neg. 21 334/103

3. Birkenau, road between sectors BI and BII, with the main gate in the background and the Women's Camp on the right, spring 1945. The photograph gives a sense of the expanse of the Birkenau site and of the relatively small number of structures remaining on the grounds only a few months after the liberation. APMO, Nr. neg. 21 334/147

4. Birkenau, human remains near Crematorium V, from corpses cremated prior to the camp's liquidation and evacuation, spring 1945. The photographer is a member of the Kraków-based Commission for the Investigation of German Crimes at Auschwitz. Photographs such as these were taken to document crimes at Auschwitz and to provide evidence at future trials. APMO, Nr. neg. 21 334/130

5. Birkenau, members of the Commission for the Investigation of German Crimes at Auschwitz on the ruins of a crematorium. At the center of the photograph, pointing, is judge Jan
Sehn, examining magistrate of the Commission for the Investigation of German Crimes at Auschwitz. On the far right is
the former Auschwitz prisoner Dr. Otto Wolken. APMO,
Nr. neg. 21 334/57

6. Auschwitz I, roof of Crematorium I, May 1945. Benches on the perimeter and a platform at the center decorated with flags and a star suggest that the Soviet Army held a gathering or ceremony here. The former gas chamber and crematorium had apparently been transformed into a ceremonial space, but clearly not in a manner honoring the victims. APMO, Nr. neg. 21 334/27

7. The first exhibition at the State Museum at Auschwitz, in the cellar of Block 4 of Auschwitz I. On the right and left are, in displays surrounded by barbed wire, items plundered from deportees. The illuminated cross at the end of the room accents not only the devotional mood of the room, but also testifies to the circumscribed and Christian character of the exhibit. APMO, Nr. neg. 3441

8. A crowd gathered in Auschwitz I for the dedication ceremonies of the State Museum, 14 June 1947. At the lectern is Prime Minister Józef Cyrankiewicz. APMO, Nr. neg. 21 390/15

9. Józef Cyrankiewicz speaking at the museum's dedication ceremonies, 14 June 1947. APMO, Nr. neg. 21 390/11

10. A Roman Catholic mass held in the courtyard between Blocks 10 and 11 of Auschwitz I, in conjunction with the museum's dedication ceremonies, 14 June 1947. The bald man in the foreground appears to be Prime Minister Józef Cyrankiewicz. APMO, Nr. neg. 21 390/9

11. Birkenau, members of the museum's protective guard at the ruins of a crematorium, 1948. APMO, Nr. neg. 22 201/7

12. Birkenau, sector BIIe. Former prisoners and members of the museum staff on a break from searching for evidence in the former Gypsy Camp, 1949. The extent of Birkenau's rapid destruction is already evident in this photograph, taken only four years after the liberation. APMO, Nr. neg. 21 308/3

13. An exhibition hall displaying prostheses, from the early 1950s. APMO, Nr. neg. 3436

14. Further evidence of Nazi crimes in an exhibition from the early 1950s, here in the form of suitcases inscribed by the deportees with their names and, in some cases, their dates of birth and cities or countries of origin. APMO, Nr. neg. 21 641/1

15. A view of a section of the "Jewish Hall" of a pre-1955 exhibit. The small banners with the flowers are from the Oświęcim Jewish Committee, the Central Committee of Jews in Poland, and the Kraków Jewish Committee. APMO, Nr. neg. 3438

16. A memorial in the cellar of Block 4, Auschwitz I. The date is unknown, but it is clear that this is from a pre-1955 exhibition. The crown of thorns in the foreground, recalling the crown of thorns worn by Jesus of Nazereth at his crucifixion, suggests the Christian notions of suffering and sacrifice. In the glass urn are presumably ashes. The letters on the triangles represent the nationalities of deportees to Auschwitz. APMO, Nr. neg. 3440

17–19. (See also opposite page) Three exhibition panels from the era of Polish Stalinism. They are noteworthy not only for their strident political tone, but also for the
absence of Auschwitz and its history in their images and texts. The first (17) bears the
inscription, "Two Camps after the Second World War," referring to the division of
the world into East and West, communist and capitalist (APMO, Fot. stara ekspozycja z przed 1955, nr. 75). The second (18) states: "40,000,000 Unemployed in the
Countries of the Marshall Plan." (APMO, Fot. stara ekspozycja z przed 1955, nr. 14).
In the third photograph (19), the prisoner states: " . . . and in West Germany the
Anglo-Saxon imperialists are re-arming my murderers . . ." (APMO, Fot. stara
ekspozycja z przed 1955, nr. 95)

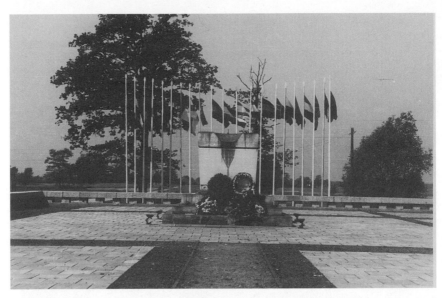

20. Birkenau, monument to the victims of Auschwitz between the ruins of Crematoria II and III. This photograph was taken in April 1955, at the ceremonies commemorating the tenth anniversary of the liberation of the camp. APMO, Nr. neg. 16053

21. A plaster model of Gas Chamber and Crematorium II from the 1955 exhibition. It remains to this day in Block 4 of Auschwitz I. The rather graphic model shows 1) victims waiting to enter the gas chamber on the left, 2) victims inside the subterranean gas chamber, and 3) the *Sonderkommando* at work in Crematorium II. The model is an attempt to represent the mass extermination at Birkenau within the confines of an exhibition in the base camp. APMO, Nr. neg. 19273

22. From the 1955 exhibition, women's hair on display in Block 4 of Auschwitz I. APMO, Nr. neg. 14445

23. Auschwitz I, Block 7: A reconstruction of a masonry barracks in the Birkenau Women's Camp, from the 1955 exhibition. This full-size diorama, part of the exhibition's section on "Living Conditions," was intended as a "true to life" representation of the camp and, in addition, was to represent Birkenau on the grounds of Auschwitz I. APMO, Nr. neg. 19362

24. The last to be visited in the 1955 exhibition, this room in the "New Laundry" emphasized international cooperation and set a less confrontational tone than that of earlier exhibits. APMO, Nr. neg. 19392

25. As the most important site for the commemoration of the war, German occupation, and Poland's martyrdom, the State Museum at Auschwitz attracted visitors and pilgrims from all walks of life. Pictured here are participants in a motorcycle rally that included a ceremonial visit to Auschwitz and Birkenau. APMO, Nr. neg. 6156

26. Commemoration of the Auschwitz dead as an intergenerational ritual: On the twentieth anniversary of the liberation, a scout and a former prisoner stand at attention next to the "Wall of Death" in the courtyard of Block 11. APMO, Nr. neg. /433

27. A crowd of thousands in Birkenau, on the occasion of the unveiling of the Monument to the Victims of Fascism, April 1967. APMO, Nr. neg. 10883

28. The Monument to the Victims of Fascism in Birkenau, at its unveiling in April 1967. APMO, Nr. neg. 10898

29. Visitors to the 1968 exhibit on "The Martyrology and Struggle of the Jews" in Block 27 of the base camp were confronted with this inscription etched in stone: "Cain, what have you done with your brother Abel?" APMO, Nr. neg. 14456

30. Exhibition on the "Martyrology and Struggle of the Jews," 1968. The panel on the left shows a resistance newspaper from the German occupation; on the right is a reproduction of a German proclamation imposing the death sentence on anyone aiding Jews. Emphasizing Polish-Jewish solidarity in suffering, the caption below reads: "Poland offered aid to its Jewish sons. Despite horrible terror, Poles did not abandon their Jewish brothers." APMO, Nr. neg. 15598

31. The final room in the 1968 exhibition on the "Martyrology and Struggle of the Jews." The text on the plaque reads: "And the Lord said to Cain, 'The blood of your brother Abel cries to me from the ground.'" APMO, Nr. neg. 14457

32. Birkenau, 7 June 1979. Pope John Paul II receives former prisoners at the papal mass. APMO, Nr. neg. 20845/30

33. The controversial building on the perimeter of Auschwitz I, known during the German occupation as the *Theatergebäude* and during the 1980s and 1990s as the Carmelite Convent. This photograph, taken in 1997, shows the former convent ten years after the Geneva agreement. Adjacent to the building is a former gravel pit where Polish prisoners were executed. On the right is a sign erected by local activists entrusting "this site of our sisters' and brothers' martyrdom to the care and prayer of the carmelite nuns" and calling for their return to "say their prayers for reconciliation between the Jewish and Polish people and for saving mankind from the threat of another tragedy." APMO, Nr. neg. 22 225/3

34. Aerial photograph of Auschwitz I. On the lower right is the visitors' reception center, once a reception center for prisoners of the camp. On the lower left is Crematorium I and its reconstructed smokestack. On the upper right is the former Carmelite Convent. PMO, 1996

35. Aerial photograph of Birkenau. On the left is sector BI. From the lower right to the upper left runs the railroad siding and the "ramp." Right of the railroad siding are sectors BII, with its remaining wooden barracks, and BIII. PMO, 1996

5 ⫴ The Internationalization of the Auschwitz Site

Auschwitz had always functioned as a register of national and international political trends, and this function only increased in the wake of the site's stabilization and revitalization. Having set aside the crude instrumentalization of the Stalinist years and achieved an unprecedented level of stability beginning in the mid-1950s, the memorial site began to attract international attention. As in the past, Poland persevered in setting its own memorial agenda for Auschwitz, only to realize by the late 1960s that it could continue to do so only at the risk of growing criticism from abroad. Three significant developments characterized the "internationalization" process at the memorial site.

First, in the 1950s the newly established International Auschwitz Committee emerged as an influential external body that helped to shape the profile of the site and to publicize it abroad. An association of former prisoners from various European countries, the IAC sponsored international conferences at Auschwitz and had an increasingly important role in organizing the site's exhibits and activities. Not least, the IAC, in its capacity as a transnational supervisory body, lent the museum a degree of international visibility and credibility that it had lacked in previous years.

Second, the International Auschwitz Committee, State Museum at Auschwitz, and Poland's Ministry of Culture initiated plans in the mid-1950s for the design and construction of a massive monument in Birkenau that would commemorate all victims of the Auschwitz complex. Abstract in form and vague in its message, the monument and the events surrounding its unveiling in April 1967 certainly furthered the memorial site's growing international character and testified to the waning relevance of a traditional Polish-national commemorative idiom at Auschwitz. At the same time, however, the

Birkenau monument failed to specify or acknowledge explicitly the suffering and death of Jews at Auschwitz, and therefore took its place in the continuum of commemorative marginalization of the Shoah at the site.

Third, in 1968—more than twenty years after the liberation of Auschwitz—the museum opened its first exhibition devoted to the "Martyrology and Struggle of the Jews" in Block 27 of the base camp. Ironically, this reintroduction of the Shoah into the Auschwitz landscape—a significant challenge to the museum's traditional orientation—occurred at the height of Poland's "anti-Zionist" campaign. Although the exhibition testified to the diversity of Auschwitz victims and, at long last, specifically and more exhaustively confronted the Jewish genocide at Auschwitz, it also became a locus of controversy because of its tendentious and misleading presentation of wartime Polish-Jewish relations.

These new vectors of memory and the narrative voices that they introduced would undermine and modify, but not destroy, the prevailing Polish-national commemorative framework at the memorial site. The internationalization of postwar Auschwitz was therefore tentative: the International Auschwitz Committee participated in setting the site's agenda for a time, but it could do so only at the cost of surrendering its independence and moral authority to the control of the Polish state. The initiative to construct an international monument at Birkenau drew upon the efforts and creativity of organizations and artists from around the world, but the monument's design would be subject to the approval of the Polish Ministry of Culture, which in the end assumed full control over its construction and the ceremonies surrounding its dedication. Finally, the addition of a Jewish exhibition was a necessary and belated thematic reinsertion of the Shoah into the memorial site's landscape. It failed, however, to articulate sufficiently the uniqueness of the Jewish experience at Auschwitz and other camps. Instead, the exhibition appeared to assimilate Jewish suffering and death into what remained of a Polish-national commemorative idiom by emphasizing Polish aid to Jews and solidarity between the two victim groups.

The State Museum at Auschwitz would emerge from the 1960s better funded, better managed, and better maintained. This was, to a great extent, the result of a growing international interest in the site as well as the desire of the Polish state to make it a fitting memorial for all of Europe. On the one hand, the stewards of memory at Auschwitz had learned in the early 1950s that no "framing" of the Auschwitz site is permanent and, perhaps more significantly, that any overtly politicized interpretive framework was bound to fail. Yet to open Auschwitz to international influence and scrutiny was also to open the site to the challenges of additional memorial narratives, illustrating once again the site's role as a register of both domestic and international political concerns.

The International Auschwitz Committee

Founded in May 1954, the International Auschwitz Committee became intimately connected to the workings of the memorial site. The committee's participation in the planning of commemorative ceremonies, exhibitions, and, most importantly, the Birkenau monument dedicated in 1967 heightened public awareness of Auschwitz and its museum. In addition, IAC involvement in the activities of the museum emphasized the international makeup of the camp's prisoners and victims. Although the Polish commemorative tradition continued to dominate the site's landscape, the addition of numerous "national exhibitions" and a monument financed and erected through international efforts ensured that Auschwitz would no longer be regarded, or ignored abroad, as a Polish memorial.

At the same time, the IAC's involvement also guaranteed that the Polish state would maintain its commitment to the museum. The Auschwitz site remained, as always, a charge of the Polish government. Beginning in the mid-1950s, however, Warsaw was compelled to consider the commemorative agendas of other prisoners' organizations, whether Austrian, French, West German, Dutch, or Yugoslavian. To that extent, the committee's presence, support, and financial support elevated the museum's status abroad and allowed it greater freedom to expand the scope of its exhibitions and activities.

Former prisoners had formed associations in many European countries, and the International Auschwitz Committee sought to unite these groups in the common goals of maintaining the memory of Auschwitz victims, representing the moral and material rights of former prisoners, spreading the ideals of the Auschwitz resistance movement, and, especially, caring for the memorial site as a witness to Auschwitz crimes.[1] This last aspect of the organization's mission was evident already in 1954, when the infant IAC initiated plans for commemorative ceremonies surrounding the tenth anniversary of the liberation, compelling the Polish authorities to undertake their own plans for the renovation of the site and organization of the April 1955 event.

In the years to follow, the committee's influence over the site grew as it convened regular international conferences at Auschwitz. A January 1957 meeting, for example, included fifty-two representatives from fourteen countries[2] and appointed a museum commission to oversee and develop the site. While respectfully acknowledging the past efforts of the Polish authorities, the group left no doubt that it intended to be an active participant in setting the agenda for the memorialization of Auschwitz in the future. Among other proposals, members of the IAC Museum Commission called for a moratorium on any further industrial or economic utilization of the memorial grounds, proposed the registration of Auschwitz on the United Nations list of sites of World Cultural Heritage,[3] and considered methods of raising funds for the Auschwitz Museum from abroad—until then a practice eschewed by the Polish government. Finally, the commission called for enhancing the international component at Auschwitz through the construction of various "national exhibitions" devoted to the struggle of individual countries under German occupation.[4] Exhibits sponsored by other states had long been a desideratum of some of the site's architects, and although a thorough analysis of them is beyond the scope of this study, it is worth noting that this form of "internationalization" only became a reality in the late 1950s and early 1960s through the initiative and support of the IAC. By then, it had secured its role not only as an advisor and public advocate of the State Museum, but also as a codeterminer of policy.

The IAC's growing participation in these years raises the question of why the Polish government and Ministry of Culture would remain open to the presence of the organization in the first place. In fact, the committee was not merely tolerated, but was encouraged as a valid and useful external influence on the character of the memorial site. It gave Auschwitz a greater international profile, explored the possibility of external funding, and was willing to help in the further development of the museum. More importantly, the Polish authorities regarded the IAC as an organization that for the most part would support rather than challenge the prevailing commemorative agenda at Auschwitz.

Even if relations between the committee and Polish authorities were not always harmonious, Warsaw generally welcomed the organization's political orientation. Officially committed to spanning partisan differences, the IAC was nonetheless clear in criticizing the presence of former Nazis in the West German government and in condemning the United States as the initiator and motor of the nuclear arms race. Moreover, the IAC remained silent on human rights issues and the nuclear presence in the Soviet Union and the Eastern Bloc. In general, then, the committee enjoyed the reputation of a leftist, Soviet-friendly, anti-NATO organization, and its ideological loyalty became especially evident in the controversy surrounding the IAC's outspoken Austrian secretary-general, Hermann Langbein.

Despite Langbein's involvement in the camp's resistance movement and his pivotal role in the IAC's formation in the mid-1950s, he soon became the object of criticism and eventual exclusion from the organization, in large part because he had emerged as a vocal critic of the German Democratic Republic. Documents of the GDR's Committee of Antifascist Resistance Fighters (*Komitee der antifaschistischen Widerstandskämpfer,* or KdAW), the sole and state-directed organization of former prisoners in that country, refer to Langbein's political improprieties: his criticism of East German prisons, his support for a former Auschwitz prisoner who had illegally fled the GDR, and his praise of West German justice in bringing former Nazi criminals to trial. In general, the KdAW regarded Langbein as, at best, ideologically suspect and divisive.[5] Polish authorities shared the East Germans' concerns, and in May 1960 ZBoWiD proposed, as a control measure, the transfer of the administrative headquarters of the organization from Vienna to Warsaw.[6] Although there were valid practical and logistical reasons for seating the committee's administrative apparatus in Warsaw, the proposed move also reflected the fear that any drastic action against Langbein, given the support that he enjoyed among the organization's "non-party" (i.e., non-communist) members, would fracture the IAC and anchor its power base in the West.[7] At issue was the independence of the committee from the governments of its constituent organizations; according to Langbein, the IAC could have international authority only if it worked independently of political parties and the dictates of governments.[8]

At the IAC general assembly in June 1960, Langbein was relieved of his duties as secretary-general. Whether of his own accord or under duress, Langbein left the IAC entirely in August 1961, publicly leveling charges that the IAC was a "communist organization."[9] His exit, as well as the transfer of the committee's power base to Warsaw, foreshadowed the strife and divisions in the IAC that would arise later in the decade. Moreover, these changes served the interests of ZBoWiD, for in the course of the 1960s the Polish organization, under the leadership of the Minister of State Security Mieczysław Moczar, would increase its power within both the Polish state apparatus and the IAC.[10]

If the IAC is to be credited with contributing to the internationalization of Auschwitz, it is also to be held partially responsible for the site's continued politicization. By initiating the development of national exhibits and organizing conferences and commemorative events, the IAC successfully broadened the museum's international profile and the scope of its mission. Polish stewards of Auschwitz were willing to tolerate the IAC and even to offer it cautious support, but within a decade the organization had sacrificed its independence by imposing considerable ideological rigidity on its ranks and by transferring its power base to Polish soil. In short, the committee was submitting itself to the political exigencies of the Polish state. This submission would become all the more apparent in the committee's efforts to construct an international monument in Birkenau and in its official silence on the institutionalized anti-Semitism of Poland's so-called anti-Zionist campaign. The "internationalization" of the Auschwitz site, motored by the efforts of the IAC, remained circumscribed by Polish control over the former camp and the public manifestations of its memory there.

The "Monument to the Victims of Fascism"

Like the idea of a memorial site, the initiative for an international monument commemorating the victims of Auschwitz had its origins in the camp itself. In 1944 the prisoner-artist and later employee of the State Museum, Jerzy Brandhuber, was commissioned by a member of the Auschwitz resistance movement to create plans for a monument in Birkenau. As Brandhuber himself described his clandestine design:

> I had an official, conspiratorial commission from colleague Benka Świer-
> czyny (from the resistance movement). . . . It was gigantic, but at that time

we counted on the fact that the entire world would provide the funds, that there would be too much money for its construction and maintenance. The entire terrain to the west of the camp in Birkenau, beginning at the crematoria, was to be leveled like a colossal roll-call square. . . . In the center a colossal smokestack, square at its base, like in a crematorium, only several times taller, fifty to sixty meters high. . . . Added to the smokestack [is] an eternal flame. . . . And all around in rows, like blocks [symbolizing prisoners] as they stood during roll-call, in formation, arranged in sectors like stones, like urns (not graves, for there were none) divided into rows of ten—like then, in the camp—five hundred, six hundred prisoners; five, six million stones. . . . And between these groupings nothing, no grass, no trees, and all around only a row of fence posts with guns and lamps. . . . And former SS men would weed the grounds to the ends of their lives.[11]

Brandhuber's vision bore no relationship to subsequent plans for a monument in Birkenau or to the actual monument dedicated in 1967, but any consideration of his 1944 sketches invites a number of broader questions associated with artistic monuments at Auschwitz and other memorial sites. Who has the authority to supervise the design and construction? What media are appropriate? How, and under whose authority is the construction of an international monument to be financed?

One cannot help but be impressed with the grandiose, if impractical scope and content of Brandhuber's vision, especially in light of the fact that it originated in Auschwitz itself at a time when surviving, not commemorating the camp experience, was the primary concern. One has perhaps the tendency or desire to lend Brandhuber's plans a higher level of "authenticity" or "expressivity" than later proposals, simply because they were not the product of artistic imagination as recalled experience, but the product of *immediate* experience in the camp. Was Brandhuber especially qualified to develop an artistic rendition of the Auschwitz experience, or were members of the International Auschwitz Committee, former prisoners themselves, especially qualified to supervise the construction of the monument? Developments in the 1960s suggested that they were not.

Brandhuber's project also raises questions of media, form, and utility— questions that can and must be asked with regard to the 1967 monument. Should there be a narrative embedded in his gigantic conglomerate of stones, symbols, and reproduced relics of the camp? What does the coalescence of these images reveal or represent? Is there a common reading of these images and, if so, is it historically accurate? How is this memorial space to function? Is it intended to be, in and of itself, a site of reflection, contemplation, and mourning, or is it to serve as stage and props for commemorative ritual like the frequent Auschwitz manifestacja?

Finally, impractical as Brandhuber's commemorative vision seems today, his description suggests that he could not imagine in 1944 that publicizing and financing the construction of such a huge monument would pose any difficulties. In fact, the lack of material resources would prove to be a continual impediment to the construction of the 1967 monument. Although support for the project came from as far away as the United States and China, funds did not simply flow in, but had to be solicited by the International Auschwitz Committee over a span of ten years. How and why could this important commemorative gesture, regarded by many as a moral duty, suffer the same fate—material neglect and political instrumentalization—as had the very Birkenau site on which it stood? The answer lies in the historical context of the monument's genesis, development, and place in the Auschwitz memorial landscape.

Analyses of the Birkenau monument and the forces behind its construction generally begin with the 1957 announcement of an artists' competition.[12] The new museum administration and IAC provided the impetus for the monument's realization, but construction of a memorial had already been under consideration for several years. The idea had emerged already in the early stages of the site's development,[13] and in November 1950 a cornerstone was laid for a monument to the victims of Auschwitz, the form of which had yet to be determined.[14] Six months later, the Ministry of Culture and Art began planning for the monument's design and construction by announcing an all-Polish artistic competition for a monument in early 1952.[15] Press reports indicate that already in January of that year a stone base equipped with an eternal flame had been erected in Birkenau near Crematorium IV. Granite blocks, extracted by prisoners of the Nazi concentration camp Gross-Rosen, were brought to the site for the construction of what was, in this era of Polish Stalinism, intended as a "monument to the victory over fascism."[16] The blocks were not, however, used for this purpose,[17] the Ministry of Culture never named a winner of the competition, and this phase of the monument project came to a halt.[18]

The State Museum revisited plans for a Birkenau monument in the early stages of its revitalization with a call for the erection of a "mausoleum" in Birkenau at a cost of 350,000 zlotys.[19] One of the museum's curators subsequently developed a proposal for such a structure. The mausoleum would be situated on the foundations of Crematorium III, where the changing room and gas chamber, decorated with symbols and sculptures to be determined by various countries whence Auschwitz deportees had come, would serve as the lower level. In addition, the crematorium's chimney was to be fully rebuilt and crowned with an eternal flame. The proposal even visualized the entire monument being constructed of bricks—some 4 million—representing what was then officially regarded as the total number of deaths in the camp complex. Revisiting a failed initiative from 1947, it went so far as to suggest the possibility of inscribing these bricks with the names of the dead.[20]

For the time being, however, pilgrims to Birkenau had to be content with a small granite block and flame. In fact, the absence of any historical inscriptions seems to have led to some confusion over the monument's meaning and significance. A French visitor, for example, concluded that the monument and its eternal flame were "erected to the memory of the 4 million Jews" who died at Auschwitz.[21] This monument was certainly not intended to commemorate specifically the suffering and death of European Jews at Auschwitz, and, ironically, it was perhaps the absence of architectonic interpretation and inscriptions at the site that allowed the visitor to arrive at this unintended conclusion.

The first large monument at the Birkenau site was a sarcophagus-like block situated between Crematoria II and III.[22] Approximately three meters in height and width, the vault sat atop an open, elevated, paved area of sixty by thirty-two meters.[23] Kazimierz Smoleń has indicated that it was a poorly built, unattractive structure that was never intended to be permanent,[24] and it is significant that this monument was erected—perhaps on the urging of the International Auschwitz Committee—specifically for the April 1955 ceremonies commemorating the liberation.[25] The inadequacy of this monument was evident in the call, only two years later, for a more elaborate structure. At its general assembly on the twelfth anniversary of the liberation, the IAC charged its newly formed museum commission with developing a concept for the monument and outlining the terms and criteria for an international artists' competition.[26] Then, at an IAC conference held in June of that year, the competition was finally announced, placing responsibility for the project firmly in the hands of the committee.[27] A paper prepared for the conference by the staff of the Auschwitz Museum emphasized the importance of the IAC's responsibility and authority in shaping the future of the memorial site:

> Those who through good fortune were able to experience the day of their liberation in Auschwitz or another concentration camp are responsible for the memorialization of those who died here. The International Auschwitz Committee has the right, indeed the duty to care for the appearance of these grounds in their name and in the name of the fraternity of all prisoners, and they should seek the most appropriate forms of memorialization.[28]

In a similar vein, the official advertisement of the artists' competition noted the particular duty of the survivor in perpetuating the memory of those who had perished in the camp.

> All these voices [of the dead] are silenced. If today anything more than a desert of ashes remains of Auschwitz-Birkenau, this is thanks to an ever-vanishing small number of survivors. The message of those who remained there must be perpetuated throughout the centuries, even if there are no longer those with tattooed arms who return to fulfill this duty. The International Auschwitz Committee has resolved that in the camp itself an international monument shall immortalize this message. . . . It shall forever characterize and capture what Auschwitz was and convey this to the world.[29]

The claims and agenda set forth in these documents had tremendous implications for the character of the Birkenau monument, for they suggested that surviving prisoners, either as individuals or as a collective, were entitled to perpetuate and objectify the memory of their fallen comrades. At issue was the authority over the project: Was the memorialization of the Auschwitz dead necessarily the privilege of the fellow prisoner, of the families of the dead, of the state, or of all three? Few would argue that fellow comrades from the camp should have been excluded from the commemorative process in any of its forms, but the fact remains that each individual survivor had his or her own "voice" or "version" of the Auschwitz experience. The Polish political prisoner who survived the base camp, for example, would recall, interpret, and memorialize Auschwitz differently than would the Soviet POW or surviving Hungarian Jew, and a wide reading of the camp's memoir literature makes such distinctions in experience and interpretation all too clear. Jochen Spielmann has perceptively suggested that the final product of the initiative, that is, the monument dedicated in 1967, clearly reflected the overwhelming presence of registered political prisoners and members of the Auschwitz resistance movement in the IAC.[30] It is clear, in any case, that members of the IAC's commission intended for the monument to convey not only suffering and death at Auschwitz, but resistance and solidarity as well.

The issue of the monument's narrative content, that is, the "message of those who remained there," was equally vexing. How was this "message" to be embodied in or communicated through a monument? The IAC never made that message precise, and it was therefore open to manifold interpretations. The competition's advertisement offered a hint, however. "The designers should never forget," it read, "that this monument should not only be suggestive of martyrdom and struggle, but also of the brotherhood that arose in common suffering and struggle—that very brotherhood, the flame of which burns more lively than the fire of the crematoria."[31] Any artistic design therefore had to address and evoke the two traditional and enduring memorial paradigms at the Auschwitz site: that of the sacrificial martyr and that of the heroic resistance fighter. To the informed analyst, the monument's proposed location at the end of the "ramp" between Crematoria II and III suggested the arrival of Jewish deportees, their murder, and cremation. Jews were not, however, mentioned in the announcement, despite the international character of the committee and the presence of many Jewish members from Western European countries. Jewish victims simply did not fit well into either of the chosen paradigms, even if they had made up the overwhelming majority of victims of industrialized murder at Birkenau.

The competition's announcement also illustrated the problem of lending the commemoration of Auschwitz victims, their "message," and their memory a degree of tangibility in the form of a monument. Would an abstract design adequately reflect and mediate the memory of all those—Jews and Gypsies, Belgians and Poles, criminals and priests—to whom the monument was dedicated? Would abstraction deprive the monument of any historical or didactic meaning? Obviously, abstract images are not as easily apprehended as the concrete, but at the same time, the vagueness of their form can make them more inclusive of the diversity of victim groups at Auschwitz. As one of the museum's position papers stated: "One must be conscious of how difficult it will be to give the proper form to such a comprehensive and rich content. For these reasons the memorial must be as monumental as the content it is intended to express."[32] One is then tempted to ask how monumental the "content" of Auschwitz is. Is it three, five, or seven meters high? Is the content worthy of concrete, granite, or marble? The point here is that the message and content of the monument—despite the competition's guidelines—remained unclear, and therefore remained open to diverse interpretations on the part of both the artists and the jury evaluating their work. Given this ambivalence, it should come as no surprise that the tasks of evaluating artists' submissions, as well as those of financing, constructing, and dedicating the monument, became painful and protracted processes.

The official evaluative jury met for the first time in April 1958. Reflecting the international character of the competition, the jury included Giuseppe Perugini (Italy) and J. B. Bakema (Netherlands) from the International Union of Architects; Henry Moore (England–chairman of the jury) and August Zamoyski (Poland/England) from the International Union of Art; Odette Elina (France) and Romuald Gutt (Poland) from the International Auschwitz Committee; and Pierre Courthion (France) from the International Association of Art Critics. More than four hundred proposals, representing the work of 685 artists and architects, were submitted from thirty-six countries as diverse as Argentina, Ceylon, Finland, New Zealand, Portugal, and the United States.[33] The Auschwitz Museum then displayed models of the submissions in a public exhibit in Blocks 16, 17, and 18 of the base camp.[34] Given the vagueness of the IAC's announcement and the diversity of submissions, the jury faced a formidable challenge—a challenge perhaps exacerbated by the composition of the jury itself. As James Young has noted:

> Members [of the jury] considered both sculptural and architectonic designs, some representative of contemporary cutting-edge work, others exemplary of early twentieth-century modernism, and still others gesturing back to romantic and figurative forms of the nineteenth century. Judging a competition in the midst of early abstract expressionism and headed by the greatest contemporary material formalist in modern sculpture [Moore], the committee faced a difficult task indeed. How would they balance the needs of a lay public against the obscure sensibilities of contemporary art, knowing that the ultimate design would have to be approved by government authorities?[35]

Unable to arrive upon a single winner, the jury instead selected seven designs to be evaluated at a subsequent meeting, which had a surprising result:

the jury accepted none of the seven proposals and requested instead that the three favored teams (the Polish group led by Oskar Hansen, an Italian collective around Julio Lafuente, and a second Italian team led by Maurizio Vitale)[36] submit further proposals, preferably as a collaborative effort of the three groups. The challenge to the jury and its inability to arrive at a decision are perhaps best explained by the words of its chairman, Henry Moore:

> The choice of a monument to commemorate Auschwitz has not been an easy task. Essentially, what has been attempted has been the creation—or, in the case of the jury, the choice—of a monument to crime and ugliness, to murder and to horror. The crime was of such stupendous proportions that any work of art must be on an appropriate scale. But, apart from this, is it in fact possible to create a work of art that can express the emotions engendered by Auschwitz? It is my conviction that a very great sculptor—a new Michelangelo or a new Rodin—might have achieved this. The odds against such a design turning up among the many maquettes submitted were always enormous. And none did.[37]

By evoking Michelangelo and Rodin, Moore emphasized the near impossibility of creating and judging an appropriate monument. Moreover, the comment reveals his perception of what that monument and its "message" were to be. For Moore, it was to be a monument "to crime and ugliness, to murder and to horror." There is here a conspicuous absence of any mention of fraternity, struggle, or heroism—those elements that were to come to the fore, according to the competition's announcement. For Moore, then, the Birkenau monument was to be a monument to crime and death rather than resistance and survival. This tension over the narrative content of the monument was likely one of the reasons why the jury had such difficulty selecting a suitable design that conformed to the wishes of the IAC and, more importantly, why the design that the jury finally approved was never faithfully reproduced on the grounds of Birkenau.

Rather than developing new designs individually, the three finalists complied with the jury's wishes and submitted a collaborative proposal. It was accepted, with some modifications, by the jury in May 1959[38] and approved by the Polish Ministry of Culture and Art the following year.[39] This design, combining elements of the proposals of all three artistic teams, called for the gate at Birkenau's main guard tower to be symbolically barred. A paved path would then run along the railroad tracks from the gate all the way to Crematoria II and III, where massive stone blocks recalling boxcars and sarcophagi were to be erected. A passage would lead from that point into a depression, at the edge of which could be viewed the ruins of the crematoria and the camp.[40]

Despite approval by both the jury and Ministry of Culture and Art, the monument was never constructed in this form. Cost was likely a significant factor. The official, and certainly legitimate, reason for the design's rejection in the end was that such a monument would violate the integrity of the memorial site, which, according to the Polish statute from July 1947, was to have the unaltered character of a "historic preserve." Aesthetic and political issues, however, may also have influenced the decision to further modify the design, for its images of the railroad siding, boxcars, and sarcophagi between the crematoria suggested the path of the unregistered Jewish deportee sent directly to the gas chamber, but evoked little of the struggle and heroism of the registered political prisoner.

In order to arrive at a solution acceptable to all, a technical commission was called to Paris in December 1961. This meeting sent the artists back once again to their drawing boards with the stipulation that the next version of the monument be severely reduced in size to fit the area between the crematoria at the end of the railroad siding; the rest of Birkenau, the commission decided, was to remain in its current state and, as ever, a charge of the Polish state.[41] These decisions reflected both the aesthetic priority of leaving the Birkenau site as "untouched" as possible and the political priority of keeping the site and its landscape firmly under Polish control. In December 1962 the IAC's board of directors met in Budapest, where they approved this proposal and prepared a new construction budget, this time utilizing less expensive Polish raw materials and labor.[42] Construction of the monument then began in 1963.[43]

Artistic concerns and a lack of unanimity had thus far characterized the process of evaluating designs for the monument, and continual concerns over the cost of the project augmented these challenges. Contrary to initial expectations, donations for the monument were not flowing in at the necessary rate, and in the end it was this lack of financial support from around Europe that would put the project once again firmly in Polish hands. Already in 1958 the IAC had called for the establishment of an international patronage committee to bolster the initiative's public image and to aid in soliciting funds.

The IAC hoped that the support of important personalities from the international scientific and cultural communities would bring greater international recognition to the monument project and encourage both private and government donations to its construction fund. In 1961 the patronage committee, which by then included notables such as Niels Bohr, Pablo Casals, and François Mauriac, issued an appeal to seventy-seven governments and sixty-five organizations worldwide. "Auschwitz-Birkenau," it stated,

> is a camp like no other. Gigantic in the immensity of the crime, gigantic in the heroism of its resistance, gigantic in its dimensions. The monument should be of commensurate dimensions.
>
> It is well that all, survivors and families of the vanished, symbolically bring their offerings for the construction of this immense tomb, but it is not possible to do it without the moral and financial participation of governments of all nations. . . .
>
> Auschwitz-Birkenau is not the cemetery of one nation,
>
> Auschwitz-Birkenau is the cemetery of the world.
>
> The International Patronage Committee is appealing to your high authority to ask for a contribution from your country to the construction of this monumental sepulchre.
>
> This gesture will be a solemn affirmation of your willingness to work with other peoples, without distinction of race, ideology, or religion, in order that there will never again be an Auschwitz.[44]

Reflecting both the broad internationalism of the monument initiative and the heroic-martyr commemorative paradigm set by the IAC in 1957, the appeal and the support of the patronage committee, if only formal, certainly lent the monument initiative a higher degree of credibility. Moreover, the committee's appeal suggested that the site was no longer the sole cultural property of the Polish state, of German history, of an organization of former political prisoners, or of the survivors of those who had perished there. Rather, Auschwitz, its memory, its continued care, and its monument were to be the responsibility of all.

Credibility and publicity, for all they were worth, did not translate into much-needed resources for the monument's construction. Auschwitz may have been a "cemetery of the world," but the world was not yet willing to offer its financial support for the erection of a monument there. Despite the efforts of the International Patronage Committee, and despite the reductions in the size and cost of the project, the lack of funds continued to threaten its viability. An accounting of donations from 1958 until 1963 reveals a wide disparity of financial support among twenty-seven different countries, both in terms of private and government donations. The patronage committee's eloquent appeal notwithstanding, in June of 1961 only three governments had offered financial support, and the 394,000 francs in the committee's coffers by 1963 were not even sufficient to begin construction of the monument, the total cost of which, in the end, would amount to some 2,000,000 francs.[45] International financial support had been so disappointing that the IAC board of directors consequently requested that Poland's Council for the Protection of Monuments of Struggle and Martyrdom, a state organization under the aegis of the Ministry of Culture and Art, assume further responsibility for the monument's construction. In May 1964 the IAC and Ministry of Culture and Art signed an agreement according to which the Council would see to the completion of the monument as planned and would assume financial responsibility for it as well.[46]

This transfer of responsibilities was a watershed in the biography of the Birkenau monument, for it represented the failure of the International Auschwitz Committee to bring to fruition its plan for an international and internationally funded memorial. A vague, yet monumental conceptualization, lack of interest abroad, the politically slanted reputation of the International Auschwitz Committee, dilatory methods on the part of the Polish Ministry of Culture and Art, and, not least, the inherent difficulty of arriving at a suitable design—these were the problems that were ultimately responsible for the failure of the endeavor as it was initially conceived in 1957. In the end, placing the future of the monument in the hands of Poland's Council for the Protection of Monuments of Struggle and Martyrdom would undermine the intended international spirit and practice of the project. Artists from around the world had submitted proposals for the competition. These, in turn, had been evaluated by an international jury. Member organizations in various countries had solicited funds under the patronage of an international committee. And yet the effort failed, not least because of insufficient financial support—a situation unimaginable to Jerzy Brandhuber as he conceptualized, behind the wires of the camp in 1944, his version of the memorial. The International Auschwitz Committee continued raising funds, but by abdicating to Poland's Council for the Protection of Monuments of Struggle and Martyrdom the responsibility for financing and construction, the IAC had effectively forfeited control over the project. It is impossible to state if, when, and in what form the memorial would have been completed had this shift in responsibility not taken place. What is clear, however, is that both the final product and the monument's dedicatory ceremonies reflected Polish commemorative practices of years past, acknowledging, yet subsuming, the diverse victims of Auschwitz into a politicized and polonized commemorative idiom.

The monument dedicated on 16 April 1967 stands on a wide platform between the ruins of Crematoria II and III. The elevated portion of the complex —the monument itself—rises from the platform at its western (rear) border to a backdrop of flagpoles and trees. It consists of a forty-meter row of block-like sandstone figures of different sizes and shapes, some resembling sarcophagi, some resembling human shapes. Right of center stands a tower fronted by vaguely human cubist figures, and fixed to the upper portion of the tower is a plate of black marble with a small triangle in the center. In front of the tower lies a stone tablet with a text documenting the award of the Polish Grunwald Cross, First Class to the victims of Auschwitz. In front of the wide row of sandstone blocks lie, at a distance of several meters, twenty-one stone tablets. At the time of the monument's unveiling, there were nineteen tablets, offering the following explanatory text in nineteen languages: "Four million people suffered and died here at the hands of the Nazi murderers between the years 1940 and 1945."[47]

The monument is abstract, and its narrative and affective content derive not from explanatory inscriptions or representational devices, but either from the monument's intrinsic form or from the foreknowledge that the visitor brings to the site. A high level of abstraction was, arguably, necessary in order for the monument to be inclusive. It was intended, after all, to honor 4 million dead from many countries. But most would argue that in this case, a greater degree of specificity regarding the identity of the victims was necessary. The sarcophagus-like sandstone forms and the cubist figures in front of the tower could be construed to resemble women, men, or children. But the reasons why these people died in Birkenau—and the fact that that the vast majority of them were Jews—would be lost on the uninformed visitor. The nineteen explanatory tablets in front of the monument lent only a modicum of identity to the victims, stating that they were 4 million "people," "victims" (in the German and Polish texts), or "men, women, and children" (as the

French text stated), and that their murderers were, depending on the language used, "Nazis" or "Hitlerites." Despite the efforts of the IAC president Robert Waitz to have the Jewish dead specifically recognized on the tablets prior to the monument's dedication, the texts remained vague.[48]

If any characterization of the Birkenau dead emerged from this recondite memorial, it was not that of the victim of the gas chambers, but that of the hero. Several features would lead the observer to this conclusion. The first was the text in Polish that remains inscribed in front of the central tower of the monument to this day. On the occasion of the monument's dedication, the Polish Council of State resolved to award the victims of Auschwitz the Order of the Grunwald Cross, First Class, the highest honor bestowed on a servant of the nation. "To the heroes of Auschwitz," the text read, "who here suffered death in the struggle against Nazi genocide, for freedom and human dignity, for peace and the brotherhood of nations. In homage to their martyrdom and heroism, the Council of State of the People's Republic of Poland awards them the Order of the Grunwald Cross, First Class."[49] Embedded in this text were the traditional and recurring themes of Auschwitz memorialization as it had been conducted over the previous twenty years: the prisoner or deportee had not died in vain, but as a martyr upholding his or her ideals, thus earning the honor and respect of the Polish nation. Above the dedicatory text was fixed the symbol of the order: a bronze symmetrical cross embossed with two swords over a shield. For the visitor unable to read the accompanying text, the cross, swords, and shield would be perhaps the only clearly recognizable images.

The design of the monument complemented the commendatory text by evoking the paradigmatic image of the political prisoner. Attached to the tower was a black marble square with an inverted triangle at its center, suggesting the symbol of the political prisoner at Auschwitz. The marble plate was a late addition to the monument. The design approved in 1962 had called for the upper half of the tower to consist of three protruding abstract figures, which were mounted as planned during the monument's construction. But as James Young relates, "For one week, the figures stood as workers cleaned the grounds in preparation for the official dedication. At the last minute, however, the carved stones were moved from their pedestal to the ground in front and replaced by a great polished square of black marble with a triangle in the middle. To this day, there has been no official explanation for this change, which we know about only through snapshots taken by workers during the installation."[50] Spielmann has also made note of this change, and speculates that the figures were moved because of the influence of "political groups . . . that declared themselves in disagreement with the fact that on the monument there was no symbol to be seen."[51] Extrapolating even further, Young suggests that

> the stones did not satisfactorily define the political character of the victims desired by the authorities. Although the triangle represents all the victims, it does so in the figure of specifically political inmates. By contrast, the different sizes of stones in the initial sculpture suggested children, who could not have been killed as political prisoners, but only as Jews. In 1967, the discerning critical eye of the authorities apparently caught this subtlety of meaning, which led them to replace human figures with a symbol of political suffering.[52]

Young's explanation is certainly credible when placed within the context of traditional Polish commemorative practice at Auschwitz. It was, above all, the memory of the political prisoner that the monument was intended to evoke, and the added triangle further suggests the political prisoner as victim. As Young indicates, this marked a further politicization of the monument, the first consequence of which was the effacement of any reference to the racial war against the Jews. In other words, the change appeared to be a last-minute attempt to elevate the political over the human element at Auschwitz—a goal that, even if it was not explicit in the design of the monument itself, was certainly achieved at its dedicatory ceremonies.

Commemoration of the twenty-second anniversary of the liberation of Auschwitz in April 1967 was the largest public event ever held at the site, and the dedication of the "Monument to the Victims of Fascism," as it was officially called, was the centerpiece of the day. In many respects it was much like other commemorative occasions at Auschwitz over the previous twenty years. Crowds, flags, and speeches were essential to the ceremonies, and the themes of antifascist resistance, patriotism, peace, and brotherhood echoed throughout. But April 16, 1967 was different. Previous observances and commemorations at the site had traditionally been public gatherings for Poles; the unveiling of the Birkenau monument, however, drew tremendous attention from abroad and can therefore be understood as the first fully "international" event held at the State Museum at Auschwitz. This may appear paradoxical, for over the previous ten years the lack of international interest and financial support from abroad had slowed construction of the monument and effectively had placed responsibility for it in Polish hands. The highly publicized April ceremonies, however, reached the wider European public and, through the presence of countless journalists, the world.

The sheer number of participants on the Birkenau moor was overwhelming. Authorities had expected a gathering of 100,000–120,000,[53] but the crowd swelled to an estimated 200,000 by the time the ceremonies concluded.[54] "On this beaming spring Sunday," a journalist recalled, "endless lines of buses, cars, and double-deck special trains rolled in from every direction to Auschwitz. For the fifty-six kilometers from Kraków the convoy took two-and-a-half hours."[55] Although the vast majority of participants were undoubtedly Poles, there were also many participants from abroad, including members of the IAC and other prisoners' organizations; representatives of the International Buchenwald, Dachau, Mauthausen, Neuengamme, Ravensbrück, and Sachsenhausen Committees; delegates of the Fédération Internationale de Résistance and the World Jewish Congress; and veterans of the Fifty-Fourth Army of the First Ukrainian Front who had liberated the camp in 1945. Also attending were members of the International Patronage Committee, the monument's evaluative jury, and the artists responsible for its design. Not least, the ceremonies were honored by the presence of former prisoners and families of those who had perished in the camp, some from as far away as Israel and Argentina.[56]

Significantly, the International Auschwitz Committee was not involved in the organization of the day's events, which had been left in the hands of ZBoWiD, the Council for the Protection of Monuments of Struggle and Martyrdom, and the Kraków and Oświęcim Party organizations. A public spectacle in every respect, the ceremonies also included the opening of a special exhibition in Auschwitz I on Nazi crimes against children and the premier performance of Krzysztof Penderecki's oratorio *Dies Irae,* commissioned for the occasion. In addition, special postcards and stamps were issued in observance of the day, and the entire Birkenau proceedings, lasting more than two hours, were broadcast on Polish Radio, Polish Television, and the European networks "Intervision" and "Eurovision."[57]

The ceremonies began with a parade of a Polish Army honor guard, followed by the singing of the Polish national anthem[58] and an address by Premier Józef Cyrankiewicz. As in the past, Cyrankiewicz used the memorial site as a political platform, and on this occasion he applauded Poland's ally, the German Democratic Republic, for drawing the proper political and socio-economic consequences from the tragedy of National Socialism. The premier was, at the same time, highly critical of the German Federal Republic for its failure to pursue Nazi criminals, for attempting to erase the bitter memory of Nazism, and for claiming, twenty-two years after the defeat of National Socialism, that it was the only legitimate government of Germany— a Germany within the borders of 1937. Yet the bulk of Cyrankiewicz's lengthy speech was devoted to a characterization of the Auschwitz crime, its brutality, and, significantly, its uniqueness. "There are other mass cemeteries in the world, if none so great as this," he stated,

> but in spite of this, they express something different, for death [at these other sites] was different. Those who fought in the Battle of Verdun, on the Somme, and at Leningrad, at Dunkirk, Tobruk, and Narvik, at Monte Cassino, Lenino, and Pommernwall, on the Normandy coast—they died a soldier's death, armed with a weapon, in combat with the enemy, in the fire of battle.
>
> They fell in battle and a different death looked them in the eyes. That is why these cemeteries express something tragic, but different from those in Auschwitz, Maidanek, Treblinka, Sobibór, and Babi Yar. For they are military cemeteries, and here are the cemeteries of genocide.

The distinction drawn by Cyrankiewicz is important, and was all too rare in the public commemorative vocabulary of postwar Poland. Noting as well that the Third Reich was the first state in history to erect death factories for women, children, and the elderly, the premier suggested, if only indirectly, that Nazi genocide had been directed against the defenseless, not on the battlefield, but in the *shtetl*, in the ghetto, and in the gas chamber. The premier's speech failed, however, to bring this line of thought to its explicit and necessary conclusion—that the victims of Nazi genocide in Europe and at Auschwitz in particular were overwhelmingly Jews. Ironically, by setting the noncombatant Auschwitz dead apart from soldiers who fell in battle, Cyrankiewicz, perhaps inadvertently, excluded them from the category of the martyr-patriot memorialized by the inscription on the monument itself "who here suffered death in the struggle against Nazi genocide."

The culmination of the day's ceremonies was the unveiling of the monument to the howl of sirens and a salvo from nearby artillery. As an additional accent, Vice-Minister of Culture Kazimierz Rusinek read a public appeal directed to all people of the world. Speaking in his capacity as secretary-general of ZBoWiD, Rusinek called to mind in this statement not only global international responsibility for the site, but also the spiritual presence of the Auschwitz dead:

> Gathered here, on the 16th of April 1967, on the largest cemetery in the world, we honor the victims of the extermination camp Auschwitz-Birkenau in the conviction that the shadows of the four million are with us and that their thoughts are in us.
> With us here are the shadows of the patriots and fighters of the antifascist resistance movement, the prisoners of war of all fronts, and the partisans who, across the entire continent, fought for human dignity. With us are the brutally murdered Jews from all of Europe; with us are those who did not go silently and humbly to their deaths, but fought in the rubble of the Warsaw Ghetto to their dying breath.

Rusinek's words were, on the one hand, unique, because specific reference to Jewish victims was not the norm at public events such as this. It appears, however, that his public appeal was an attempt to imbue the victims of the Shoah with a degree of heroism more typically associated with the resistance fighter and soldier. Rather than distinguishing the victims of genocide, as had Cyrankiewicz, from heroes of the battlefield and underground, the vice-minister armed the Jews and praised the heroes of the Warsaw Ghetto as archetypal Jewish martyrs. Although the Jewish dead at Birkenau may have been effaced from the monument itself, Rusinek's public appeal aimed at their assimilation among the fighters and martyrs of Auschwitz I.

The speech by Robert Waitz, president of the International Auschwitz Committee, was one of the most remarkable moments of the day. Recalling camp's inhumane conditions and the mechanics of the extermination process, the content of the address was unusual in at least one respect: it explicitly referred to the high percentage of Jews among those murdered at Auschwitz.

> Among the four million victims, the overwhelming majority were Jews. Auschwitz was, among other camps, the largest center for their extermination. This extermination took on a special character. It dealt the entire Jewish

population—men, women, and children—a decisive blow. This extermination was typical mass genocide. If not for the victory of the allies, the European Jews would have fully fallen victim to the Nazi "Final Solution." The Nazis intended to prepare a similar fate for other peoples.[59]

Distinguishing Jewish victims in this way would today be intrinsic to any speech on an occasion such as this. In April 1967, however, it was exceptional, as noted by a number of journalists from abroad. The New York Jewish newspaper *Aufbau* observed, for example, that "the course of the ceremonies did not live up to even the smallest expectations of human decency . . . that three-fourths of the victims of Auschwitz could not in any way be mentioned in the ceremonies."[60] The *Frankfurter allgemeine Zeitung* likewise criticized the lack of a Jewish presence in the day's events, stating that the ceremony "had the character of a performance of the Polish state."[61] In fact, the only "events" of the day dedicated specifically to Jews were recitations of Kaddish by several Jewish groups—Greek, Israeli, American—at the Hebrew and Yiddish commemorative tablets in front of the monument. These informal rituals were not, however, part of the day's official program, but were small, independently organized gatherings.[62] Other Jews also held their own individual commemorative observances. An American journalist recounted, for example, how

> an old woman clambered on the steel-and-concrete ruins of the camp's Crematory III today after the ceremony had ended, the bands departed, the speeches made. She swayed rhythmically from side to side as she silently read from her prayer book the Kaddish, the Jewish prayer for the dead. . . . The old woman finished the prayer, kissed the book and returned it to the shopping bag she had held between her feet while she prayed. From the bag she took a candle that Jews light on the anniversary of a loved one's death. She lit it, put it in a sheltered spot deep in the rubble of the furnace, climbed down to the ground and left silently. . . . Men and women came, said silent prayers and tried to control their weeping. They placed small bouquets or single flowers on the rubble of Crematory III. Their flowers touched the heart no less than the hundreds of formal wreaths that had been placed on the monument by delegations and governmental representatives.[63]

According to some Western observers, Jews had been forbidden to recite their prayers in the context of the official proceedings.[64] Whether this was the case or not, it is clear that aside from Waitz's speech and the brief references of Cyrankiewicz and Rusinek, the only commemoration of the specifically Jewish dead at Auschwitz occurred outside the event's official agenda—a stark reminder of the all-encompassing, yet ultimately exclusive commemorative choreography and rhetoric of the day. Jews were the object not of explicit, but only implicit commemoration. Their memory, publicly assimilated into the memory of non-Jewish dead at Auschwitz, could only be honored privately. Moreover, it is significant that specific recognition of the Jewish dead at Auschwitz was introduced by guests, speakers, and pilgrims from abroad. Polish choreographers of the day welcomed an international presence at the event, but that international presence had to remain tentative and on the margins, lest it too obviously introduce the Shoah into the Auschwitz narrative.

Criticisms of the day's proceedings were appropriate, but in light of the commemorative traditions at Auschwitz over the preceding two decades it is surprising that the content of the ceremonies caused such a stir among foreign observers. For example, a German journalist, struck by the politicized character of the event, observed:

> More and more, or so it seems from this ceremony, Auschwitz-Birkenau is to become a symbol of the present political struggle and Polish resistance against the occupation. Publications and the inscriptions on the memorial plaques of the monument do not distinguish between the hundred thousand political prisoners who died here and the millions of men, women, and children who, defenseless and without resistance, were gassed here because of their faith and hair color.[65]

Contrary to this writer's claim, this was not a new direction in state-sponsored commemoration at Auschwitz, nor was the memorial site "becoming a symbol of the present political struggle." It had served for twenty years as a political arena for the Warsaw government, and the April 1967 ceremonies were only the latest point on a continuum of political instrumentalization.

The historian Michal Borwicz, one of the few scholars to address this issue in those years, placed the ceremonies in the context of the "anti-Zionist campaign" of the late Gomułka years. Although that context is certainly appropriate, his claim that the monument's dedication was the "official start of the campaign aimed to 'dejudaize' the Auschwitz necropolis"[66] is misleading, for it suggests that "dejudaization" at the site was a new phenomenon. Marginalization, neglect, and understatement of the Jewish presence were not, after all, new at Auschwitz. April 1967 was simply one manifestation of a twenty-year tradition, albeit on a larger and more publicized scale. What these contemporary analyses revealed, then, was a lack of familiarity with the established currents of Polish martyrology and memory at postwar Auschwitz. If criticism of commemorative rhetoric and practices proliferated in the aftermath of the April 1967 ceremonies, they should be regarded not only as a response to the manipulations of the past undertaken there, but also as a function of the growing public profile and internationalization of the memorial site.

Auschwitz and the "Anti-Zionist" Campaign

For two decades, murdered Jews had been marginalized or assimilated into official public memory at Auschwitz. The late 1960s, however, saw the removal of living Jews from the Polish state and society. The so-called "anti-Zionist" campaign, along with the resulting purges and emigration of Jews, stands as one of the great blemishes in postwar Polish history. Anti-Jewish outbursts, repressive government measures, and internal purges were not unknown in postwar Polish society. Anti-Semitism, both latent and overt, racial and political, had always existed; there were pogroms in 1945–46; the "Polish October" in 1956 saw the removal of Jews from high-level positions in the state apparatus, some because they were regarded as Stalinists, while others were condemned by opponents of the democratic revival and reform of the early Gomułka era.[67] The "anti-Zionist" campaign of the late 1960s, however, was a broad movement within the party that elicited condemnation from around the world. The campaign was certainly directed from above, but it found a receptive, or at least passive audience at various levels of society, and was also the first case of official Polish anti-Semitism that directly intersected with the state of affairs at Auschwitz. This was, in this era of the internationalization of the site, an illustration of how political developments in Poland and abroad could influence the interpretation and representation of history there.

Political anti-Semitism in Poland—always officially condemned by the regime—and the marginalization of Jewish memory at Auschwitz had over-lapped, but still operated independently of one another for some twenty years. The communist regime's stance on the Jewish past had certainly influenced the landscape and commemorative ritual at the Auschwitz site, but beginning in 1967 there was a clear and obvious relationship between anti-Semitism at the state level and the configurations of official memory of Auschwitz, both in Polish society at large and at the State Museum. One manifestation of this was the attempt to revise scholarship and public opinion on the issue of relative Jewish and Polish suffering during the Second World War. In addition, state-supported anti-Semitism in Poland caused a near-fatal fracture in the International Auschwitz Committee, severely undermining its independence and in-ternational credibility. Most significantly, the "anti-Zionist campaign" had a direct, if paradoxical, effect on the character of the Auschwitz Museum. It did not result in continued or intensified exclusion of the Jews from official mem-ory at the Auschwitz site; instead, state-sponsored anti-Semitism resulted in a new exhibition block devoted to Jewish suffering and struggle.

The anti-Jewish measures of the late 1960s[68] were neither a spontaneous outburst of popular anti-Semitism nor the sole property of the communist re-gime. The post-October euphoria over Gomułka and his 1956 reforms did not last long; by the late 1950s there was popular discontent over economic stagna-tion, unfulfilled expectations of democratic reform and cultural liberalization, and the enduring, if weakened, Stalinist presence and praxis in the state appa-ratus.[69] In the decade following Gomułka's rise to power, anti-Semitism seemed rather dormant on the surface, but within the PZPR it became an im-portant political issue in a growing factional struggle.

For years there had existed within the party a so-called "Partisan" faction composed predominantly of former resistance fighters and veterans who, as they believed, had laid the groundwork for the communist assumption of power in postwar Poland, only to lose their influence to a Moscow-trained elite. These nationally minded, yet devoted, communists had also been frus-trated by the post-October reforms, such as Gomułka's more liberal and tol-erant stance toward the Roman Catholic Church and toward critics of the regime. At the head of the Partisan group, which by the 1960s included many new and younger functionaries, stood General Mieczysław Moczar, minister of the interior, president of ZBoWiD, and Gomułka's main rival for power within the party apparatus.

Gomułka's policy toward Jews within the party was aimed at their gradual disappearance from the echelons of power, either through attrition or an occasional demotion, but not through large-scale purges. A "Jewish question" therefore existed within the PZPR, but was not used as a powerful political weapon. It was primarily General Moczar who, in the words of Łukasz Hirszowicz,

> transformed the Jewish issue into an instrument for gathering support in the party *apparat* and among the public. Moczar aimed at supreme power—that is, at replacing Gomułka—and harping on the Jewish issue and arranging limited purges of Jewish personnel was a way of both strengthening his faction and undermining the position of the Gomułka leadership which, in this context, could be presented as "soft on the Jews," linked with the Jews (real and imaginary), and even as almost Jewish.[70]

Moczar had been covertly preparing for anti-Jewish measures since the early 1960s, when, as minister of the interior, he named Tadeusz Walichnowski as head of the Department of Nationalities and began collecting data and keeping files on Poles of Jewish heritage. The Six-Day War in June 1967 provided Moczar and his faction with the perfect occasion to intensify anti-Jewish measures, to draw Gomułka into the fray, and to destabilize the party's upper cadres. As the noted Polish author Andrzej Szczypiorski recalled:

> [H]istory smiled graciously for the new generation of party functionaries. At the peak of power sat people of Jewish origin. Meanwhile, in the Sinai Desert Jews were smashing up the armies of Nasser's Egypt, an ally of the Soviet Union. There was nothing simpler than to declare war on the supporters of Zionism, who occupied lucrative posts in the apparatus of power. These functionaries had never been Zionist but had always been loyal Communists. Just because of that, the fight against them proved to be easier. Who in Poland would sympathize with the fate of a party gang that was guilty of so many misdeeds during the Stalin era?[71]

Poland's new anti-Israel stance thus gave Gomułka cause to intensify measures against Jews within the party in the name of "anti-Zionism," "anti-imperialism," and the fight against "cosmopolitans." It would be inappropriate, however, to see a direct causal nexus between the Six-Day War and the anti-Jewish measures of the months and years to follow. Instead, the war served as a pretext for the acceleration and intensification of purges already underway,[72] and in exploiting the Arab-Israeli conflict, Gomułka initiated a reaction within the party and society that with the help of Moczar's machinations developed a dynamic of its own.

Familiar stereotypes emerged once again. Polish citizens of Jewish descent were now associated not with Jewish-inspired communism (the so-called żydokomuna), but with the vestiges of Stalinism. Jews were not true Poles, but cosmopolitans without a fatherland who, because of their (alleged) Zionist and imperialist leanings, were undermining the fabric of Polish socialism and the Polish nation. The defamation, discrimination, and purging reached its peak in March of the following year, when antigovernment protests, led mostly by students and initiated in response to censorship and lack of democracy in public life, swept across the country. Seeking to link the protesters and dissent in general with an unreliable Jewish element, the purges extended to nearly all areas of public life: the party, bureaucracy, economics, education, and the arts. Gomułka and Moczar were using the anti-Jewish measures at cross-purposes, however. Gomułka, by casting Poland's remaining Jews in role of scapegoat, hoped to exploit the anti-Semitic frenzy as a form of "negative integration," thereby solidifying the regime and status quo in the country. Moczar, on the other hand, intended to destabilize Gomułka's hold on power and then fill the vacuum.[73] The result was international condemnation from outside the Soviet bloc and, by the time the hysteria waned in late 1968, the exclusion of some nine thousand "Zionist traitors" from the ranks of the party and the emigration of twenty thousand Polish Jews. A prewar Jewish community of 3 million had numbered in 1967 only thirty thousand (that is, less than 1 percent of the population), and after the witch-hunts of the late 1960s, only some ten thousand remained.[74]

Developments at Auschwitz in 1967 and 1968 may be only a footnote in the broader history of the "anti-Zionist" campaign, but the months of anti-Jewish agitation loomed large in the history of the memorial site. The campaign had, as noted above, three major consequences: an attempt to revise scholarship and public opinion regarding relative Jewish and Polish Gentile suffering during the Second World War; the fracture and near disintegration of the International Auschwitz Committee; and the attempt to restore some of Poland's international credibility by the erection of an exhibition in Block 27 of the base camp dedicated to the "Martyrology and Struggle of the Jews."

For two decades Polish historians and the stewards of memory at Auschwitz had included Poland's Jewish victims of the Holocaust in the larger and less precise categories of national losses. The conventional claim was that Poland lost some 6 million citizens in the war, among them many Jews. Relative Polish and Jewish losses had never been a contentious issue, however, until that issue became useful for anti-Jewish propaganda purposes. Beginning late in the summer of 1967, a number of articles appeared attacking the most recent (1966) edition of the *Wielka Encyklopedia Powszechna* (Great Universal Encyclopedia), a respected Polish reference work, for supposed inaccuracies regarding human losses suffered in Poland during the war. According to one journalist condemning the publication, the *Encyklopedia* entry on "Hitlerite Concentration Camps"[75] had minimized Poland's non-Jewish losses by stating that "in the extermination camps approximately 5.7 million died (ca. 99 percent Jews, ca. 1 percent Gypsies and others)." This "manipulation" of historical facts, the author implied, was the inspiration of imperialist West German and American anti-Polish propaganda bent on minimizing Polish losses during the war and defaming Poland's good name.[76]

The total number of extermination camp victims cited in the 1966 edition of the *Encyklopedia* was inflated, but the number of Jewish deaths relative to other victim groups—according to the article approximately 99 percent— was accurate. In an atmosphere of anti-Jewish agitation, however, the possibility of Polish wartime losses being diminished through a comparison to Jewish losses was intolerable and constituted cause for revision of the official historical record. In November 1967 the vice-minister of culture and head of ZBoWiD, Kazimierz Rusinek, attacked the *Encyklopedia* and the historian responsible for this entry, Janusz Gumkowski.[77] Rusinek argued that it was misleading to differentiate, as Gumkowski had, between the concentration camp and extermination camp. To do so, he claimed, confused the reader, gave undue emphasis to the "final solution," and silenced the losses of other nations.[78] That Rusinek chose this particular moment to attack Gumkowski and the *Encyklopedia* makes clear that he was less concerned about overcoming distortions of scholarship than about finding yet another outlet for the regime's anti-Semitic campaign. The *Encyklopedia*'s "errors" were but a pretext for the purging of Jewish members of the editorial staff, some of whom were even imprisoned.[79]

Gumkowski's successor at the central commission, Czesław Pilichowski, then published, at the height of the anti-Jewish campaign, two revisionist articles in the PZPR organ *Trybuna Ludu.*[80] These were not works of corrective scholarship, but a clumsy effort to unmask what Pilichowski argued were the distorting claims of "Zionist" propaganda. In the second article, for example, the author portrayed Polish Gentiles as heroic rescuers even as he advocated further investigation of the role of the Jewish Councils in the ghettos, the activities of Jewish police in the extermination process, and Jewish collaboration with the Gestapo. Many of the "Zionists" and "nationalists" who had collaborated, the author claimed, were now to be found in Western countries and Israel.[81]

Marginalization of the Shoah had been a central characteristic of postwar Polish memory of the occupation, and Poles had never been encouraged to focus on Jews as victims of Nazi persecution. Even if publications such as these were not a major revision of the official historical record, they did represent a renegotiation of Polish considerations of the Shoah. At the very least, they encouraged the reader to regard statistics (and even Polish statistics, such as those provided in the 1966 edition of the *Encyklopedia*) on Jewish wartime deaths with skepticism or to dismiss them outright as "Zionist" fabrications. The propagandists of the campaign were quick to suggest that Jewish behavior during the occupation was not patriotic and self-sacrificing like that of Gentile Poles, but self-serving and ultimately treasonous[82]—in other words, like the behavior of the "Zionists" and "imperialists" working to undermine the reputation and integrity of the Polish people and state. The implication was that the Jewish dead at Auschwitz were no longer worthy of the designation "martyr," and that their behavior was to be regarded with suspicion— effectively moving them into what Primo Levi has described as the "gray zone" within the triangle of perpetrator, victim, and bystander.[83] Politically motivated changes to the official historical record, such as these, in combination with the broader anti-Semitic measures undertaken by the Polish state, had serious repercussions for the further internationalization of the Auschwitz site, including the crippling fracture of its weakened patron, the International Auschwitz Committee.

After relinquishing its control over the construction of the Birkenau monument to the Polish Council for the Protection of Monuments of Struggle and Martyrdom in 1964, the International Auschwitz Committee slowly came under the control of ZBoWiD. Throughout the 1960s ZBoWiD had steadily increased its influence within Polish governing circles, so that by the early 1970s it was no longer simply a party front organization, but had earned itself the reputation of a center of power in the Polish state and an agitator of anti-Jewish propaganda and policy.[84] With Mieczysław Moczar at its head, ZBoWiD's control over the International Auschwitz Committee would solidify to such an extent that it would hold the IAC dependent on annual subsidies of one million zlotys, and even would have the power to name the committee's secretary-general.[85]

The IAC's loss of independence to ZBoWiD, combined with its failure to confront the anti-Semitic measures in Poland, eventually led Professor Robert Waitz of France to tender his resignation as president of the committee in March 1968. Compelling his decision were a number of specific factors ranging from inability to work with the IAC secretary-general Mieczysław Kieta, whom he regarded as ZBoWiD's puppet, to the refusal of the Polish authorities to acknowledge Jewish deaths in Birkenau, to the inappropriate date—the Sunday following the end of Passover—set for the dedication of the new Jewish exhibition in Auschwitz I. In general, however, Waitz's withdrawal from the IAC was in response to the committee's acquiescence to ZBoWiD control and its unwillingness to challenge the policies and rhetoric of Poland's campaign against Jews. As Waitz stated in his letter of resignation:

> In recent weeks, particularly during the commemoration of the Warsaw Ghetto Uprising and during the opening of the Jewish block at the Auschwitz Museum, numerous Polish leaders have not ceased opposing Jews and Zionists to justify their position against Israel and the measures that they have taken against Jews in Poland.
>
> These leaders, and among them Vice-Minister Rusinek, secretary-general of ZBoWiD, are against anti-Semitism when it relates to the millions of victims of Hitlerite racism, but they are against Israel, the refuge of several thousand Auschwitz survivors. They use the dead against the living.
>
> Personally, I cannot disassociate the one from the other. I cannot accept, under current conditions, a secretary-general of the IAC so tightly bound to ZBoWiD.[86]

Several months later Waitz publicly condemned the IAC, calling the IAC's Warsaw headquarters "an immediate creation of ZBoWiD." Lamenting the committee's lack of independence, Waitz claimed that "the interests of the eighteen organizations made up of national groups of former prisoners in all of Europe and in Israel are in the hands of the Polish government. We know its stance towards the Jews. It is all scandalous."[87]

Waitz's exit from the IAC presidency portended further divisions within the organization, as member organizations split along East-West lines over the committee's stance toward developments in Poland. Organizations from the capitalist countries protested the IAC's silence with regard to events in Poland, while government-sponsored organizations in the communist states supported Poland or at least refrained from commenting on its anti-Jewish excesses. The East German Committee of Antifascist Resistance Fighters, for one, lent its full support to the Poles by taking the position that it was not Waitz's principles that compelled him to resign, but pressure placed upon him by various Jewish groups.[88]

In 1968 the Austrian, Belgian, French, and Dutch member organizations suspended their activities with the IAC because of the Warsaw office's intransigence on the "Zionist" issue or, to be more precise, the unwillingness of the Poles and their allies to take a stand on the issue at all. According to one Austrian member, silence for Western opponents of the "anti-Zionist" crusade was no less than a betrayal both of their Jewish comrades in the camp and of the very mission of the International Auschwitz Committee, for its silence in the face of institutionalized Polish anti-Semitism had rendered the IAC useless, unable to carry on its work, and morally bankrupt.[89] The international organization that bore the name "Auschwitz" was founded in the spirit of the underground resistance, dedicated to the fight against racism, committed to perpetuating the memory of the camp, and charged as a caretaker and patron of the memorial site. But by submitting to institutionalized anti-Semitism, the IAC had failed in its mission, squandering the respect of the living and dishonoring the legacy of the dead. Severely weakened, the IAC no longer appeared able to shape or even to influence the uses and manifestations of memory at the State Museum. The International Auschwitz Committee's presence at Auschwitz since the mid-1950s had contributed to the site's continuing instrumentalization; the absence of an international and effectual IAC, however, opened the door in 1968 to a particularly conspicuous form of political exploitation: the new exhibition on the "Martyrology and Struggle of the Jews 1933–1945."

In April 1968 a small crowd gathered in front of Block 27 of the Auschwitz base camp for the dedication of this new exhibit. The first of its kind, this "Jewish pavilion" holds a paradoxical place in the history of the memorial site, for it opened even as "Zionists" were allegedly undermining the stability of Polish society and the integrity of the Polish state. The exhibit therefore prompts the question of why there was a need for such an exhibition at all. Scholars who have addressed the postwar history of the Auschwitz site either have indicated that the exhibit was closed after the Six-Day War of June 1967[90] or have referred only to a revised exhibition opened in 1978.[91] In fact, Block 27 was opened at the height of the anti-Semitic purges in the spring of 1968. In the years to follow it was closed from time to time, but not permanently, and museum records indicate that nearly fifty thousand people—a not insignificant number—visited the exhibition from 1968 to 1975.[92] Contrary to what one might assume, the presence of an exhibition on the martyrology of the Jews was not at all intolerable to the Polish authorities during the campaign against "Zionism." Nearly the opposite is true: Polish authorities were intent on opening the exhibition in 1968 when the campaign was reaching its apex, and it was the Polish government that facilitated the exhibition's rapid completion and dedication in April of that year.

In its early years the State Museum at Auschwitz had devoted a small room specifically to the memory of Jews murdered in the camp, but not until the 1960s did the museum staff and the International Auschwitz Committee initiate plans for a separate "Jewish Block" in response to the growing interest in establishing "national exhibitions" in Auschwitz I. Czechoslovakia and Hungary opened their exhibitions in 1960, followed by the German Democratic Republic and the Soviet Union in 1961.[93] Intended to enhance the international component at the site, these exhibitions were primarily devoted to the history of different countries while under Nazi occupation. As such, they did not describe in detail the fate of Czechs, Hungarians, or Soviet citizens in the Auschwitz camp, but emphasized instead suffering and, especially, resistance on the home front.[94] These additions to the museum reflected a growing openness to other memorial narratives at Auschwitz, and, by encouraging the visitor to consider the suffering of other nations, they competed with the dominant Polish-national commemorative agenda at the site.

Block 27, however, remained a special case, for it was neither a "Polish" nor an "Israeli" pavilion, but a "Jewish" pavilion developed by Poles, Polish Jews, and Israelis. When the IAC and ZBoWiD initiated plans for a Jewish exhibition in 1964,[95] the ZBoWiD secretary-general Rusinek rejected out of hand any possibility of developing it as an "Israeli" pavilion. According to Rusinek, the Jews murdered in Auschwitz had not been citizens of Israel, and the State of Israel had no right to "represent the Jewish nation" or "those Jews who are citizens of other states."[96] The argument appears sensible, but raises the question of why countries such as Poland or the GDR were entitled to represent in their exhibitions the lot of "Germans" or "Poles" during the war. Those countries were entitled to speak for Polish and German émigrés around the world; Israel, on the other hand, was not allowed to present the fate of European Jews at the hands of the Germans.

Already in 1964—three years prior to the collapse of Polish-Israeli relations—there were likely other factors at work in this prohibition against an exclusively Israeli exhibition: early signs of "anti-Zionist" agitation within ZBoWiD and in other Polish government circles, the fear that an exhibition organized by Israelis would place too great an emphasis on Jews' resistance and heroism as Jews rather than as Poles or communists, and the obvious concern that Israelis would portray Jewish persecution both at Auschwitz and across Europe as being far more extensive and deadly than that suffered by other victim groups. Any or all of these concerns may have influenced the decision to keep Block 27 firmly under the control of Poles. It is also worth noting that Rusinek made clear that "the Jewish block should have as its main theme, first and foremost, Polish Jews."[97] In other words, even if the Auschwitz Museum did not fully assimilate the annihilation of Europe's Jews into the Polish wartime tragedy, the exhibition was, nonetheless, to depict Jewish martyrdom in a restrictive and simplified Polish context, free from the complex and transnational realities of Nazi racial ideology.

Progress on the exhibition was slow until 1967, when it became politically expedient to hasten the process. By October of that year Tadeusz Hołuj of the Auschwitz Museum had prepared a preliminary draft of its blueprints, which a review commission approved and then passed on to the journalist Jan Zaborowski and the noted author Andrzej Szczypiorski for editing.[98] The exhibit was based on three main programmatic principles: first, "to show the fate, in successive steps in the history of Hitlerism, of Jews and those designated by Hitlerism as Jews"; second, "[t]o show the common fate that united Jews and German democrats during the development of the Third Reich, and that united Jews and other European peoples during the development of [Nazi] imperialism . . . especially the solidarity in struggle, suffering, and persecution on Polish territory"; and third, "[t]o pay homage to the 5 million Jews, the first victims of Hitlerism, and to all Europeans, mainly Poles, who offered aid to the Jews, defended them, and showed solidarity towards them in their struggle and suffering."[99]

Block 27 steadfastly adhered to these principles.[100] Its entrance led to a dark corridor bordered by illuminated red columns, where the visitor faced a stone bearing a paraphrase from the fourth chapter of Genesis: "Cain, what have you done with your brother Abel?" The exhibition then attempted to answer this accusatory question. The first hall was intended to chronicle the origins of anti-Semitism in modern German society and to describe how it was applied to National Socialist ideology. By documenting the writings of nineteenth-century German intellectuals such as Fichte, Lagarde, and Treitschke, and then citing their echo in Hitler's *Mein Kampf* and other Nazi tracts, the exhibit could demonstrate the progression and historical continuity in German anti-Semitic ideology.

"Construction of the Third Reich" was the exhibition's second theme. Relying heavily on documentary photographs, the displays in Hall 2 depicted both the base (capital, the military) and superstructure (the Nazi Party, *Sturmabteilung* terror, concentration camps, propaganda) of fascist power in Germany. This hall also illustrated the plight of German Jewish immigrants, as well as the indifference of many European countries to their fate. Poland, however, was a notable exception; according to the exhibition, it had been a leader among nations in providing aid to Jews fleeing Hitler's Germany.

The next room of the exhibit introduced the visitor to the early phases of the occupation in Poland. The destruction of war, summary executions, police terror and roundups, and, not least, the construction of the Auschwitz camp were all portrayed as events and measures affecting Jew and non-Jew alike. "Jews to the ghettos—Poles to the prisons," read one epigraph, while another, situated above a map of Europe surrounded by barbed wire, reminded the visitor that "Poland was conquered, but still maintained the heroic fight"—a fight common to both Poles and Jews and undertaken to avert a common fate. The exhibition thus attempted to show parallels between the Jewish and non-Jewish experience during wartime occupation, because the treatment of Polish Jews—ghettoization, deportation, and, finally, annihilation—seemed to embellish a more comprehensive Polish wartime suffering.

The next section of the exhibit addressed more directly and specifically the persecution of Jews in occupied Poland, whether in the countryside, in the camps, or in the ghettos. Facing the entrance was a brick barrier simulating a wall of the Warsaw Ghetto, and fixed to it were documents illustrating aspects of the Jews' plight there: terror, hunger, epidemics, and death. A thematic shift then juxtaposed the horror of the camps and ghettos with the indifference of nations free from Nazi occupation. The accusation of indifference was not limited to the governments of the United States and Western European countries, for the exhibition also condemned the World Jewish Congress and Jewish organizations in the United States for failing to come to the aid of European Jews. The similarity of these attacks to contemporary Polish government rhetoric, which was bent on portraying "world Zionism" as self-serving and imperialist,[101] is too striking to be coincidental: while Jews around the world were indifferent to the plight of their own, Poles, by contrast, were altruistic and heroic in their aid to Jews. Moreover, it was solidarity in the face of common suffering that characterized Polish-Jewish relations under German occupation: "All Poland suffered; all Poland fought; all Poland wanted victory." Claims such as these may have drawn upon century-old notions of Polish-Jewish solidarity in opposition to a foreign occupier,[102] but in this context they were undoubtedly intended to challenge those international visitors to the Auschwitz site who, at the apex of the "anti-Zionist" agitation in April 1968, may have regarded Poles as an anti-Semitic people with a record of indifference or even complicity in the face of Jewish suffering.

"Extermination," both in the mobile killing units and in the death camps, was the theme of the next exhibition hall. Treatment of this issue, however, was kept to a minimum in order to avoid thematic duplication of Block 4 of the main exhibition, entitled "Extermination of Millions."[103] Instead, this hall emphasized mobile killing operations in the eastern regions under German occupation, the Wannsee Conference, and the execution of the Final Solution and its application in other killing centers like Bełżec, Treblinka, and Sobibór. To detail the Auschwitz extermination process in Block 27 would certainly have duplicated some of the information offered in Block 4; but, more importantly, an emphasis on mass extermination at Auschwitz in the context of a Jewish exhibition might lead the visitor to the conclusion that the camp's extermination process was directed mainly toward Jews. As legitimate as that conclusion would have been, in 1968 it was not in Poland's interest to encourage what was regarded as a "Zionist" contention that genocide was directed toward Jews and Jews only.

The final hall of Block 27 had a votive rather than didactic atmosphere. At the center of the dimly lit room stood an illuminated, yellow-green glass column resembling a plume of smoke or gas. At its base, projected from above, was the image of the label from a can of Zyklon-B. Visible within this opaque column were shapes that merged into the contours of a human form.

If there was a salient theme in this exhibition, it was the theme of shared struggle, suffering, and death—a fate common to both Poles and Jews. It is ironic that Andrzej Szczypiorski, one of the exhibition's early editors, subsequently became one of the most eloquent voices condemning the sort of distortion and obfuscation of the historical record that the 1968 Jewish pavilion exemplified. In Szczypiorski's words:

> We were not dying together, we were dying separately! Our fate during the occupation was not a shared fate. Those who now claim that we were dying together, shoulder to shoulder, like brothers under the same sentence of death, are not telling the truth. . . . It is a question of the completely different way the Nazis treated Jews and Poles. On account of his Jewishness a Jew was condemned to death. On account of his Polishness a Pole was condemned to life under the rule of force, to a life of poverty, humiliation, repressive measures, terror, and also random murder. However, the planned, industrialized murder on a mass scale in the gas chambers of Treblinka, Auschwitz, Chelmno or Belzec did not embrace the Poles. Whoever says otherwise engages in a falsification of history.[104]

Szyczypiorski's passion with respect to this issue is perhaps what led him to resign from the exhibition's review commission, for Block 27 failed to recognize, to use his words, the "completely different way the Nazis treated Jews and Poles."

The very presence of a Jewish pavilion at the Auschwitz site made it impossible to remain silent about the Jewish presence in the Auschwitz camp, but that presence could be relativized, assimilated into a larger Polish tragedy, and put to political use at the height of the "anti-Zionist campaign." In light of the protests, purges, and anti-Semitic rhetoric at the time, the Warsaw regime could exploit the new exhibition and, therefore, the memory of Auschwitz Jews in the hope of gaining political currency or redeeming lost international credibility. Officially, of course, there was never any campaign against Jews in Poland, but rather measures and propaganda directed against "Zionists." Therefore, as far as the regime was concerned, accusations of

Polish anti-Semitism were unwarranted. The Polish state had erected a special Jewish exhibition at the Auschwitz Museum—an exhibition documenting Poland's bravery and solidarity in defending Jews during the occupation. In short, the exhibition was an antidote intended primarily for foreign consumption to counter the effects of Poland's anti-Semitic campaign.[105] Block 27 was an attempt to restore Poland's international credibility, but the exhibit was clumsy in its execution and transparent in its hypocrisy.

Not surprisingly, the new Jewish pavilion damaged the regime's credibility more than it helped restore it. Not only did the exhibition itself elicit criticism from abroad, but its dedication ceremonies only served to confirm in the eyes of foreign observers the Polish government's anti-Jewish agenda.[106] The event was scheduled for 21 April, the Sunday following Passover, virtually guaranteeing that few, if any, Jews from abroad would attend. Moreover, according to the French newspaper *Tribune Juive*, invitations were sent late, and entry visas were refused for members of foreign Jewish delegations.[107] The dedication ceremonies therefore attracted only 150–200 people.[108] In his dedicatory address, Minister of Culture Lucjan Motyka sought, in the words of one journalist, "to steer a middle ground between the Government's 'anti-Zionist' policy and its proclaimed concern for Poland's 30,000 remaining Jews."[109] He condemned Israel's aggression in the Middle East but, at the same time, issued a warning against letting the campaign against Jews spin out of control.[110] Motyka appears to have been attempting to assume a posture of compromise, but in reference to the exhibition, he situated the Shoah in the context of Poland's wartime destruction:

> Mass executions, concentration and work camps, forced resettlement, along with murder and plunder, deportation to the Reich for slave labor—these are some of the elements of the criminal activities that, in the event of a Hitlerite victory, would surely conclude with the biological destruction of the Polish nation. It was in the framework of that action that the destruction of peoples of Jewish extraction was undertaken in the most cruel manner.[111]

Thirty years later, the minister's words offer a concise, descriptive summary of official memory at Auschwitz, whether in Block 27, at the Birkenau monument, or in the museum's permanent exhibition. It is certainly appropriate to place this interpretation of wartime history within the context of Poland's anti-Jewish policies of the late 1960s, but the tone and content of the minister's speech represented the intensification and culmination of a twenty-year tradition of assimilating the Jewish Shoah into a Polish wartime catastrophe.

The 1968 Jewish exhibition was a clear illustration of what was, and has remained, the central dilemma in the memorialization of Auschwitz: how to emphasize the uniqueness of the Shoah while, at the same time, contextualizing it in the broader narrative of all Nazi crimes of oppression and murder. The Polish response to the dilemma in the spring of 1968 was manipulative and misleading. At the height of the "anti-Zionist" campaign, failure to recognize the Jewish presence at Auschwitz would have incurred further charges of Polish anti-Semitism. At the same time, the exhibition in Block 27 was appropriately—and perhaps inevitably—condemned as a disingenuous attempt to deflect further criticism of Poland's anti-Semitism and anti-Zionism. As facile as post hoc condemnations of the Jewish pavilion may be, it is worth noting that this dilemma, revisited numerous times in the decades to follow, remains an object of controversy to this day.

The tentative internationalization of the Auschwitz site did not destroy the paradigms that had guided Poland's public memorialization of the camp since 1945, but undermined them. Resilient as it had been over the years, Poland's dominant memory of Auschwitz could not remain completely unchanged in the wake of the international pressures and revisionary impulses of the 1960s. These pressures and revisionary impulses came, to use Henry Rousso's term, in the form of new official and organizational carriers of Auschwitz memory. The International Auschwitz Committee, the Birkenau monument, and the new Jewish pavilion challenged Poland's official and circumscribed memory of Auschwitz. With the International Auschwitz Committee as its patron, the State Museum at Auschwitz could no longer represent Auschwitz history solely within the confines of a Polish-national commemorative idiom; with the Birkenau monument attracting both visitors and international media attention, Poland was suddenly held accountable for its traditional neglect of the Jewish presence at the memorial site; with Polish-Jewish relations irrevocably damaged by the measures of the anti-Zionist campaign, the Polish government took the clumsy and palliative step of opening an exhibition dedicated to the martyrology and struggle of the Jews to regain some of its international credibility. These external pressures challenged Poland's prevailing notions of Auschwitz memory and reinserted the Shoah, if only indirectly and tentatively, into the Auschwitz landscape.

Poland's commemorative framework was resistant, but not rigid. The introduction of external carriers of memory in the 1960s began a process by which dominant and official modes of commemoration at the memorial site would be forced to yield to a more vernacular understanding of Auschwitz, its significance in Polish history, and its role in the commemorative culture of the 1970s and 1980s.

6 ⫴ The Power and Limits of a Commemorative Idiom

John Paul II at the "Golgotha of Our Age"

THE INTERNATIONALIZATION OF the memorial site was certainly a watershed in its history, for Poland's dominant memory of Auschwitz could not remain unchanged in the wake of the international influences and the introduction of new carriers of memory in the 1960s. By comparison, the next decade was relatively calm. Relatively few major changes were made to the site in the 1970s, and it is therefore tempting to regard that decade as a period of stability or even entrenchment. If the first twenty-five years of the State Museum at Auschwitz were characterized by repeated and alternating attempts to refashion and then to restore the framework of collective memory there, the period from Gomułka's fall from power in December 1970 to the end of the decade was a period of peaceful discontinuity in the broader history of the memorial site. The 1955 exhibition remained largely intact while the museum opened several new "national pavilions"; the International Auschwitz Committee, foreign organizations, and the Polish government organized regular demonstrations and commemorative ceremonies; foreign dignitaries paid their respects to the Auschwitz dead during visits to Poland; the number of pilgrims and tourists to the site grew steadily. The coexistence of these disparate elements suggests a modus vivendi among the various claimants to memory. Under the surface, however, changes in the symbolic value and public uses of Auschwitz were underway, forcing the museum and the Polish state to respond to an ever-growing variety of commemorative constituencies and external pressures, both domestic and foreign.

This chapter focuses on these responses as it addresses several developments at the Auschwitz site in the 1970s. First, there were a number of initiatives to revise the memorial site's exhibits and landscape. These efforts included, in the first half of the decade, an attempt to restructure the main exhibition and to transform radically the way in which the visitor was to experience the site. Although ineffective in the end, this initiative reflected the museum staff's growing concerns about the limitations of the 1955 exhibition. It also marked an effort to accentuate the history of mass extermination at the site and to overcome the traditional neglect of the Birkenau site as a destination, both physical and intellectual, for the Auschwitz visitor. Moreover, the discussions of the future of the memorial site in the early 1970s presaged many of the debates over the site in the wake of communism's fall in 1989.

Second, this chapter addresses one of the most significant changes to the memorial site during these years: the dedication of a totally remodeled exhibition on the "Martyrology and Struggle of the Jews" in 1978. Like the reform efforts of the early 1970s, the new exhibit was the result of Polish government initiative and the efforts of the museum staff. Even if undertaken partly in response to the foreign policy needs of the time, the remodeling of Block 27 was also an attempt to remedy the mistakes of the past (specifically, the unsatisfactory 1968 Jewish exhibition), giving the history of the Shoah at Auschwitz and elsewhere a more prominent place at the memorial site and making it more accessible and relevant to a broader commemorative constituency.

Auschwitz, by all appearances, was becoming more "international," but major political and social transformations were underway in Poland—transformations that would signal the collapse of communism and, in the process, would allow for the forceful assertion of a Polish-national and specifically Polish-Catholic vision of Auschwitz free from the ideological demands of the state. This chapter, therefore, also examines the growing visibility and significance of Polish Roman Catholic commemoration at Auschwitz in the 1970s. Beginning with ceremonies in 1972 honoring the beatification of Father Maksymilian Kolbe and culminating in a papal mass on the fields of Birkenau in 1979, the Polish Catholic Church successfully used the Auschwitz grounds as a stage and a sanctuary for a specifically Christian, Polish-national commemorative ritual. The visit of John Paul II to Birkenau in June 1979 and his homily there before tens of thousands of his faithful were more than an enormous open-air mass, more than a nationalist ritual, and more than a requisite stop on the itinerary of Poland's favorite son. John Paul II's pilgrimage—and it was understood as such—to Poland's "golgotha" represented the triumph of Polish vernacular notions of Auschwitz and its role in postwar Polish culture. The triumph expressed in the papal visit to Auschwitz also democratized the site and "liberated" it from the political constraints of the past. In this lies a paradox: John Paul II's presence at Auschwitz was, on the one hand, a confirmation and legitimation of the Polish-national commemorative idiom, but at the same time, it opened the site to international media attention and the controversies of the 1980s, 1990s, and beyond.

Reform and Revision at Auschwitz in the 1970s

Writing of the transfer of power from Władysław Gomułka to Edward Gierek in 1970, Michael Steinlauf observed that "[w]ith Gomułka's fall, Polish communism assumed its terminal configuration."[1] Indeed, one tends to associate the so-called "Gierek era," spanning the years from Edward Gierek's appointment as first secretary of the Polish United Workers' Party in 1970 until the birth of the Solidarity movement in 1980, as a period of initial optimism, unfounded hopes, and, in the end, economic and political collapse.

Władysław Gomułka had survived the events of 1968 and the anti-Zionist campaign, and in 1970 had concluded Poland's most important diplomatic agreement in decades: the treaty normalizing relations with the Federal Republic of Germany. In that same year, however, deteriorating economic conditions, strikes, and bloody government reprisals marked the end of Gomułka's fourteen years at the helm of the PZPR. Edward Gierek took over the post of first secretary in December 1970 amid hopes for economic stability and social peace.

This much he achieved, at least for the first few years of his regime. After quelling the unrest of December 1970 and early 1971, Gierek worked to establish himself as a leader different from Gomułka. He appeared as an approachable, less ideological politician who showed a genuine concern for the workers. Moreover, Gierek was successful in ousting compromised members of the old regime, including Józef Cyrankiewicz and the ZBoWiD leader Mieczysław Moczar, who was removed from his post in the Ministry of the Interior in April 1971 and effectively neutralized by the end of that year.[2]

During Gierek's first years, Poland enjoyed a level of apparent economic prosperity and a degree of cultural liberalization unseen since 1956. Real wages increased, national income rose; for the average Pole, this was a period of relative prosperity and progress. The regime remained true—at least officially—to its Marxist-Leninist precepts, but ideology appeared to be giving way to political opportunism and a renewed form of nationalism that the state upheld in its propaganda as the "moral-political unity of the Polish nation."[3] Gierek did, in fact, play the patriotic card in a variety of ways, perhaps most effectively in his initiative to rebuild the Royal Castle in Warsaw, a symbol of Nazi destruction but also a symbol of national pride. In the area of cultural politics, Gierek sought a level of accommodation with non-party elements in society. The state relaxed censorship, reached a rapprochement with the Roman Catholic Church, and allowed for greater freedom of expression in culture and the arts.

It was in this atmosphere of economic optimism and more relaxed control over cultural policy that a renewed debate emerged over the future of the Auschwitz site and its exhibitions—a debate that predated by some twenty years many of the same discussions of the postcommunist era. Auschwitz was no longer a political instigator, but its landscape and exhibitions remained embedded in the domestic and foreign policy context of the period. Already in 1970, only two years after the "anti-Zionist" campaign, individuals and organizations concerned with the workings of the memorial site began to address publicly a number of issues relating to the state of the Auschwitz Museum and its future. The Kraków Club of Catholic Intelligentsia, a forum for reform-minded Catholics, sponsored a publicized discussion on "Auschwitz after Twenty-Five Years," which centered on the educational mission of the memorial site and how that mission could be more effectively fulfilled in the future. Participants included, among others, the Auschwitz survivor Władysław Bartoszewski; writer, former prisoner, and longtime museum affiliate Tadeusz Hołuj; representatives of the State Museum at Auschwitz; and the Rector of the Oświęcim Catholic parish. According to an account of the meeting, a significant portion of the discussion focused on the problems associated with mass tourism at the site: traffic congestion, souvenir stands, the presence of a hotel on the museum grounds, irreverent behavior, and the like. In addition, the discussants expressed concern over the accessibility of the site and its exhibitions, and the ways in which the "Auschwitz experience" was conveyed at the site. Perhaps the museum should be less accessible? Perhaps people should visit the site only on their own initiative, and not in organized groups? What is to be renovated or reconstructed? Is one's understanding of the "martyrdom" of Auschwitz victims limited by Christian notions of martyrdom, or can such notions be accessible to all?[4]

The International Auschwitz Committee, still in a crisis over Poland's campaign against Jews and the resulting East-West split, also took up some of these issues in the fall of 1970, when the West German weekly *Stern* published an article that was highly critical of the management and atmosphere of the Auschwitz Museum. The number of visitors from the Federal Republic of Germany had increased steadily over the course of the 1960s, especially through the efforts of organizations on the political left like the Sozialistische Jugend (Socialist Youth), otherwise known as the "Falken," and Aktion Sühnezeichen (Action Reconciliation), an organization of the protestant churches dedicated to reconciliation work and social service abroad.[5] Over the years, the travel seminars, pilgrimages, and other forms of "political tourism" sponsored by these organizations became more visible in the West German and Polish press, while the *Ostpolitik* (policy toward the East) of the new social democratic government in Bonn continued to direct attention toward Poland as the key to the Federal Republic's efforts to achieve détente with its eastern neighbors.[6] In an article reflecting the growing West German interest in People's Poland, *Stern* journalist Erich Kuby criticized the Polish government for turning the State Museum into a "modern tourist center."[7] Kuby indicted the State Museum on several counts: tourist facilities, from an ice cream stand to a hotel, had been incorporated into the grounds and structures of the former camp; young people were permitted to walk around with radios blaring; and the museum had shown a general "lack of instinct" as to the proper way of commemorating the Auschwitz dead. Perhaps most embarrassing to the Poles was Kuby's use of the lack of reverence shown at the Auschwitz site as a springboard for his discussion of Poland's mistreatment of its Jews during the recent "anti-Zionist" campaign. The new secretary-general of the IAC, Roman Gesing, replied to this criticism by maintaining that visitors to the site were not tourists, but students of history, and that the Auschwitz *"sanktuarium"*—the only one of its type in the world—should not be shrouded in silence, but should accommodate the thousands of voices that came to learn from its history.[8]

Criticism of the site was increasing in the international press, bringing many of the problems there into the public view.[9] Not surprisingly, throughout the first half of the 1970s the museum was a recurring topic of discussion for the PZPR and its provincial authorities in Kraków. Participants at the Sixth Party Congress in December 1971, for example, voiced criticisms of the museum in a variety of areas: services for the hundreds of thousands of visitors per year were insufficient; elements of the exhibition devoted to the martyrdom of the Polish nation were inadequate; Birkenau was not receiving proper care; and the national exhibits required party review and approval. The nature of these criticisms and the response submitted by museum director Kazimierz Smoleń suggest that although Auschwitz was "on the map" of the higher party leadership, few were familiar with its inner workings or the economic and political constraints that it faced. Smoleń, for example, pointed out that state subsidies for conservation work at the memorial site were woefully inadequate and that as early as 1969 the museum had already developed extensive blueprints for an exhibit entitled "The Struggle and Martyrdom of the Polish Nation during the Hitlerite Occupation." The Ministry of Culture and Art had rejected these plans, however, because they did not adequately address issues of underground resistance in Auschwitz and the surrounding region.[10]

Although the Auschwitz Museum can hardly be regarded as a "preoccupation" of the Warsaw government, it continued to attract the attention of state and party authorities. This was likely the result of the site's growing visibility as a destination for foreign dignitaries and diplomats in the early 1970s. Expressions of a new era of East-West détente, the visits of West Berlin mayor Klaus Schütz in 1969,[11] West German foreign minister Walter Scheel in November 1970,[12] and a delegation of West German Social Democrats led by Herbert Wehner in February 1971[13] all testified to the growing importance of Auschwitz as a destination for foreign and especially West German visitors to Poland. Among other visitors from the West in the years to follow were United Nations secretary-general Kurt Waldheim in July 1972,[14] the West German ambassador to Poland in December of that year,[15] French president Valéry Giscard d'Estaing in June 1975,[16] and U.S. president Gerald Ford the following month.[17] As always, the Polish state placed great value on these official visits. They not only gave visibility to the Auschwitz Museum and its history, but also offered, if only indirectly, legitimacy to Polish foreign policy goals, whether West German recognition of the Oder-Neisse Line, Franco-Polish cooperation in the effort toward European peace, or support for the Conference on Security and Cooperation in Europe that resulted in the Helsinki Accords signed immediately after Ford's visit to Poland in 1975. All this suggests that Auschwitz was increasing in importance as a diplomatic stage in this era of détente, even as the site grew in its role as an arena for political demonstrations and regular commemorative ceremonies. High-level diplomatic visits and events such as the twenty-fifth anniversary of the State Museum at Auschwitz, the fifth anniversary of the dedication of the Birkenau monument, or the thirtieth anniversary of the liberation made all the more evident the need for the Ministry of Culture and Art and the Auschwitz Museum to address some of the problems at the site.

In response, the PZPR Provincial Committee in Kraków convened a commission of experts charged with evaluating the current status of the museum and making recommendations for the future. The commission, which included museum directors from around the country as well as members of the Auschwitz Museum's staff,[18] met on ten different occasions between July 1973 and April 1974.[19] An April 1974 letter from Tadeusz Hołuj to the PZPR Provincial Committee's Department of Propaganda (apparently the party had solicited Hołuj's opinion on the matter of the Auschwitz Museum) gives a glimpse of the wide variety of issues and the far-reaching changes that were under consideration at the time.[20] One proposal, apparently intended to emphasize the diverse backgrounds of the camp victims, called for changing the name of the museum to "Museum in Auschwitz-Birkenau: Monument to the Martyrdom of the Nations." Among other matters under discussion were the removal of all enterprises, factories, and stores in the near vicinity of the museum; the removal from Auschwitz I of all museum workers' apartments, the reception building's "hotel," and other accommodations for overnight guests; the revision and modernization of the main exhibition and national exhibitions; and the raising of the age of admission to the museum to eighteen. In his responses to these proposals, Hołuj noted that, in one form or another, all had been discussed in the past.[21] With a view to the more recent history of the site, it is worth noting that even today several of these matters remain unresolved and open to debate.[22]

The final report issued by the commission of experts and sent on to the Central Committee of the PZPR was not as far-reaching as some of the preliminary recommendations suggested, but it did include a number of innovative proposals. For example, the commission called for a comprehensive urban development plan for the areas surrounding and lying between Auschwitz I and Birkenau, the removal of all economic enterprises in the immediate vicinity of the museum, and the regulation of traffic and tourist services. With respect to the exhibitions, the commission recommended that the 1955 main exhibition be remodeled extensively and that the museum develop a permanent introductory exhibit in the reception building, that is, the former Aufnahmegebäude built in 1944. This exhibit was to introduce the visitor to the general themes of the museum: the rise of German fascism, the development of concentration camps and extermination centers, the crimes of the Nazi state before and during World War II, the history of the Auschwitz complex, and the pursuit and punishment of Nazi criminals after the war. Emphasizing the need for greater international exposure and participation in the activities of the museum, the report stated that in the future the museum would have to provide information to visitors in five languages. It also called for the further development of national exhibits in the former base camp and, at the same time, expressed concern that some of the current exhibits had been designed without consulting Polish authorities and were consequently not "at the desired level." The commission also repeated the demand for an exhibit on the "Struggle and Martyrdom of the Polish Nation, 1939–1945."[23] As noted above, the museum had developed plans for such an exhibition in 1969 and subsequently revised those plans according to the wishes of the Ministry of Culture and Art. The exhibit was to open in 1973, but for reasons that are unclear it remained an elusive goal until a "Polish pavilion" was finally opened in 1985.[24]

The commission's final report centered primarily on issues relating to Auschwitz I, its problematic tourist atmosphere, and its exhibitions. But the report had little to say about the future of Birkenau beyond calling for it to be maintained, as in the past, as a historic preserve with the International Monument to the Victims of Fascism as a central site for the commemoration of Auschwitz victims. Recognizing the report's limitations, several members of the museum staff addressed directly the problems at Birkenau, the most prominent of which was the low number of visitors there. Appealing directly to the provincial PZPR authorities, these five historians submitted a bold proposal for the radical transformation of the memorial site's exhibitions and the visitors' route through the camp. They claimed that a large percentage of visitors failed to visit Birkenau and that they were

> leaving Oświęcim with an undoubtedly distorted image of the former KL Auschwitz. Not even the most lively explanations of museum guides . . . are

a substitute for the eloquence of the huge Birkenau grounds, with the remains of primitive barracks and traces of immediate mass extermination preserved there: ruins of crematoria and gas chambers."[25]

Their solution to this problem was to locate the State Museum's main reception center, along with an introductory exhibit, in front of the entrance to the former Birkenau camp. This would ensure "that all visitors, without exception, become acquainted in the first place with the unique grounds of Brzezinka (Birkenau), and not, as it has been until now, with the incomparably less eloquent grounds of the former Auschwitz base camp."[26] Such a proposal marked, in effect, a change in both pedagogical orientation and historical interpretation. The presence of Birkenau had never been totally silenced at the museum but like the history of the mass extermination of Jews and Gypsies there, had been relegated to the periphery of the exhibitions and the experience of most visitors. The new proposal called for the theme of mass extermination to have the highest priority at the museum, with the life of the registered prisoner (the major emphasis of the 1955 exhibit) as a secondary point. The former base camp was not to fall into disuse, but was to reflect its own history and to continue to house the various "national pavilions" and artistic exhibitions.

It is not clear how the provincial PZPR representatives responded to this proposal or whether there was any attempt to integrate its recommendations with those of the party's commission of experts. In the end, neither the commission's recommendations nor the suggestions of the museum's team of historians came to fruition. According to one museum historian, the faltering Polish economy was responsible for the lack of action on either plan. The oil crisis, a weakening export market, inflation, and food shortages in the mid-1970s led to a wave of protests and strikes, and without additional resources specifically earmarked for the museum's renovation, it was impossible to undertake any major changes.[27]

Economic factors undoubtedly stood in the way of fulfilling the commission's recommendations, but it is also necessary to take into account the political and ideological dimensions of the museum staff's courageous proposal. Only a few years after the "anti-Zionist" campaign and the studied efforts of the regime to minimize the record of Jewish wartime deaths in Polish lands, a radical reorientation of the memorial site and its exhibitions toward the remains of Birkenau would have been too great a pedagogical shift for the party Central Committee and the Ministry of Culture. To make the issue of mass extermination at Birkenau the primary focus of a visit to Auschwitz would certainly have been to deviate from the traditional uses of the site that had prevailed in decades past. Over the course of the 1960s the State Museum at Auschwitz had opened itself, albeit hesitantly, to new commemorative agendas and commemorative narratives from abroad, but none of these had required the de-emphasis of the Polish-national memorial paradigm at the site. It was one thing for member organizations of the International Auschwitz Committee to protest Poland's treatment of Jews during the anti-Zionist campaign; it was quite another to require every visitor to the memorial site to view the selection ramp and crematoria of Birkenau before viewing the barracks and Block 11 of the base camp.

As if to head off any undesirable preoccupation with non-Polish deaths at the Auschwitz complex, the PZPR organ *Trybuna Ludu*, in its coverage of the thirtieth anniversary of the liberation in January 1975, included an article about a West German television documentary that was misleading viewers with "a falsified image of 'KL Auschwitz,'" representing it as a camp for the extermination of Jews and Gypsies." The documentary, *Trybuna Ludu* alleged, also failed to emphasize that the Polish nation had suffered the highest percentage of casualties among the nations subject to Nazi aggression, and that the Nazis had "planned, and partially carried out, the biological extermination of the Polish people."[28]

For the domestic audience, the party was determined to avoid dividing the "Polish people" who suffered at Auschwitz—whether Jews or Gentiles, political prisoners or the racially persecuted—into various victim groups. At the same time, however, the authorities were certainly aware of the site's problems and poor image among some foreign observers. In November 1974 an article highly critical of the museum had appeared in the *New York Times*. "Nearly 30 years after Auschwitz concentration camp was closed down," the article began, "the underlying horror of the place seems diminished by the souvenir stands, Pepsi-Cola signs and the tourist attraction atmosphere." The article offered scathing criticism of the behavior of visitors as well as of the tourist services (a snack bar, cafeteria, hotel) and souvenirs available at the site. Moreover, the *Times* correspondent noted the desolation of Birkenau, where the "vast area and the ruined condition of its barracks, barbed-wire aprons and gas chambers evidently make it less attractive to tourists."[29] Although the authorities may have responded only minimally to these criticisms, it is clear that the Ministry of Culture and Art was aware of them and was sensitive to the "image problem" at the State Museum at Auschwitz.[30]

The broad problems under discussion in the early 1970s bear a striking similarity to issues that have been the subject of debate—at times heated—in the postcommunist era. There is a tendency to ascribe the origins of conflict and controversy over postwar Auschwitz to the more recent past, as if the history of the State Museum prior to 1989 were shrouded in mystery, its exhibitions and public demonstrations conforming to the ideological proclivities and political exigencies of the regime. Although this image is not entirely incorrect, it is nonetheless misleading; Poles began to confront, albeit only tentatively, some of the challenges and problems associated with mass tourism, conservation, and the relative emphasis given to Birkenau as a site of mass extermination well before the emergence of the Carmelite Convent controversy and the fall of communism. Ideology and economics had always stood in the way of far-reaching changes to the State Museum at Auschwitz, but it was clear that change was necessary.

Throughout the 1970s the regime's relationship to the State Museum at Auschwitz was characterized by its desire to uphold the former camp as a site of Polish national martyrdom while at the same time making it more accessible to an international public. This ambivalence, evident in the failed reform efforts in the first half of the decade, manifested itself once again in its latter years, this time in the renovation and rededication of a new Jewish exhibition in Block 27 of the base camp in 1978. The inadequacy and tendentious nature of the Jewish exhibition opened during the "anti-Zionist" agitation of 1968 was undoubtedly clear to members of the museum staff as well to the authorities in Warsaw. Although approximately eighty thousand visitors to the museum passed through Block 27 in the ten years of its existence,[31] the exhibit was frequently closed[32] and generally saw far fewer visitors than most of the other "national" exhibitions. It is impossible to determine whether the low number of visitors to Block 27 was due to lack of interest, or because it was inaccessible, or both. In any case, in the years 1971 through 1975, for example, the museum recorded 35,903 visitors to the Jewish exhibition (nearly half of whom were from abroad) and 49,698 to the Danish exhibit;[33] in 1973 approximately 7,800 visited Block 27, compared to more than 55,000 who viewed the

Soviet Union's pavilion and more than 10,000 who visited the exhibit of the German Democratic Republic.[34]

Inadequate and embarrassing, the exhibit on the "Martyrology and Struggle of the Jews" was in desperate need of renovation, especially given the ever-growing numbers of international visitors to the site. Documents from the Ministry of Culture and Art indicate that a review commission for the exhibition began its work in February 1977. The commission called for the immediate closure of the current Jewish pavilion and for the posting of information in five languages explaining why the exhibit was closed. That the commission saw it necessary to explain the reason for closing the exhibit suggests that Block 27 was, at least at that point in 1977, generally accessible to the public and of sufficient importance that visitors might misinterpret a locked door on Block 27. The commission met on several occasions over the ensuing months and solicited the assistance of research centers abroad, including the Holocaust Martyrs' and Heroes' Remembrance Authority (Yad Vashem) in Jerusalem, France's Centre de Documentation Juive Contemporaine, and the Rijksinstitut Voor Oorlags Documentatie in the Netherlands. Moreover, those responsible for the new exhibition's blueprints, including Tadeusz Hołuj and Emeryka Iwaszko from the museum's educational department, worked with Warsaw's Jewish Historical Institute.[35] Contact and cooperation with institutions abroad were indeed characteristics unique to this exhibition among the various "national pavilions" at Auschwitz I; in all other cases, individual countries were fully responsible for planning and creating their own exhibitions with relatively little, if any, input from other countries or from the Polish side.[36]

The exhibition's dedication ceremonies on 17 April 1978 began a series of events commemorating the thirty-fifth anniversary of the Warsaw Ghetto Uprising and were attended by representatives from the Ministry of Culture and Art and ZBoWiD, by delegates from Yad Vashem and Israeli organizations of former prisoners and resistance fighters, as well as by international organizations like the World Jewish Congress, International Auschwitz Committee, and the World Organization of Jewish Fighters, Partisans, and Camp Prisoners.[37] Like the opening of the previous Jewish exhibition almost exactly ten years before, the April 1978 ceremonies combined the relative novelty of a focus on Jewish wartime losses with current political concerns and traditional commemorative themes. Although the disingenuous and overtly politicized references to Polish-Jewish solidarity in resistance and death were absent from the new exhibition, Janusz Wieczorek, head of the Council for the Protection of Monuments of Struggle and Martyrdom, echoed many of the themes of 1968 in his dedicatory address: common suffering and common resistance among Jews and Poles, resistance in the Warsaw Ghetto and in the Auschwitz camp, the injustices of anti-Polish propaganda, and the challenges of the early postwar period.[38] Referring to the wartime losses of Polish citizens, Wieczorek stated:

> Poland after the war did not easily make up for the six million lives lost. Among the slaughtered and murdered were students and intellectuals, physicians and clerics, cultural figures, workers, and farmers. Many of them were of Jewish descent. For us they were Poles; they thought and felt in Polish; they were the co-authors of our material and spiritual culture. We never separated them, and their loss is for us as irreparable as for the Jewish nation.[39]

Wieczorek's words were directed at both a Polish and an international audience. As though to instruct his Polish audience, he noted the contributions of Jews to Polish culture; as though to reassure an audience abroad, Wieczorek emphasized that Poles continued to lament the irreparable loss of so many Jews in their midst. But unlike the exhibition itself, Wieczorek's speech did not emphasize the unique aspects of Jewish suffering under the Nazis. Instead, it served to "polonize" the Jewish experience in what today would seem rather crass terms. Wieczorek described sites of Jewish suffering and genocide—Auschwitz, Treblinka, Łódź, Białystok, and Sobibór—as "stations of the cross of Polish Jews and Jews from other European lands."[40] Not only is this a peculiar metaphor, coming as it did from the lips of an official of the communist state, but Wieczorek's words also cloaked the specifically Jewish element of suffering at Auschwitz and elsewhere in the terms and experience of the (Christian) Polish martyr. "For us they were Poles," Wieczorek stated. This assertion was undoubtedly intended as an affirmation of Polish tolerance, and Wieczorek may have been drawing upon a secular, civic, and assimilationist notion of citizenship and national identity that had been associated with elements of reformist and leftist Polish politics —from romantic nationalism to positivism to socialism—for generations.[41] At the same time, however, his comments revealed the severe limitations of nationalism as a dominant leitmotiv at the Auschwitz memorial site. The

198 | *Auschwitz, Poland, and the Politics of Commemoration*

claim that Poles "never separated" Jews during the occupation rings tolerant and patriotic. But the claim was untrue, and where the Poles did not separate the Jews, the Nazis did.

Like his predecessors on such occasions, Wieczorek also was quick to draw current political lessons from the Auschwitz past. In a manner reminiscent of that of the speakers at the 1968 exhibition, he was highly critical of Western European countries and the United States, accusing the West of failing to respond to the Jews' plight during the war. Despite Polish warnings, reports, and documentation of Nazi crimes against Jews, Western responses were slow and indifferent, unlike the valiant and heroic efforts of Poles who had sacrificed much in assisting their Jewish fellow citizens. Moreover, argued Wieczorek, those drawing meaning from the new exhibition and from the history of the Auschwitz camp ought to join in protest against all wars, cruelties, and new weaponry. "[I]n the name of the millions of victims of the Second World War," he claimed, "in the name of all murdered Poles, Jews, Russians, and citizens of other nationalities, we join the worldwide protest against the production of the neutron bomb."[42]

The transparency and provocative tone of these words notwithstanding, the exhibition itself was a great improvement over the 1968 pavilion. The *Jerusalem Post,* for example, described the new Jewish exhibit as "similar to that of the Yad Vashem permanent exhibition in Jerusalem,"[43] while a representative of that institution mounted a mezuzah on the door of Block 27[44]—an act that appeared to convey the Israeli institute's blessing on the new exhibition. Covering approximately one thousand square meters, the new exhibit did away with the tendentious and glaringly propagandistic material of the 1968 exhibit, although it did retain many of the same themes as its predecessor: the evolution of Nazi anti-Jewish policy in the 1930s and in the occupied East, the ghettoization of Jews in occupied Poland, the "final solution," Jewish resistance to Nazi genocide, and Polish aid to Jews, with Żegota upheld as a salient example.[45] The new exhibit also retained a concluding "Hall of Memory," with a well-known quotation from the book of Genesis. But whereas the 1968 exhibit had begun with the question, "Where is Abel your brother?" as if to accuse the German and vindicate the Pole, the 1978 exhibit concluded with a simple lament from the same story, describing the effects and grief of loss: "And the Lord said to Cain, 'The blood of your brother Abel cries to me from the ground.'"

The 1968 exhibition in Block 27 was intended as an antidote (for foreign consumption) to Poland's campaign against "Zionism." Ten years later, after the diplomatic successes of détente, the economic hopes of the early Gierek years, and the strikes, shortages, and revolts of 1976, Poland's domestic and foreign-policy needs were far different. One contemporary analyst argued that the dedication of a new exhibit at Auschwitz was part of a general shift in Poland's attitude toward Israel, evident in the invitation to Israeli representatives to participate not only in an event at Auschwitz but also in ceremonies commemorating the Warsaw Ghetto Uprising. Authorities from Yad Vashem reciprocated, in effect, by awarding "Righteous Gentile" medals to twenty-two Poles at a ceremony in Warsaw—the first time Yad Vashem had held such a ceremony on Polish soil.[46] Likewise, a *Jerusalem Post* editorial welcomed the opening of the new exhibition in Block 27 as a "bit of thaw in the frost which has covered Polish relations with the Jewish people since 1967." The editorial went on to point out Poland's "special debt to the Jewish people," for "they [the Poles] were also oppressors without whose active collaboration the Nazis could not have carried out their genocide against the Jewish people with such grisly efficiency."[47]

Understandably, the Polish state and Polish society were not willing to admit in 1978—nor have they ever been willing to admit—any sort of collective and nationwide collaboration in the crimes of the Holocaust, and it is only in the last twenty years that many have begun to confront more vigorously the roles of ethnic Poles under the occupation as bystanders[48] to the Shoah and even as perpetrators[49] of atrocities against Jews and others. The opening of a new exhibition at Auschwitz was certainly not intended as a step in the direction of acknowledging any form of "collective guilt." But it was a step toward repairing some of the damage that had been done to Polish-Jewish relations and Polish-Israeli relations in the wake of the 1967 Six-Day War. Recognizing this, the *Jerusalem Post* continued:

> The act at Auschwitz this week marks the first recognition the Polish government has given to the tragedy that befell Jews as Jews and not only as Polish nationals at Auschwitz. That this is not a solitary act but part of a series of events, even if not a full-blown new departure in policy, is shown by the presence in Israel of a Polish delegation to commemorate the name of that remarkable Jewish-Polish educator, Janusz Korczak. Both events are welcome, as will be any additional gestures Warsaw may be contemplating

to cement relations with the Jewish people. Cynics would argue that these steps are not simply part of a new perception in Warsaw of Poland's moral debt to the Jews, but an attempt by the dollar-hungry Polish economy to woo the American Jewish community.[50]

A diplomatic advance toward Israel, a "debt" to the Jewish people for Poland's role in the crimes of the Shoah, Poland's need for American economic support and therefore the support of American Jews—all these are cited here as motivations for the renovation and rededication of the Jewish exhibition at Auschwitz. One should also leave room, however, for the possibility that authorities in the Ministry of Culture and Art and the staff at the Auschwitz Museum were responding, if not to a "moral debt," then at least to a certain moral imperative by replacing the politicized and embarrassing 1968 version of Block 27 with an exhibit more collaborative in its origins and more accurate in its historical presentation. The new exhibit on the "Martyrology and Struggle of the Jews," if imperfect, remains to this day a fixture of the Auschwitz site and is now the most frequented among the "national pavilions" at the museum.[51] As such, it can certainly be counted among the most successful of the museum's attempts to respond to a more international commemorative constituency and to document and present the crimes of the Shoah to a larger and more cosmopolitan audience.

The Prisoner-Martyr and the Pilgrim-Pope

Growing in its appeal to a broader commemorative constituency, the State Museum appeared to be making progress toward a more accurate and historically specific representation of the crimes at Auschwitz. At the same time, it was maintaining its role as a memorial to Poland's wartime suffering. These two trends were not mutually exclusive, for the Polish-national idiom in the iconography and commemorative practice at Auschwitz had been a constant throughout the first thirty years of the museum's existence and had withstood the challenges of Stalinist ideology, political upheaval, economic deprivation, and anti-Semitic agitation. At times, of course, the PZPR or Ministry of Culture and Art cultivated that idiom, but the Polish state had seldom encouraged development of its Roman Catholic element. In the early postwar years government officials could be seen participating in worship services at the memorial site, and in the early 1950s the Patriot Priests movement had worked to introduce an ideologically circumscribed Roman Catholic presence at Auschwitz. But the Marxist state had never encouraged the inclusion of a broad and vernacular Catholic element in the commemorative culture at Auschwitz. Nonetheless, Roman Catholic faith and ritual had always been present at Auschwitz and had manifested themselves over the years in a variety of ways, whether in the vocabulary of commemoration at Auschwitz (martyrdom, golgotha, sacrifice), in occasional worship services at the site, or in the observances and ceremonies held annually on All Saints' Day.

In the 1970s, however, Catholicism gained greater prominence at the site. One of Poland's great equalizers, Catholicism knew not the differences of class, education, privilege, or, in the rather unusual context of People's Poland, political affiliation, for practicing Catholics among the ranks of the Polish United Workers' Party were not unusual. Moreover, Catholicism was intimately bound to the identity of the Polish people and nation—a nation that was, in the aftermath of the Second World War, for the first time relatively homogenous and that could, with justification, claim to be "Catholic," that is, faithful to Rome, and ardent in its devotion to the Marian cult. As crucial as the link between Church and nation is for our understanding of Polish identity in this period, it is important not to mystify that relationship, as if its two components were synonymous or as if the Church, as the transcendent and spiritual element in that partnership, were devoted solely to "otherworldly" pursuits. Even as the Church was enjoying greater tolerance and sympathy as a spiritual force in the 1970s, it was also gaining acceptance and power as a reformist and oppositional force in Polish society—a force that always had its own institutional interests and political agendas and that always was eager to expand upon them.

It is not surprising, then, that the Roman Catholic Church entered the public arena at Auschwitz in the 1970s. The memorial site, better known for state-sponsored commemorative ceremonies and demonstrations than for Church rituals, was nonetheless an appropriate and highly symbolic sanctuary for Catholic observances. Auschwitz, as the most important memorial in Poland, could increase the Church's visibility and underscore the Church's historical relevance for the suffering nation. At the same time, Catholicism could give redemptive meaning to Auschwitz, helping it to transcend both nihilism and Marxist materialism in order to reach the liberating heights of selfless sacrifice and martyrdom. The complementary themes of sacrifice and martyrdom had dominated Catholic ritual at Auschwitz for decades, and in the 1970s these themes came to center on two personalities: the prisoner-martyr Maksymilian Kolbe and the pilgrim-pope John Paul II. For hundreds of thousands of Poles, to honor Father Kolbe and to celebrate Pope John Paul II was to give expression to their most intimately Polish notions of patriotism, national sacrifice, and Catholic virtue.

On the morning of 15 October 1972 an enormous crowd gathered on the grounds of Birkenau for a holy mass in honor of Father Maksymilian Kolbe, the Franciscan friar and priest who died a martyr's death at Auschwitz in 1941. Described by one journalist as a "national church celebration" and "one of the largest religious gatherings since the war,"[52] the event was an unprecedented demonstration of Roman Catholic religiosity and national unity at the Auschwitz memorial site. In years past, political demonstrations and state-sanctioned commemorative ceremonies had drawn tens of thousands to Oświęcim, but this was the first time that an event of primarily religious character had assumed such enormous proportions, attracting an estimated ninety thousand participants.[53] Beyond this, however, the mass was significant because it set a precedent for Roman Catholic commemorative events at the site in the years ahead, most prominently, the visit of John Paul II to Auschwitz seven years later.

Known today chiefly for his voluntary death in the place of another Auschwitz prisoner, Maksymilian Kolbe was one of the most prominent Roman Catholic leaders in interwar Poland. Described by one historian as "one of the church's outstanding evangelists,"[54] Kolbe was a foreign missionary and the founder of the Knights of the Immaculata, an organization dedicated to the conversion of non-Catholics, and especially Freemasons. In 1927 Kolbe founded a monastery called Niepokolanów, or "City of the Immaculata," which became one of the largest monasteries in the world and the seat of Poland's largest publishing enterprise. The publishing house issued several newspapers, including the unsophisticated, anti-Semitic, and highly popular *Mały Dziennik* (Little Daily). This newspaper expressed a militant, defensive Catholicism that was opposed to liberalism and secularism, as well as to communism and National Socialism.[55] To brand Kolbe an anti-Semite on the basis of this and other publications is perhaps too simple, but the fact remains that he was responsible, if indirectly, for supervising the publication of anti-Semitic literature at Niepokolanów.[56]

Kolbe was arrested at Niepokolanów in February 1941 for offering assistance and shelter to refugees, among them Jews.[57] He was transported in May to Auschwitz, where he was given the number 16,670. On 29 July 1941, in retaliation for the escape of an inmate, the camp authorities sentenced ten prisoners to death by starvation. Kolbe offered to take the place of one of the men sentenced, Franciszek Gajowniczek, who had a family. Höss's representative Fritzsch allowed the substitution, and Kolbe was locked in the cellar of Block 11 along with nine others. Kolbe survived in the bunker for more than two weeks and was killed on 14 August 1941 by a phenol injection.[58] His sacrificial death immediately took on a symbolic, even folkloric meaning for other prisoners at Auschwitz and beyond; over the course of the next twenty-five years, Kolbe was honored at Auschwitz and across Poland as the prototypical martyr-patriot. Largely through the efforts of Cardinal Karol Wojtyła, the archbishop of Kraków who later became Pope John Paul II, Kolbe was beatified—the first step toward possible canonization—in October 1971. To mark this occasion, there was a mass held at the Wall of Death in Auschwitz I, and the ceremonies held a year later on a much larger scale were to celebrate the first anniversary of his beatification.

By all accounts an event of massive scale, the celebration on 15 October 1972 began with the early-morning arrival of pilgrims from across Poland. Many came in buses from parishes around the country, others from surrounding areas, on foot. The day included a visit by an official Church delegation to Auschwitz I and to the cell where Kolbe was incarcerated, a wreath-laying ceremony at Birkenau monument, and, finally, the celebration of mass at the Birkenau site.[59] The official Church delegation included not only Cardinal Wojtyła but also the Polish primate, Cardinal Stefan Wyszyński; the head of the American episcopate, Cardinal John Król of Philadelphia; and the prefect of the Sacred Congregation of the Clergy in Rome, Cardinal John Joseph Wright. The presence of the latter two clerics marked the first official visit of American prelates to a communist country since World War II.[60] Franciszek Gajowniczek was present and gave a short speech expressing his gratitude "for the gift of life" that he had received through the sacrifice of Father Kolbe. Polish primate Stefan Wyszyński also addressed the crowd and proclaimed the victory of love and life over hatred and death. "You see that hatred has not succeeded here," the cardinal asserted. "These barbed-wire fences once charged with electricity have rusted, the guard posts are rotting and the barracks are sinking in to the ground, and the crematoriums are themselves burned out. . . . What remains here in this land is the faith in life and resurrection."[61]

The Polish press offered little coverage of the ceremonies to honor Father Kolbe and did not mention the enormous crowds in its reports. It is likely that the local political authorities were somewhat shaken by the level of public enthusiasm for the event, for the crowd was one of the largest ever to gather at the site. Only two weeks after the Kolbe commemoration, the Provincial Office of Internal Affairs denied a Church request to convene an event at Auschwitz on All Saints' Day. The Kraków diocese appealed this decision, but the authorities stood firm, citing the need to preserve the character of the memorial site and the artifacts remaining there.[62]

Concern for the preservation of the site was entirely legitimate, yet the local party and administrative authorities, who had allowed and even organized their own mass convocations there on a regular basis, were certainly not eager to see unofficial, Catholic, and potentially oppositional gatherings at Auschwitz or anywhere else. The Kolbe ceremonies served as a warning flag of sorts and were a vivid reminder that the vernacular symbols attached to Auschwitz were perhaps as powerful as those employed by the state. For many of the faithful, Maksymilian Kolbe represented the ideal of the Polish political prisoner. He was a patriotic Pole, a leader of the Church, and a fearless prisoner who was willing to give his life for another. And for many, his was a prisoner-paradigm more accessible than that of the communist prisoner (with whom many Poles could not identify), the Soviet prisoner of war (who, for many, represented another occupation force), or the Jew (who, even if a Polish citizen, represented for some an alien force that was outside the scope of the Polish national community). The martyr-priest was also a symbol of the Roman Catholic Church—an institution tolerated by the Gierek regime, but regarded as oppositional and nonconformist nonetheless. Finally, Kolbe as a historical icon also spoke to the people's sense of loss and to their hopes and ideals. His death was a symbol of the deaths of tens of thousands of Polish political prisoners, devout Catholics among them, who were murdered in Auschwitz. He was also a model of Christian charity, and even if his sacrificial act was beyond the reach of the average Catholic, it still represented something more holy and transcendent than the deeds of the communist underground fighter. Likewise, Kolbe's death, tragic as it was, remained something more explicable and redemptive than the death of a Jewish victim of the gas chamber, for unlike the Jew at Auschwitz, Kolbe died so that another might live.

The October 1972 ceremonies honoring Maksymilian Kolbe were the first large-scale, exclusively Roman Catholic convocation at Auschwitz, and they set a precedent for such gatherings in the future. The event also foreshadowed conflict. Since the 1960s the Auschwitz site had been opening itself, at times unwillingly, to a more international and diverse constituency. Albeit belatedly, the State Museum had begun to address and to exhibit the history of the Jewish genocide at Auschwitz in its plans for the future of the Birkenau site and in a new exhibition in Block 27. Yet the growth of a commemorative cult surrounding the person and sacrifice of Maksymilian Kolbe (and later, the person of Pope John Paul II) placed Auschwitz and its meaning—at least for the adherents of that cult—squarely within a Polish-Catholic memorial framework. Furthermore, the infusion of a specifically Catholic commemorative agenda appeared not only to polonize, but also to Christianize the most honored site of Jewish destruction. The contradictory and arguably anti-Semitic past of Father Kolbe and the presence of ninety thousand Catholics attending mass at Birkenau are only two reminders of the problems associated with these conflicting currents of memory. It would be far too simplistic to claim, as did one analyst in the late 1980s, that "as early as 1971, the beatification of Kolbe was the first stone of a gigantic design: to transform the Holocaust into a Polish-Catholic event."[63] Conspiracy theories such as this distort the agenda and exaggerate the power of the Polish Roman Catholic Church at that time. Nevertheless, the use of Auschwitz as a stage for mass Catholic worship and commemorative ceremony in 1972 opened the State Museum, the Polish state, and the Polish people to criticism of their stewardship of the site and foreshadowed many of the controversies associated with John Paul II's visit to Auschwitz in 1979 and its aftermath.

When Cardinal Karol Wojtyła was elected by the papal conclave in Rome on 16 October 1978, shock waves reverberated throughout Poland. It was an occasion for public and private rejoicing for the majority of Poles, and a moment of grave concern for the regime. According to Edward Gierek, when he heard the news of Wojtyła's election, he said to his wife: "A Pole has become pope. What a great event for the Polish nation and what complications this means for us."[64] The Gierek regime was struggling with economic problems, a continuing lack of political credibility, and, in the aftermath of the strikes and repression of 1976, a seething public resentment that had thus far been channeled into more peaceful avenues of opposition like the Committee for Defense of the Workers. That resentment, however, was threatening to explode at any time. The election of John Paul II put Gierek on the defensive, and in the midst of a public mood of rejoicing and celebration, the government was forced, in effect, to relinquish its leadership role and to follow the sentiments of the people. As one contemporary analyst wrote:

> While the population rushed to the telephone, opened bottles, hung out Polish flags or merely sat happily weeping in front of the television screen, the Party leadership went into emergency session. . . . A handsome message of congratulations was despatched to Rome, sounding the only note available to the Party at such a moment: nationalism. "For the first time in the history of the papal throne, it is occupied by a son of the Polish nation, which is building the greatness and prosperity of its socialist fatherland with the unity and cooperation of all its citizens."[65]

Although it may have not been obvious at the time, this was one of the turning points in the history of People's Poland, and it is difficult to appreciate, in the post-communist era, the impact of John Paul II's election. National pride aside, the pope's election enlivened Polish society, gave Poland's political opposition a new self-confidence, and sent to the forefront of the world stage the opposition's religious and human rights concerns—concerns that had been growing for decades, but especially since the strikes and government reprisals of 1976. Viewing the Pope's election in the context of the broader oppositional movement, historian Jan Józef Lipski recalled,

> After October 16, 1978, all of Poland lived, as it were, in a state of intoxication and expectancy. Joy over the election of a Polish pope merged with hopes more difficult to specify. This mood was accompanied not only by an intensification of religious life but also by ever more daring public manifestations of unofficial, genuine patriotism, in its noble rather than obscurantist version; by the growth of the spirit of social resistance in defense of human dignity and truth in public life; by a recognition of the duty to bear responsibility for all national and social life; and by increased courage, for which John Paul II appealed.[66]

The sum of all these sentiments was, in the long run, the undoing of communist authority in Poland. In the shorter term, however, they intensified and converged nine months later on the occasion of the pope's visit to his homeland and, more specifically, during his visit to the Auschwitz memorial site. Religious devotion, patriotism, resistance against oppression, courage—the pope used the backdrop of Auschwitz to emphasize both the historical legacy of these virtues, embodied in the selflessness of Maksymilian Kolbe, and their relevance in Poland's current situation.

Karol Wojtyła was born in 1920 in the small town of Wadowice, not far from Oświęcim. He studied at Kraków's Jagiellonian University and also in an underground seminary during the German occupation. Ordained as a priest in 1946, Wojtyła went on to earn his doctorate and become a professor of moral theology and social ethics in Kraków and Lublin. One of the Polish Church's brightest young minds, he was named bishop of the Kraków diocese in 1958, then archbishop in 1963. He was appointed to the College of Cardinals by Pope Paul VI in 1967.

At the time of Karol Wojtyła's election to the papacy in 1978, the Catholic Church in Poland was emerging as a social force more powerful than it had been for several decades. Contrary to the hopes and efforts of the PZPR, Roman Catholicism had not waned in importance and influence in the years since World War II. According to a study undertaken in the early 1980s, more than 93 percent of Polish citizens were baptized Roman Catholics, and as many as two-thirds of PZPR members considered themselves Roman Catholics. Since 1945, the number of churches in Poland had increased, and the number of priests had doubled. In a public opinion survey completed for Polish Radio in the early 1980s, 94 percent of those surveyed stated that the Catholic Church inspired confidence; 90 percent said that the nascent Solidarity movement inspired confidence; and only 32 percent made the same claim for the PZPR.[67] It was not only the Church's antimaterialist and anticommunist stance in the postwar era that helped to enhance its status as an institution of national integrity and oppositional goals; for nearly two centuries the Church had cultivated and maintained the role of national and moral defender of the Polish people, offering continuity and stability in the face of partition, war, revolt, revolution, and the secularist ideologies of the twentieth century.

This traditional role of the Church contributed to a tendency among the people "to find national reaffirmation against foreign influence and a psychological consolation through religious institutions and symbols."[68] For many Poles in the postwar era, Soviet communism was the most pernicious "foreign influence," and it was only natural that the Church was a strong and stable rallying point for opposition to the communist regimes in their various forms.[69] The Church was traditionally at the forefront of struggles for the survival of national identity, and even when it appeared to fail, it was still able to maintain its status as a defender of cultural continuity. Hence, Catholicism in Poland easily took on the mantle of martyrdom, elevating its status in the eyes of a devout and politically refractory population.

Since Edward Gierek's rise to power in the early 1970s, the Catholic Church had enjoyed an improvement in relations with the state. This was evident already in 1971, when the state had allowed the pilgrimage of Polish delegations to Rome for the beatification of Maksymilian Kolbe[70] and had likewise permitted the ceremonies honoring Kolbe at Auschwitz in October of the following year. Moreover, the state had relented somewhat in its struggles with the episcopate over the construction of new churches. At the same time, the Church was becoming increasingly attentive to the struggle of the Polish worker, and although refraining from endorsing any specific oppositional movement or activity, it inevitably became a rallying point for oppositional sentiment. In Gierek's Poland, less repressive than the Poland of his predecessors, the Church could forge stronger links both with workers and with secular intellectuals. It quickly emerged as a leader in the defense of human dignity and freedoms, in the restoration of society's informal social and political ties, and in helping many to recognize that the "fundamental issue under the system of decomposing communism was not ideological but moral."[71] Cardinal Stefan Wyszyński, in his cautious dealings with the state over the previous decades, had helped to prepare the Church to assume this role—and the Church did so with great effect after the election of John Paul II.

From the beginning of his papacy, John Paul II placed human dignity and human rights at the forefront of his mission. His first encyclical, *Redemptor Hominis,* confirmed what appeared to be a humanistic orientation in the Roman Catholic Church that had been growing for years. Issued in March 1979, the encyclical articulated the centrality of human dignity in the redemptive act of Christ and the mission of the Church. "Since man's true freedom," John Paul II wrote, "is not found in everything that the various systems and individuals see and propagate as freedom, the Church, because of her divine mission, becomes all the more the guardian of this freedom, which is the condition and basis for the human person's true dignity."[72] The encyclical was intended to speak to all the faithful, but was written against the background of the pope's own experience and the historical experience of the Polish people, whether under the German occupation of the Second World War or under communism in the decades that followed.[73] It was only fitting, then, that the pope carry this message directly to his homeland, where he would recapitulate the themes of love, redemption, dignity, and liberation through faith.

Plans for the pope's visit to Poland were announced in March 1979 and were the result of extensive negotiation between the Polish episcopate, the Vatican, and the Polish government. John Paul II had originally intended to visit Poland in May 1979, on the nine-hundredth anniversary of the martyrdom of St. Stanisław. The state, however, would not agree to this, for Stanisław, a bishop dismembered on the orders of his king, was a figure too easily identified with the Church's resistance to civic authority.[74] When the papal visit was finally announced for June, the regime made it clear, on the one hand, that it would avoid confrontation, embracing the new pontiff as a "son of the Polish nation" and a moral leader; on the other hand, the government was eager to counter speculation, both in Poland and in the Western press, that it was weakening in the face of a powerful Church. Thus, the state and Church would continue to work together to achieve the common goals of the Polish People's Republic, but the Pope's visit would not change the secular character or undermine the authority of the communist state. Following the announcement of the pope's visit, Mieczysław Rakowski, editor in chief of *Polityka* and member of the PZPR Central Committee, wrote in the pages of his weekly that the pope's visit would "neither level nor eliminate the differences" between Church and state and would not change the secular character of the Polish state. As though issuing a warning, Rakowski continued, "And if there are those in the Catholic camp who believe that the secular character of our state can be weakened, it is necessary to make it clear to them that this is an illusion."[75]

In the end, it was Rakowski who appeared to be harboring illusions. The pope's visit and the overwhelming public response to it revealed much about the regime, for those nine days in June confirmed that the people could organize, order, participate in, and celebrate an event of national significance without the direction of the state. Moreover, there was an obvious gulf between the ideals of the pope and the respect that he commanded on the one side, and the crumbling authority of the Gierek regime on the other. Describing what was, in effect, the pope's eclipse of the communist leadership, one analyst wrote, "Wojtyła offered hope to Poles, while Gierek could offer only material austerity. Wojtyła spoke of truth, while Gierek spoke of an imaginary national unity which was propped up by the work of regime censors."[76] Writing in the same vein, not long after the pope's pilgrimage to his homeland, Andrzej Szczypiorski recalled

> It is astonishing what tricks history sometimes likes to play! That which so many people concerned with Polish sovereignty tried to build with such difficulty, sacrifice and expenditure of effort—one man managed to create in the course of a week.
>
> The whole world was dumbfounded during the visit of Pope John Paul II to his native country. All the strivings, exertions and efforts of 35 years on the part of the communist regime turned out to be not only sterile, but a glaring failure. The myth so painstakingly created and fostered by the party was quickly buried for ever.[77]

Putting it more succinctly, Jan Nowak later wrote, "The pontiff's visit left people with a marked sense of their own strength and their rulers' weakness."[78] This is why many have regarded John Paul's 1979 visit as an important milestone in the collapse of European communism. Jan Józef Lipski, for example, has claimed that "[s]piritually, Poland before June 1979 and Poland after June 1979 seemed to be two different countries,"[79] and according to the pope's friend Marek Skwarnicki, Poland's "freedom shock" occurred not with the legalization of Solidarity or with the elections of 1989, but in the summer of 1979.[80] "After that," writes Norman Davies, "the die was cast. The crack in the crust of the Polish communists' world had been opened."[81]

All of this suggests that although John Paul II's visit to Poland was a spiritual pilgrimage and conferral of status and recognition on the Polish Church and its faithful, it was also a highly political act. The Church had assured the communist leadership that the visit would have an exclusively spiritual character,[82] yet the pope's itinerary, the masses he celebrated, his speeches and homilies, and the enthusiastic public response testified to an unavoidable political current. That the Church with its thousands of volunteers could organize the visit, arrange transportation, and provide the necessary forces for security and crowd control—all largely without the help of the state—emphasized both the power of spontaneous, unofficial social organization and the weakness of the regime.[83]

There are no exact figures available for the number of people who took to the streets, squares, and open fields to see the pope, but estimates range from six[84] to fifteen[85] million, or between one-sixth and more than one-third of the country's population. Contemporary reports suggest that during the visit people appeared inspired, more generous, and, in the words of Adam Michnik, "metamorphosed into a cheerful and happy collectivity, a people filled with dignity."[86] Ironically, it was as though Marx's prediction had been turned on its head: at least for the duration of the pope's visit, the state was "withering away," while the masses organized themselves not under the banner of communism, but under the guidance of the Church. It is also significant that not all the millions who turned out to participate in the events of the pope's visit were devout believers. For those who were not, the pontiff's presence was an opportunity to voice opposition to the government and, in a way, their allegiance to the West, symbolized by Poland's allegiance to the Roman Church.[87]

Although John Paul II's speeches and the presence of millions who came to hear them must be regarded as political acts in their political context, the pope consciously refrained from provoking the authorities. Upon his arrival at Warsaw's Okęcie airport, he stated:

> My visit is dictated by a strictly religious motive. At the same time, I warmly desire my present visit to serve the great cause of rapprochement and cooperation among nations, to serve mutual understanding, reconciliation and peace in the world of today. And I want my visit to bear the fruit of internal unity for my compatriots and to help in the further satisfactory development in the relations between the State and Church in my beloved homeland.[88]

Benign as these goals may seem, they nonetheless carried political weight, for in them were themes repeated throughout the pope's visit: the unbreakable relationship between Roman Catholicism and the Polish nation, the right of every nation to govern itself and to shape its own future, the universal validity of human rights, the moral power and immediate relevance of Catholic tradition and doctrine in Polish public life, the broad and international significance of the Polish Church's struggles and demands, and a resurgent messianism based not in the tropes of Polish romantic nationalism, but in a new Christian and Slavic message calling for spiritual unity in Europe across the East-West divide.[89] The pope emphasized different elements of his "programme" at different stages along his itinerary. Thus, in his speech while meeting with Gierek, the pope stressed that peace can be achieved only on the basis of respect for "the objective rights of the nation."[90] In his sermon on 2 June at Warsaw's Victory Square, he emphasized the unbreakable link between the Polish nation and Christianity, and the centrality of Christ in the history all peoples, and especially the history of the Polish people.[91] At Gniezno, the historic cradle of Polish Christianity, the pope emphasized his unique mission as a Slav and as a Pole to work toward the spiritual unity of Europe.[92]

Each of the stops on John Paul II's itinerary was intended to highlight a significant aspect of Polish history and culture, or a tradition of the Church in Poland. Warsaw was the capital city destroyed in World War II; Wadowice, the town of the pope's birth; Częstochowa, home to the Jasna Góra monastery and the Black Madonna;[93] Kraków, a great center of learning, Catholic tradition, and, more recently, Catholic opposition. Oświęcim, then, was an obvious destination for John Paul II. Unlike other stops on his nine-day itinerary, a visit to the grounds of the former camp had the full support of the regime. From the regime's perspective, Auschwitz was not a Catholic shrine or site of traditional Catholic pilgrimage, nor was it a center of Polish Catholic tradition. Auschwitz was, however, a site that affirmed the unity of oppression and resistance, for the suffering of the Polish nation at Auschwitz did not recognize boundaries of class or religion or ideology. Moreover, an acknowledgment of the Red Army's liberation of Auschwitz and the bravery of the camp's underground resistance could perhaps offer the regime a modicum of legitimacy.[94]

The Polish episcopate, however, did not include a visit and mass at the Auschwitz site in order to mollify the regime, although this was perhaps an added benefit. Auschwitz was crucial because more than any other site on the itinerary, it was a place where the pope could symbolically and effectively articulate and integrate the broader themes of his pilgrimage. Auschwitz was a site of patriotic unity called forth by the memory of those Poles who had suffered and sacrificed there. Auschwitz was where the pope could "safely" emphasize his creed of basic and unalterable human and civil rights, for nowhere had the rights of the individual been violated more than there. Furthermore, Auschwitz was a site that in recent years had attracted increasing international attention. Better known around the world than Częstochowa or perhaps even Kraków, the former camp could function as an international stage for John Paul's mission and message. Auschwitz and its history could also demonstrate the indissoluble link between the suffering Polish nation and the Catholic Church. The Polish Church was a martyr church, and there was no more poignant a symbol of this than the grounds of the former camp, where Maksymilian Kolbe and countless, nameless others had given their lives for a faith so inseparable from their identity as Poles. Finally, for the pope and his faithful, Auschwitz was a site of redemption, where those who perished for the faith experienced, through their sacrifice, the victory of salvation.

Shortly after three o'clock in the afternoon on 7 June, John Paul II arrived in a white helicopter at the base camp of the Auschwitz complex.[95] He was accompanied by Vatican dignitaries as well as representatives of the Church hierarchy from abroad, including Cardinals John Król of Philadelphia and Joseph Ratzinger of Germany. He was also accompanied by representatives of the Polish state, including the minister of foreign affairs, ZBoWiD president Stanisław Wroński, the director of the state's office of religions Kazimierz Kąkol, as well as representatives of the provincial leadership of the PZPR.[96] Among other members of the retinue were Kazimierz Smoleń, who welcomed the Pope to the grounds of the State Museum and accompanied him through the camp, and Franciszek Gajowniczek, the man whose life was spared by Father Maksymilian Kolbe's offer to take his place in the bunker of Block 11.

John Paul II proceeded from the main gate of Auschwitz I to Block 11, where, in Maksymilian Kolbe's cell, the pope paid homage to the priest who, according to one journalistic account, had "become a symbol of the highest of Christian values."[97] Although John Paul II was on a pilgrimage to "Auschwitz" broadly defined, this cell appeared to be the most important destination for the pope personally. To visit the Franciscan's cell was to recognize both the place and act of his martyrdom, and it was one stage in the pope's decades-long effort toward Kolbe's canonization. John Paul II then proceeded to the courtyard next to Block 11, where, in the presence of his entourage, he laid flowers and knelt at the Wall of Death in prayer.[98] Ritual reverence at the Wall of Death was part of nearly every "state visit" to Auschwitz, but it was also in keeping with the traditions of Polish Catholics. The gesture was not only a demonstration of the pope's personal devotion, but also appeared to offer his blessing to a site "sanctified" by the blood of thousands of martyrs and revered as such by pilgrims to Auschwitz throughout the decades.

While the ceremony at Auschwitz I, intimate and subdued, was reserved for the pope and accompanying dignitaries, the papal mass became the largest public event ever held on the grounds of the State Museum. Throughout the morning, tens of thousands gathered on the fields of Birkenau. As one journalistic account described the anticipatory mood there:

> The press center is situated not far from the gates of the extermination camp. We waited there about two hours, at the entrance of walls and wires, the whole time regarding the hundreds of thousands of people that this same camp engulfs, not in order to exterminate them, but to become the site of the final victory of love over hate. The altar is situated on the "ramp." In front of it sat former prisoners of concentration camps. Next to it, the press, and likewise an area for priests concelebrating the most holy mass with John Paul II. Red chasubles and stoles on the shoulders of the priests awaiting the Bishop of Rome. Hot and sultry, humid air. A huge and growing crowd among the chimneys that remain from the disintegrated barracks. . . . After hours of anticipation the white helicopter bringing the pope and his escorts arrives. They land in the main camp. The anticipation grows. Finally an aerial cavalcade arrives. People spring onto benches, fall into silent song and prayer. On the elevated altar appears at the fore a cross, then the red of liturgical vestments of concelebrating priests overflows the steps, and John Paul II finally appears.[99]

When the pope arrived, he changed his vestments in a former women's barracks and proceeded to the main altar erected for the mass. The altar was situated directly over the railroad siding built in 1944 to bring Jewish deportees to their deaths. Above the altar rose a gigantic, rough-hewn cross adorned at its center with a ring of barbed wire. Symbolizing a crown of thorns, the wire linked the suffering and death of Auschwitz victims to the passion of Christ. From one arm of the cross hung a banner resembling a camp uniform and bearing the red triangle of the Polish political prisoner. The triangle was inscribed with the number 16,670—the number worn by Maksymilian

Kolbe.[100] Kolbe and his legacy were central to the event at Birkenau, just as they had been at Auschwitz I, and the mark of his uniform on the altar's cross ensured that his presence would tower, both literally and figuratively, over the proceedings.

Kolbe's death was understood and celebrated as an act of love, sacrifice, redemption, and victory, and these themes resonated throughout the entire mass, from the liturgy and readings to the pope's homily.[101] The scripture readings were taken from I John 3:13–16 ("By this we know love, that he laid down his life for us; and we ought to lay down our lives for the brethren.");[102] Psalm 116 ("I kept my faith, even when I said, 'I am greatly afflicted'; I said in my consternation, 'Men are all a vain hope.' . . . I will offer to thee the sacrifice of thanksgiving and call on the name of the Lord. I will pay my vows to the Lord in the presence of all his people.");[103] and John 15: 12–16 ("This is my commandment, that you love one another as I have loved you. Greater love has no man than this, that a man lay down his life for his friends.").[104] The readings were intended as directives for the faithful gathered at Birkenau, but they were also illustrations of the sacrificial death of Christ mirrored in the sacrificial death of Maksymilian Kolbe. Guided by his faith, Kolbe had followed these directives and modeled himself after Christ; in the midst of hatred and misery, he had demonstrated his love, offered himself as a sacrifice, and thereby gained redemption and the final victory of salvation.

In his homily,[105] John Paul II expanded on this theology of redemption by addressing an additional text from the First Letter of John: "[A]nd this is the victory that overcomes the world—our faith."[106] That victory, at Christ's crucifixion and at Auschwitz, was, in the pope's words, a "victory through love, which enlivens faith to the point of the final witness." The supreme example of the "final witness" at Auschwitz was Maksymilian Kolbe, described by John Paul II as an ordinary man of humble origins beatified "by God's grace and the Church's judgement." Described in this manner, Kolbe was to represent all martyrs at Auschwitz—the "everyman-martyr," as it were—and to stand as a model of devotion and sacrifice for all believers. In the words of Marek Skwarnicki, writing the following week in *Tygodnik Powszechny:*

> The deed of Blessed Maksymilian Kolbe, of which John Paul II spoke at the mass celebrated here has, moreover, such a huge dimension for posterity, for it gives a name to the man among the millions of anonymous other victims. It

also gives a name to all those nameless ones who found it in themselves to undertake similar acts or even gestures upholding hope then and now.[107]

In the Polish vernacular understanding of Auschwitz and its victims, Kolbe was the ideal prisoner: he was selfless, patriotic, and, unlike the prisoner of the political left so often valorized in the past, he was also the personification of the highest ideals of Christian charity. His victory, however, was not unique. As the pope continued in his homily:

> But was Father Maksymilian Kolbe the only one—he, who won the victory that was felt by his fellow prisoners, and is felt by the Church and the world to this day? Certainly many others won similar victories as, for example, the death in a gas chamber of the Carmelite Sister Benedicta of the Cross, known in the world as Edith Stein, by trade a philosopher, a distinguished student of Husserl who became one of the standouts of contemporary German philosophy, and who came from a Jewish family living in Wrocław.

To include Edith Stein among those who had won the victory through sacrificial death was certainly in keeping with Catholic theology and the pope's soteriology of Auschwitz. Here Sister Benedicta of the Cross, a Jewish convert to Catholicism, was counted among the faithful who died at Auschwitz, yet her death was not the result of voluntary sacrifice. She was sent to Westerbork, a transit camp mainly for Jews to be deported from the Netherlands. From there she was deported to Auschwitz along with several dozen other Catholics, among them nuns and monks, whom the Nazi authorities defined as Jews. Arriving at Auschwitz on 8 August 1942, she was deemed unfit to work, and sent to the gas chamber.[108] Stein was not killed as a martyr of her Catholic faith or her political convictions; she was the victim of Nazi genocide, killed as a Jew at Auschwitz among a million others.

The historical obfuscation was not new, but the context was. For decades, demonstrations at Auschwitz had proclaimed a certain inclusivity for the Jewish victims of the camp, whether the inclusivity of Polish nationality, of communism, or of international solidarity in suffering. Yet the failure to recognize Jews—or any other victim group—as a particular category of deportee and prisoner was to neglect the historical uniqueness of their experience in the camp and the reasons for their persecution. For the pope to evoke Stein's memory in the context of his homily at Birkenau, the site of her death, was perhaps only natural and may also have been intended as a gesture of inclusivity and reconciliation between Catholics and Jews. After all, the pope was including Stein among those who had died for the faith and thereby won the victory of salvation. Did this inclusion, however, suggest that all Jews who died at Auschwitz partook in that "final victory," or was that victory limited to Christians? In any case, the pope's words, if not very controversial at the time, were not a useful step toward Jewish-Catholic reconciliation in the long term. In subsequent years and especially during the Carmelite convent controversy of the 1980s, John Paul II's reference to Stein became a symbol of what many regarded as his continuing effort to bring the Shoah and Auschwitz under the banner of Catholicism.

The pope's invocation of Edith Stein was not his only reference to the murder of Jews at Auschwitz. Later in his homily, he paid homage to all the victims at the site, as it were, of their crucifixion:

> I have, of course, come to pray with all of you here today, with all of Poland, and with all of Europe. Christ wishes that the successor to Saint Peter gives witness before the entire world to the greatness of contemporary man and his misery, to his defeat and to his victory. Therefore I come and kneel at the Golgotha of our age, at these tombs, largely nameless like a great tomb of the unknown soldier. I kneel before all the tablets, one after another, in Birkenau, on which are inscribed a memorial to the victims of Auschwitz in the following languages . . .

The pope went on to recite the nineteen languages on the tablets before the Birkenau monument. His remarks, as he stated, were addressed to all in the audience. Likewise, his naming of victims' languages acknowledged the ecumenism of suffering at Auschwitz. Yet his choice of metaphor endowed the site with Christian symbolism and meaning. "Golgotha," the place of Christ's crucifixion, was a site of suffering on behalf of others and therefore a site of redemption, but it can be understood as such only from a Christian perspective.

John Paul II then singled out three tablets among the nineteen:

> I pause together with you, dear participants in this gathering, for a moment before the tablet with an inscription in Hebrew. The inscription calls forth the memory of that nation whose sons and daughters were marked for total extermination. This nation has its origins with Abraham, the "father of

our faith" (Romans 4:12) as expressed by Paul of Tarsus. The very nation that received from the God Yahweh the commandment "Thou shalt not kill" experienced its own death in special measure. No one may pass by this tablet with indifference. And another chosen tablet—the tablet with an inscription in Russian. I add no comment. We know of which nation this tablet speaks. We know of the contribution of this nation to the freedom of the peoples in the last horrible war. One may not pass by this tablet with indifference.

And finally, the tablet in the Polish language. Six million Poles perished during the last war—one-fifth of the nation. It was yet another stage in the centuries-old struggle of that nation, of my nation, for its fundamental rights among the nations of Europe, one more cry for the right to its own place on the map of Europe, one more painful reckoning with the conscience of contemporary humanity.

One can only speculate, on the basis of context and the broader agenda of the pope's visit, on the reasons for which he chose to emphasize the suffering of these three peoples. For John Paul II to single out the Jews as victims of a policy of total extermination appears today as an obvious and necessary element of any public address at the site. Given the context or, more specifically, the history of public events at Auschwitz, the pope's acknowledgment of the Shoah was unusual and was certainly the first such acknowledgment there before an audience of three hundred thousand people.[109] Was it sufficiently explicit? Was it sufficiently instructive for a Polish public for whom Auschwitz stood, in the first place, as a site of their nation's martyrdom?

According to Robert Wistrich, John Paul II's 1979 visit to Poland and Auschwitz marked the beginning of a leitmotif of his work: his continuing concern over the problem of Jewish suffering during the Second World War.[110] It was, to be sure, the first visit of a pope to a former Nazi camp, and John Paul II was clear in singling out the Jews as "that nation whose sons and daughters were marked for total extermination," thereby setting their history apart from that of Poles, Russians, and others at Auschwitz. Some contemporary observers considered the words of John Paul II restrained, sensitive, and intended as a gesture of reconciliation toward Jews;[111] others regarded them as symbolic of a larger process of integrating the suffering of Jews at Auschwitz into a broader Polish or international holocaust, or of a plan to polonize and Christianize the memorial site and its history.[112] The reality was, of course, far more complex, as events in the two decades since have shown.[113] On the one hand, John Paul II has always been insistent on the absolute validity of Christian claims to showing the path to salvation. At the same time, genuine concern for the Jews and the fight against anti-Semitism have been trademarks of Wojtyła's work since his youth, and his papacy has resulted in significant advances in relations between Catholics and Jews.[114] In any case, the pope's visit to Auschwitz heralded a new era in Polish-Jewish and Jewish-Catholic relations, but it also foreshadowed Polish-Jewish conflicts over the site in the decades to follow.

There is no reason to doubt that John Paul II's reference to the Soviet dead at Auschwitz was a sincere recognition of the thousands of Soviet prisoners of war who perished there as well as the soldiers who died in the region's liberation. It may, however, have been a slight concession to the authorities. According to one biography, Cardinal Macharski of Kraków had received a letter from Stanisław Kania, Gierek's eventual successor, noting that John Paul II had not mentioned the six hundred thousand Soviet soldiers killed in the fight for Poland's liberation.[115] It is not clear whether this influenced the pope, but his acknowledgment of Soviet wartime losses was bound to calm the authorities somewhat, while the restraint of his words ensured that his audience would not equate them with the hyperbolic praise traditionally lavished on the Red Army by representatives of the government.

References to Poland's wartime losses were not at all unusual in the context of large public events at the Auschwitz site. John Paul II, however, placed these losses not in their usual context of the fight against fascism or World War II, but in the broader context of the continuing struggle for Polish national independence. National uniqueness, Polish national messianism, and of course the martyrdom of the Polish nation in the last war were all common themes at Auschwitz, but the pope interpreted Poland's wartime sacrifice as a fight "for its fundamental rights among the nations of Europe." Describing Poland's struggle as "one more painful reckoning with the conscience of contemporary humanity," John Paul II was appealing to the higher ideals of European liberalism and nationalism. The pope's words were not overtly political, but circumspect. Yet they did convey—for the first time at the State Museum at Auschwitz—an antiestablishment message, for to evoke the goal of national independence and freedom from external oppression was to draw a historical parallel to Poland's contemporary situation. Constrained by an unwanted and corrupt government, unable to shape its own future, and still under the watchful eye of the Soviet Union, Poland would wait another ten years to govern itself independently. Many would argue, however, that the process of achieving that independence began during John Paul II's visit in 1979.

National sovereignty was not the only political theme addressed in the pope's homily, for John Paul II used the history of the Auschwitz camp to affirm other presentist goals. For much of the State Museum's history, Polish political leaders had used the memorial site as an arena to demonstrate and to rally support for the regime and its policies. In 1979, however, the authority of John Paul II and his Church transformed it into a forum for opposition. Affirming the principles of universal human rights, the pope referred again to the redemption and victory won by Maksymilian Kolbe and Sister Benedicta of the Cross "at this place built upon hatred and the contempt for man in the name of a mad ideology, at this place built upon cruelty." Linking the Auschwitz past to a central theme of his first encyclical, *Redemptor Hominis,* the pope then stated:

> At the site where humanity, the dignity of man, was so horribly trampled upon, man was victorious.
>
> It should surprise no one that the pope born and raised on this soil, the pope, who came to the see of Saint Peter from Kraków, from that archdiocese where the Auschwitz camp is located, that this pope began the first encyclical of his pontificate with the words "Redemptor Hominis" and dedicated it in its entirety to the cause of man, to the dignity of man, to the threats against man—and finally to the rights of man—indispensable rights, which can so easily be trampled upon and annihilated by man! To do so it is enough to put him in a different uniform, arm him with the apparatus of violence, with the means of destruction; to do so it is enough to impose upon him an ideology, in which the rights of man are subordinated to the demands of the system, subordinated as if they did not exist at all.

It was natural, even imperative that John Paul II's visit to Poland include a pilgrimage to Auschwitz. Karol Wojtyła had long had a personal relationship to the site, its history, its horrors, and its postwar role as a sanctuary for pilgrimage and prayer. As pope, however, he used it as a stage for clear, if restrained, comment on the current state of human rights in Poland and the world. The destruction of individual rights at Auschwitz was part of the Nazi past, but sounding a presentist chord, the pope emphasized the basic fragility of individual rights and how easily they are subject to the brutality of any regime. To a discontented Polish public on the verge of revolt, the references to a "different uniform," an "apparatus of violence," an alternative "ideology" and the "demands of the system" were clear.

Effectively blending the spiritual with the temporal once again, John Paul II resumed the human rights theme later in the homily, as he cited the United Nations Universal Declaration of Human Rights, Pope John XXIII's encyclical *Pacem in terris,* and even Paweł Włodkowic, a fifteenth-century rector of Kraków's Jagiellonian University. Włodkowic, in the pope's words, "proclaimed the necessity of securing the following rights of nations: the right to exist, the right to freedom, the right to independence, the right to one's own culture, the right to honorable development. 'Where power is more at work than love,' Włodkowic wrote, 'one seeks that which is in one's own interest and not in the interest of Jesus Christ, and from there easily departs from the rule of God's law.'" The foundation of all human rights, John Paul II affirmed, lay not only in the common declarations of the nations or the words of a pope, but also in the dictates of God. "I speak," he concluded, "not only on behalf of those who perished, the four million victims of this huge field. I speak in the name of all nations whose rights are disregarded and violated. I speak because I am obligated, we are all obligated, to the truth. I speak because I am obligated, we are all obligated, to the care of man."

John Paul II's homily was addressed to Poles and to their situation, but it is important to stress that he was also addressing an international audience at a site of suffering not only for Poland, but for many nations. His recitation of the languages on the various tablets at Birkenau emphasized this, as did his reference to "all nations whose rights are disregarded and violated" and the prayers he recited in various languages at the conclusion of his homily. The values the pope was upholding were universal, as were the threats against them—hatred, intolerance, oppression, violence, and war.

In this sense, it is appropriate to regard the pope's visit and his homily at Auschwitz as a contribution to the "internationalization" of the site that had begun some fifteen years before. Like much of the rest of John Paul II's visit, the papal mass and visit at Auschwitz were covered in the mass media around the world, and this substantially increased the museum's international visibility. Newspapers, radio reports, and television broadcasts showed the memorial site not only as a locus of Catholic pilgrimage, but also as a venue for the condemnation of war and the proclamation of universal values. Since the 1960s Auschwitz had been responding to a growing and more complex assortment of commemorative constituencies. It was already "on the map" of the international public. As the years ahead would reveal, representatives of various victim groups and many nations would not only make use of the public space at Auschwitz, but also would make claims to the features and uses of its memorial landscape.

Yet there remained a particularly Polish calling associated with John Paul II's message at Auschwitz. As Neil Acherson rather melodramatically wrote in June 1979:

> He has restored to Poland the mystic belief in a national mission. A hundred years ago, the visionary Tuwiański [Towiański] formulated "Messianism," the idea that Poland was the collective reincarnation of Christ, to be crucified in every generation for the redemption of the world. That fanaticism died finally in the holocaust of the Warsaw Rising in 1944. And yet, in the new form of a faith that Poland has been chosen through its suffering to show mankind how to find peace and be saved, Messianism is resurrecting on the Vistula. And, in the heart of a great and very homesick man, on the Tiber.[116]

A Slavic pope, called by God to witness to the spiritual renewal in Europe and to defend the dignity of mankind, John Paul II was also carving out a new role for himself and for Poland. Whether the "fanaticism" to which Acherson refers died in Warsaw or was suppressed by the postwar regime remains open to debate. It is, in any case, clear that a new national spirit and mission were awakened by the presence of John Paul II, and nowhere was this more obvious than at Birkenau. John Paul II and his faithful were to carry the banner of the dreadful Auschwitz past, but they were also compelled to seek and to find in that past a clear redemptive meaning. Victory was won at Auschwitz by countless Poles like Kolbe—won through faith, love, and willing sacrifice. Motivated by virtues like these, Poles could bring the lessons of Auschwitz to bear on their own struggles for freedom, human dignity, and the rights of the nation. In short, a Polish sense of mission could be a motor of social change.

The effects of the pope's 1979 visit on the social and political landscape of his homeland were immediate and enormous. As if attempting to return to the status quo ante, the next month Edward Gierek unveiled a new monument to

Bolesław Bierut in Lublin;[117] but in reality, the regime was repeatedly forced to confront the legacy of John Paul II's visit. The Catholic writer Bohdan Cywiński had accurately predicted that "[t]he papal visit will be a time of sowing, the moral harvest will come later."[118] Without a doubt, the pope had a liberating effect on a population that, emboldened by his visit and the weakness of the regime, would initiate a wave of strikes a year later and form the nationwide independent trade union "Solidarity." Unique in its nationalism and Catholicism, but broadly appealing in its call for individual rights and democratization, the Solidarity movement laid the foundation of Poland's revolution in 1989 and of the other revolutionary movements that swept East-Central Europe in that year.

The effects of the pope's visit to Auschwitz were perhaps less immediate, but were no less important for the future of the memorial site. Most obviously, the visit of John Paul II publicized the site, its history, and the pope's interpretation of that history. When used as a pulpit for the pope's theology, Auschwitz served not only as an example of fascism, racism, and war, but also as an example of faithlessness, hate, and the absence of a Christ-centered view of human relations. In his sermon at Warsaw's Victory Square on the day of his arrival, John Paul II had strongly emphasized the necessity of a Christ-centered interpretation of history, and especially of Polish history. "Without Christ it is impossible to understand the history of Poland," the pontiff stated, "above all as the history of the people who have traveled and are traveling the road of life in this land." "Without Christ," he continued, "it is impossible to understand this nation that has a past so splendid and at the same time so frightfully difficult. . . . It is impossible to understand the history of Poland from Stanisław at Skalka to Maksymilian in Auschwitz unless we apply to them as well the sole and basic criterion of understanding which bears the name of Jesus Christ."[119] Likewise, for John Paul II it was impossible to understand the true meaning of Auschwitz and its place in Polish history without Christ. Christ, he believed, was the model of love and sacrifice who motivated the martyrs at Auschwitz; he was the martyr-prototype who had won the victory for all the faithful departed. In short, Christ lent Auschwitz and its history a redemptive value that would vanish in his absence.

In the aftermath of the pope's visit a Polish journalist claimed, "Humanity was wounded and has not entirely healed. That is why the mass of John Paul II in 1979 has an unusual meaning. Because here everything in history that terrifies the living shows its weakness in the face of an omnipotent and merciful God. . . . The mass at Birkenau was a triumph."[120] An acclamation such as this was undoubtedly meaningful for many Polish Catholics and accurately reflected their sentiments at the time. It was also typical of the euphoric responses to the pope's visits at Auschwitz and elsewhere. Removed from its context, however, the claim that "an omnipotent and merciful God" was evident among the ruins of Birkenau was difficult for many to accept, and reflects today a certain Christian triumphalism or, at the very least, a desire to "baptize" the site and to explain its history from an exclusively Christian perspective. Over the preceding thirty-five years Auschwitz had been explained in a variety of ways, the stewards of its memory seeking a redemptive history in the themes of patriotism, resistance, communism, antifascism, anti-Americanism, and a host of other temporal dogmas considered serviceable at any given moment. According to the pope, however, redemption was not to be found in the temporal and secular act, but in the timeless and divinely inspired sacrifice of Christ and his many disciples among the prisoners of the camp.

The pope had acknowledged the diversity of languages on the tablets at the foot of the Birkenau monument and had chosen to single out the Jews, Russians, and Poles among the victims. Yet his deeds and words at Auschwitz suggested that the most important thing about Auschwitz, "the birthplace of the patron of our century," was Maksymilian Kolbe's sacrificial death—a death that symbolically redeemed the camp and its prisoners. Although intended to be inclusive, this theology of Auschwitz was limiting in its effect, for it made sense only within the traditions of Polish nationality and Catholicism. At the same time, many Poles undoubtedly experienced this theology as liberating, for it offered their vernacular understanding of Auschwitz and its significance a degree of legitimacy that official Auschwitz narratives had denied. "Auschwitz as the final stage in the development of German fascist imperialism" or "Auschwitz as golgotha?" The former was based in materialist philosophy, but the latter was far easier for the ordinary Pole to understand. Free of state-sponsored ideologies and contrived histories, the pope's Auschwitz could now be commemorated in the context of Polish national tradition and using the vocabulary of Polish Catholicism.

Paradoxically, however, by freeing Auschwitz from the cant and state-directed choreography that had characterized the memorial site throughout much of its history, John Paul II also opened Auschwitz and the stewards of its memory to criticism and controversy. Thus, to uphold the suffering of Jews, Poles, and Russians at Auschwitz was to fail to specify the suffering of other victim groups. To invoke the martyr's death of Maksymilian Kolbe was to raise questions about Kolbe's nationalism and his supervision of anti-Semitic publications before the war and, more broadly, the anti-Semitic traditions of the Polish Church. To uphold the death of Edith Stein as a sacrificial death for the faith was to blur the historical distinction, drawn by the Nazis, between Catholic political prisoners and "racial" Jews who happened to have converted to Catholicism. To refer to Auschwitz as the "Golgotha of our age" was a poignant and effective use of metaphor, but the image associated Auschwitz with the sentiments of Polish messianism and located it within the purview of Christian culture. To celebrate mass at Birkenau was a moving recognition of the martyrs of Auschwitz and of the former camp's place in the postwar identity of the Polish nation, but the mass was also a Christian ritual held on what was regarded by many as the world's largest Jewish burial ground.

It was in this way that the Pope's visit both legitimized the Polish-national commemorative framework at Auschwitz and marked the beginning of that framework's collapse. Over the course of the 1980s, public discussion and commemoration of the war, occupation, and genocide dramatically increased the value of Auschwitz as a metonym for all three—and increased the stakes of the debates over the memorial site's future. Should there be a place for specifically (or exclusively) Christian, Jewish, Romani, Polish, Russian, or German commemoration at Auschwitz, now that the site appeared relieved of the Marxist ideology and vague internationalism of the past? If so, what are the appropriate sites and symbols of memory? Who is to have proprietorship over them? The questions were not new, and since 1979 they have been raised again and again, whether in the context of the Carmelite Convent controversy, in reference to the presence of religious symbols at the memorial site, or in connection with plans for the future of the grounds. And if public debate over Auschwitz continues to the present day, it is in part the result of the "liberation" of the memorial site that began during the papal visit of June 1979.

Epilogue ⫿

Poland and Auschwitz in the 1980s

> O earth, cover not my blood, and let my cry find no resting-place.
>
> Job 16:18

THIS BOOK BEGAN WITH the premise that the images of Auschwitz captured in January 1945 have been blurred in the decades since the camp's liberation. Neither the physical characteristics of Auschwitz nor its meaning remained static, but instead were modified by age, the elements, and especially by the diverse and often competing narratives of the camp complex's history. Moreover, the cultural imperatives and political exigencies of the postwar Polish state and society modified and even distorted the landscape and memory of Auschwitz. This work has attempted to account for, to explain, and to evaluate many of these postwar images as they have been manifested at Auschwitz from the camp's liberation through the 1970s. Some of these images were accurate and appropriate representations of the camp's history, while others distorted the historical record, but all must be understood in relation to the memorial site's function as a locus of public commemoration and education.

Various carriers of public wartime memory have converged at the State Museum at Auschwitz, and at this point of intersection—the primary memorial site of the Polish People's Republic—the stewards of Auschwitz memory have preserved and destroyed the artifacts of history. They have erected monuments, developed, transformed, and effaced interpretive exhibits, and choreographed votive commemorative ceremonies and noisy political demonstrations. In these ways Auschwitz memory was constructed, maintained, and modified—all within a shifting, yet sturdy, political and cultural framework based in postwar

Polish culture and politics. Supporting that framework were the three prevailing characteristics of memory: first, the Polish-national martyrological idiom; second, its marginalization of the Shoah; and third, its political instrumentalization. Originating in the first postwar years, these characteristics proved remarkably persistent elements of official memory at Auschwitz. The Polish state mobilized the site and its meanings in the service of political goals, but at the same time, postwar Auschwitz remained a register of how Poles perceived themselves and their history, state agendas notwithstanding. The image of the heroic resistance fighter, the memorial site as the golgotha of the Polish nation, the legacy of shared suffering and solidarity among those persecuted by the Nazis—notions of Auschwitz such as these aided Poles in the process of confronting the tragedy and loss they experienced during the German occupation. They also lent the memorial site, and especially the base camp, a certain mystical permanence and transcendence as an icon of Polish postwar identity.[1]

Public expressions of Auschwitz memory were not always misleading, tendentious, or the result of deliberate political manipulation; many of the exhibitions and commemorative rituals at the site were the result of good faith and honest effort on the part of their organizers, and reflected the complex and diverse history of the camp. But when viewed in combination, the three main elements of collective memory helped to construct a dominant narrative context for Polish considerations of Auschwitz in the postwar years. Much of this book has been devoted to explaining and even indicting the narratives and forms of representation employed at the memorial site, but this should not be understood as a universal condemnation of frameworks of interpretation or narratives. "No memory," as Martin Jay has written, "can ever survive the death of its original holder without the collective will to keep it alive."[2] This should remind us that the total absence of any narrative context or memorial framework at Auschwitz would leave us with little other than a pure chronicle of the events that took place there or a faceless landscape devoid of any artifacts or images of the past. Minimalist representations of the past, stripped of any stylized or aestheticized interpretation, may appear as "neutral containers" for the facts of history, but the postwar history of the memorial site shows how elusive "neutrality" can be. Neutral and objective representation of the Auschwitz past is, strictly speaking, an impossible goal. But the effort to reach that goal is hardly an idle task. Thus, collective memories converging on Auschwitz, although evolutionary and vulnerable to manipulation of the historical record, nonetheless remain necessary, if imperfect, vehicles for conveying the stories and lessons of the past to the present.

The memorialization of Auschwitz involves certain risks, and the stewards of memory and their mentors at the State Museum at Auschwitz have demonstrated both the value and the potentially tragic cost of representing the past at the memorial site. The framework of memory at postliberation Auschwitz, grounded in postwar Polish politics and commemorative culture, has been anything but neutral; instead, it has alerted us to the dangers of tendentious and even irresponsible representations of the historical record. But that framework and its commemorative narratives cannot simply be explained away as a clumsy historicization of Auschwitz, as the result of transferential "narrative fetishism,"[3] or, in the words of one scholar, as a "churlish denial of the history of others."[4] Rather, the complexity of the camp's history, differing forms and agendas of commemoration, the pull of Polish culture and politics, and, not least, the metonymical status of Auschwitz in Poland and around the world have subjected the memorial site to various and at times contradictory demands.[5]

These demands have proliferated since John Paul II's visit, and in this sense, 1979 marked a turning point for postwar Auschwitz. The museum's appearance has not changed radically in the past twenty years, but its agenda, its political and cultural context, and the ways in which it is understood and used by the Polish and international public certainly have changed. Part of the "internationalization" process initiated in the 1960s and the "democratization" process in the aftermath of the pope's visit, new commemorative constituencies have emphasized and modified the role of Auschwitz as a national and international symbol. These changes have opened the site to controversy and have suggested additional avenues of research into its more recent history.

The increase in the symbolic value of Auschwitz and growing interest in the history and memorialization of the camp in the 1980s took place at a time when many Europeans and North Americans were turning their attention to the legacy of the war and the Holocaust. In July and August 1979, shortly after the pope's visit, an American delegation of the President's Commission on the Holocaust led by Elie Wiesel visited Poland and Auschwitz.[6] In September it issued a report to President Jimmy Carter, and the following year, the United States Congress established the U.S. Holocaust Memorial Council, which would supervise the planning and construction of a memorial museum in Washington, D.C. In the two German states, in Poland, and in many other European countries, the years 1979 and 1980 began a series of "forty-years-after" anniversaries commemorating the outbreak of war and the invasions and occupations of various countries. Perhaps most importantly, the international community recognized the growing visibility and symbolism of Auschwitz in 1979 when the United Nations Education, Scientific and Cultural Organisation (UNESCO) inscribed the Auschwitz grounds on its World Heritage List. "By virtue of its activities," the nominating documents stated, "the Museum makes an important contribution to the struggle for world peace and security."[7] UNESCO elected to enter Auschwitz on the list "as a unique site and to restrict the inscription of other sites of a similar nature."[8] The decision to add Auschwitz to the list increased and further institutionalized the site's international significance. Moreover, to limit the inscription of other such sites of genocide—whether those of the Third Reich or those of other regimes—was to elevate and universalize Auschwitz as the premier symbol of National Socialism's brutality and, according to the committee's recommendation, as an "irrefutable and concrete witness to one of the greatest crimes which has been perpetrated against humanity."[9]

The universal importance of the memorial site as a "concrete witness" was reflected in the expanding number of visitors to the site in the 1980s—especially West German visitors and Jewish visitors from Israel, the United States, and around the world.[10] Chapter 6 noted the pilgrimages and politicized tourism of West German organizations at Auschwitz in the 1970s. These groups had increased their presence at the site to such an extent that by 1983 there were already more than fifty Aktion Sühnezeichen groups a year at Auschwitz.[11] The participants in these seminars—not mere tourists—volunteered their labor at the site, undertook research in the museum archives and library, and met with former prisoners. The growing presence of these young pilgrims and volunteers began to cast the Auschwitz site in a new role, for this memorial to the painful history of Polish-German relations and the Shoah was emerging as a symbol of penitence, dialogue, and reconciliation. Aktion Sühnezeichen worked closely with the International Auschwitz Committee and, where necessary, with the state authorities responsible for tourism and youth exchanges. To this extent, their agenda fit within Poland's traditional framework of memory at Auschwitz, but the organization's growing visibility in Poland and at home was symbolic of a general opening of the site in the aftermath of John Paul II's visit.

Efforts to expand the site's role as a forum for dialogue and reconciliation continued throughout the 1980s and became centered on the construction and dedication in 1986 of an International Youth Meeting Center—a hostel and conference center near the base camp that was erected with West German funds at a cost of more than 4.2 million marks.[12] In the years since its founding, it has functioned as a forum for academic conferences and youth exchanges among groups from Germany, Poland, Israel, and other countries. The center, the continuing efforts of Aktion Sühnezeichen, as well as the pilgrimages and travel seminars of hundreds of different educational and political groups have established a continuing German presence at the memorial site and have publicized it at home. With Germany unified and cold-war travel restrictions lifted, Germans now comprise the third-largest visitor group to Auschwitz, after visitors from Poland and from the United States.[13]

Growth in the number of German visitors to the memorial site in the 1980s and 1990s paralleled an increase in Jewish visitors from around the world, especially from the United States and Israel. In the U.S., the airing of the television miniseries *Holocaust* and government initiatives aimed at the institutionalization of Holocaust remembrance—most prominently the formation of the U.S. Holocaust Memorial Council—added to the already growing public and academic interest in the subject. Moreover, the growth of American travel to the countries of Eastern Europe encouraged an expanding interest in the history and meaning of the Shoah and in what was becoming its most prominent symbol: Auschwitz. In Israel, Holocaust remembrance took an increasingly prominent place in that country's political and popular culture throughout the 1980s.[14] Holocaust commemoration was not only a moral imperative for Jews in Israel; it could also demonstrate the triumph of survival and legitimize Israel's strong defense of its citizens and Jewish interests in general. Moreover, for many, a visit to Auschwitz provided a link between memory and identity. For Jews around the world, the symbolic value of Auschwitz was growing exponentially, to the extent that it had become the primary symbol of the Shoah and, for some, a symbol of the Shoah only.[15]

At the same time, in the 1980s Poland was experiencing a difficult and, for some, cathartic confrontation with its past that centered around relations between Poles and Jews during the war and after. This had tremendous implications for Poland's traditional framework of memory at Auschwitz and the future of the memorial site itself. John Paul II's visit signaled the emergence in the 1980s of a new national "patriotic-symbolic-religious language" of re-emerging "traditions."[16] "What this entailed at Auschwitz . . . ," according to Michael Steinlauf, "was the emergence of a symbolic palimpsest: not the eradication of the old narrative with its marginalization of the memory of Jews, but the development of a new narrative layer that only partially covered the old."[17] John Paul II had "overwritten" the old narrative at Auschwitz with a vocabulary and religiosity that celebrated the martyrdom of Maksymilian Kolbe and would help to institutionalize a Roman Catholic presence at the memorial site. At the same time, however, the pope upheld the memory of the Shoah for his countrymen at Birkenau, breaking the capsule, as it were, in which the vexing issue of Polish-Jewish relations in wartime and under the PZPR regime had lain dormant.

If John Paul II provided the catalyst for a more open conversation about Polish-Jewish relations, the independent trade union movement Solidarity provided the political and social context. Winning legal status as the first independent trade union in the communist bloc, Solidarity not only encouraged the revival of nationalism and the Polish insurrectionary spirit, but also called for greater cultural openness, thereby encouraging a more thorough historical self-examination and a more honest commemoration of the past. In an open letter to *Polityka,* for example, Solidarity supporters Jan Józef Lipski, Władysław Bartoszewski, and others called for a new confrontation with "the problem of Polish-Jewish relations" and the "so-called 'Jewish question,'" and went on to condemn the "anti-Semitic campaign" of 1968 and to call for the rehabilitation of those who suffered because of it.[18] Although the writers of this letter were not necessarily representative of the Solidarity movement as a whole, it was demands such as these, as well as the freedoms won from the state, that allowed for the emergence of a more fruitful, if painful, reassessment of relations between Jews and Poles during and since the war. It is no accident that so many of the participants in the debates over Jewish-Polish relations in the 1980s and 1990s were intimately connected with Solidarity.

An additional factor spurring public discourse about Polish-Jewish relations was the airing of Claude Lanzmann's film *Shoah,* which premiered in Paris in 1985. Lanzmann's film was more than nine hours long and was composed of interviews with witnesses to the Holocaust—bystanders, perpetrators, and victims. The official Polish press and many critics abroad condemned the film as tendentiously anti-Polish, especially in its characterization of Poles as indifferent and ignorant bystanders. The polemics that resulted were angry, and rehearsed familiar refrains: an anti-Polish conspiracy was at work and the film was "yet another attempt to justify Nazi crimes and erase from European memory German plans for the biological annihilation also of the Polish nation."[19] Despite the discomfort it may have caused, the film nonetheless caused many Poles to reassess their assumptions about the nature and character of Nazi occupation policy, and it brought the problem of wartime relations between Poles and Jews into the public sphere as a matter of debate—rather than as a matter of government propaganda, as in 1967–68.

Finally, Poland's confrontation with its past in the 1980s was furthered by a controversy among intellectuals that was publicized in the print media. It began with the publication in January 1987 of an article in *Tygodnik Powszechny* entitled "The Poor Poles Look at the Ghetto." Its author, literary critic Jan Błoński, argued that to the extent that Poles had attempted to confront or to discuss the Nazi destruction of Jews, their responses had generally been limited to apologetics and attempts to justify Polish behavior during the Holocaust. Poles, he claimed, were fearful of being accused of participating in the crimes or of having regarded them with indifference. The way out of this fear and the way to avoid reflex defensive reactions, according to Błoński, was for Poles to "stop haggling, trying to defend and justify ourselves. We must stop arguing about the things that were beyond our power to do, during the occupation and beforehand. Nor must we place blame on political, social, and economic conditions. We must say first of all—Yes, we are guilty."[20] Błoński did not claim that the Poles were guilty of any direct involvement in the genocide of the Jews (making, of course, the obvious exception for blackmailers and informants). Rather, the Poles were guilty of an "insufficient effort to resist." "[I]f only," Błoński wrote, "we had behaved more humanely in the past, had been wiser, more generous, then genocide would perhaps have been 'less imaginable,' would probably have been considerably more difficult to carry out, and almost certainly would have met with much greater resistance than it did. To put it differently, it would not have met with the indifference and moral turpitude of the society in whose full view it took place."[21]

The article prompted passionate responses in the Polish press,[22] and the debates that ensued were even the subject of academic conferences in Poland and abroad. One powerful response expressing the sentiments of many Poles was that of the Solidarity activist Władysław Siła-Nowicki, who enumerated several of the common defenses against accusations of Polish complicity or indifference: Poland had traditionally been a haven for Jews; before 1939, Jews had dominated certain professions and disproportionately controlled wealth, while at the same time retaining their separateness and alien character; no European nation had done more to help the Jews than Poland, and it was in Poland that the risks associated with assistance to Jews had been the greatest; it was not only Jews who had been killed under the occupation, but Poles as well; there had been no quislings in Poland and no collaborative government, but a massive underground resistance that sentenced to death those who betrayed Jews to the Nazis.[23] Siła-Nowicki's defense also offered the following:

> I am proud of my nation's stance in every respect during the period of occupation and in this include the attitude towards the tragedy of the Jewish nation. Obviously, the attitudes towards the Jews during that period do not give us a particular reason to be proud, but neither are they any grounds for shame, and even less for ignominy. Simply, we would have done relatively little more than we actually did.[24]

Responses such as these were not unusual, nor were the attitudes expressed therein particularly new. But the controversy in the second half of the 1980s over relations between Jews and Poles during the occupation marked a turning point. For the first time in forty years, scholars and publicists both in Poland and abroad were participating in a relatively open, and certainly contentious, re-evaluation of their history.

This, then, was the context for the controversy over the convent at Auschwitz, and it is no accident that it erupted at roughly the same time that many Poles were attempting to come to terms with their wartime past and with the issue of Polish-Jewish relations. The ensuing and increasingly hostile debate over the convent brought to the surface and to the international media many of the decades-old tensions between the competing narratives of Jewish and Polish suffering at Auschwitz, further straining relations between Poles and Jews, and between Jews and Roman Catholics. The source of the controversy lay in conflicting notions of the symbolic and didactic value of the Auschwitz site, what James Young has appropriately described as "a micro-study in the conflict between Jewish and Polish memory."[25] Its origins, however, go back to August 1984, when ten Carmelite nuns were granted permission to occupy an unused building just beyond the wires of Auschwitz I.[26] The building, known during the occupation as the *Theatergebäude,* had served as a theater for the Polish troops stationed on the grounds before the war and was later used as a warehouse for, among other things, canisters of Zyklon-B. The building bordered on the confines of Auschwitz I, was included among those structures to be preserved according the Polish government's 1979 agreement with UNESCO, and was therefore part of the "museum."

Various structures that were once part of the camp complex had been used over the decades for a variety of different purposes: the Aufnahme-gebäude built in 1944 as a reception building for prisoners now provided a reception center, complete with food and lodgings, for visitors to the site; the Lagererweiterung had long served as housing for the local population and barracks for the Polish army; the *Kommandatur* (command headquarters) of the base camp contained staff apartments; nearby garages were used by Poland's state-run bus lines. It was perhaps with this in mind that the Oświęcim town authorities and the archbishop of Kraków, Cardinal Franciszek Macharski, granted permission for the nuns to occupy and use the building as a house of penance, prayer, atonement, and honor for the martyrs of the camp. Shortly thereafter, a Belgian Catholic group launched an international fund-raising appeal in support of the convent that the group claimed would function as "a spiritual fortress and a guarantee of the conversion of strayed brothers from our countries, as well as proof of our desire to erase outrages so often done to the Vicar of Christ."[27]

The convent controversy arose from a three-way conflict involving the growing role of Auschwitz as a symbol of the Shoah, traditional Polish narratives of Auschwitz, and Polish sensitivities that emerged in the aftermath of the pope's visit—sensitivities over Polish national identity and the newly opened debate on Polish-Jewish relations. Understandably, Jews were disturbed by the presence of the convent and saw it as a misappropriation and exploitation of the grounds. The convent was, for many Jews, a symbol of persecution at the hands of Christians and, moreover, served only to reinforce the character of the site as a Polish symbol. "Elsewhere," as one commentator remarked, "contrition would be appropriate. Catholic prayers would be in order for the thousands of Gypsies and other non-Jewish prisoners, mainly Poles, who had also been killed in Auschwitz, but not for that one people which had been marked by the Third Reich to be killed during World War II simply because of the accident of birth."[28] As far as this and many other critics were concerned, the nuns were unwilling to recognize the "otherness" of Jews, and by praying for the Jewish dead, insisted on bringing them into the fold of Christianity. In short, the presence of a convent at Auschwitz was perceived by many Jews as a "Christianization" or, at the very least, a universalization of the Shoah.

Protests against the convent grew louder, and in 1986 European Jewish and Roman Catholic leaders met in Geneva to find a solution to the problem. In February of the following year, they agreed that within two years the convent would be relocated as part of a center for "information, education, meeting and prayer" situated near, but clearly outside, the territory of the former camp. Furthermore, the Geneva accord stated that "[t]here will, therefore, be no permanent Catholic place of worship on the site of the Auschwitz and Birkenau camps. Everyone will be able to pray there according to the dictates of his own heart, religion, and faith."[29]

It appeared, then, that the conflict was defused, at least for a time; but the terms of the agreement met stiff opposition from the Catholic Church in Poland, the Carmelite sisters, and the Polish public. The two-year deadline passed without construction of the new center, and in the summer of 1989 the growing hostility between Poles and Jews was exacerbated, when a group of American Jewish protesters led by Rabbi Avraham Weiss of New York held demonstrations at the convent. Denied access, they scaled the convent fence and began to pray and sound a horn. Polish workmen at the site demanded that they leave, and then poured paint and water on the protesters, roughed them up, and physically removed them from the grounds.[30] This open conflict would have been unimaginable only a few short years before, and it signaled not only the memorial site's growing role as an arena for protest of various kinds, but also the more tolerant and open political and social climate. Michael Steinlauf has pointed out that Poland's first free elections in decades—held in the summer of 1989—accompanied these protests. Likewise, the Poles' first experience with a press free of censorship brought them reports of the convent controversy.[31]

Coverage of the conflict was not limited to Polish newspapers, for it was reported internationally. The conflict was exacerbated in August 1989, when Cardinal Macharski, in an unfortunate comment, publicly referred to a "violent campaign of accusations and insinuations on the part of some Jewish circles in the West" and called for the rejection of the Geneva agreement.[32] In a homily later that month, the Polish primate Józef Glemp implied that the protesters had been attempting to assault the nuns and destroy the convent. Jews, the cardinal also suggested, should not speak to Poles "from the position of a nation above all others," but should put an end to the anti-Polish campaign in the media, "which are, in many countries, at [their] disposal."[33] Several weeks later, the Israeli prime minister Yitzhak Shamir was quoted as saying that the cardinal's remarks mirrored an organic Polish anti-Semitism and that the Poles "suck it in with their mother's milk."[34] Thus, what had begun as a controversy over the appropriate use of memorial space at Auschwitz had become a revisitation of stereotypes of the causes and nature of the poor state of Polish-Jewish relations. Aware that the controversy was escalating to an ugly exchange of accusations, the Vatican, reaffirming its commitment to the Geneva agreement, announced that it would fund the construction of a new convent and center for interfaith dialogue near Auschwitz I. Ground was broken in February 1990, and the Carmelite sisters finally occupied their new quarters in 1992.

Jewish reactions of pain and anger to the presence of the convent were certainly understandable; in permitting the sisters to occupy the former Theatergebäude, Polish Catholics and civil authorities had demonstrated a lack of sensitivity to and understanding of the site's symbolic value for Jews around the world. Polish responses to Jewish protests—at times clumsy and at times aggressive—were grounded in far more than what some simply regarded as Polish anti-Semitism. Emboldened by an increasingly Catholic commemorative culture at Auschwitz and accustomed as they were to regarding the camp (and especially Auschwitz I) as a site of their nation's martyrdom, many Poles were baffled by the claims made on the site by others. After all, had Auschwitz I not been constructed for Polish political prisoners? Birkenau, Cardinal Glemp had made clear in his homily, was the more appropriate memorial site for Jews. To many Poles, Jewish objections to the convent were an offense to their religious practice, cultural sensibilities, and commemorative traditions.

Perhaps adding to the Poles' sense of bewilderment was an overlooked irony: the Carmelite convent was certainly not the first physical expression of Roman Catholic religiosity at the memorial site.[35] In 1983 a church had been opened at Birkenau in the former Kommandantur—a large building just outside the site's perimeter and not officially part of the State Museum, but obviously part of the camp's original architecture. The structure and its towering cross were easily visible to visitors at Birkenau, but this obvious Catholic presence had thus far elicited little, if any, protest.[36] The lack of response to the church, arguably a far greater affront to Jewish memory than a convent at the base camp, affirms the tremendous metonymical value of the terminus "Auschwitz" as opposed to "Birkenau" and, significantly, the way in which most have linked symbolism of the Shoah to that portion of the memorial grounds known as "Auschwitz." The concept of "Auschwitz" extends beyond the confines of the original camp, of course, but it is nonetheless ironic that preoccupation with the status and symbolism of Auschwitz I reflects— perhaps more by accident than by design—Poland's success in directing the public's attention to a site primarily connected with Polish, and not Jewish, suffering. As a result of the durable framework of memory at Auschwitz, the base camp had prevailed, in a manner, over Birkenau as the primary locus memoriae of the Shoah.

The Carmelite convent controversy was undoubtedly the most publicized, but certainly not the first, manifestation of the larger conflict between Jewish and Polish memory at Auschwitz. Differing symbols and competing narratives surrounding the public representation of Auschwitz had existed and conflicted for decades, and one analyst has suggested that the outbreak of the controversy was perhaps less remarkable than the fact that it had not occurred sooner.[37] Yet it is not at all surprising that the convent controversy erupted in the 1980s. John Paul II had opened the site and its meaning to debate and even to protest. The cultural and spiritual legacy of his visit further enabled the emergence of an emboldened Catholicism and national-insurrectionary spirit, while at the same time, the status of Auschwitz as a symbol of the Shoah grew exponentially throughout the decade. These forces converged at the memorial site to shake the foundation and undermine the structural integrity of Poland's commemorative framework. Thus, the controversy was not a sudden and spontaneous eruption of Jewish-Catholic tension or merely a manifestation of animosity between Poles and Jews, but a reflection and registration of conflicting historical emplotments and commemorative forces associated with Auschwitz memory at the site since the 1940s.

"Nothing is more unbecoming a sacred space," one observer of the convent controversy has suggested, "as a turf war."[38] The debate over the Auschwitz Carmelites was an unfortunate, even ugly, battle over the stewardship of public memory and its manifestations at a site better suited to reflective silence and mourning. But the controversy did have a number of positive results. It marked an important stage in the continuing internationalization process at Auschwitz. Jewish protests from abroad, the engagement of Catholic leaders from around Europe, international media attention, and the scholarly debates and publications confronting the convent issue emphasized more clearly than ever that the symbolism of Auschwitz and its memorial landscape were not the sole property of its Polish caretakers or the Polish state.

Recognizing this, in the fall of 1989 the new Polish prime minister Tadeusz Mazowiecki directed the Polish Ministry of Culture to call for a special International Council of the Auschwitz-Birkenau State Museum to consider the future of the memorial site. Composed of prominent scholars from around the world as well as former prisoners and Polish officials, the council met in May 1990 and agreed to several principles to guide the work of the State Museum in the future. These included the recommendation that the exhibitions and inscriptions at the memorial site show that 1.6 million were murdered there, that over 90 percent of them were Jews, and that Jews and Gypsies were the only victim groups condemned to die at Auschwitz for the "crime" of birth. Moreover, the council agreed that the museum should also make clear that tens of thousands of non-Jews, and especially Poles, died at Auschwitz, a camp that was central to the Nazis' efforts to destroy the Polish nation.[39]

Broadly speaking, the formation of the new Auschwitz Council marked a major shift in official public memory—a shift that corresponded to the change in political regime that its initiator, Tadeusz Mazowiecki, symbolized. The fall of communism in Poland, although not the sole cause of this "changing of the memorial guard,"[40] certainly broadened responsibility for the site's future and invited the introduction of new and more accurate narratives into historical representation and commemorative practice at the State Museum. More specifically, the council's recommendations, which are still being implemented, included the clearest and most effective interpolation of the Shoah at the memorial site to date. Like the controversies surrounding the forms and expressions of Jewish memory at Auschwitz in the late 1960s, growing international influence at the memorial site during the convent controversy and following the fall of communism reinserted the Jewish presence into the Auschwitz landscape—a process by which this crucial and neglected aspect of Auschwitz history reemerged, despite the durability of traditional narrative contexts and despite the mythopoetic meaning cultivated at the site in decades past. In this sense, it is reassuring that memory, dominant narrative, and their public manifestations at Auschwitz have yielded in this way to historical fact.

The recent revision of official memory and the attendant correction of its physical registrations at the memorial site are perhaps best exemplified by the fate of the commemorative tablets in front of the Birkenau monument. On the recommendation of the Auschwitz Council, the inscriptions reading "Four million people suffered and died here at the hands of the Nazi murderers between the years 1940 and 1945" were removed. In 1994 a new tablet was added, and all existing tablets were inscribed with the text: "For ever let this place be a cry of despair and a warning to humanity where the Nazis murdered about one and a half million men, women, and children, mainly Jews from various countries of Europe. Auschwitz-Birkenau, 1940–1945."[41] The State Museum has also added extensive interpretive inscriptions (in Polish, English, and Hebrew), maps, and photographs along the visitors' routes in Auschwitz I and Birkenau[42] and, significantly, an impressive exhibition in Birkenau's "Sauna," a reception building for prisoners that had stood dormant and decaying for more than fifty years. Moreover, plans have been undertaken to link Auschwitz and Birkenau with a walkway, to preserve the so-called *alte Judenrampe* (old Jewish ramp) where deportees disembarked prior to 1944, and to create a comprehensive agenda for the development and preservation of the memorial site as a whole. Revisions and corrections such as these will continue in the years ahead. They will serve as explanatory markers, will lend greater didactic value to the site as a whole, and will contribute to a more accurate and accessible representation of the past. But in a larger sense, they also represent the growing plurality of memory at Auschwitz.

The plurality of memory may well be a good thing, but the diversity of commemorative voices at Auschwitz has not introduced harmony at the site. The fall of the communist regime and attendant changes in Poland that occurred in 1989 enabled the museum, in the words of its vice-director, "to open an incomparably greater number of doors to the West and, conversely, ensured that circles in the West interested in the subject could voice their opinions with the certainty that they would be heard in Poland."[43] As the memorial site opened itself to opinions and agendas from the outside, debates proliferated over a wide variety of issues: the official Polish ceremonies on the fiftieth anniversary of the camp's liberation, the presence of religious symbols (crosses and stars of David) on the grounds of Birkenau, the "crosses controversy" at Auschwitz I, plans for a commercial center near the base camp, or development of designs for a nightclub in a building that once housed the camp's tannery, to name only some of the most publicized controversies. All of these testify to the unresolved character of the site and the ever-growing need to accommodate new constituencies in the memorialization undertaken there.

The plurality of memory at Auschwitz has also been reflected in the number and diversity of visitors. The site draws more than five hundred thousand visitors annually, visitors who are individual carriers of memory from across Europe and around the world. Although Polish schoolchildren no longer participate in universally obligatory excursions to the site, nearly half of all visitors to Auschwitz are Poles. In 2000, however, the majority came from abroad: from the United States (46,838), Germany (34,671), Britain (19,169), Italy (17,705), Israel (17,315), and France (16,289).[44] These visitors also represent official and organizational vectors of memory. Although the state-sponsored demonstration has become a rarity at Auschwitz, commemorative ceremonies organized by groups in Poland and from abroad are now common. Whether the annual international March of the Living, the highly-structured pilgrimages of Israeli schoolchildren and students, the continuing work of Aktion Sühnezeichen volunteers, a Romani ceremony commemorating the liquidation of the "Gypsy Camp," or Roman Catholic observances on the anniversary of Maximilian Kolbe's death—all attest to the multiplicity of meanings assigned to Auschwitz over the past two decades and the multiplicity of demands that the memorial site will face in the future.

The State Museum at Auschwitz has, of course, always worked within a Polish political and cultural context. But as it responds to the needs of a growing constituency at home and abroad, the museum will undoubtedly incorporate these "international" demands into its changing memorial framework. In an era of increasing cultural and political pluralism, it is worth considering the emergence of these controversies in the context of academic and public disputes over Polish-Jewish relations and the relevance of the memorial symbols of the past. Indeed, the highly charged responses to Jan T. Gross's account of the 1941 massacre of Jews at Jedwabne[45] encourage us to consider both the reality of wartime relations between Poles and Jews and, no less, the ways in which Polish scholars and the public at large have memorialized—or effaced—the most painful aspects of that reality from their collective memory of the occupation. Gross has sparked what is probably the greatest historiographical controversy in Poland since the fall of communism, and although the debates surrounding his work have sometimes been bitter, they have set the stage for a continuing forum of discussion that may well prove to be liberating and, in a sense, cathartic.

Just as future analyses of Polish-Jewish relations will necessarily take this controversy into account, so too will changes to the State Museum at Auschwitz be founded in a broader and more inclusive awareness of the needs and expectations of visitors, the commemorative agendas of various victim groups, and, not least, recent scholarship on Poland's history during the German occupation. Likewise, the multiplicity of meanings attached to Auschwitz and its memorial site will undoubtedly increase in the years ahead. The continued existence of the State Museum at Auschwitz is guaranteed, and Auschwitz I, with its plasticity and extensive exhibitions, will retain its didactic importance and authorial voice. The future of Birkenau is less clear. Neglect has been an enduring characteristic of this memorial site, but because of the addition of interpretive inscriptions to its landscape, because of the restoration work undertaken there, and, not least, because of its role as a stage for Jewish commemorative ritual, the wreckage of Nazi Germany's largest extermination center cannot remain as muted as it has been in the past. Rather, Birkenau will be a participant in an increasingly important dialogue between the two memorial sites at the State Museum at Auschwitz.

Over the past fifty years the Auschwitz base camp and Birkenau have stood in opposition to one another as contrasting manifestations of public memory. This work has been critical of Poland's neglect of the Birkenau site and of the thematic assimilation of its history. Birkenau does not, and should not, define Auschwitz memory as a whole, but it should occupy a central position in the tableau of commemorative images and rituals at the State Museum. Through the years of the Polish People's Republic, Birkenau was of secondary importance, its grounds and structures languishing and decaying in the shadow of the base camp. Efforts to focus the public's attention on Birkenau—most often in the form of the mass political rally—were usually little more than attempts to translate the commemorative vocabulary of Auschwitz I onto the page of Birkenau. These efforts failed, for as the Monument to the Victims of Fascism and its dedicatory ceremonies illustrated, the narrative idiom of Auschwitz I, lacking any specific reference to the Shoah, struck many observers as recondite, inappropriate, and even offensive when staged on the Birkenau cemetery. In sum, for many years Birkenau appeared most useful for the size of its commemorative space, not for its history or for the memories evoked by its physical characteristics, whether artifactual or artificial.

The contrast between the two sites and the different ways that they have been used are also products of their history, reflecting the respective functions of the camps during the occupation. Auschwitz I, as a camp primarily intended for the incarceration and exploitation of registered prisoners, has naturally been a locus for commemoration of the martyr-prisoner—the prisoner who survived, if not in body, then at least in the spirit of heroic sacrifice. The base camp was therefore an ideal foundation for the Polish framework of memory constructed there. Although intended as a multiplier of the martyrological idiom, the Birkenau site has, by contrast, been suggestive of the unregistered deportee/victim—an object of commemoration with little, if any, redemptive value. The iconography and ritual of Auschwitz I functioned to articulate notions of patriotic heroism, national sacrifice, and socialist solidarity, while heroism and dignity seemed to be lost in the desolation, neglect, and indeterminacy of Birkenau. And it is the history of the Birkenau site, especially the murder of a million of Europe's Jews there, that has given the terminus "Auschwitz" its metaphorical value in the indeterminacy of the postwar world. The memorial site at Auschwitz I, utilizing the conclusive referents of the past to inspire hope and decision in the future, was the locus of commemorative redemption. Birkenau was the expression of death and despair.

The contrast between the redemptive and non-redemptive characters of the two sites has been expressed more recently in terms of a dialogue, as memorialists of Auschwitz assess the limitations of the base camp's redemptive narrative framework, especially as it relates to the historical reality of genocide at Birkenau. This critical reevaluation and the conclusions of this analysis reveal a paradox: for decades the cant of martyrology and political agendas has muted the voice of Birkenau, yet the redemptive instrumentalization of Auschwitz I has also emphasized the inappropriateness, and ultimately the inapplicability, of this prevailing memorial construct for the grounds at Birkenau. In other words, the sense of pain and loss evoked by Birkenau would, paradoxically, be lessened without the physical presence and salvatory tropes of Auschwitz I. Cultural and political imperatives have guided and fortified the physical presence of Auschwitz I, and its dominant narrative has muted the voice of Birkenau. At the same time, however, Auschwitz I has prevented, both figuratively and literally, the pastoralization or total effacement of Birkenau. This is what distinguishes Birkenau from the sites of other killing centers in occupied Poland. At Bełżec, for example, it is not only the lack of physical remains or explanatory inscriptions that makes it the object of indifference; the juxtapositional element is also absent. At the State Museum at Auschwitz, however, it is the redemptive orchestration of the Stammlager that accents Birkenau's more poignant voice.

The dialogue between the two sites and even the conflict over their respective meaning and symbolism will continue to shape the memorial grounds at Auschwitz. With a view to the future, it would seem that a representational synthesis of meanings and symbolisms is necessary—a synthesis that emphasizes not only the mechanics of the Auschwitz crimes, but the motivations for them as well; a synthesis that gives all victim groups their rightful places in the memorialization of Auschwitz; a synthesis that sufficiently articulates the experience of both the unregistered and the registered deportee; a synthesis that upholds the historical significance and symbolic importance of both the base camp and Birkenau. Such a synthesis was, and will remain, an elusive goal, for the meaning and symbolism of the site derives not only from its wartime history, but also from the competing and contradictory memories that converge there. Changes at the memorial site, a diversity of visitors, and the expanding variety of exhibitions all testify to the multiplicity of narratives that exist—and belong—at Auschwitz. They also remind us that any attempt to forge a common memory at the site is not only impossible, but also undesirable.

Auschwitz memory will remain controversial and even embattled, and as indecorous as disputes over its public manifestations may appear, they will also secure the site against the indifference or effacement that has threatened it in the past. "O earth, cover not my blood, and let my cry find no resting-place." demands Job. His entreaty is also an admonition, and the struggles over the shapes and uses of memory at Auschwitz may well ensure that his cry may "find no resting-place." Job's soliloquy, however, also reminds us of an enduring dilemma associated with the memorialization of Auschwitz. "If I speak," he states, "my pain is not assuaged, and if I forbear, how much of it leaves me?"[46] The tension between the vocal and the mute, between redemptive and non-redemptive manifestations of public memory at Auschwitz will define the site and its meaning in the years ahead, but Auschwitz memory cannot be expressed solely in terms of one or the other. The future of Auschwitz will reflect a variety of narratives, and in setting their agenda for the site, the stewards of memory will undoubtedly reflect upon its biography.

Notes

Preface

1. Tadeusz Chowaniec, "Epilog," *Zeszyty Oświęcimskie* 7 (1963): p. 148.

2. The memorial site as an institution has alternatively and most commonly been referred to as the Państwowe Muzeum w Oświęcimiu (frequently abbreviated as PMO) or State Museum in Oświęcim. The Polish government and the museum have been criticized at times for using in the museum's official title the Polish name for the adjacent town and the camp that bore its name, the common assumption being that this was an attempt to "polonize" the site and its history. There are, however, two simple reasons why the word "Auschwitz" was not used. First, in postwar Poland the name "Auschwitz" has sometimes, if erroneously, been regarded as a Nazi invention (as was, for example, the name "Litzmannstadt," given to the Polish city of Łódź during the German occupation) even though the German name Auschwitz goes back to the thirteenth century. Second, usage of Polish forms of foreign proper nouns is a strong linguistic tradition. Thus, the first president of the United States is known as Jerzy Washington, the largest city in the United States is Nowy York, and the author of *Capital,* is Karol Marks. On the origins and development of the name "Auschwitz" and the town Auschwitz/Oświęcim, see Debórah Dwork and Robert Jan van Pelt, *Auschwitz 1270 to the Present* (New York: W. W. Norton, 1996), pp. 17–37 and p. 383. The museum's official name is now "Państwowe Muzeum Auschwitz-Birkenau w Oświęcimiu," or the State Museum Auschwitz-Birkenau in Oświęcim. Although the Auschwitz museum was not officially opened until June 1947, this analysis will frequently use the terms "museum" or "State Museum at Auschwitz" to describe the entire memorial site as of 1946, that is, when former prisoners of the camp began their conservation work there.

3. Geoffrey H. Hartman, introduction to *Holocaust Remembrance: The Shapes of Memory* (Oxford: Basil Blackwell, 1994), p. 4.

Introduction

1. See, for example, Maurice Halbwachs, *The Collective Memory,* trans. Francis J. Ditter, Jr. and Vida Yazdi Ditter (New York: Harper and Row, 1980); Geoffrey H. Hartman, ed., *The Longest Shadow: In the Aftermath of the Holocaust* (Bloomington:

Indiana University Press, 1996); idem., *Holocaust Remembrance;* Patrick Hutton, *History as an Art of Memory* (Hanover, N.H.: University of Vermont/University Press of New England, 1993); Amos Funkenstein, "Collective Memory and Historical Consciousness," *History and Memory* 1, no. 1 (spring-summer 1989): pp. 5–26; James E. Young, "Memory and Monument," in *Bitburg in Moral and Political Perspective,* ed. Geoffrey H. Hartman (Bloomington: Indiana University Press, 1986); Michael C. Steinlauf, *Bondage to the Dead: Poland and the Memory of the Holocaust* (Syracuse: Syracuse University Press, 1997). See also James Young's acclaimed study *The Texture of Memory: Holocaust Memorials and Meaning* (New Haven: Yale University Press, 1993), especially pp. 113–54, which are concerned with memorials in Poland, specifically the Auschwitz and Maidanek sites.

2. As of this writing, there is no monograph concerned primarily with the postwar Auschwitz site, although a number of articles and book chapters have addressed the subject. Noteworthy among them are: Jonathan Huener, "Geneza Państwowego Muzeum w Oświęcim-Brzezinka i jego koncepcja, 1945–1947," *Zeszyty Oświęcimskie* 23 (2002): pp. 7–28; Tomasz Goban-Klas, "Pamięć podzielona—pamięć urażona: Oświęcim i Auschwitz w polskiej i żydowskiej pamięci zbiorowej," in *Europa po Auschwitz,* ed. Zdzisława Macha (Kraków: Universitas, 1995), pp. 71–91; Timothy W. Ryback, "Evidence of Evil," *New Yorker,* 15 November 1993, pp. 68–81; Kazimierz Smoleń, "Działalność upowszechnieniowa Państwowego Muzeum w Oświęcimiu," *Biuletyn Towarzystwa Opieki nad Oświęcimiem* 1–2 (1987): pp. 17–31; Jean-Charles Szurek, "Le camp-musée d'Auschwitz," in *A l'Est, la mémoire retrouvée,* ed. Alain Brossat, et al. (Paris: Editions la Découverte, 1990), pp. 535–65; Jonathan Webber, *The Future of Auschwitz: Some Personal Reflections* (Oxford: Oxford Centre for Postgraduate Hebrew Studies, 1992); Emeryka Iwaszko, "Wystawy Państwowego Muzeum w Oświęcimiu w latach 1945–1973," *Muzea Walki* 8 (1975): pp. 215–19. Readers may also consult the epilogue to Dwork and van Pelt, *Auschwitz 1270 to the Present.* In addition, the April-May 1990 issue of the Polish Catholic journal *Znak,* entitled "Auschwitz po 50 latach. Czym był? Jakie ma dziś znaczenie?" contains a number of articles on the significance of the memorial site in Poland and elsewhere. Moreover, there have been several publications focusing on the Carmelite convent controversy at Auschwitz, most notably, Władysław T. Bartoszewski, *The Convent at Auschwitz* (London: The Bowerdean Press, 1990) and Carol Rittner and John K. Roth, eds., *Memory Offended: The Auschwitz Convent Controversy* (New York: Praeger, 1991). There are several unpublished manuscripts on the history of the Auschwitz site. These include a master's thesis—largely an administrative history—by a former employee of the State Museum, Henryk Płuszka, "Działalność Państwowego Muzeum w Oświęcimiu w XXX-leciu (1947–1977)" (master's thesis, Wyższa Szkoła Pedagogiczna im. Komisji Edukacji Narodowej, Kraków, 1978). There are also at least two more recent master's theses, Maria R. Avery, "Preserving Memory at Auschwitz: A Study in

Polish-Jewish Historical Memory" (master's thesis, Central Connecticut State University 1999); and Jaime Ashworth, "The Iconography of Destruction: A Historical Portrait of the Auschwitz-Birkenau State Museum" (master's thesis, Jagiellonian University, Centre for European Studies, 2001), which is an overview of the history of the site that emphasizes the visual experience of the visitor. Finally, a thorough analysis of the origins of the Birkenau monument is the Ph.D. dissertation by Jochen Spielmann, "Entwürfe zur Sinngebung des Sinnlosen. Zu einer Theorie des Denkmals als Manifestation des 'kulturellen Gedächtnisses': Der Wettbewerb für ein Denkmal für Auschwitz" (Ph.D. diss., Freie Universität Berlin, 1990).

3. Given the magnitude of the crimes committed at Auschwitz and the postwar memory associated with them, it is surprising that historians have not devoted even more attention to the camp complex. For several decades researchers at the State Museum Auschwitz-Birkenau have published their findings in *Zeszyty Oświęcimskie* (Auschwitz Notebooks)—also published in German as *Hefte von Auschwitz*. Among more recent works is the most exhaustive treatment of the camp's history by a single author: Danuta Czech's monumental chronicle *Kalendarz wydarzeń w KL Auschwitz* (Oświęcim: Wydawnictwo Państwowego Muzeum w Oświęcimiu-Brzezince, 1992), published in English as *Auschwitz Chronicle, 1939–1945* (New York: Henry Holt & Co., 1990) and in German as *Kalendarium der Ereignisse im Konzentrationslager Auschwitz-Birkenau 1939–1945* (Reinbeck bei Hamburg: Rowohlt, 1989). Useful as well is *Anatomy of the Auschwitz Death Camp* (Bloomington: Indiana University Press, 1994), a collection of articles and essays by an international consortium of scholars, edited by Yisrael Gutman and Michael Berenbaum and published in association with the United States Holocaust Memorial Museum. For the general history of the camp, the contributions by Yisrael Gutman ("Auschwitz—An Overview"), Raul Hilberg ("Auschwitz and the 'Final Solution'"), and Franciszek Piper ("The Number of Victims") are particularly useful. Readers of Polish should also consult the five-volume anthology edited by Wacław Długoborski and Franciszek Piper, *Auschwitz 1940–1945: Węzłowe zagadnienia z dziejów obozu* (Oświęcim: Wydawnictwo Państwowego Muzeum Oświęcim-Brzezinka, 1995). Piper's introduction (pp. 11–28 of volume 1) serves as a useful summary of the development and current state of historical research on the Auschwitz complex. The English translation is now available as *Auschwitz, 1940–1945: Central Issues in the History of the Camp* (Oświęcim: Auschwitz-Birkenau State Museum, 2000). A useful and briefer anthology now available in English is Franciszek Piper and Teresa Świebocka, eds., *Auschwitz: Nazi Death Camp* (Oświęcim: Auschwitz-Birkenau State Museum in Oświęcim, 1996). In addition, Debórah Dwork and Robert Jan van Pelt have accounted for the transformation of the unremarkable town of Oświęcim into the "concentrational city" known as Auschwitz in *Auschwitz 1270 to the Present* (New York: Norton, 1996). Among more dated analyses are: Filip Friedman, *To jest Oświęcim!* (Warszawa: Państwowe

Wydawnictwo Literatury Politycznej, 1945); Ludwik Rajewski, *Oświęcim w systemie RSHA* (Warszawa: E. Kuthan, 1946); Central Commission for the Investigation of Nazi Crimes in Poland, *Concentration Camp Oświęcim* (Warszawa: Wydawnictwo Prawnicze, 1955); as well as the numerous editions of three Polish standard works, Jan Sehn, *Concentration Camp Oświęcim-Brzezinka* (Warszawa: Wydawnictwo Prawnicze, 1957, 1961); Kazimierz Smoleń, ed., *From the History of KL Auschwitz* (Oświęcim: Państwowe Muzeum, 1976); and Józef Buszko, ed., *Auschwitz: Nazi Extermination Camp* (Warsaw: Interpress, 1985).

4. The work first appeared in Poland as *Sąsiedzi: Historia zagłady żydowskiego miasteczka* (Sejny: Pogranicze, 2000) and the following year in English as *Neighbors: The Destruction of the Jewish Community in Jedwabne, Poland* (Princeton: Princeton University Press, 2001).

5. In addition to the works by Steinlauf, Young, and others cited in note 1, above, see also Henry Rousso, *The Vichy Syndrome: History and Memory in France since 1944* (Cambridge: Harvard University Press, 1991); Pierre Nora, "Between Memory and History: Les Lieux de Mémoire," trans. Marc Roudebush *Representations* 26 (1989): pp. 7–25; and the essays by Friedlander and others in Saul Friedlander, ed., *Probing the Limits of Representation: Nazism and the "Final Solution"* (Cambridge: Harvard University Press, 1992).

6. See especially Steinlauf, pp. 56–61.

7. Young, *Texture of Memory,* p. 15.

8. Hutton, for one, has warned the historian against the dangers inherent in an overweening focus on memorial images: "[T]he historians' recent interest in memory is tied to the postmodern emphasis on the images and forms of its representation. The problem with such an approach, however, is that it reduces the memory of the past to the history of its images. It makes of rhetorical practice itself a level of reality that intervenes between historians and the events, personalities, and ideas of the past that they would study." Hutton, *History as an Art of Memory,* p. 22.

9. Upper Silesia and the Wartheland were geographic and administrative designations for two western areas of prewar Polish territory annexed and incorporated by Nazi Germany. The *Generalgouvernement* (General Government) was a separate territorial administration, much like a colony, in the interior of occupied Poland. It was under the authority of Governor General Dr. Hans Frank and included cities such as Warsaw, Kraków (its capital), Lublin, and Lwów. In 1939, approximately 1.4 million Jews lived in this region.

10. So-called "functionary prisoners" were those who were were charged with special supervisory or administrative tasks in the camp and consequently enjoyed a priveleged status in the prisoner hierarchy.

11. "KL" was a common German abbreviation for *Konzentrationslager* (concentration camp).

12. Czech, *Kalendarz*, p. 52.

13. That is, prisoners who were assigned serial numbers, blocks, and work, as opposed to those deportees (overwhelmingly Jews, but also Gypsies) who were brought in mass transports, subjected to selections, and killed shortly after arrival. Smaller groups of Poles, Soviet POWs, and others were also killed in this manner.

14. Contrary to popular belief, the practice of tattooing prisoners was not common to all Nazi concentration camps, but was unique to Auschwitz.

15. Primo Levi, *If This Is a Man: Remembering Auschwitz* (New York: Simon & Schuster, 1986), pp. 19–20.

16. See Primo Levi, *The Drowned and the Saved* (New York: Simon & Schuster, 1988), pp. 36–69.

17. Gutman, "Auschwitz—An Overview," p. 27.

18. Levi, *If This Is a Man*, p. 20.

19. Officially designated *Pferdestallbaracke, OKH-Typ 260/9* (horse stall barracks, Army High Command—model 290/9), the huts measured forty by ten meters.

20. Registered prisoners, exploited as a labor resource, were usually considered replaceable and therefore expendable. The SS administration was little concerned with the continued health of the prisoner and was consequently unwilling to expend what it regarded as unecessary food resources for the physical sustenance of the prisoner-worker. However, when prisoners became a more valuable source of labor (particularly in the later years of the war), efforts were made to improve their diet. For example, in an effort to make maximum use of the prisoners' labor, a ban on the sending of food parcels to some concentration camp inmates was lifted in October of 1942. To the extent that the contents of these parcels were not immediately added to the larders of the SS, they did help some prisoners to prevent or to postpone starvation. At Auschwitz, Jewish prisoners and Soviet POWs were not permitted to receive parcels. See Tadeusz Iwaszko, "Zakwaterowanie, odzież i wyżywienie więźniów," in Długoborski and Piper, 2:44–47.

21. Tadeusz Iwaszko, "Zakwaterowanie," p. 45.

22. Gutman, "Auschwitz—An Overview," p. 28.

23. Franciszek Piper, *Die Zahl der Opfer von Auschwitz aufgrund der Quellen und der Erträge der Forschung 1945 bis 1990* (Oświęcim: Verlag Staatliches Museum in Oświęcim, 1993), pp. 171, 200.

24. The distinction made here is essential, but, as is usually the case when generalizing about the history of Auschwitz, runs the risk of oversimplification. Gypsies, although for the most part registered prisoners, were killed in the gas chambers by the thousands, and other types of deportees, such as Gentile Poles (of whom about ten thousand were deported to Auschwitz and killed without registration as prisoners) and Soviet POWs, were also subjected to extermination by gassing and mass execution by shooting, hanging, or lethal injection. This fact notwithstanding, the

treatment of Jews at Auschwitz remains unique—unique because that treatment was based solely on contrived racial definitions, because the number of Jews killed far exceeded that of other victim groups, and, not least, because of the uncompromising thoroughness with which the killing of Jews was undertaken and was continued even as the German fronts in the east were collapsing. The oft-quoted words of historian Eberhard Jäckel were intended to emphasize the singularity of the Shoah among other instances of mass murder and genocide, but certainly apply to the Jewish fate at Auschwitz as well: "Never before had a state with the authority of its responsible leader determined and proclaimed its intention to kill, as completely as possible, a specific group of people inclusive of the old, women, children, and babies, and to implement this decision with all the power at the state's command." Eberhard Jäckel, "Die elende Praxis der Untersteller: Das Einmalige der nationalsozialistische Verbrechen läßt sich nicht leugnen," *Die Zeit,* 12 September 1986.

25. The term *Muselmann* (plural, *Muselmänner*) or "Muslim" was camp slang for an inmate who had lost the will to live and was near death. Emaciated, unresponsive to the blows of a Kapo or the aid of a fellow prisoner, the *Muselmann* rarely returned to health. The origins of this term are unknown.

26. Hilberg, "Auschwitz and the 'Final Solution,'" p. 81.

27. Rudolf Höss, *Commandant of Auschwitz: The Autobiography of Rudolf Hoess* (Cleveland: World Publishing, 1959), p. 205.

28. Like the "selections" of registered prisoners, the selections of newly arrived deportees on the railroad platforms were usually carried out by an SS doctor. Pregnant women, the elderly, and young children were generally considered unfit for work and consequently seldom survived the selection process. There were, however, many instances in which entire transports of Jews—men, women, and children—were gassed upon arrival without regard to age, sex, or state of health.

29. Members of the Sonderkommando undoubtedly led the most deplorable existence of all Auschwitz prisoners. Not only did they serve as participants in the killing actions, but as a rule they were killed after a few months by the SS in order to destroy any eyewitness evidence of the killing operations.

30. Quoted in Franciszek Piper, "Gas Chambers and Crematoria," in Gutman and Berenbaum, p. 170.

31. Ibid., p. 166. See also Franciszek Piper, "Zagłada," in Długoborski and Piper, 3:132.

32. See Piper, *Die Zahl der Opfer,* and idem, "The Number of Victims," in Gutman and Berenbaum, pp. 61–76. The estimates listed here rely on these two sources.

33. For a discussion of the origins, significance, and subsequent revision of the figure of 4 million Auschwitz victims, see Andrzej Strzelecki, *Ostatnie dni obozu Auschwitz* (Oświęcim: Państwowe Muzeum Oświęcim-Brzezinka, 1995), pp. 52–53; and Franciszek Piper, *Auschwitz: How Many Perished? Jews, Poles, Gypsies . . .* (Kraków: n.p., 1992).

34. Martin Gilbert, *The Holocaust: The Jewish Tragedy* (London: Collins, 1986), p. 287, n. 853. The estimates of the number of dead at these sites are from Raul Hilberg, *The Destruction of the European Jews* (New York: Holmes & Meier, 1985), 3:1219.

35. In the words of the French historian Annette Wieviorka, "The mission that has devolved to testimony is no longer to bear witness to inadequately known events, but rather to keep them before our eyes. Testimony is to be a means of transmission to future generations." See Annette Wieviorka, "On Testimony," in Hartman, ed., *Holocaust Remembrance*, p. 24.

36. The distinction between history and memory that has so preoccupied scholars in recent years is a relatively new phenomenon and first emerged in the twentieth century with the pioneering work of the French sociologist Maurice Halbwachs. Henry Rousso, for example, has claimed that the distinction between memory and history did not exist at all in nineteenth-century France, an era of "history as memory," when history functioned to legitimate the French state and to forge a national feeling. Nineteenth- and twentieth-century Polish historiography has also been steeped in such a tradition; despite or, arguably, because of the absence of a sovereign nation-state, Polish historians often chronicled and evaluated past events in terms of their relationship to the *ideal* of the nation-state. See Jan T. Gross, *Polish Society under German Occupation: The Generalgouvernement, 1939–1944* (Princeton: Princeton University Press, 1979), pp. 7–9; and Piotr Wandycz, "Historiography of the Countries of Eastern Europe: Poland," *American Historical Review* 97, no. 4 (October 1992): pp. 1011–25. As Rousso writes, "Thus a new field of study has been opened up for historians: the history of memory, that is, the study of the evolution of various social practices and, more specifically, of the form and content of social practices whose purpose or effect is the representation of the past and the perpetuation of its memory within a particular group or the society as a whole." Rousso, p. 3. See also Nora, pp. 9–15; Hutton, *History as an Art of Memory*, p. 9; and Halbwachs, *The Collective Memory*, pp. 80–86.

37. See Robert Bellah et al., *Habits of the Heart: Individualism and Commitment in American Life* (New York: Harper & Row, 1985), pp. 152–55.

38. Nora, p. 8.

39. Jacques Le Goff, *History and Memory*, trans. Steven Rendall and Elizabeth Clamen (New York: Columbia University Press, 1992), p. 97.

40. Rousso, p. 2.

41. Nora, pp. 7, 12–25.

42. Although the State Museum at Auschwitz covers approximately 1.8 square kilometers, making it the largest memorial site of a former camp, that surface area represents less than one-twentieth of the total area of the so-called Auschwitz "area of interest" defined in 1941.

43. Written in 1925, Halbwachs's posthumously published *Les Cadres sociaux de la mémoire,* (Paris: Presses Universitaires de France, 1952) was the pioneering work in the

field of collective memory. English translations of parts of this work are available in: Maurice Halbwachs, *On Collective Memory* (Chicago: University of Chicago Press, 1992) and Halbwachs, *The Collective Memory,* as cited above. For a lucid and concise synopsis of Halbwachs's work on memory see Hutton, *History as an Art of Memory,* pp. 73–90.

44. Halbwachs, *On Collective Memory,* pp. 38–40. See also Jan Assmann, "Kollektives Gedächtnis und kulturelle Identität," in *Kultur und Gedächtnis,* ed. Jan Assmann and Tonio Hölscher (Frankfurt am Main: Suhrkamp, 1988), p. 13; and Paul Connerton, *How Societies Remember,* (Cambridge: Cambridge University Press, 1989), p. 3.

45. Patrick Hutton, "Collective Memory and Collective Mentalities: The Halbwachs-Aries Connection," *Historical Reflections/Réflexions historiques* 15 (1988): p. 314. The postulate that memory of the past is forced to adapt to the present is described by Jan Assmann as the "reconstructivity" of cultural memory: "Das kulturelle Gedächtnis verfährt rekonstruktive, d.h., es bezieht sein Wissen immer auf eine aktuell gegenwärtige Situation." Assmann and Hölscher, p. 13.

46. Hutton, *History as an Art of Memory,* p. 7.

47. Halbwachs, *On Collective Memory,* p. 51.

48. Ibid., p. 182. See also Geoffrey H. Hartman, introduction to *Holocaust Remembrance,* p. 5.

49. Hartman, for example, has pointed out that memorial narratives often limit "the subversive or heterogeneous facts, invented to nationalize consensus by suggesting a uniform and heroic past." See "Public Memory and its Discontents," in Hartman, ed., *The Longest Shadow,* pp. 104–5. Along these lines, Bellah and his colleagues have noted that among the "communities of memory" they discuss, an "honest" community will remember "stories not only of suffering received but of suffering inflicted." See Bellah, et al., p. 153.

50. Hutton, "Collective Memory and Collective Mentalities," p. 314.

51. Le Goff, p. 97; David Middleton and Derek Edwards, introduction to *Collective Remembering,* ed. David Middleton and Derek Edwards (London: Sage, 1990), p. 9; Hutton, *History as an Art of Memory,* pp. 7, 88.

52. Friedländer, introduction, pp. 2–3.

53. Ibid., p. 3.

54. Rousso, p. 219.

55. Ibid., pp. 219–20.

56. Ibid., p. 4.

Chapter 1

1. For accounts of the 14 June 1947 ceremonies at Oświęcim, see Ludwik Rajewski, "Oświęcim 14.6.1940–14.6.1947," *Wolni Ludzie,* 15 June 1947; *Wolni Ludzie,* 1 July

1947; *Gazeta Ludowa,* 16 June 1947; *Ilustrowany Kurier Polski,* 17 June 1947; Polski Związek byłych Więźniów Politycznych, "14.VI.1947 R.," in *Kalendarz b. więźnia politycznego na rok 1948* (Śl.-Dąbrowski: n.p., 1947), pp. 120–23; *Times* (London), 16 June 1947; *New York Times,* 15 June 1947.

2. *Gazeta Ludowa,* 16 June 1947; Cyrankiewicz quoted in *Mosty,* 17 June 1947.

3. *Dziennik Polski,* 17 June 1947.

4. Quoted in Czesław Stanisławski and Wojciech Rawicz, "Podniosłe dni Oświęcimia: Otwarcie muzeum martyrologii polskiej," *Wolni Ludzi,* 1 July 1947.

5. Quoted and translated in Norman Davies, *God's Playground: A History of Poland* (New York: Columbia University Press, 1982), 2:136; translation modified by the author based on Maria Konopnicka, *Wybór poezji* (Warszawa: n.p., 1953), p. 196.

6. Jakub Karpiński, *Poland since 1944: A Portrait of Years* (Boulder: Westview Press, 1995), p. 15.

7. In fact, leaders of the PPR were even known to participate in processions on Roman Catholic holidays. See Krystyna Kersten, *The Establishment of Communist Rule in Poland, 1943–1948* (Berkeley: University of California Press, 1991), pp. 211–13. Also noteworthy is the participation of the new prime minister Józef Cyrankiewicz in the Roman Catholic mass celebrated in conjunction with the opening ceremonies of the State Museum at Auschwitz.

8. For discussions of the Polish press in the early postwar years, the extent of its pluralism and freedom, as well as its repression and censorship, see Jakub Perkal, "Polityczna historia prasy w Polsce w latach 1944–1984," in *40 lat władzy komunistycznej w Polsce,* ed. Irena Lasota (London: Polonia, 1986), pp. 151–58; Mieczysław Ciecwierz, *Polityka prasowa 1944–1948* (Warszawa: Państwowe Wydawnictwo Naukowe, 1989); Arthur Bliss Lane, *I Saw Poland Betrayed: An American Ambassador Reports to the American People* (Indianapolis: Bobbs-Merrill, 1948), pp. 171–72.

9. Padraic Kenney, *Rebuilding Poland: Workers and Communists, 1945–1950* (Ithaca: Cornell University Press, 1997), p. 27.

10. Kersten, *Establishment,* p. 145.

11. Norman Davies, *Heart of Europe: A Short History of Poland* (Oxford: Oxford University Press, 1986), p. 82.

12. Ibid., p. 102.

13. The historian Krystyna Kersten estimates that in July 1946 there were approximately 245,000 Jews in Poland, mostly in the so-called "recovered territories" of western Poland put under Polish administration at the Potsdam Conference. See Kersten, *Establishment,* p. 215. See also Józef Adelson, "W Polsce zwanej Ludowa," in *Najnowsze dzieje Żydów w Polsce,* ed. Jerzy Tomaszewski (Warszawa: Wydawnictwo Naukowe WDN, 1993), p. 387. Although estimates of Holocaust survivors, the number of Jews residing in Poland, or the number of Jewish immigrants to Poland after the liberation vary greatly, the point is that these figures represent only a small fraction of the prewar population.

14. Institute of Jewish Affairs, *The Anti-Jewish Campaign in Present-Day Poland* (London: Institute of Jewish Affairs, 1968), p. 6.

15. Michal Borwicz, "Polish-Jewish Relations, 1944–1947," in *The Jews in Poland*, ed. Chimen Abramsky, et al. (Oxford: Basil Blackwell, 1986), p. 193; Lucjan Dobroszycki, "Restoring Jewish Life in Post-War Poland," *Soviet Jewish Affairs* 3, no. 2 (1973): pp. 66–67. The most comprehensive treatment of the Kielce pogrom to date remains Bożena Szaynok, *Pogrom Żydów w Kielcach, 4 lipca 1946* (Warszawa: Wydawnictwo Bellona, 1992).

16. Dobroszycki, p. 67. Jan T. Gross has noted that "[g]iven the general level of disorder at the time, and the fact that many victims were not killed *qua* Jews but as targets of political violence or armed robbery, only a fraction of these deaths can be attributed to anti-Semitism. Still, one must be careful about the circumstances of each episode for, as it turns out, even victims of robberies could be deliberately targeted because of their ethnicity." Jan T. Gross, "A Tangled Web: Confronting Stereotypes Concerning Relations Between Poles, Germans, Jews, and Communists," in *The Politics of Retribution in Europe: World War II and its Aftermath*, ed. István Deák, Jan T. Gross, and Tony Judt (Princeton: Princeton University Press, 2000), pp. 106–7.

17. *Życie Warszawy*, 15 August 1945. See also the *Życie Warszawy* article of 8 April 1945, in which the author regards anti-Semitism as a long-maintained Polish tradition, but also as a pernicious vestige of the fascist occupation.

18. While acknowledging the prevailing public perception of the żydokomuna in early postwar Poland, Jan T. Gross has recently made a strong case against the traditional claims that Jews welcomed the Soviet occupation of eastern Poland in 1939, and likewise that Jewish survivors in Poland enthusiastically and disproportionately supported the goals of the Soviet-inspired regime in the early postwar years. See Gross, "Tangled Web," pp. 92–105.

19. See Michael Checiński, *Poland: Communism—Nationalism—Anti-Semitism* (New York: Karz-Cohl Publishing, 1982), pp. 7–18; Borwicz, "Polish-Jewish relations," pp. 192–93; Kersten, *Establishment*, pp. 218–20; Adelson, pp. 400–401, 405; Włodzimierz Borodziej, "Polen und Juden im 20. Jahrhundert. Zum Fortleben von Stereotypen nach dem Holocaust," in *Polen nach dem Kommunismus*, ed. Erwin Oberländer, (Stuttgart: Fritz Steiner Verlag, 1993), pp. 76–77. For a contemporary analysis of this problem see Stanisław Ossowski, "Na tle wydarzeń Kieleckich," *Kuźnica* 38 (56) (1946): 1–4.

20. Władysław Bartoszewski, "The Founding of the All-Polish Anti-Racist League in 1946," *Polin* 4 (1989): 245.

21. Institute of Jewish Affairs, p. 6; Checiński, pp. 8–10; Kersten, *Establishment*, pp. 219–20; Andrzej Szczypiorski, *The Polish Ordeal: The View from Within* (London: Croom Helm, 1982), p. 75.

22. Steinlauf, p. 49.

23. See, for example, Borwicz, "Polish-Jewish Relations," p. 191–193; Adelson, pp. 400–401; Isaac Deutscher, "Remnants of a Race," *Economist* (London) 150, no. 5342 (12 January 1946): pp. 15–16.

24. Shneiderman, p. 24.

25. Kazimierz Wyka, "Potęga ciemnoty potwierdzona," *Odrodzenie,* 23 September 1945, quoted and translated in Shneiderman, pp. 45–46. The same argument has subsequently been advanced in Alexander Smolar, "Jews as a Polish Problem," *Daedelus* 116, no. 2 (spring 1987): p. 41, and more recently in Antony Polonsky, "Beyond Condemnation, Apologetics, and Apologies: On the Complexity of Polish Behavior toward the Jews during the Second World War," in *The Fate of the European Jews, 1939–1945: Continuity or Contingency?* ed. Jonathan Frankel, vol. 13 of *Studies in Contemporary Jewry* (New York: Oxford University Press), p. 204.

26. Examples of publications on Auschwitz based on information provided by the resistance include *The Camp of Disappearing Men: A Story of the Oświęcim Concentration Camp, Based on Reports from the Polish Underground Labor Movement* (New York: n.p., 1944); *The Camp of Death* (London: n.p., 1944); and *Obóz śmierci. Zbiór relacji z obozu w Oświęcimiu opublikowanych w kraju przez ruch mas pracujących Polski* (London: n.p., 1943). For a more comprehensive treatment of the collection and distribution of materials on the camp by prisoners see Henryk Świebocki, *Ruch oporu,* vol. 4 of Długoborski and Piper.

27. It is worth noting again in this context that approximately half of the some 147,000 non-Jewish Poles deported to Auschwitz survived.

28. Franciszek Piper, "Liczba ofiar," in Długoborski and Piper, 3:171.

29. *Życie Warszawy,* 24 August 1945.

30. *Życie Warszawy,* 28 July 1946.

31. *Życie Warszawy,* 15 May 1945.

32. *Życie Warszawy,* 4 January 1946.

33. *Gazeta Ludowa,* 15 February 1945.

34. See, for example, Friedman; *Dziennik Polski,* 11 February 1945; ibid., 8 April 1945; Ocalały (Anonymous Survivor), "Koniec Oświęcimia," *Życie Warszawy,* 1 March 1945. Secondary accounts of the liberation itself are to be found in Andrzej Strzelecki, *Ewakuacja, likwidacja i wyzwolenie KL Auschwitz* (Oświęcim: Państwowe Muzeum w Oświęcimiu, 1982), pp. 212–27; Jerzy Ptakowski, *Oświęcim bez cenzury i bez legend* (London: Myśl Polska, 1985), pp. 130–33; Jon Bridgman, *The End of the Holocaust: The Liberation of the Camps* (Portland, Ore.: Areopagitica Press, 1990), pp. 22–29; and Czech, *Kalendarz,* pp. 860–63.

35. Franciszek Piper, "The Number of Victims at KL Auschwitz," in Piper and Świebocka, p. 186.

36. *Życie Warszawy,* 2 March 1945.

37. On the founding of the CKŻP, see David Engel, "The Reconstruction of

Jewish Communal Institutions in Postwar Poland: The Origins of the Central Committee of Polish Jews, 1944–1945," *Eastern European Politics and Societies* 10, no. 1 (1996): 85–107; see also Steinlauf, pp. 46–47.

38. *Życie Warszawy*, 15 March 1945; *Dziennik Polski*, 11 April 1945.

39. In an apparent political concession to Poland's East German allies, the name of the commission was changed in the early 1950s to Główna Komisja Badania Zbrodni Hitlerowskich w Polsce (Central Commission for the Investigation of Hitlerite Crimes in Poland). See Lucy Dawidowicz, *The Holocaust and the Historians* (Cambridge: Harvard University Press, 1982), p. 168, n. 17.

40. *Życie Warszawy*, 9 May 1945.

41. See Strzelecki, *Ostatnie dni obozu Auschwitz*, pp. 52–53, as well as the discussion of previous estimates and the background of the author's research in the introduction to Piper, *Die Zahl der Opfer*, pp. 7–19, and idem., "Liczba ofiar," in Długoborski and Piper, 3:171–78. It was, above all, Piper's pioneering research in the 1980s that definitively broke the symbolic barrier of the number 4 million for Polish historiography.

42. On these revisions see Czesław Łuczak, "Szanse i trudności bilansu demograficznego Polski w latach 1939–1945," *Dzieje Najnowsze* 26, no. 2 (1994): 9–14.

43. Piper, *Die Zahl der Opfer*, p. 18.

44. Główna Komisja Badania Zbrodni Niemieckich w Polsce, *German Crimes in Poland* (Warszawa: Wydawnictwo Głównej Komisji Badania Zbrodni Niemieckich w Polsce, 1946), pp. 14–16. This English-language publication is an abridged version of early issues of the commission's ongoing periodical, the *Biuletyn Głównej Komisji Badania Zbrodni Niemieckich w Polsce*.

45. *Dziennik Polski*, 3 October 1945; ibid., 10 November 1945; *Życie Warszawy*, 5 October 1945, and 18 November 1945.

46. *Życie Warszawy*, 29 January 1946, 28 February 1946, 16 April 1946; *Dziennik Polski*, 16 April 1946.

47. Tadeusz Cyprian, "Dlaczego nie zabijamy bez sądu?," *Życie Warszawy*, 8 March 1947.

48. *Życie Warszawy*, 12 March 1947, 15 March 1947, 20 March 1947, 23 March 1947.

49. Bartoszewski, *Convent at Auschwitz*, p. 10.

50. Alfred Woycicki, "Oświęcim, 14.VI.1940–14.VI.1947," *Dziennik Polski*, 11 June 1947.

51. Brian Porter, *When Nationalism Began to Hate: Imagining Modern Politics in Nineteenth-Century Poland* (New York: Oxford University Press, 2000), p. 27. On the origins and transformations in Polish romantic messianism, see also part three of Andrzej Walicki, *Philosophy and Romantic Nationalism: The Case of Poland* (Oxford: Clarendon Press, 1982), pp. 237–333.

52. Dawidowicz, pp. 89–90.

53. Quoted in Davies, *God's Playground*, p. 9.

54. Antoni Symonowicz, "Nazi Kampaign Polish Culture," in *1939–1945 War Losses in Poland*, ed. Roman Nurowski (Poznań: Wydawnictwo Zachodnie, 1960), p. 83.

55. *Mosty*, 17 July 1947.

56. "Wydział Muzeów i Pomników Martyrologii Polskiej," Archiwum Akt Nowych, Warsaw (hereafter AAN), zespół: Ministerstwo Kultury i Sztuki, Centralny Zarząd Muzeów, Wydiał Muzeów i Pomników Walki z Faszyzmem, syg.: 1.

57. Ibid.

58. *Życie Warszawy*, 2 March 1945.

59. "Wydział Muzeów i Pomników Martyrologii Polskiej," AAN, zespół: Ministerstwo Kultury i Sztuki, Centralny Zarząd Muzeów, Wydiał Muzeów i Pomników Walki z Faszyzmem, syg.: 1.

60. Ibid.

61. Jan T. Gross, *Polish Society under German Occupation*, pp. 185–86; Raul Hilberg, *Perpetrators, Victims, Bystanders: The Jewish Catastrophe, 1933–1945* (New York: HarperCollins, 1992), p. 204.

62. *Życie Warszawy*, 8 June 1946. See also Zygmunt Klukowski, "How the Eviction of the Poles by the Germans from the Area of Zamość Was Carried Out," in Główna Komisja, *German Crimes in Poland*, 2:67–85.

63. Główna Komisja, *German Crimes in Poland*, 1:14.

64. Ibid., p. 23.

65. *Życie Warszawy*, 22 March 1947.

66. *Dziennik Polski*, 21 April 1945.

67. J. A. Szczepański, "Prawo narodu żydowskiego," *Dziennik Polski*, 19 April 1947. The time factor has also been cited by Jan T. Gross, who has claimed that "[t]here is little doubt that the Poles would have become victims of genocide, in turn, if time had allowed." See Gross, *Polish Society under German Occupation*, p. 49.

68. Hilberg, *Destruction*, 2:520–21; idem., 3:1001–1002. See also Gross, *Polish Society under German Occupation*, pp. 42–91.

69. Hilberg, *Destruction*, 3:999.

70. In addition to evidence cited by Hilberg and others, entries in Hans Frank's diary also reveal a certain tension in the Nazi leadership between the desire to annihilate the Poles, on the one hand, and the need to exploit them for labor, on the other. Moreover, SS and police leader Friedrich Wilhelm Krüger is recorded as noting that it would be in the interests of the Third Reich to keep in the Zamość region those Poles positively disposed towards the Nazi regime and those of a certain "racial value." See Hans Frank, *Das Diensttagebuch des deutschen Generalgouverners in Polen 1939–1945*, vol. 20 of *Quellen und Darstellungen zur Zeitgeschichte* (Stuttgart: Deutsche Verlags-Anstalt, 1975), pp. 590–91, 603. See also in this regard Czesław Madajczyk, "Was *Generalplan Ost* Synchronous with the Final Solution?" in *The Shoah and the War*, ed. Asher Cohen, Yehoyakim Cochavi, and Yoav Gelber (New

York: Peter Lang, 1992), pp. 145–59. For decades, many historians in communist Poland and many authors in the West were committed to demonstrating that the plight of Poles under the occupation was more severe than many scholars of the Shoah and World War II have been willing to admit or that in some cases Poles were treated as badly as or worse than Jews. Such authors have also generally emphasized the extent of Polish aid rendered to Jews during the occupation. See, for example, Władysław Żarski-Zajder, *Martyrologia ludności Żydowskiej i pomoc społeczeństwa polskiego* (Warszawa: Związek Bojowników o Wolność i Demokrację, 1968); Stefan Korboński, *The Jews and the Poles in World War II* (New York: Hippocrene, 1989); Richard Lukas, *Forgotten Holocaust: The Poles under German Occupation, 1939–1945* (New York: Hippocrene, 1997); Tadeusz Piotrowski, *Poland's Holocaust: Ethnic Strife, Collaboration with Occupying Forces, and Genocide in the Second Republic, 1918–1947* (Jefferson, N.C.: McFarland and Company, 1998); Peter Stachura, "Poles and Jews in the Second World War," chapter 6 in *Poland in the Twentieth Century* (New York: St. Martin's Press, 1999), pp. 97–111. The most effective rebuttal to those who have argued that Poles and Jews faced a common fate under the German occupation is Yisrael Gutman and Shmuel Krakowski, *Unequal Victims: Poles and Jews during World War II* (New York: Holocaust Library, 1986).

71. This theme is covered extensively in chapter 5.

72. *Życie Warszawy*, 1 June 1946.

73. *Życie Warszawy*, 15 May 1945.

74. *Życie Warszawy*, 14 June 1947.

75. Webber, p. 10.

Chapter 2

1. Kazimierz Smoleń, interview by the author, audio recording, Oświęcim, Poland, 11 April 1994.

2. "Apel do b. więźniów politycznych w sprawie Muzeum w Oświęcimiu," PZbWP, okólnik nr. 5/47, AAN, zespół: 415, syg.: 13.

3. "Memoriał byłych więźniów obozu oświęcimskiego w sprawie wzięcia pod opiekę terenu obozu w Oświęcimiu," AAN, zespół: Ministerstwo Kultury i Sztuki, Centralny Zarząd Muzeów, Wydział Muzeów i Pomników Walki z Faszyzmem. syg.: 19b.

4. A Nazi term for ethnic Germans living outside the Reich.

5. See Strzelecki, *Ostatnie dni obozu Auschwitz*, pp. 57–58; Zygmunt Woźniczka, "Z działalności polskiego i radzieckiego aparatu represji na Górnym Śląsku w 1945 roku," in *Obozy pracy przymusowej na Górnym Śląsku*, ed. Andrzej Topola (Katowice: Wydawnictwo Uniwersytetu Śląskiego, 1994), pp. 51–76. There are also records

of 52 German POWs working at the State Museum at Auschwitz as late as October 1948, although it is unclear where they were housed. Składnice Akt Państwowego Muzeum w Oświęcimiu (hereafter SkAPMO), teczka: Depozyty pieniężne 1948.

6. Genowesa Przybysz, "Relacja, pielęgniarka,, szpital ob. PCK [Polskiego Czerwonego Krzyża (Polish Red Cross)]," 25 April, 22 and 24 May 1973, Archiwum Państwowego Muzeum w Oświęcimiu (hereafter APMO), syg.: Ośw/Przybysz/1745.

7. Ernst Dittmar, "Wspomnienie," 17 June 1985, APMO, syg.: Wsp/Dittmar/904.

8. Ibid.; Joanna Jakobi, "Relacja pielęgniarka Joanny Jakobi n/t założenia szpitala PCK na terenie b-obozu w Oświęcimiu, pracy w tym szpitalu oraz personelu lekarskiego," 21 May 1973, APMO, syg.: Ośw/Jakobi/1733a; Smoleń, interview, 11 April 1994; Adam Żłobnicki, "Relacja b. więźnia KL Auschwitz Adama Żłobnickiego Nr. 165010 odnośnie pracy w Muzeum a w szcególności dziejów niektórych obiektów poobozowych na terenie KL Auschwitz I i II," 18 November 1981, APMO, syg.: Ośw./tom 96.

9. Smoleń, interview, 11 April 1994.

10. Kazimierz Smoleń, "Sprawozdanie z X-letniej działalności Muzeum w Oświęcimiu-Brzezince," 10 October 1956, APMO, syg.: Ref/63.

11. PZbWP, "Protokół z pierwszego posiedzenia Zarządu Głównego obytego dn. 6.II.1946 r.," AAN, zespół: 415, syg.: 5.

12. PZbWP, okólnik nr. 5, 7 July 1946, AAN, zespół: 415, syg.: 12.

13. Letter, Cyrankiewicz to Michał Rola-Żymierski, 30 April 1946, AAN, zespół: 415, syg.: 52; Żłobnicki, "Relacja," APMO; Kazimierz Smoleń, interview by the author, audio recording, Oświęcim, Poland, 8 December 1993; "Obóz w Oświęcimiu pod ochroną władz," *Dziennik Polski,* 16 April 1946.

14. Letter, Cyrankiewicz to Rola-Żymierski.

15. Kazimierz Smoleń, interviews by the author, audio recording, Oświęcim, Poland, 8 December 1993 and 24 August 1994.

16. Żłobnicki, "Relacja," APMO; Tadeusz Szymański, "Relacja b. więźnia KL Auschwitz Tadeusza Szymańskiego odnośnic początków swojej pracy w PMO-B oraz przedmiotów znalezionych po wyzwoleniu na terenie byłego KL Auschwitz," 7 November 1985, APMO, syg.: Ośw/Szymański/2621.

17. Smoleń, interview, 24 August 1994. According to Smoleń, victims arriving in transports often had hidden valuables that were not always extracted by members of the Sonderkommando, who had no interest in adding to the coffers of the SS.

18. Irena Woźniakowska, "Tam było więcej śmierci niż chleba," *Dziennik Polski,* 4 March 1947.

19. "Memoriał byłych więźniów," AAN; *Echo Chełmna,* 16 September 1946.

20. Wincenty Hein, "Relacja b. więźnia KL Auschwitz Hein Wincenty nr?, odnośnie pobytu w kl Auschwitz . . . a następnie historii Państwowego Muzeum w OB," 20 September 1973, APMO, syg.: Ośw/Hein/2083.

21. *Naprzód,* 23 March 1947.

22. Hein, "Relacja," APMO.

23. "Protokół spisany w dniu 29. lipca 1946 r. z odbytej komisji rozdziału baraków dla ludności Gromady Brzezinki," SkAPMO, protokóły z narad, protokóły z obowiązań. Rok: 1946, 1949, 1954, 1957, 1964, 1965, 1966. Administracja.

24. *Gazeta Ludowa,* 20 October 1946.

25. Żłobnicki, "Relacja," APMO.

26. "Sprawozdanie z posiedzenia rozszerzonego Prezydium Zarządu Głównego P.Z.B.W.P. odbytego w Sekretariacie Zarządu Głównego w dniu 30.VIII.1946 r.," AAN, zespół: 415, syg.: 5.

27. The *Lagererweiterung,* or camp extension area, refers to the section of Auschwitz I built after 1942, when the base camp was expanded to include not only a greater area, but additional structures such as barracks and work halls. This area was not included as part of the State Museum, its barracks used instead for the Polish Army and as housing for the local population. See Irena Strzelecka, "Budowa, rozbudowa oraz rozwój obozu i jego filii," in Długoborski and Piper, 1:58–59; Dwork and van Pelt, pp. 359–60.

28. Żłobnicki, "Relacja," APMO.

29. Ibid.; Szymański, "Relacja," APMO.

30. Krystyna Szymańska, "Relacja Krystyny Szymańskiej dot. działalności w pierwszych latach powojennych w Krakowskiej Komisji Badania Zbrodni Niemieckich," 9 March 1990, APMO, syg.: Ośw/Szymańska/3010.

31. Ibid. Despite the Liquidation Office's suspicious handling of deportees' property, the number of artifacts in the possession of the State Museum at Auschwitz today stretches the imagination. Władysław T. Bartoszewski found, for example, that in 1989 the museum's collection included 79 cubic meters of shoes, irons, and cutlery, 2,479 kilograms of glasses, razors, and buttons, 3,500 suitcases, 29,000 toothbrushes, and 460 prosthetic limbs. See Bartoszewski, *Convent at Auschwitz,* p. 157.

32. Szymański, "Relacja," APMO.

33. *Express Wieczorny,* 5 November 1946.

34. Szymański, "Relacja," APMO.

35. *Echo Chełmna,* 16 September 1946.

36. Lucjan Motyka, interview by the author, audio recording, Warsaw, Poland, 1 December 1994.

37. Hein, "Relacja," APMO.

38. Smoleń, interview, 24 August 1994; Szymański, "Relacja," APMO.

39. Stanisław Peters, "Oświęcim," *Dziennik Polski,* 4 April 1947.

40. Tadeusz Szymański, "Wzmianki o początkach Muzeum w Oświęcimiu o odnajdywaniu na terenie byłego KL Auschwitz różnych dokumentów i rzeczy przywożonych przez więźniów," November 1985, APMO, syg.: Ośw/Szymański/2659.

41. Ibid.

42. "Scenariusz filmu *Muzeum w 25-leciu*," APMO, syg.: S/Iwaszko, Szymański/64.

43. Smoleń, interview, 11 April 1994.

44. Hein, "Relacja," APMO.

45. This block was subsequently designated Block 4. For the purpose of clarity, this analysis will always refer to it as Block 4.

46. Emeryka Iwaszko, "Wystawy Państwowego Muzeum w Oświęcimiu," p. 215.

47. Smoleń, interview, 8 December 1993.

48. APMO, Dz. IX/2, wystawa przed 1955 r.

49. *Express Wieczorny,* 5 November 1946.

50. Hein, "Relacja," APMO; Żłobnicki, "Relacja," APMO.

51. The PZbWP was the largest organization of former prisoners and by the spring 1947, counted 177,000 members. On the work of the PZbWP see Czesław Łeski, "Jak pracuje nasz Związek," *Wolni Ludzie,* 1 May 1947; Mieczysław Wróblewski, "Wstęp do inventarza" (1977), Polski Związek b. Więźniów Politycznych Hitlerowskich Więzień i Obozów Koncentracyjnych, Zarząd Główny, Zarządy Wojewódzkie, Koła /1940/1946-49/-1952, AAN, zespół: 415.

52. Among the PZbWP's most prominent members were Józef Cyrankiewicz, who was named prime minister after the January 1947 election, Minister of Justice Henryk Świątkowski, Vice-Minister of Justice Tadeusz Rek, and Ludwik Rajewski, director of the Ministry of Culture's Department of Museums and Monuments of Polish Martyrology. "Apel do b. więźniów politycznych," AAN; Łeski.

53. Alfred Woycicki, "Głos ma Naród" [protocol of the December 1946 conference], AAN, zespół: 415, syg.: 52.

54. *Wolni Ludzie,* 1 May 1947; Woycicki, "Oświęcim, 14.VI.1940–14.VI.1947,"

55. Hein, "Relacja," APMO.

56. Woycicki, "Głos ma Naród," AAN.

57. Krystyna Żywulska, *Przeżyłam Oświęcim* (Warszawa: Wiedza, 1946); Zofia Kossak, *Z otchlani. Wspomnienia z lagru* (Częstochowa: Wydawnictwo Księgarni Wł. Nagłowskiego, 1946); Seweryna Szmaglewska, *Dymy nad Birkenau* (Warszawa: Czytelnik, 1946). Szmaglewska's memoir quickly became one of the most widely read accounts of life and death in Auschwitz and has been published in at least six Polish editions. See Anna Pawełczyńska, *Values and Violence in Auschwitz: A Sociological Analysis* (Berkeley: University of California Press, 1979), p. 25, and the *Życie Warszawy* article of 17 June 1947 which credits Szmaglewska with acquainting the public with the concept of "Birkenau."

58. A 1955 memorandum of the Department of Museums and Monuments of the Struggle against Fascism indicates that by the end of 1946, 60 percent of the structures on

the grounds of the Auschwitz memorial site been destroyed. Most of the structures were in Birkenau. "Notatka Służbowa," AAN, zespół: Ministerstwo Kultury i Sztuki, Centralny Zarząd Muzeów, Wydział Muzeów i Pomników Walki z Faszyzmem, syg.: 21.

59. *Życie Warszawy,* 22 April 1947; *Naprzód Dolnośląski,* 31 May 1947.

60. Quoted in "Najstraszliwsze muzeum świata na miejscu martyrologii milionów ludzi. Rozmowa z prof. Rajewskim o planach organizacji muzeum," *Express Wieczorny,* 24 February 1947.

61. "Zasady rozplanowania muzeum w byłym obozie koncentracynym w Oświęcimiu," SkAPMO, teczka: Projekty ekspozycji w blokach wystawowych 1947–1949.

62. "Zasady rozplanowania muzeum w byłym obozie koncentracynym w Oświęcimiu," AAN, zespół: 415, syg.: 13.

63. *Wolni Ludzi,* 15 June 1947.

64. *Opinia,* 16 June 1947.

65. *Dziennik Ludowy,* 17 June 1947. The first large exhibit on the Shoah and fate of the Jews at Auschwitz was not opened until 1968. See chapter 5.

66. Smoleń, interview, 11 April 1994; Motyka, interview.

67. Also noteworthy in this context is Ciecwierz's contention that press censorship in the early postwar years, especially after a reorganization of press and propaganda institutions in the spring of 1947, did make a clear effort to understate or delete important "Jewish issues," such as the participation of Poles of Jewish background in the regime's administrative elite or Polish complicity in the murder of Jews by the Germans during the occupation. See Ciecwierz, pp. 178, 289–90. On transformations in the provisional government's policies toward the press, see also Perkal, pp. 151–58.

68. Alfred Rosenberg was a leading racial theorist of the Nazi Party who wrote on the alleged Jewish world conspiracy and the evils of Bolshevism and Zionism. After the invasion of the Soviet Union in July 1941 he was appointed minister for the occupied eastern territories. Motyka is using Rosenberg simply as a metaphor for Nazi racial principles in general.

69. Motyka, interview.

70. J. L. Lindsay, "It wasn't like this . . . ," *New Statesman and Nation* 36 (1948): p. 259.

Chapter 3

1. Quotations from the rally's speeches are from "Nigdy więcej obozów koncentracyjnych! Wielkie zgromadzenie b. więźniów politycznych w Oświęcimiu," *Wolni Ludzie,* 1 May 1949. Beginning in 1949, official ceremonies commemorating the liberation of Auschwitz were no longer held in January. Because of concerns over

winter weather, they were moved to April, which then became the traditional month for such observances.

2. For a general introduction to the Stalinist period in Poland, see A. Kemp-Welch, ed., *Stalinism in Poland, 1944–1956: Selected Papers from the Fifth World Congress of Central and East European Studies, Warsaw, 1995* (New York: St. Martin's Press, 1999); Davies, *God's Playground* 2:577–86.)

3. Krystyna Kersten, "The Terror, 1949–1954," in Kemp-Welch, pp. 79, 82, 94.

4. In June 1947 the ministry formed a historical commission to guide the museum in its work. The commission was to submit recommendations to the museum, which would then send its exhibition plans to the Department of Museums and Monuments of Polish Martyrology in the Ministry of Culture. This office would send its recommendations for the plans to the ministry's Council for the Protection of Monuments of Martyrdom. The council would then return proposals, if approved, to the ministerial office, which would then forward them on to the Auschwitz Museum for implementation. Ministerstwo Kultury i Sztuki, "Odpis do Dyrekcji Muzeum Państwowego w Oświęcimiu," 16 July 1947, SkAPMO, teczka: Projekty ekspozycji w blokach wystawowych 1947–1949; "Sprawozdanie z konferencji w Oświęcimiu w dniu 6. i 7.VII 1947 r.," SkAPMO, teczka: Projekty ekspozycji w blokach wystawowych 1947–1949; Smoleń, inteview, 11 April 1994; Hein, "Relacja," APMO; Ustawa z dnia 2 lipca 1947 r. o upamiętcieniu męczeństwa narodu polskiego i innych narodów w Oświęcimiu, *Dziennik Ustaw Rzeczypospolitej Polskiej* 52, ustawa 265, pp. 826–27.

5. "Informacja dla Wydziału Propagandy o Państwowym Muzeum w Oświęcimiu i Brzezince," AAN, PZPR, Kom. Cent. syg.: 237/XVIII/81.

6. See, for example, *Dziennik Polski*, 15 July 1947.

7. Wincenty Hein, "I tu obowiązuje realizm polityczny," *Dziennik Polski*, 11 August 1947.

8. Władysław Długocki, "Dyskutujemy dalej na temat: Czym ma być Oświęcim?," *Dziennik Polski*, 27 August 1947. For other voices in the discussion over the site's future see, for example, Adolf Gawalewicz, "Czym ma być Oświęcim," *Dziennik Polski*, 11 August 1947; and *Polska Ludowa*, 27 July 1947.

9. "Protokół z posiedzenia Rady Ochrony Pomników Walki i Męczeństwa w dniach 23 i 24 marca 1948 r.," AAN, zespół: Ministerstwo Kultury i Sztuki, Centralny Zarząd Muzeów, Wydział Muzeów i Pomników Walki z Faszyzmem, syg.: 1A.

10. Stanisław Kłodziński, "Wytyczne dla Państwowego Muzeum w Oświęcimiu," *Wolni Ludzie*, May 1948.

11. Motyka, interview; Smoleń, interviews, 8 December 1994, 11 April 1994, and 24 August 1994.

12. Ciecwierz, p. 76; Piotr Kuncewicz, *Leksykon polskich pisarzy współczesnych* (Warszawa: Graf-Punkt, 1995), pp. 147ff; R. F. Leslie, *The History of Poland since 1863* (Cambridge: Cambridge University Press, 1980), p. 323.

13. Jerzy Putrament, "Notatki o Oświęcimiu," *Odrodzenie* no. 23 (6 June 1948): p. 3.

14. Ibid.

15. Ibid.

16. Smoleń, interview, 11 April 1994.

17. Kuncewicz, p. 467.

18. Kazimierz Koźniewski, "Drażliwy problem," *Przekrój* no. 179 (12–18 September 1948): p. 3. The article was reprinted in its entirety in the PZbWP organ *Wolni Ludzie*, 15–30 September 1948, sparking a lively response from former prisoners and their families.

19. Koźniewski, p. 3.

20. Ibid., p. 4.

21. Ibid.

22. Smoleń, interviews, 11 April 1994 and 24 April 1994.

23. Motyka, interview.

24. In April 1943 the Germans announced the discovery, in the Katyn Forest near Smolensk, of mass graves containing the remains of more than 4,000 Polish officers who the Germans claimed had been executed by the Soviets. Moscow dismissed the claim as a German propaganda attempt to sow discord among the Allies at a crucial point in he war, while the Polish government in exile in London demanded an investigation conducted by the International Red Cross. Moscow terminated its relations with the government in exile, and for fifty years denied responsibility for the massacre, which remained a vivid reminder of Soviet brutality in the unofficial memory of Poles. On Katyn see Janusz K. Zawodny, *Death in the Forest: The Story of the Katyn Forest Massacre* (Notre Dame, Ind.: University of Notre Dame Press, 1962.)

25. Smoleń, interview, 11 April 1994.

26. Hein, "Relacja," APMO.

27. See, for example, "Słuszny artykuł," in *Kuźnica* no. 39 (26 September 1948), p. 12.

28. Ludwik Rajewski, "Jeszcze 'Oświęcim' (na marginesie dyskusji w związku z artykułem pt. 'Drażliwy problem')," AAN, zespół: Ministerstwo Kultury i Sztuki, Centralny Zarząd Muzeów, Wydział Muzeów i Pomników Walki z Faszyzmem, syg. 21; Tadeusz Myszkowski, "Stare buty i okulary . . . w odpowiedzi na 'Drażliwy problem,'" *Wolni Ludzie*, 15 October 1948; Ludwik Rajewski, "'Drażliwy Problem' po raz czwarty," *Wolni Ludzie*, 15 November 1948; Wincenty Hein, "Czym jest Muzeum Oświęcimskie," *Dziennik Polski*, 19 November 1948; Konstanty Przybysławski, "Jeszcze raz 'Drażliwy Problem,'" *Tygodnik Powszechny*, 12 December 1948.

29. Myszkowski.

30. Untitled, undated manuscript of the Ministry of Culture and Art, SkAPMO, teczka: Projekty ekspozycji w blokach wystawowych 1947–1949.

31. Cited in Rajewski, "'Drażliwy problem,'" and in "Zestawienie liczby zwiedzających Państwowego Muzeum w Oświęcimiu," 19 January 1949, SkAPMO, teczka: Projekty ekspozycji w blokach wystawowych 1947–1949.

32. "Zestawienie frekwencji zwiedzających Państwowe Muzeum w Oświęcim-Brzezince," SkAPMO, teczka: Dział III, podkładki do sprawozdań rocznych.

33. "Informacja dla Wydziału Propagandy," AAN.

34. Tadeusz Hołuj, "Projekt bloku 21 'Walka i zwycięstwo,'" SkAPMO, teczka: Projekty ekspozycji w blokach wystawowych 1947–1949.

35. "Protokół z konferencji Prezydium Rady Ochrony Pomników Walki i Męczeństwa, Komisji Fachowej Rady, przedstawicieli Ministerstwa Kultury i Sztuki, Komisji Historycznej przy Państwowym Muzeum w Oświęcimiu oraz przy współudziale Dyrekcji Państwowego Muzeum w Oświęcimiu i zaproszonych gości," 3 April 1949, SkAPMO, teczka: Projekty ekspozycji w blokach wystawowych 1947–1949.

36. Ibid.

37. Tadeusz Hołuj, "Podstawa do opracowania bloku 15 w Państwowym Museum w Oświęcimiu," 6 July 1949, SkAPMO, teczka: Projekty ekspozycji w blokach wystawowych 1947–1949.

38. Ibid.

39. Memorandum, Tadeusz Wąsowicz do Naczelnej Dyrekcji Muzeów, Wydział Pomników Męczeństwa i Walki, Warszawa, 2 February 1949, SkAPMO, teczka: Projekty ekspozycji w blokach wystawowych 1947–1949; Tadeusz Hołuj, "Projekt bloku 21 'Walka i zwycięstwo,'" SkAPMO, teczka: Projekty ekspozycji w blokach wystawowych 1947–1949; "Protokół Posiedzenia Komisja Fachowej Rady Ochrony Pomników Walki i Męceństwa w dniu 18 marca 1949 r.," SkAPMO, teczka: Projekty ekspozycji w blokach wystawowych 1947–1949; Letter, Prezydium Rady Ochrony Pomników Walki i Męczeństwa do Komitetu Centralnego PZPR, Wydział Kultury, 14 July 1949, AAN, zespół: PZPR. KC. syg.: 237/XVIII/81.

40. "Informacja dla Wydziału Propagandy," AAN.

41. Teresa Torańska, *Them: Stalin's Polish Puppets* (New York: Harper and Row, 1987), p. 314.

42. Ibid., pp. 320–21. See also Checinski, pp. 90–91, and Jaff Schatz, *The Generation: The Rise and Fall of the Jewish Communists of Poland* (Berkeley: University of California Press, 1991), pp. 255–63.

43. For information on ZBoWiD, its predecessor organizations, and its formation in September 1949, see M. Wróblewski, "Wstęp do inwentarza" (1977), AAN, zespół: 415/Polski Związek byłych Więźniów Politycznych, Zarząd Główny, Zarządy Wojewódzkie, Koła /1940/1946–49/-1952; Janina Mróz-Krzos, "Wstęp do inwentarza" (1977), AAN, zespół: Związek Bojowników z Faszyzmem i Najazdem Hitlerowskim o Niepodległość i Demokrację (1939–1944), 1945–1949, 1950–1951; *Die*

Welt, 17 May 1972; Włodzimierz Lechowicz, "Międzynarodowa współpraca organizacji kombatanckich," in *Zbowidowcy. Tradycje i zadania*, ed. Mikołaj Łomacki and Jadwiga Szulc-Łyskowa (Warszawa: Wydawnictwo ZG ZBoWiD/Książka i Wiedza, 1969), pp. 366–71; and T. R., "Schemat organizacyjny Związku Bojowników," in Łomacki and Szulc-Łyskowa, pp. 391–94.

44. Quoted in *Dziennik Polski*, 17 April 1950. For additional accounts of the day's events see *Rzeczpospolita*, 17 April 1950; and *Trybuna Robotnicza*, 17 April 1950.

45. Quoted in *Kurier Szczeciński*, 17 April 1950.

46. *Dziennik Polski*, 17 April 1950.

47. Torańska, p. 338; Jörg K. Hoensch and Gerlind Nasarski, *Polen. 30 Jahre Volksdemokratie* (Hannover: Fackelträger-Verlag Schmidt-Küster, 1975), pp. 185–89; Jan Nowak, "The Church in Poland," *Problems in Communism* 31, no. 1 (January-February 1982): pp. 5–7. The most comprehensive treatment of the organization is Jan Żaryn, "'Księża Patrioci'—geneza powstawania formacji duchownych katolickich," in *Polska 1944/45–1989: Studia i materiały*, ed. Krystyna Kersten, et al. (Warszawa: Instytut Historii PAN, 1995), 1:123–49.

48. Żaryn, pp. 124–26, 138–40; Richard F. Starr, *Poland 1944–1962: The Sovietization of a Captive People* (New Orleans: Lousiana State University Press, 1962), p. 258.

49. Jerzy Laudański, "Wstęp do inwentarza" (1977), AAN, zespół: 425/Główna i Okręgowe Komisje Księży przy ZBoWiD 1950–1955.

50. *Życie Warszawy*, 18 June 1950.

51. Ibid. For additional accounts of the day's ceremonies see *Głos Wielkopolski*, 19 June 1950; *Rzeczpospolita*, 18 June 1950; *Rzeczpospolita*, 19 June 1950.

52. Letter, Józef Cyrankiewicz, prezes Rady Ministrów, do Komisji Księży przy ZBoWiD, 17 June 1950, AAN, zespół: 425/Główna i Okręgowe Komisje Księży przy ZBoWiD 1950–1955, syg.: 19.

53. Jerzy Ros, "Wyznanie wiary. Trzy razy Oświęcim," *Kurier Codzienny*, 19 June 1950.

54. Laudański.

55. Henryk Matysiak, ZBoWID, Zarząd Główny, "Notatka sprawozdawca," do Komitetu Centralnego PZPR, Wydz. Propagandy Masowej, AAN, zespół: PZPR, Kom. Cent., syg.: 237/XVIII/81.

56. Ibid.; Letter, Jerzy Bogusz, Wydział Propagandy KC PZPR, do tow. Sarewicza, 12 July 1950, AAN, zespół: PZPR, Kom. Cent. syg.: 237/18/81. Wąsowicz's tenure at the museum did not end, however, until his death in November 1952.

57. Matysiak, "Notatka sprawozdawca," AAN; Letter, Ministerstwo Kultury i Sztuki do E. Kowalskiego, Dyr. FIAPP, 9 August 1950, Związek Kombatantów Rzeczypospolitej Polski i Byłych Więźniów Politycznych (hereafter ZKRPiBWP), syg.: 17/246.

58. Protokół konferencji komisji, powołane przez Ministra Kultury i Sztuki na

wniosek C.K. PZPR—ustalenia programu Muzeum w Oświęcimiu w dniu 20.VIII.1950 r., ZKRPiBWP, syg.: 17/246.

59. "Protokół z posiedzenia Komisji Programu Muzeum w Oświęcimiu w dniu 11 października 1950 r." and "Protokół z posiedzenia Komisji Plastycznej Państwowego Muzeum, odbytego dnia 4 października 1950 roku," SkAPMO, teczka: 853 Projekty zmian ekspozycji w blokach wystawowych, protokoły 1950–1952.

60. "Protokół z posiedzenia Komisji Plastycznej," SkAPMO; "Protokół z posiedzenia w Państwowym Muzeum w Oświęcimiu w dniu 6 października 1950 r.," and "Protokół nr. 3 z posiedzenia zespołu kierowniczego Państwowego Muzeum w Oświęcimiu w dniu 7.X.1950 r.," SkAPMO, teczka: 853 Projekty zmian ekspozycji w blokach wystawowych, protokoły 1950–1952.

61. "Protokół z posiedzenia Komisji Programu Muzeum," SkAPMO.

62. Ibid.

63. "Protokół, 10.VII.50," SkAPMO, teczka: Protokoły: —Konieczności 1974–77, Odzysku materiałów 1971, Z obrad Międzynarodowej Konferencji Muzeów martyrologii 1972, uszkodzeń, zniszczeń, lub kradzieży eksponatów 1948–51. On changes in the composition and role of the Central Committee of Jews in Poland see Schatz, pp. 253–55.

64. "Protokół konferencji komisji, powołane przez Ministra Kultury i Sztuki na wniosek C.K. PZPR—ustalenia programu Muzeum w Oświęcimiu w dniu 20.VIII.1950 r.," ZKRPiBWP, syg.: 17/246.

65. "Protokół z odbioru i wycenienia wykonanego wnętrza bloku 15, ilustraującego temat 'Źródła ludobójstwa,' w dniu 14 grudnia 1950 r.," SkAPMO, teczka: 853 Projekty zmian ekspozycji w blokach wystawowych, protokoły 1950–1952; "Protokół z posiedzenia Komisji Programu Muzeum," SkAPMO.

66. "Protokół z posiedzenia Komisji Programu Muzeum," SkAPMO. In the archives of the State Museum at Auschwitz are numerous photographs illustrating the exhibitions in these years, many of which include texts such as those cited here. Unfortunately, few of these photographs are dated and marked, making it difficult to determine the locations of their subjects at the museum. APMO, teczka: Fot: stara ekspozycja z przed 1955; APMO, Dz. IX/2, wystawa przed 1955 r.

67. Smoleń, interview, 11 April 1994.

68. Stefan Dybowski, *Problemy rewolucji kulturalnej w Polsce Ludowej* (Warszawa: Ludowa Spółdzielnia Wydawnicza, 1953), p. 231.

69. "Protokół z posiedzenia Komisji Programu Muzeum," SkAPMO; Smoleń, interview, 11 April 1994.

70. Hein, "Relacja," APMO.

71. "Narada produkcyjna Wydziału Plastycznego przy Państwowe Muzeum w Oświęcimiu," 26 April 1951, "Protokół z przeglądu bloków muzealnych w dniu 12.7.1951 r.," "Protokół z narady produkcyjnej odbytej w Wydziale Plastycznym w

dniu 26 lipca 1951 r.," and "Protokół z narady produkcyjnej odbytej w Wydziale Plastycznym w dniu 16 listopada 1951 r.," SkAPMO, teczka: 853 Projekty zmian ekspozycji w blokach wystawowych. Protokoły 1950–1952.

72. Smoleń, interview, 11 April 1994.

73. Letter, Paweł Hoffman, Kierownik Wydziału Kultury Komitetu Centralnego PZPR, do Wicepremiera Józefa Cyrankiewicza, Sekretarz KC PZPR, November 1953, AAN, zespół: PZPR, Kom. Cent., syg.: 237/XVIII/81.

74. Stefan Wiernik, director of the State Museum at Auschwitz, 1953–54.

75. Hein, "Relacja," APMO; Smoleń, who succeeded Wiernik as director in late 1954, also supports Hein's conclusion that the government intended to let the museum die a slow death. Smoleń, interview, 11 April 1994.

76. "Wykaz uczestników zjazdu w dniu II.X.53 r.," AAN, zespół: PZPR, Kom. Cent. syg.: 237/XVIII/81; Odpis (deposition), Stefan Wiernik do Ministerstwa Kultury i Sztuki, 26 October 1953, AAN, zespół: PZPR, Kom. Cent. syg.: 237/XVIII/81.

77. Letter, Minister Kultury i Sztuki do PZPR, Komitetu Centralnego, Wydział Kultury, AAN, zespół: PZPR, Kom. Cent. syg.: 237/XVIII/81.

78. "Odpis z notatki w sprawie Muzeum w Oświęcimiu," AAN, zespół: PZPR, Kom. Cent. syg.: 237/XVIII/81.

79. Hein, "Relacja," APMO.

80. Zbigniew Drożdż, Odpis (deposition), 11 October 1953, AAN, zespół: PZPR, Kom. Cent. syg.: 237/XVIII/81.

81. "Odpis z notatki w sprawie Muzeum w Oświęcimiu," AAN, zespół: PZPR, Kom. Cent. syg.: 237/XVIII/81.

82. Smoleń, interview, 8 December 1993.

Chapter 4

1. For analyses of post-Stalinist/pre-October developments in Poland, see Nicholas Bethell, *Gomułka: His Poland, His Communism* (New York: Holt, Rinehart and Winston, 1969); Checiński, chapters 8 and 9; Jörg K. Hoensch, *Geschichte Polens* (Stuttgart: Verlag Eugen Ulmer, 1983), chapter 6; Jakub Karpiński, *Countdown. The Polish Upheavals of 1956, 1968, 1970, 1976, 1980. . .* (New York: Karz-Cohl Publishing, 1982); Peter Raina, *Political Opposition in Poland, 1954–1977* (London: Poets and Painters Press, 1978); Konrad Syrop, *Spring in October. The Story of the Polish Revolution of 1956* (Westport, Conn.: Greenwood Press, 1976); and Szczypiorski, *Polish Ordeal,* chapter 5.

2. Quoted in Karpiński, *Countdown*, p. 34.

3. Bethell, p. 196.

4. Józef Światło defected to the West in late 1953, and in December 1954 Radio Free

Europe began to broadcast Światło's descriptions of the functioning of PZPR authority and the links between Soviet institutions, the party, and the UB.

5. Jan B. De Weydenthal, *The Communists of Poland: An Historical Outline* (Stanford, Calif.: Hoover Institution Press, 1986), p. 79.

6. Szczypiorski, although noting that the role of the Security Service in Poland under Stalinism was not as great as that of the secret police in Hungary or the Soviet Union, states nonetheless: "In every enterprise, in every office, in every institution, security agents held sway, and their opinions counted in the party apparatus." Szczypiorski, *Polish Ordeal*, p. 51.

7. Stefan Żółkiewski, "O aktualnych dyskusjach literackich," *Nowe Drogi*, June 1955; quoted in Peter Raina, *Political Opposition*, p. 32.

8. Hołuj, "Sprawa wiecznej pamięci," p. 3. Hołuj's assessment is remarkable on two counts: first, his overt criticism testifies to the radical relaxation of censorship during the early "thaw," and second, the propagandistic exhibitions to which he was referring were, in part, his own creation.

9. "Kosztorys orientacyjny dla remontu, odbudowy i rekonstrukcji muzeum w Oświęcimiu i na Brzezince," AAN, zespół: Ministerstwo Kultury i Sztuki, Centralny Zarząd Muzeów, Wydział Muzeów i Pomników Walki z Faszyzmem, syg.: 21.

10. An organization of former prisoners from various European countries, the IAC would exert a profound influence on the character of the memorial site in the years ahead. A more thorough discussion of the committee follows in chapter 5.

11. "Décisions du Comité International d'Auschwitz réuni à Vienne, les 22 et 23 mai 1954," Stiftung Archive der Parteien und Massenorganizationen der ehemaligen Deutschen Demokratischen Republik im Bundesarchiv Berlin (hereafter SAPMO), Bestand VVN/KdAW, syg.: 74/4.

12. "10-lecie oswobodzenia Obozów Koncentracyjnych Oświęcim-Brzezinka," SkAPMO, segregator 852/"Popularyzacja miejsc pamięci od 1947"; Hołuj, "Sprawa wiecznej pamięci," p. 3; "Muzeum, które jest przestrogą dla świata," *Za Wolność i Lud* (May 1955): pp. 19-20; "Uchwała Nr. 39 Sekretariatu KC w sprawie Muzeum w Oświęcimiu," AAN, zespół: Ministerstwo Kultury i Sztuki, Centralny Zarząd Muzeów, Wydział Muzeów i Pomników Walki z Faszyzmem, syg.: 21.

13. Smoleń contends that this initiative was the result of a fact-finding visit by a PZPR/Ministry of Culture joint commission in late 1954. Smoleń, interview, 24 August 1994.

14. Smoleń, interviews, 8 December 1993, 11 April 1994, 24 August 1994.

15. Smoleń, interview, 24 August 1994.

16. Ibid.

17. "Scenariusz Wystawy Stałej Państwowego Muzeum w Oświęcimiu," 3 February 1955, APMO, syg.: S./Smoleń/6.

18. The exhibition was completed none too soon. On 17 April the final touches

were still being applied to the exhibition, and as Prime Minister Cyrankiewicz began viewing the exhibition in Block 4, Kazimierz Smoleń was still attempting to complete the work in Block 11. Smoleń, interviews, 11 April 1994, 24 August 1994.

19. "Décisions du Comité International d'Auschwitz," SAPMO; Letter, Komitee der Antifaschistischen Widerstandskämpfer an Polnischen Informationsdienst, 14 March 1955, SAPMO, Bestand VVN/KdAW, syg.: 75/4.

20. "Décisions du Comité International d'Auschwitz," SAPMO; Letter, Comité International d'Auschwitz to Komitee der Antifaschistischen Widerstandskämpfer, 3 March 1955, SAPMO, Bestand VVN/KdAW, syg.: 74/4.

21. "Sprawozdanie z pracy działu nauków—oświatowego Państwowego Muzeum w Oświęcimiu . . . wybrana na zebraniu POP PZPR Państwowego Muzeum w dniu 12.X.55," SkAPMO, segregator: D-1/Plan pracy, sprawodawczość, statystyka wg. działów.

22. "Aufruf der 250 internationalen Delegierten aus 17 Ländern Europas anläßlich der internationalen Gedenkfeiern des 10. Jahrestages der Befreiung des Konzentrationslagers Auschwitz," SAPMO, Bestand VVN/KdAW, syg.: 75/4.

23. Wilhelm Detlefsen, "Nie wieder Auschwitz! Eine ungewöhnliche Reise durch Polen," *Die Kirche der Heimat. Evangelisch-lutherisches Gemeindeblatt in Schleswig-Holstein, Hamburg und Nordschleswig* 31, no. 10 (2 May 1955). For additional accounts of the day's proceedings see Jerzy Rawicz, "W Oświęcimiu," *Trybuna Ludu*, 19 April 1955; *Trybuna Ludu*, 18 April 1955; *Życie Warszawy*, 19 April 1955; *Za Wolność i Lud* (May 1955).

24. Nikolaus Zils, "In Auschwitz—nach 10 Jahren!," SAPMO, Bestand VVN/KdAW, syg.: 74/4.

25. "Uchwała Nr. 39 Sekretariatu KC w sprawie Muzeum w Oświęcimiu," AAN.

26. "Rahmenprogramm der Feierlichkeiten die in Polen aus Anlaß des 10. Jahrestages der Befreiung the Konzentrationslager stattfinden werden," ZKRPiBWP, syg.: 17/251.

27. "Ansprache der Vorsitzenden des französischen Auschwitz-Komitees, Frau Professor Marie Normand, als Sprecherin der 17 ausländischen Delegationen internationaler Widerstandskämpfer und ehemaliger Häftlinge des Konzentrationslagers Auschwitz auf der großen Gedenkkundgebung am Ehrenmal der 4 millionen Opfer in Birkenau am 17. April 1955," SAPMO, Bestand VVN/KdAW, syg.: 75/4.

28. Ibid.

29. "Przemówienie Prezesa Rady Ministrów Józefa Cyrankiewicza," *Trybuna Ludu*, 18 April 1955.

30. *Trybuna Ludu*, 18 April 1955; Detlefsen; "Rahmenprogramm der Feierlichkeiten," ZKRPiBWP.

31. Jerzy Rawicz, "W Oświęcimiu."

32. Hermann Pörzgen, "Auschwitz, wie es heute ist. In dem ehemaligen Konzentrationslager," *Frankfurter allgemeine Zeitung*, 20 October 1956.

33. Zils, SAPMO.

34. Jerzy Brandhuber, "Das Staatlich Museum in Auschwitz. Organization, Tätigkeit, Gesamtarbeiten für 1957," SAPMO, Bestand VVN/KdAW, syg.: 75/4; Letter, Kazimierz Smoleń to Vice-Minister of Culture and Art Lucjan Motyka, 2 June 1956, AAN, zespół: Ministerstwo Kultury i Sztuki, Centralny Zarząd Muzeów i Pomników Walki z Faszyzmem, syg.: 22.

35. Dwork and van Pelt, pp. 359–60.

36. Letter, Smoleń to Motyka, AAN.

37. Pörzgen.

38. "Pilgerfahrt nach Auschwitz," quoted from a German translation, SAPMO, Bestand VVN/KdAW, syg.: 74/4; *Le Déporté*, no. 80 (February–March 1955).

39. "Muzeum, które jest przestrogą dla świata."

40. Hołuj, "Sprawa wiecznej pamięci," p. 3.

41. Unless otherwise noted, all subsequent references to the 1955 exhibition are based on the "Scenariusz wystawy stałej," APMO, and from the photograph collection "Fotografia, DZ. IX/1, wystawa stała z 1955 r.," APMO.

42. Smoleń, interview, 11 April 1994.

43. Ibid.

44. Ibid.

45. Ibid.

46. A survey conducted by the museum staff in 1958, for example, concluded that the hair displayed was one of the three "artifacts" at the site (the Block of Death (Block 11) and Crematorium I being the other two) that made the greatest impression upon visitors. "Wyniki badań ankietowych przeprowadzonych przez Państwowe Muzeum w Oświęcimiu wśród zwiedzających w okresie od 7 maja 1958 r. do 31. grudnia 58," SkAPMO, teczka: Sprawozdania 1961 r. Dz. III.

47. "Protokół konferencji ustalenia programu Muzeum w Oświęcimiu," ZKRPiBWP.

48. Maksymilian Kolbe's significance is discussed more extensively in chapter 6.

49. *Neue Zürcher Zeitung*, 15 August 1964.

50. Pörzgen.

51. Hołuj, "Sprawa wiecznej pamięci," p. 3.

52. Czesław Ostańkowicz, "Żeby ziemia nie parowała cyklonem," *Nowe Sygnały* 8, no. 11 (23) (1957): pp. 1, 3. The author's parenthetical insertions "pre-October" refer to the period preceeding the "Polish October" of 1956, that is, when Władysław Gomułka assumed leadership of the PZPR, ushering in a spirit of reform and greater independence from the Soviet Union.

53. See, for example, Lucjan Wolanowski, "Ajschylos niczego nie widział—świeczka, która by zgasła ze wstydu. Dwa reportaże oświęcimskie, których wolałbym nigdy nie pisać," *Świat* 11, no. 13 (1957): pp. 8–9, 18; Mieczysław Kieta, "Oświęcim 1959," *Wieści* 3, no. 4 (25 January 1959): p. 4.

54. Henryk Poznański, "Notatka w sprawie upamiętnienia miejsc walk i straceń oraz reaktywowania Rady Ochrony Pomników Walki i Męczeństwa," AAN, zespół: Ministerstwo Kultury i Sztuki, Centralny Zarząd Muzeów, Wydział Muzeów i Pomników Walki z Faszyzmem, syg.: 1.

55. Letter, Smoleń to Motyka, AAN.

56. Smoleń, "Sprawozdanie z X-letniej działalności Muzeum," APMO.

57. Ibid.

58. Smoleń, interview, 11 April 1994.

59. "Notatka służbowa rozmowy w Urzędu Rady Ministrów w sprawach związanych z działalnością Międzynarodowego Komitetu Oświęcimskiego oraz Państwowego Muzeum w Oświęcimiu," SkAPMO, segregator: D-1/Plan pracy, sprawodawczość, statystyka wg. działów.

60. "Sprawozdanie z działalności muzeum za okres 1961–1965 i projekt planu na lata 1966–1970," APMO, syg.: Mat/1040. The allocation of such funds, if inadequate, nonetheless enabled the former director to claim with pride, "Since 1955 not a single structure here has collapsed." Smoleń, interview, 24 August 1994.

61. Kazimierz Smoleń, "Blisko 4 miliony zwiedziło Muzeum," *Za Wolność i Lud* (January, 1963): pp. 15–16.

62. "Zestawienie frekwencji zwiedzyjących," SkAPMO.

Chapter 5

1. "Statut des Internationalen Auschwitz-Komitees," SAPMO, Bestand VVN/KdAW, syg.: 75/2.

2. Jacques Coubard, "Le comité international d'Auschwitz se réunit dans l'ancien camp de concentration," *L'Humanité*, 30 January 1957. This article notes the participation of representatives from the German Democratic Republic, Federal Republic of Germany, Austria, Belgium, Denmark, France, the Netherlands, Hungary, Norway, Poland, Switzerland, Sweden, Yugoslavia, and the USSR.

3. The grounds and structures of the State Museum at Auschwitz were added to the UNESCO World Heritage List in 1979.

4. "Protokoll der am 28. u. 29.I.1957 abgehaltenen Sitzung der Kommission für die Ausstattung des Museums in Auschwitz," SAPMO, Bestand VVN/KdAW, syg.: 74/4; "Resolutionsentwurf der Museums-Kommission," SAPMO, Bestand VVN/KdAW, syg.: 74/4. On the development of the various "national exhibitions" at the site, see Kazimierz Smoleń, "Wystawy narodowe w Oświęcimiu," *Muzea Walki* 13 (1980): pp. 53–59.

5. "Protokoll der Komitee-Sitzung am 23.VI.1958," SAPMO, Bestand VVN/KdAW, syg.: 3/K 57/58; Curt Posener, "Zu internationales Auschwitz-Komitee (Langbein)—Bericht vom 29.VII.59," SAPMO, Bestand VVN/KdAW, syg.: 75/2;

"Bericht über die Generalversammlung des Internationalen Ausschuß[*sic*]-Komitee in Warschau vom 14. bis 17. April 1962," SAPMO, Bestand VVN/KdAW, syg.: 75/2; Memorandum, Moldt, Botschaft der Deutschen Demokratischen Republik in der Volksrepublik Polen, an Helmer, 2. Europäische Abteilung, Ministerium für Auswärtige Angelegenheiten, 7 April 1961, SAPMO, Bestand VVN/KdAW, syg.: 75/2.

6. Memorandum, ZBoWiD to IAC members, 26 May 1960, SAPMO, Bestand VVN/KdAW, syg.: 75/2.

7. Memorandum, Moldt, Botschaft der Deutschen Demokratischen Republik in der Volksrepublik Polen.

8. Spielmann, "Entwürfe," pp. 95–96.

9. "Bericht über die Generalversammlung des Internationalen Ausschuß[*sic*]-Komitee," SAPMO.

10. In his 1971 publication, Paul Lendvai claimed that in the course of the 1960s ZBoWiD assumed control over the IAC. While this is an exaggeration, the fact remains that the Polish veterans' and prisoners' organization was without a doubt the most powerful among the constituent groups of the IAC, and that Moczar spared no efforts in attempting to make the IAC's agenda conform to his own. See Lendvai, *Antisemitism without Jews* (New York: Doubleday, 1971), p. 190.

11. This is a translation of the description found in a letter from Brandhuber to Janina Jaworska, reproduced in Janina Jaworska, "*Nie wszystek umrę . . .*": Twórczość plastyczna Polaków w hitlerowskich więzieniach i obozach koncentracyjnych, 1939–1945* (Warszawa: Książka i Wiedza, 1975), pp. 50–51.

12. Scholarship on this theme is limited, and the most important works are the analyses of Spielmann, "Entwürfe," and Young, *Texture of Memory*, pp. 128–44.

13. See, for example, *Gazeta Robotnicza*, 4 November 1946.

14. *Kurier Szczeciński*, 14 November 1950. Former Minister of Culture and Art Włodzimierz Sokorski also described the politicized considerations of a monument when, in 1950, the designs of Mexican sculptor Alfaro Siqueiros were rejected after being considered by both Jakub Berman and Bolesław Bierut. Włodzimierz Sokorski, *Wspomnienia* (Warszawa: Krajowa Agencja Wydawnicza, 1990), pp. 229–30.

15. Letter, Ministerstwo Kultury i Sztuki, Wydział Muzeów, to Sekretariat Generalny F.I.A.P.P., 8 May 1951, and letter, Ministerstwo Kultury i Sztuki to ZBoWiD, 16 June 1951, ZKRPiBWP, syg.: 17/246; *Nowa Kultura* 3, no. 6 (10 February 1952); Jadwiga Jarnuszkiewiczowa, "Z zgadnień rzeźby pomnikowej (po konkursie oświęcimskim)," *Przegląd Artystyczny* 7, no. 4 (1952): pp. 24–26.

16. *Dziennik Zachodni*, 26 January 1952; *Głos Pracy*, 26–27 January 1952; Jerzy Rawicz, "Oświęcim mobilizuje do walki," *Za Wolność i Lud*, 2 February 1952.

17. Smoleń, "Sprawozdanie z X-letniej działalności Muzeum," APMO; Ostańkowicz, "Żeby ziemia nie parowała cyklonem," p. 1.

18. Hołuj, "Sprawa wiecznej pamięci," p. 3; Smoleń, "Sprawozdanie z X-letniej działalności Muzeum," APMO.

19. "Kosztorys orientacyjny dla remontu," AAN.

20. Tadeusz Szymański, "Projekt realizacji planu budowy mauzoleum w obozie śmierci Brzezinka," AAN, zespół: Ministerstwo Kultury i Sztuki, Centralny Zarząd Muzeów, Wydział Pomników Walki z Faszyzmem, syg.: 22.

21. *Le Déporté* no. 80 (February/March 1955).

22. "Das Staatliche Museum in Auschwitz. Die Frage des Denkmals," SAPMO, Bestand VVN/KdAW, syg.: 74/4.

23. Spielmann, "Entwürfe," p. 83.

24. Smoleń, interview, 24 August 1994.

25. "Décisions du Comité International d'Auschwitz," SAPMO.

26. Letter, Hermann Langbein to KdAW, 16 November 1956, SAPMO, Bestand VVN/KdAW, syg.: 78/12.

27. The most comprehensive analysis of the competition and subsequent evaluations of the submissions is in Spielmann, "Entwürfe."

28. "Das Staatliche Museum in Auschwitz. Die Frage des Denkmals," SAPMO.

29. Quoted in Spielmann, "Entwürfe," p. 78.

30. Ibid., pp. 81, 140.

31. Ibid., p. 79.

32. "Das Staatliche Museum in Auschwitz. Die Frage des Denkmals," SAPMO.

33. Tadeusz Hołuj, "Wielki konkurs," *Przegląd Kulturalny* 20 (15 May 1958): p. 1.

34. Ibid.; *Echo Krakowska*, 26 January 1959.

35. Young, *Texture of Memory*, pp. 134–35.

36. Photographic reproductions of the proposals of these three teams are set out in ibid., pp. 136–37.

37. Quoted from Henry Moore, *The Auschwitz Competition*, in ibid. p. 135.

38. "Bericht, IAK-Generalversammlung, 25–27 June 1960," SAPMO, Bestand VVN-KdAW, syg.: 75/2; Spielmann, "Entwürfe," p. 94.

39. "Bericht, IAK-Generalversammlung, 25–27 June 1960," SAPMO; Comité International d'Auschwitz, *Informationsbulletin* no. 1 (December 1960).

40. Young, *Texture of Memory*, pp. 138–39.

41. Comité International d'Auschwitz, *Informationsbulletin* no. 1 (14) (January 1962).

42. "Historia budowy pomnika międzynarodowego w Oświęcimiu," Biblioteka Państwowego Muzeum w Oświęcimiu (herafter BPMO), teczka: "Odsłonięcie pomnika," tom VII/132; Comité International d'Auschwitz, *Informationsbulletin* no.12 (25) (December 1962).

43. Young, *Texture of Memory*, p. 139.

44. Comité International d'Auschwitz, *Informationsbulletin* no. 2 (January–March 1961). Cited here is the author's translation from the German.

45. The three governments that had earmarked funds for the monument were

those of Albania (1,000 French francs), Belgium (24,069 francs), and France (200,000 francs). The level of support from private citizens also varied drastically. For example, a total of 16 francs had come from Czechoslovakia, 18 from Norway, 37 from Venezuela, 724 from Switzerland, 2,140 from Hungary, 4,844 from the Federal Republic of Germany, 35,978 from Italy, and 177,463—the highest amount—from Poland. Two absences are worthy of note: no contributions—neither private donations nor state subsidies—had come from the German Democratic Republic, and the Polish government had refrained from providing any formal financial support, although the reasons for this are unclear. "Internationaler Fond für das Denkmal in Auschwitz," 6 June 1963, SAPMO, Bestand VVN/KdAW syg.: 75/2.

46. "Historia budowy pomnika międzynarodowego w Oświęcimiu," BPMO; Comité International d'Auschwitz, *Informationsbulletin* nos. 6–7(43–44) (June–July 1964).

47. In 1994 one new tablet and twenty new inscriptions were added. In 2002 a twenty-first tablet and inscription in Ladino were added. The new texts are discussed in the epilogue.

48. "Lettre du Professeur Robert Waitz," in *Auschwitz selon Varsovie ou chambres à gaz 'déjudaïsées,'* ed. Michel [Michał] Borwicz and Joseph Weinberg (Paris: Association Indépendente des Anciens Déportés et Internés Juifs de France, 1970), pp. 18–20. In his letter of resignation as president of the IAC, reproduced in this publication, Waitz wrote: "Likewise, the word 'Jewish' does not figure on the bronze tablets in front of the monument, although of the 4 million people, more than 3 million Jewish men, women, and children were massacred by the Nazis in Auschwitz During the months that preceeded this inaugural ceremony I had attempted in vain to alert the general secretariat to the reaction this would cause."

49. Comité International d'Auschwitz, *Informationsbulletin* nos. 3–5 (76–78) (March–May 1967).

50. Young, *Texture of Memory*, p. 141.

51. Spielmann, "Entwürfe," p. 100.

52. Young, *Texture of Memory*, p. 141.

53. "Program uroczystości odsłonięcia międzynarodowego pomnika w Oświęcimiu-Brzezince," BPMO, teczka: "Odsłonięcie pomnika" tom VII/132.

54. Bernard Marguerite, "Deux cent mille personnes ont assistés à l'inauguration du monument international élevé à la mémoire des victimes du fascisme," *Le Monde,* 18 April 1967; Henry Kamm, "Monument Unveiled for 4 Million Killed at Auschwitz Camp," *New York Times,* 17 April 1967.

55. *Der Tagesspiegel,* 18 April 1967.

56. Comité International d'Auschwitz, *Informationsbulletin* nos. 3–5 (76–78) (March–May 1967).

57. "Program uroczystości odsłonięcia," BPMO; "Informationsbulletin über die

Vorbereitung zur Enthüllung des Internationalen Denkmals in Auschwitz, nr. 1,"
January 1967, BPMO, teczka: "Odsłonięcie pomnika," tom VII/132; Państwowe
Muzeum w Oświęcimiu, "Biuletyn," April 1967, BPMO; Comité International
d'Auschwitz, *Informationsbulletin* nos. 3–5 (76–78) (March–May 1967).

58. "Program uroczystości odsłonięcia," BPMO. The most thorough description of the 16 April ceremonies, including transcripts of the day's speeches quoted
here, is found in Comité International d'Auschwitz, *Informationsbulletin* nos. 3–5
(76–78) (March–May 1967).

59. At least two observers from abroad noted that Waitz spoke in French and
that his address was not translated, thus making the content of his speech beyond the
control of the Polish authorities. The implication here is that had Polish officials
been aware of what he was going to say, they would have censored his speech. It is
doubtful, however, that such strict censorship would have been applied in this case,
because copies of the speech were distributed to the press, and excerpts from it were
subsequently published across Poland. See Georges Wellers, "Quelques impressions
du pélerinage d'Auschwitz," *Le Déporté* no. 5 (May 1967): p. 7; and Kamm.

60. Quoted in *Die Welt,* 22 April 1967.

61. *Frankfurter allgemeine Zeitung,* 18 April 1967.

62. Bernard Marguerite; Kamm; Franz von Hammerstein, "Bericht betr.:
Gedenkstätte Auschwitz," 10 May 1967, Evangelisches Zentral-Archiv Berlin (hereafter EZA), syg.: 97/94/183.

63. Kamm.

64. Marguerite; Michal Borwicz, "Auschwitz 'Judenrein,'" in Borwicz and Weinberg, pp. 1–15; Kamm.

65. *Frankfurter allgemeine Zeitung,* 18 April 1967.

66. Borwicz, "Auschwitz 'Judenrein,'" p. 1.

67. Josef Banas, *The Scapegoats: The Exodus of the Remnants of Polish Jewry*
(London: Weidenfeld and Nicolson, 1979), p. 29.

68. This phase in postwar Polish politics has been the object of considerable
scholarly attention in the past thirty years. For more general treatments of Polish-
Jewish relations that offer analyses of developments in the late 1960s, see, for example,
Borodziej, pp. 71–79; Checiński; Łukasz Hirszowicz, "The Jewish Issue in Post-War
Communist Politics," in *The Jews in Poland,* ed. Chimen Abramsky, Maciej Jachim-
czyk, and Antony Polonsky (Oxford: Basil Blackwell, 1986), pp. 199–208; Krystyna
Kersten, *Polacy. Żydzi. Komunizm. Anatomia Półprawd, 1939–68* (Warszawa: Nieza-
leżna Oficyna Wydawnicza, 1992); Steinlauf, pp. 75–88. Works specifically addressing
the events of the late 1960s include Borwicz and Weinberg; J. Atkins, "Poland in 1968.
Chronicle of Events," *Polish Review* 14, no. 1 (1969): pp. 91–117; Jerzy Eisler, *Marzec
1968: Geneza, przebieg, konsekwencje* (Warszawa: Państwowe Wydawnictwo
Naukowe, 1991); Jörg K. Hoensch, "Gegen 'Revisionismus' und 'Zionismus.' Go-

mułka, die 'Partisanen' und die Intellektuellen, 1964–1968," in *Zwischen Tauwetter und neuem Frost. Ostmitteleuropa 1956–1970,* ed. Hans Lemberg, vol. II in *Reihe historischer und landeskundlicher Ostmitteleuropastudien* (Marburg: Herder, 1993), pp. 79–92; Institute of Jewish Affairs, *The Anti-Jewish Campaign in Present-Day Poland: Facts, Documents, Press Reports* (London: Institute of Jewish Affairs, 1968); Jakub Karpiński, "The Events of March 1968 and Their Historical Background," in John S. Micgiel, Robert Scott, and Harold B. Segel, eds., *Proceedings of the Conference on Poles and Jews—Myth and Reality in the Historical Context* (New York: Columbia University Institute on East Central Europe, 1986), pp. 508–14; Dariusz Stola, *Kampania antysyjonistyczna w Polsce, 1967–1968* (Warszawa: Instytut Studiów Politycznych Polskiej Akademii Nauk, 2000); and Banas, as well as the detailed contemporary analysis of Lendvai, pp. 89–239.

69. Banas, pp. 65, 81; Hoensch, "Gegen 'Revisionismus' und 'Zionismus,'" p. 80.

70. Hirszowicz, p. 202.

71. Szczypiorski, *Polish Ordeal,* p. 77. It is also worth noting that the Six-Day War posed a peculiar problem for Polish governing circles, for there were reports of widespread jubilation among Poles after the decisive Israeli victory—this despite the fact that (or perhaps because) the Soviet Union and its allies had declared their support for the defeated Arab states and broken off diplomatic relations with Israel. The popular reaction provides an interesting example of Polish ambivalence towards Jews, illustrating how not only Poland's Jewish past, but also Israel's victorious present could serve as a political instrument. As Szczypiorski writes on page 77: "The large majority of Poles were elated by the Israeli successes in the Middle East. After all, Israeli commandants apparently spoke to one another in Polish. Therefore it was a kind of Polish military success, performed by proxy by Polish Jews. The famous saying that 'the Polish Jews have beaten the Russian Arabs' best illustrates the mood of the community at the time."

72. Hirszowicz, p. 203.

73. Ibid., p. 202.

74. Hoensch, "Gegen 'Revisionismus' und 'Zionismus,'" p. 79.

75. "Obozy koncentracyjne hitlerowskie," *Wielka encyklopedia powszechna,* vol. 8 (Warszawa: Państwowe Wydawnictwo Naukowe, 1966), pp. 87–89.

76. Krzysztof Kulicz, "Fałsz w encyklopedii," *Stolica,* 13 August 1967. See also Jacek Wilczur, "Prawda obowiązek konieczność," *Za Wolność i Lud,* 1–15 September 1967, p. 13. See also Atkins, p. 91; Lendvai, pp. 187–90.

77. A scholar of high reputation, Gumkowski was then serving as director of the Central Commission for the Investigation of German Crimes in Poland.

78. Kazimierz Rusinek, "Hitlerowskie obozy koncentracyjne," *Polityka,* 11 November 1967.

79. Borwicz, "Auschwitz 'Judenrein,'" pp. 7–8.

80. Czesław Pilichowski, "Straty i lokalizacja" and "Pomóc i współnictwo," *Trybuna Ludu*, 23 and 25 May 1968.

81. Pilichowski, "Pomóc i współnictwo."

82. This theme was echoed a month later for publication abroad in the foreign-language editions of *Polska*. See Jerzy Piórkowski, "Aus dem Notizbuch des Redakteurs," *Polen* 15, no. 6 (166) (June 1968): p. 2.

83. Levi, *The Drowned and the Saved*, pp. 36–69.

84. An internal memorandum of the East German Ministry of Foreign Affairs even went to the extent of referring to ZBoWiD as a "state within a state." Memorandum, Ministerium für Auswärtige Angelegenheiten der DDR, Abt. Benachbarte Länder, Sektion VR Polen, 16 June 1972, SAPMO, Bestand VVN/KdAW, syg.: 76/4.

85. Letter, Robert Waitz to IAC Board of Directors, 8 October 1969, SAPMO, Bestand VVN/KdAW, syg.: 74/1; Johann Hüttner, "Bericht über meine Tätigkeit in Warszawa v. 6.4.–11.4.1972," SAPMO, Bestand VVN/KdAW, syg.: 60/1; idem., "Bericht über die Sitzung der Arbeitsgruppe zur Vorbereitung der Generalversammlung und der Sitzung der Leitung des Internationalen Auschwitz Komitees vom 16.–18. Juni 1977 in Warszawa," SAPMO, Bestand VVN/KdAW, syg.: 74/1.

86. Waitz, letter of resignation as president of the International Auschwitz Committee, 6 May 1968, reprinted in "Dé-Mission," *Tribune Juive* (Strasbourg), 20 October 1968, pp. 28–9; also reprinted in Borwicz and Weinberg, pp. 18–20.

87. "Une déclaration du professeur Waitz, après sa démission de la présidence du Comité International d'Auschwitz," *Les dernières nouvelles du Haut-Rhin Colmar*, 25 September 1968.

88. Bruno Baum, "Bericht über die Leitungstagung des IAK am 11. und 12. Oktober 1969 bei Wien." SAPMO, Bestand VVN/KdAW, syg.: 74/1.

89. Letters, Felix Rausch to IAK member organizations, 30 December 1969, and Felix Rausch to IAK members and member organizations, 19 May 1970, SAPMO, Bestand VVN/KdAW, syg.: 74/1.

90. Young, *Texture of Memory*, p. 130.

91. See, for example, Iwona Irwin-Zarecka, *Neutralizing Memory: The Jew in Contemporary Poland* (New Brunswick: Transaction Publishers, 1989), pp. 153–54; Charles Hoffman, *Gray Dawn: The Jews of Eastern Europe in the Post-Communist Era* (New York: HarperCollins Publishers, 1992), p. 278; Jochen Spielmann, "Museen, Ortee, Eintrittszeiten," in *Die Unsichtbare Lager: Das Verschwinden der Vergangenheit im Gedenken*, ed. Reinhard Matz (Reinbeck bei Hamburg: Rowohlt, 1993), p. 170.

92. "Działalność Państwowego Muzeum w Oświęcimiu w r. 1975 i w latach 1971–1975," APMO, materiały—sprawozdania muzeum 1966–1968–1976, nr. inw.: 120.

93. "Referat na temat dotychczasowej działalności i założeń programowych w zakresie upamiętnienie miejsc walk i straceń," AAN, zespół: Ministerstwo Kultury i Sztuki, Centralny Zarząd Muzeów, Wydział Muzeów i Pomników Walki z

Faszyzmem, syg.: 1. Other exhibitions included those by Yugoslavia (constructed in 1963), Belgium (1965), Denmark (1968), Bulgaria (1977), and Austria (1978). Smoleń, "Wystawy narodowe," pp. 53–59.

94. Dorota Grela, "'Wystawy narodowe w muzeum oświęcimskim przejawem międzynarodowej solidarności w walce o pokój,' wygłoszony na III konferencji w Oświęcimiu, 18–20.9.1979 r.," APMO. syg.: Ref/Grela, D./445.

95. "Biuletyn nr. 9/64, Państwowe Muzeum w Oświęcimiu," MKiSz, syg.: 667/39, 18/64.

96. Letter, Kazimierz Rusinek, ZBoWiD, to Zarząd Główny Międzynarodowy Komitet Oświęcimski, 12 February 1964, APMO, syg.: S./73a.

97. Ibid.

98. "Notatka służbowa w sprawie projektu scenariusza wystawy w bloku 27 & tezy robocze które będą składały się na treść wystawy p.t. "Walka i zagłada Żydów," APMO, syg.: S./73a/; "Zarys scenariusz bloku żydowskiego," APMO, syg.: S./73a/. According to a letter from Andrzej Szczypiorski to the author, dated 29 December 1999, Sczczypiorski's involvement in the project was minimal and brief.

99. "Scenariusz bloku nr. 27" in "Scenariusz i materiały dotyczące ekspozycji bloku 27 martyrologii Żydów w okresie hitlerowskim, plany itp.," APMO, syg.: S./zbiorowy/53.

100. Unless otherwise noted, any further description and analysis of the exhibit is based on photographs from the Archive of the State Museum at Auschwitz (Dział X/3, "Blok nr. 27, 'Historia martyrologii Żydów'—stara ekspozycja"), and the main planning document for the exhibition: "Scenariusz bloku nr. 27," APMO

101. See Pilichowski, "Straty i lokalizacja" and "Pomóc i współnictwo," as well as Walichnowski, "Die Rolle der zionistischen Bewegung in der antikommunistischen Kampagne und der Rehabilitation der Bundesrepublik," *Polen* 15, no. 6 (166) (June 1968): pp. 17–22, 39–44.

102. Theodore R. Weeks has described a "vision of Jews and Poles shoulder to shoulder defending their shared homeland against the Russian invader" in the early 1860s as a "myth of 1863." Obviously, the exhibition in Block 27 was not evoking anti-Russian sentiment, but rather the notion of common resistance against, in this case, the Germans. See Theodore R. Weeks, "Poles, Jews, and Russians, 1863–1914: The Death of the Ideal of Assimilation in the Kingdom of Poland," *Polin* 12 (1999): p. 243.

103. Tadeusz Hołuj, "Uwagi ogólne do scenariusza bl. 27," APMO, syg.: Scen/Zbior/53.

104. Quoted in Charles Hoffman, *Gray Dawn*, p. 284. Szczypiorski's observation is also quoted in Susanne Benzler, "Die vollendete Sinnlosigkeit. Noch einmal: Auschwitz," *Vorgänge* 30, no. 113 (October 1991), p. 57.

105. Letter, Andrzej Szczypiorski to the author, 29 December 1999; Emeryka Iwaszko, interview with the author, Oświęcim, Poland, 17 November 1994.

106. The French newspaper *Tribune Juive,* for example, wrote of the exhibition "tendentiously and indifferently falsifying the history of the massacre of more than three million Jews brought from all of Europe." *Tribune Juive* (Strasbourg), 10 May 1968. The exhibition and its opening ceremonies were also referred to by Professor Robert Waitz in his letter of resignation from the presidency of the IAC, dated 6 May 1968. In Waitz's words: "Formal guarantees as to the objectivity of this exhibition had been provided. Thousands of documents have been furnished by the Centre de Documentation Juive de Paris and by Yad Vashem in Israel. The plan of the exhibition was supposed to be sent to those two institutions prior to the end of 1967. Nothing has been done. My letters have received no response, as well as those concerning the important questions that I have raised over the years. The opening of the Jewish block at the Auschwitz Museum took place on 21.IV.68. The members of the Executive Committee of the IAC had been informed of this opening only by a letter from the Warsaw General Secretariat dated 10 April. Under these conditions, no Jewish delegation could go to Auschwitz and be present at the opening of the Jewish block. This indicates that the opening of the Jewish block was the product of haste." *Tribune Juive* (Strasbourg), 20 October 1968. For accounts of the opening ceremonies and Motyka's speech, see also Jonathan Randal, "Pavilion Honors Auschwitz Dead," *New York Times,* 22 April 1968, and *Jerusalem Post,* 23 April 1968.

107. *Tribune Juive* (Strasbourg), 10 May 1968.

108. APMO, Fotografia, Dział XI, nos. 14015–14023.

109. Randal, p. 3.

110. *Jerusalem Post,* 23 April 1968.

111. "Blok poświęcony martyrologii Żydów w Oświęcimiu. Przemówienie min. L. Motyka," *Trybuna Ludu,* 23 April 1968.

Chapter 6

1. Steinlauf, p. 89.

2. Keith John Lepak, *Prelude to Solidarity: Poland and the Politics of the Gierek Regime* (New York: Columbia University Press, 1988), pp. 50, 55–59.

3. Jerzy Lukowski and Hubert Zawadzki, *A Concise History of Poland* (Cambridge: Cambridge University Press, 2001), p. 268.

4. Józefa Hennelowa, "Problem Oświęcimia," *Tygodnik Powszechny,* 8 March 1970.

5. On the activities of these two organzations at Auschwitz, see Jonathan Huener, "Antifascist Pilgrimage and Rehabilitation at Auschwitz: The Political Tourism of *Aktion Sühnezeichen* and *Sozialistische Jugend,*" *German Studies Review* 24, no. 3 (October 2001): pp. 513–32; Michael Schmidt, *Die Falken in Berlin, Antifaschis-*

mus und Völkerverständigung: Jugendbegegnung durch Gedenkstättenfahrten,
1954–1959 (Berlin: Elefanten Press, 1987); Susanne Orth, ed., *"Wie soll ich singen . . ."*:
10 Jahre Internationale Jugendbegegnungsstätte Auschwitz (Berlin: Aktion Sühnezeichen Friedensdienste, 1996); Rudolf Dohrmann, "Schritte der Versöhnung," *Zei-*
chen 12, no. 4 (December 1984): pp. 4–5; Jerzy Piórkowski, "Hoffnung," *Polen* 15, no.
161 (January 1968): pp. 14–18. Established in 1959, Aktion Sühnezeichen was divided
into two separate organizations after the construction of the Berlin Wall. The East
German organization initiated its travel seminars to Auschwitz in 1965; the West Berlin/
West German branch, in 1967. It was the Western organization, however, that remained the main force behind the initiative in the decades to follow.

6. Analysis of the Museum's "Memorial Book," or guest register, for the years
1966–72 suggests a marked increase in the number of West German groups beginning
in 1969. Księga Pamiątkowa, 1966–1972, APMO, syg.: Mat/1140.

7. Erich Kuby, "Zoppot, Weltbad ohne Welt," *Stern* 23, no. 35 (1970): pp. 42–49.

8. Comité International d'Auschwitz, *Informationsbulletin* no. 10 (119) (October 1970).

9. See, for example, Bernhard Heimrich, "Block 13 in Auschwitz blieb geschlossen," *Frankfurter allgemeine Zeitung,* 19 December 1972, which criticizes the presence
of an East German exhibition in the absence of a West German exhibition, and *New
York Times,* 3 November 1974, which echoes many of the criticisms voiced by Kuby,
describes the tastelessness of souvenir stands, and notes the lack of visitors to
Birkenau.

10. Ministerstwo Kultury i Sztuki, Wydział Muzeów, syg.: 84–4a, 37A.

11. Comité International d'Auschwitz, *Informationsbulletin* nos. 6–7 (103–104)
(June–July 1969).

12. Comité International d'Auschwitz, *Informationsbulletin* no. 12 (121) (December 1970).

13. Księga Pamiątkowa, 1966–1972, APMO, syg.: Mat/1140; Comité International
d'Auschwitz, *Informationsbulletin* no. 3 (124) (March 1971).

14. Księga Pamiątkowa, 1966–1972, APMO, syg.: Mat/1140.

15. *Frankfurter allgemeine Zeitung,* 19 December 1972.

16. Comité International d'Auschwitz, *Informationsbulletin* no. 8 (173) (August
1975).

17. *New York Times,* 30 July 1975.

18. Teresa Świebocka, "Historia i współczesność dyskusji wokół strefy ochronnej byłego obozu," *Pro Memoria* 9 (June 1998): p. 116.

19. "Raport w sprawie Muzeum w Oświęcimiu." APMO, syg.: /Opr./189.

20. Letter, Tadeusz Hołuj to Kierownik Wydziału Propagandy, Komitet
Wojewódzki PZPR w Krakowie, 20 April 1974. APMO, syg.: Opr./189/.

21. Ibid.

22. In recent years the name of the museum has been changed, the "hotel" in the former Aufnahmegebäude has been removed, and most of the national exhibitions have been closed (e.g., those of the German Democratic Republic and Czechoslovakia) or remodeled. On the other hand, members of the museum staff still occupy apartments on the grounds of Auschwitz I, approximately 80 percent of the 1955 exhibition is still in use, and controversy over the presence of economic enterprises near the borders of the former camps continues unabated. For an overview of the issue of borders and the presence of a "protective zone" around the camp, see Świebocka, "Historia i współczesność," pp. 115–119.

23. "Raport w sprawie Muzeum w Oświęcimiu." APMO.

24. Smoleń, "Działalność upowszechnieniowa," p. 18.

25. Letter, Cegłowska, Piper, Strzelecka, Strzelecki, and Świebocka to Provincial Committee of the PZPR, Kraków. APMO, syg.: Opr./189.

26. Ibid.

27. Świebocka, "Historia i współczesność," p. 116.

28. Daniel Luliński, "Fałszowanie prawdy o Oświęcimiu w telewizji RFN," *Trybuna Ludu*, 28 January 1975.

29. *New York Times*, 3 November 1974.

30. Ministerstwo Kultury i Sztuki, Wydział Muzeów, 69A/teczka "Martyrologia i walka Żydów wystawa w Muzeum w Oświęcimiu i zarządzania, 1974–1978."

31. Smoleń, "Wystawy narodowe," p. 57.

32. Letter, Andrzej Szczypiorski to the author, 29 December 1999.

33. "Działalność Państwowego Muzeum w Oświęcimiu w r. 1975 i w latach 1971–1975," APMO.

34. "Działalność Muzeum w Oświęcimiu w 1973 r. i zamierzenia w 1974 r.," Ministerstwo Kultury i Sztuki, Wydział Muzeów, 38A, "Państwowe Muzeum w Oświęcimiu 1973–1975."

35. "Sprawozdanie z wykonanych prac związanych ze zmianą wystawy 'Martyrologia i walka Żydów,' Ministerstwo Kultury i Sztuki, Wydział Muzeów, 84–4a, 37A, "Muzeum w Oświęcimiu 1970–1977."

36. Dorota Grela, "Wystawy narodowe w muzeum oświęcimskim," APMO.

37. Alexander Zvielli, "Jewish Pavilion Re-opens on Site of Auschwitz," *Jerusalem Post*, 18 April 1978; *Gazeta Południowa*, 18 April 1978.

38. *Dziennik Polski*, 18 April 1978.

39. Ibid.

40. *Życie Warszawy*, 18 April 1978.

41. On this notion, see Porter, pp. 37–42, 160–63, 172; Stanislaus A. Blejwas, *Realism in Polish Politics: Warsaw Positivism and National Survival in Nineteenth-Century Poland* (New Haven: Yale Concilium on International and Area Studies, 1984), pp. 99–100; Weeks, pp. 242–56.

42. *Gazeta Południowa,* 18 April 1978.

43. Zvielli, "Jewish Pavilion Re-opens."

44. Ibid.

45. *Życie Warszawy,* 18 April 1978; *Trybuna Ludu,* 18 April 1978; *Przekrój,* 7 May 1978.

46. Alexander Zvielli, "Poland Seen Warming to Israel," *Jerusalem Post,* 20 April 1978, p. 3.

47. Editorial, "Poland Makes a Gesture," *Jerusalem Post,* 18 April 1978.

48. This was the focus of a debate in Poland in the late 1980s sparked by Jan Błoński's 1987 article "The Poor Poles Look at the Ghetto," *Tygodnik Powszechny,* 11 January 1987. Aspects of the debate, which is discussed in the epilogue, are chronicled, documented, and analyzed by some of its participants in Antony Polonsky, ed., *'My Brother's Keeper?': Recent Polish Debates on the Holocaust* (London: Routledge, 1990).

49. This much more recent debate has centered around revelations concerning the 1941 massacre, by Poles, of the Jews of Jedwabne, a village northeast of Warsaw. The historian Jan T. Gross was responsible for unearthing this history, which has had a tremendous echo and has been the cause of acrimonious debate over the past three years. See Gross, *Neighbors,* as well as the collection of Polish responses to and criticisms of Gross's claims in William Brand, ed., *Thou Shalt Not Kill: Poles on Jedwabne* (Warsaw: Towarszystwo "Więź," 2001).

50. Editorial, "Poland Makes a Gesture," *Jerusalem Post,* 18 April 1978. In an article published only two days later, the Israeli journalist Alexander Zvielli cited "an urgent need for Jewish support in the U.S. for the passage of a bill in Congress according Poland most-favoured-nation status" as a further motivation for Poland's apparent opening to Israel and Jewish communities around the world. Zvielli, "Poland Seen Warming to Israel."

51. In 1993, for example, Block 27 saw nearly 66,000 visitors, or approximately one-seventh of all visitors to the memorial site in that year. Although that ratio may not appear high, it is important to bear in mind that the previous exhibition in Block 27 saw only approximately 80,000 visitors over the entirety of its existence, that is, from April 1968 until early 1977. "Państwowe Muzeum w Oświęcimiu, sprawozdanie z działalności w 1993 r.," BPMO; Smoleń, "Wystawy narodowe," p. 57.

52. James Feron, "150,000 at Auschwitz Pay Homage to Polish Martyr," *New York Times,* 16 November 1972.

53. This is the number of participants as estimated by the internal bulletin of the State Museum at Auschwitz (SkAPMO, Biuletyn Państwowego Muzeum w Oświęcimiu No. 10, 7 November 1972), and is a much more conservative figure than the estimate of 150,000 offered by Feron.

54. Ronald Modras, *The Catholic Church and Antisemitism: Poland, 1933–1939* (Amsterdam: Harwood Academic Publishers, 2000), p. 41.

55. Ibid., pp. 41–42.

56. Ibid., pp. 398–99.

57. Paul Johnson, *John Paul II and the Catholic Restoration* (New York: St. Martin's Press, 1981), p. 131.

58. Czech, *Kalendarz,* pp. 64, 76, 79. Franciszek Gajowniczek, a devout Catholic, survived both Auschwitz and Sachsenhausen. After returning to Poland after the war, he became a lay missionary of sorts for the ideals exemplified by Maksymilian Kolbe. Gajowniczek was present at the beatification of Kolbe in Rome, at the ceremonies at Auschwitz in October 1972, and again during Pope John Paul II's visit to Auschwitz in June 1979. On Gajowniczek's biography see Diana Dewar, *Saint of Auschwitz: The Story of Maximilian Kolbe* (San Francisco: Harper and Row, 1982), pp. 116–22.

59. "Program uroczystości w dniu 15.X.1972 r. oraz plan organizacyjnego zabezpieczenia uroczystości na terenie b. obozu zagłady w Brzezince w dniu 15.X.1972 r.," SkAPMO, teczka: Personalne-administracjne,1969–72.

60. *Życie Warszawy,* 17 October 1972; *New York Times,* 8 September 1972.

61. Feron.

62. Prezydium Wojewódzkiej Rady Narodowej w Krakowie, Urząd Spraw Wewnętrznych, decyzja, Kraków, dnia 9.XI.1972 r., SkAPMO, teczka: Personalne-administracjne, 1969–72.

63. Sergio I. Minerbi, "The Kidnapping of the Holocaust," *Jerusalem Post,* 25 August 1989.

64. Edward Gierek, *Edward Gierek: Przerwana dekada* (Warszawa: Wydawnictwo Fakt, 1990), p. 135.

65. Neal Acherson, *The Polish August: The Self-Limiting Revolution* (New York: Viking Press, 1982), p. 122.

66. Jan Józef Lipski, *KOR: A History of the Workers' Defense Committee in Poland, 1976–1981* (Berkeley: University of California Press, 1985), p. 332.

67. Suzanne Hruby, "The Church in Poland and Its Political Influence," *Journal of International Affairs* 36, no. 2 (fall/winter 1982/1983): p. 317.

68. Ibid., p. 318.

69. In fact, among the churches of Eastern Europe, Polish Catholicism had remained profoundly suspicious of the Ostpolitik initiated under John XXIII and Paul VI, fearing that the Vatican was yielding far too much to the atheistic regimes of the Soviet client states. See Dennis Dunn, "The Vatican's Ostpolitik: Past and Present," *Journal of International Affairs* 36, no. 2 (fall/winter 1982/1983): pp. 253–54.

70. Tadeusz Cieplak, "John Paul II and Eastern Europe," *Nationalities Papers* 8, no. 2 (1980): p. 235.

71. Steinlauf, p. 91. On the reformist and oppositional role of the Catholic Church in these years see also Szczypiorski, *Polish Ordeal,* pp. 107–8.

72. Pope John Paul II, *The Redeemer of Man—Redemptor Hominis* (Boston: Daughters of St. Paul, n.d.), p. 23.

73. George Huntston Williams, *The Mind of John Paul II: Origins of His Thought and Action* (New York: The Seabury Press, 1981), p. 307.

74. Johnson, p. 73; Gierek, p. 136.

75. Mieczysław Rakowski, "Interes nadrzędny," *Polityka* 33, no. 10 (10 March 1979): p. 1.

76. Lepak, p. 188.

77. Andrzej Szczypiorski, "The Limits of Political Realism," *Survey* 24, no. 4 (109) (autumn 1979): pp. 28–29.

78. Nowak, p. 13.

79. Lipski, p. 331.

80. Quoted in Tad Szulc, *Pope John Paul II: The Biography* (New York: Scribner, 1995), p. 308.

81. Davies, *Heart of Europe*, p. 17.

82. Gierek, p. 136

83. Acherson, *The Polish August*, p. 277. Of the same phenomenon Timothy Garton Ash has written: "For nine days the state virtually ceased to exist, except as a censor doctoring the television coverage. Everyone saw that Poland is not a communist country—just a communist state." Ash, *The Polish Revolution: Solidarity* (New York: Charles Scribner's Sons, 1983), p. 29.

84. Alex Alexiev, "The Kremlin and the Vatican," *Orbis* 27, no. 3 (fall 1983): p. 556.

85. Szczypiorski, *Polish Ordeal*, p. 112.

86. Adam Michnik, *Letters from Prison and Other Essays* (Berkeley: University of California Press, 1985), p. 160.

87. Adam Michnik, "Demonstration der Sehnsucht nach Freiheit," *Der Spiegel* 33, no. 23 (4 June 1979): p. 117; Nowak, pp. 12–13; Szczypiorski, "The Limits of Political Realism," p. 30.

88. Dominique Le Corre and Mark Sobotka, eds., *John Paul II in Poland—Jan Paweł II na Polskiej Ziemi* (Bagnolet: Le Corre, 1979), p. 18.

89. This list relies in part on Dieter Bingen, "The Catholic Church as a Political Actor" in *Polish Politics: Edge of the Abyss*, ed. Jack Bielasiak and Maurice D. Simon (New York: Praeger, 1984), p. 216.

90. Radio Free Europe, Research and Analysis Department, *The Pope in Poland* (Munich: Radio Free Europe Research, 1979), p. 44.

91. *Tygodnik Powszechny*, 10 June 1979.

92. *Trybuna Ludu*, 4 June 1979; *Życie Warszawy*, 4 June 1979; Radio Free Europe, pp. 70–71.

93. The Black Madonna refers to the monastery's icon of the Virgin Mary—

according to legend, painted by Saint Luke. It is the most important locus of Marian devotion and pilgrimage in Poland.

94. John Vinocur, "Pope Prays at Auschwitz: 'Only Peace!,'" *New York Times,* 8 June 1979.

95. *Tygodnik Powszechny,* 17 June 1979.

96. *Słowo Powszechne,* 8 June 1979; Kazimierz Kąkol, *Spowiedź pogromcy kościoła* (Olsztyn: Ethos, 1994), p. 174.

97. *Słowo Powszechne,* 8 June 1979.

98. Comité International d'Auschwitz, *Biuletyn Informacyjny* nos. 7–8 (220–221) (July–August 1979).

99. Marek Skwarnicki, n.t., *Tygodnik Powszechny,* 17 June 1979.

100. *Słowo Powszechne,* 8 June 1979; Vinocur.

101. The entire liturgy of the Birkenau mass is reproduced in Jan Paweł II, papież, *Pielgrzymka do ojczyzny: przemówienia i homilie Ojca Świętego Jana Pawła II* (Warszawa: Instytut Wydawniczy Pax, 1979), pp. 286–89.

102. Verse 16, from the *Revised Standard Version.*

103. Verses 10–11, 17–18 RSV.

104. Verses 12–13 RSV.

105. Although the homily was reproduced in part in newspapers across the country, I rely principally on the version reproduced in *Znak* 31, nos. 301–302 (7–8) (July–August 1979): pp. 767–71. Incomplete English translations, on which I have relied in part, are found in John Paul II, pope, *Return to Poland: The Collected Speeches of John Paul II* (London: Collins, 1979), pp. 124–29; and Radio Free Europe, pp. 66–79.

106. Chapter 5, verse 4 RSV.

107. Skwarnicki.

108. Czech, *Kalendarz,* p. 221.

109. Records from the State Museum at Auschwitz do not give an estimate of the number of participants in the papal mass. The conservative estimate of 300,000 is from *Der Spiegel* 33, no. 24 (11 June 1979): p. 113. Skwarnicki, in *Tygodnik Powszechny,* 17 June 1979, simply described the "hundreds of thousands of people," while in a contemporary journalistic account, Neal Acherson referred to "a million men, women, and children" at the papal mass. See Neal Acherson, "The Pope's New Europe," *Spectator* 242, no. 7875 (16 June 1979): p. 7.

110. Robert S. Wistrich, "John Paul II on Jews and Judaism," *Partisan Review* 67, no. 1 (Winter 2000): p. 107.

111. See Darcy O'Brien, *The Hidden Pope. The Untold Story of a Lifelong Friendship That is Changing the Relationship between Catholics and Jews: The Personal Journey of John Paul II and Jerzy Kluger* (New York: Daybreak Books, 1998), pp. 279–80; Williams, p. 328.

112. See, for example, Minerbi, who even speculated "that there is a kind of collu-

sion between the Catholic Church and the Communist government in Warsaw, whose common objective is ignoring the unique tragedy of the Holocaust for the Jews."

113. In the words of Michael Steinlauf, "John Paul also visited Auschwitz. His words at a mass, widely reprinted and hailed in Poland as marking a new stage in the Church's relationship to the memory of the Holocaust, offered a foretaste of the reconciliations but also of the new conflicts that the new era would inspire." Steinlauf, p. 95.

114. Wistrich, "John Paul II on Jews and Judaism," p. 100; James Carroll, "The Silence," *New Yorker* 73, no. 7 (7 April 1997): p. 67.

115. Carl Bernstein and Marco Politi, *His Holiness: John Paul II and the Hidden History of Our Time* (New York: Doubleday, 1996), p. 221.

116. Acherson, "The Pope's New Europe," p. 8.

117. Karpiński, p. 214.

118. Quoted in Nowak, p. 13.

119. *Tygodnik Powszechny,*10 June 1979.

120. Skwarnicki.

Epilogue

1. Relevant in this context is Eric Santner's discussion of "working through" the past by means of what Freud described as *Trauerarbeit,* or the "work of mourning" and, by contrast, the "narrative fetishism . . . consciously or unconsciously designed to expunge the traces of the trauma or loss that called that narrative into being in the first place." See Santner, "History Beyond the Pleasure Principle: Some Thoughts on the Representation of Trauma," in Friedländer, pp. 143–54.

2. Martin Jay, "Of Plots, Witnesses, and Judgments," in Friedländer, p. 107.

3. Santner, pp. 143–54.

4. Geoffrey Hartman, "Public Memory and its Discontents," p. 104.

5. Saul Friedländer has made note of this problem as it relates to writing the history of the "Final Solution," stating that "the nature of the events that we are dealing with may lead to various approaches in terms of representation, and the outright negation of most of them would not do justice to the *contradictory demands* raised by the evocation of this past." Friedländer, introduction, p. 6.

6. Comité International d'Auschwitz, *Bulletin d'Information* no. 9 (222) (September 1979).

7. "Auschwitz Concentration Camp," World Heritage List nomination dossier no. 31, submitted by the government of the People's Republic of Poland, inscribed on the World Heritage List by the World Heritage Committee at its third session, Luxor, Egypt (22–26 October 1979), collection of the UNESCO World Heritage Centre, Paris, France.

8. World Heritage Committee, report of the third session of the committee (Luxor, Egypt, 22–26 October 1979), UNESCO Doc. CC-79/CONF.003/13.

9. Ibid.

10. In discussing changing Western attitudes to the memorial site, Steinlauf has noted, "So long as Poland, in western eyes, continued to exist in a never-never land behind the Iron Curtain, there was little inclination to connect the word Auschwitz with the place called Oświęcim. In the 1980s, this isolation began to be broken." Steinlauf, p. 118.

11. *Zeichen* 9, no. 1 (January 1983): p. 6.

12. Christoph Heubner, "Eine Vision wurde Realität," *Zeichen* 14, no. 3 (fall 1986): pp. 4–5. Funds for the center's construction came primarily from private West German donations, although the West German federal and state governments also participated in the financing.

13. "Frekwencja zwiedzających w 2000 r.," Państwowe Muzeum Auschwitz-Birkenau w Oświęcimiu, 8 August 2001.

14. On the role of the Holocaust in Israeli state-building and political identity as well as growing significance of the Holocaust in the 1980s in Israeli culture, see Tom Segev, *The Seventh Million: The Israelis and the Holocaust,* trans. Haim Watzman (New York: Hill and Wang, 1993), especially chapters 22–28, pp. 396–507, and Young, *Texture of Memory,* pp. 209–81.

15. Webber, p. 9. Describing the growth in the symbolic value of Auschwitz for Jews, Webber has written: "For two generations after the war, Auschwitz was largely the subject of a *self*-imposed silence. Jewish religious leaders, for example, largely shied away from the memory of the Holocaust. . . . Today the position has been totally reversed. . . . The slogans, stereotypes, and generalizations Jews conventionally use to comprehend the Holocaust—or, as I should prefer to say, to mythologize the Holocaust—these slogans converge today on the duty to remember." Ibid., p. 20.

16. Steinlauf, p. 117.

17. Ibid.

18. Letter to the editor, *Polityka,* 12 December 1980, quoted in Steinlauf, p. 101.

19. *Rzeczpospolita,* 2 May 1985, quoted in Steinlauf, p. 111.

20. Błoński, in Polonsky, *'My Brother's Keeper?'* p. 44. This is a translation and reprint of Błoński's *Tygodnik Powszechny* article of 11 January 1987.

21. Ibid., p. 46.

22. Jerzy Turowicz, "Polish Reasons and Jewish Reasons," *Yad Vashem Studies* 19 (1988): 379–88.

23. Władysław Siła-Nowicki, "A Reply to Jan Błoński," in Polonsky, *'My Brother's Keeper?'* pp. 59–68. This is a translation and reprint of Siła-Nowicki's *Tygodnik Powszechny* article of 22 February 1987.

24. Ibid., p. 62.

25. Young, *Texture of Memory,* p. 144.

26. For a concise chronology of the events surrounding the controversy, as well as the thoughtful analyses of many authors on the subject, see Carol Rittner and John K. Roth, eds., *Memory Offended: The Auschwitz Convent Controversy* (New York: Praeger, 1991). The most thorough and balanced treatment of the issue by a single author is Władysław T. Bartoszewski's *Convent at Auschwitz.*

27. Quoted in Young, *Texture of Memory,* p. 146. According to Young, the "Vicar of Christ" refers here to Pope Pius XII, head of the Roman Catholic Church during the Second World War.

28. Monty Noam Penkower, "Auschwitz, the Papacy, and Poland's 'Jewish Problem,'" *Midstream* 36, no. 6 (August/September 1990): p.14.

29. Quoted in Rittner and Roth, p. 22.

30. Accounts of the incident vary considerably. I rely here on Bartoszewski, *Convent,* pp. 86–87, in which the author bases his account on the report in the Solidarity daily *Gazeta Wyborcza.*

31. Steinlauf, p. 120.

32. Quoted in Steinlauf, p. 120.

33. Quoted in Rittner and Roth, p. 224.

34. Quoted in ibid., p. 24.

35. In the early 1950s there was a barracks in Auschwitz I used as a chapel. Likewise, a local administrative document from November 1972 (Prezydium Wojewódzkiej Rady Narodowej w Krakowie, Urząd Spraw Wewnętrznych. Decyzja. Kraków, dnia 9.XI.1972 r. SkAPMO, teczka: Personalne-administracjne 1969–72.) refers to a "chapel" at the memorial site.

36. To the best of this writer's knowledge, the first public protest against the presence of the church was in August of 1994, when Rabbi Avraham Weiss returned to the memorial site with a group of American demonstrators.

37. Emanuel Tanay, "Auschwitz and Oświęcim: One Location, Two Memories," in Rittner and Roth, p. 101.

38. Ronald Modras, "Jews and Poles: Remembering at a Cemetery," in Rittner and Roth, p. 54.

39. Young, *Texture of* Memory, pp. 151–52. On the work of the council see also Teresa Świebocka, "The Auschwitz-Birkenau Memorial and Museum: From Commemoration to Education," *Polin* 13 (2000): p. 295. In January 2000 Prime Minister Jerzy Bużek announced the formation of a new advisory body, the International Auschwitz Council, to carry on the work of its predecessor.

40. Young, *Texture of Memory,* p. 150.

41. The tablets' inscriptions are in the various languages of the prisoners. New languages on the 1994 tablets included Belorussian, Croatian, Dutch, Serbian, Slovakian, and Ukrainian. The original texts in Bulgarian, Danish, Spanish, Flemish, and Serbo-Croatian were not replaced. A tablet and inscription in Ladino were added in 2002.

Jarosław Mensfelt, Robert Placzek, Państwowe Muzeum Auschwitz-Birkenau w Oświęcimiu, Dział Wystawiennicy, correspondence with the author, 10 April 2003.

42. Świebocka, "The Auschwitz-Birkenau Memorial and Museum," pp. 295–96.

43. Krystyna Oleksy, "Historical Truth Comes First," *Pro Memoria* 7 (July 1997), p. 8.

44. "Frekwencja zwiedzających w 2000 r."

45. See Gross, *Sąsiedzi* and *Neighbors,* as well as Brand.

46. Job 16: 6 RSV.

Bibliography

A Note on Sources

Some of the archival collections listed below may have been reorganized since re-search for this study was completed. The Składnice Akt Państwowego Muzeum w Oświęcimiu, or Administrative Archives of the State Museum at Auschwitz, was, for example, under reorganization during the course of my research there. All citations in this bibliography and in the notes are based on the file names and call numbers at the time of my research. I have provided full bibliographic information below for newspaper and magazine articles only in cases where authors' names were provided.

Archival Collections of Unpublished Documents

Berlin

Evangelisches Zentral-Archiv Berlin (EZA)

Stiftung Archiv der Parteien und Massenorganizationen der ehemaligen Deutschen Demokratischen Republik im Bundesarchiv Berlin (SAPMO)

> Bestand VVN
> Bestand VVN/KdAW
> Bestand Seketariat des ZK
> Bestand Sozialistische Einheitspartei Deutschlands, Zentralkomitee, Beschlüsse
>> Politbüro

Oświęcim

Archiwum Państwowego Muzeum Auschwitz-Birkenau w Oświęcimiu (APMO)

> Fotografia, Dział IX/1, wystawa stała z 1955 r.
> Fotografia, Dział IX/2, wystawa przed 1955 r.
> Fotografia, Dział IX/4, wystawa czasowa z okazji 50-ciolecia powstania PMO
> Fotografia, Dział XI, uroczystości
> Fotografia, stara ekspozycja z przed 1955
> Księgi Pamiątkowe
> Materiały

Materiały-sprawozdania muzeum 1966–1968–1976
Opracowania
Oświadczenia
Polski Związek byłych Więźniów Politycznych
Referaty
Scenariusze
Wspomnicnia

Biblioteka Państwowego Muzeum Auschwitz-Birkenau w Oświęcimiu (BPMO)

Składnice Akt Państwowego Muzeum Auschwitz-Birkenau w Oświęcimiu (SkAPMO)

852/Popularyzacja miejsc pamięci od 1947
853/Projekty zmian ekspozycji w blokach wystawowych. Protokoły 1950–1952
D-1/Plan pracy, sprawodawczość, statystyka wg. działów
Dział III, podkładki do sprawozdań rocznych
Korespondacje 1970–73, Dz. III.
Projekty ekspozycji w blokach wystawowych 1947–1949
Protokóły z narad. Protokóły z obowiązań. Rok: 1946, 1949, 1954, 1957, 1964, 1965, 1966. Administracja
Sprawozdania 1961 r. Dz. III

Warsaw

Archiwum Akt Nowych (AAN)

Biuro Polityczne KC PPR: protokóły posiedzeń, protokóły komisji gospo-
darczej, wiejskiej, komunikacyjnej, administracyjno-samorządowej,
teoretyczno-propagandowej i kulturalno-oświatowej istniejących przy BP
Ministerstwo Kultury i Sztuki. Centralny Zarząd Muzeów. Wydiał Muzeów i
Pomników Walki z Faszyzmem
Ministerstwo Kultury i Sztuki. Dopływ wewn. z PKPG
PPR, Komitet Centralny, Sekretariat. Partie i organizacje działające wśród
ludności żydowskiej
Polska Partia Robotnicza. Komitet Centralny 1944–1948
Związek Bojowników z Faszyzmem i Najazdem Hitlerowskim o
Niepodległość i Demokrację (1939–1944), 1945–1949, 1950–1951
237/PZPR. Komitet Centralny
415/Polski Związek byłych Więźniów Politycznych, Zarząd Główny, Zarządy
Wojewódzkie, Koła /1940/1946–49/–1952
416/Związek Bojowników z Faszyzmem i Najazdem Hitlerowskim o
Niepodległość i Demokrację

425/Główna i Okręgowe Komisje Księży przy ZBoWiD 1950–1955

Ministerstwo Kultury i Sztuki (MKiSz)

Wydział Muzeów

Ministerstwo Sprawiedliwości, Archiwum Głównej Komisji Badania Zbrodni Przeciwko Narodowi Polskiemu:

Zespół Nr. 126. Konzentrationslager Auschwitz /Obóz Koncentracyjny w Oświęcimiu/ 1940–1945
Zespół Nr. 185. Ministerstwo Kultury i Sztuki. Wydział Muzeów i Pomników Martyrologii Polskiej. 1945–1951, 1958, 1960–1962
Zespół Nr. 190. Archiwum Jana Sehna. 1938–1944, 1945–1965

Związek Kombatantów Rzeczypospolitej Polski i Byłych Więźniów Politycznych (ZKRPiBWP)

Newspapers and Magazines

Dziennik Ludowy
Dziennik Polski
Dziennik Zachodni
Echo Chełmna
Echo Krakowska
Economist
Express Wieczorny
Frankfurter allgemeine Zeitung
Gazeta Ludowa
Gazeta Południowa
Gazeta Robotnicza
Głos Pracy
Głos Wielkopolski
Ilustrowany Kurier Polski
Informationsbulletin/ Biuletyn Informacyjny/ Bulletin d'Information (Comité International d'Auschwitz)
Jerusalem Post
Kurier Codzienny
Kurier Szczeciński
Kuźnica
Le Monde
Mosty

Naprzód
Naprzód Dolnośląski
Neue Zürcher Zeitung
New York Times
New Yorker
Nowa Kultura
Nowe Drogi
Nowe Sygnały
Opinia
Polityka
Polska Ludowa
Rzeczpospolita
Spectator
Der Spiegel
Stern
Stolica
Survey
Świat
Der Tagesspiegel
Times (London)
Tribune Juive
Trybuna Ludu
Trybuna Robotnicza
Trybuna Wolności
Tygodnik Powszechny
Die Welt
Wolni Ludzie
Za Wolność i Lud
Zeichen
Die Zeit
Znak
Życie Literackie
Życie Warszawy

Oral Interviews

Cienciała, Stanisław (former Auschwitz prisoner, former associate of the State Museum at Auschwitz). Interview by author. Audio recording. Oświęcim, Poland, April 1994.

Iwaszko, Emeryka (director of pedagogy, State Museum at Auschwitz). Interview by author. Audio recording. Oświęcim, Poland, 17 November 1994.

Motyka, Lucjan (former Auschwitz prisoner, former Minister of Culture and Art). Interview by author. Audio recording. Warsaw, Poland, 1 December 1994.

Smoleń, Kazimierz (former Auschwitz prisoner, former member of the Historical Commission at the State Museum at Auschwitz, director of the State Museum at Auschwitz, 1955–1990). Interview by author. Audio recording. 8 December 1993; 11 April 1994; 24 August 1994.

Szymański, Tadeusz (former Auschwitz prisoner, former employee of the State Museum at Auschwitz). Interview by author. Audio recording. Oświęcim, Poland, 24 August 1993.

Zbrzeski, Jerzy (former employee of the State Museum at Auschwitz). Interview by author. Audio recording. Oświęcim, Poland, April 1994; 25 August 1994.

Articles, Books, and Published Documents

Abramsky, Chimen, Maciej Jachimczyk, and Antony Polonsky, eds. *The Jews in Poland.* Oxford: Basil Blackwell, 1986.

Acherson, Neal. "The Holy Circus Rolls On." *Spectator* 242, no. 7874 (9 June 1979): 8–9.

———. *The Polish August: The Self-Limiting Revolution.* New York: Viking Press, 1982.

———. "The Pope's New Europe." *Spectator* 242, no. 7875 (16 June 1979): 7–8.

Adelson, Józef. "W Polsce zwanej Ludowa." In *Najnowsze dzieje Żydów w Polsce,* edited by Jerzy Tomaszewski, 387–477. Warszawa: Wydawnictwo Naukowe WDN, 1993.

Adorno, Theodor W. *Eingriffe.* Frankfurt am Main: Suhrkamp, 1971.

Alexiev, Alex. "The Kremlin and the Vatican." *Orbis* 27, no. 3 (fall 1983): 554–65.

Ash, Timothy Garton. *The Polish Revolution: Solidarity.* New York: Charles Scribner's Sons, 1983.

Ashworth, Jaime. "The Iconography of Destruction: A Historical Portrait of the Auschwitz-Birkenau State Museum." Master's thesis, Jagiellonian University, 2001.

Assmann, Jan. "Kollektives Gedächtnis und kulturelle Identität." In *Kultur und Gedächtnis,* edited by Jan Assmann and Tonio Hölscher, 9–19. Frankfurt am Main: Suhrkamp, 1988.

Atkins, J. "Poland in 1968. Chronicle of Events." *Polish Review* 14, no. 1 (1969): 91–117.

August, Jochen. "Chancen und Aufgaben von Jugendbegegnung in Oświęcim." In

"Wie soll ich singen . . .": 10 Jahre Internationale Jugendbegegnungsstätte Ausch-witz, edited by Susanne Orth, 68–77. Berlin: Aktion Sühnezeichen Friedens-dienste, 1996.

Augustyn, O. *Za drutami obozu koncentracyjnego w Oświęcimiu.* Kraków: Powściągliwość i Praca,1945.

Avery, Maria R. "Preserving Memory at Auschwitz: A Study in Polish-Jewish His-torical Memory." Master's thesis, Central Connecticut State University, 1999.

Banas, Josef. *The Scapegoats: The Exodus of the Remnants of Polish Jewry.* London: Weidenfeld and Nicolson, 1979.

Bartoszewski, Władysław. "The Founding of the All-Polish Anti-Racist League in 1946." *Polin* 4 (1989): 243–54.

Bartoszewski, Władysław T. *The Convent at Auschwitz.* London: The Bowerdean Press, 1990.

Bartov, Omer. "An Idiot's Tale: Memories and Histories of the Holocaust." *Journal of Modern History* 67 (March 1995): 55–82.

Bauman, Zygmunt. *Modernity and the Holocaust.* Ithaca, N.Y.: Cornell University Press, 1989.

Bellah, Robert, et al. *Habits of the Heart: Individualism and Commitment in Ameri-can Life.* New York: Harper & Row, 1985.

Benzler, Susanne. "Die vollendete Sinnlosigkeit. Noch einmal: Auschwitz," *Vorgänge* 30, no. 113 (October 1991): 56–68.

Bernstein, Carl and Marco Politi. *His Holiness: John Paul II and the Hidden History of Our Time.* New York: Doubleday, 1996.

Bethell, Nicholas. *Gomułka: His Poland, His Communism.* New York: Holt, Rine-hart, and Winston, 1969.

Bingen, Dieter. "The Catholic Church as a Political Actor." In *Polish Politics: Edge of the Abyss,* edited by Jack Bielasiak and Maurice D. Simon, 212–40. New York: Praeger, 1984.

Blejwas, Stanislaus A. *Realism in Polish Politics: Warsaw Positivism and National Survival in Nineteenth-Century Poland.* New Haven: Yale Concilium on Inter-national and Area Studies, 1984.

Błoński, Jan. "The Poor Poles Look at the Ghetto." In *'My Brother's Keeper?': Re-cent Polish Debates on the Holocaust,* edited by Antony Polonsky, 34–48. Lon-don: Routledge, 1990.

Borodziej, Włodzimierz. "Polen und Juden im 20. Jahrhundert. Zum Fortleben von Stereotypen nach dem Holocaust." In *Polen nach dem Kommunismus,* edited by Erwin Oberländer, 71–79. Stuttgart: Fritz Steiner Verlag, 1993.

Borwicz, Michal. "Auschwitz 'Judenrein.'" In *Auschwitz selon Varsovie ou cham-bres à gaz 'déjudaïsées,'* edited by Michaı Borwicz and Joseph Weinberg, 1–15.

Paris: Association Indépendente des Anciens Déportés et Internés Juifs de France, 1970.

————. "Polish-Jewish Relations, 1944–1947." In *The Jews in Poland,* edited by Chimen Abramsky, et al., 190–198. Oxford: Basil Blackwell, 1986.

Borwicz, Michal and Joseph Weinberg, eds. *Auschwitz selon Varsovie ou chambres à gaz 'déjudaïsées.'* Paris: Association Indépendente des Anciens Déportés et Internés Juifs de France, 1970.

Brand, William, ed. *Thou Shalt Not Kill: Poles on Jedwabne.* Warsaw: Towarzystwo "Więź," 2001.

Bridgman, Jon. *The End of the Holocaust: The Liberation of the Camps.* Portland, Ore.: Areopagitica Press, 1990.

Brumberg, Abraham, ed. *Poland: Genesis of a Revolution.* New York: Random House, 1983.

Buszko, Józef, ed. *Auschwitz: Nazi Extermination Camp.* Warsaw: Interpress, 1985.

The Camp of Death. London: n.p., 1944.

The Camp of Disappearing Men: A Story of the Oświęcim Concentration Camp, Based on Reports from the Polish Underground Labor Movement. New York: n.p., 1944.

Carroll, James. "The Silence." *New Yorker* 73, no. 7 (7 April 1997): 52–68.

Central Commission for the Investigation of Nazi Crimes in Poland. *Concentration Camp Oświęcim.* Warszawa: Wydawnictwo Prawnicze, 1955.

Checinski, Michael. *Poland: Communism—Nationalism—Anti-Semitism.* New York: Karz-Cohl Publishing, 1982.

Chowaniec, Tadeusz. "Epilog." *Zeszyty Oświęcimskie* 7 (1963): 145–54.

Ciecwierz, Mieczysław. *Polityka prasowa 1944–1948.* Warszawa: Państwowe Wydawnictwo Naukowe, 1989.

Cieplak, Tadeusz. "John Paul II and Eastern Europe." *Nationalities Papers* 8, no. 2 (1980): 233–39.

Cole, Tim. *Selling the Holocaust: From Auschwitz to Schindler. How History Is Bought and Sold.* New York: Routledge, 1999.

Connerton, Paul. *How Societies Remember.* Cambridge: Cambridge University Press, 1989.

Coubard, Jacques. "Le comité international d'Auschwitz se réunit dans l'ancien camp de concentration." *L'Humanitié,* 30 January 1957.

Cyprian, Tadeusz. "Dlaczego nie zabijamy bez sądu?" *Życie Warszawy,* 8 March 1947.

Cyrankiewicz, Józef. "Oświęcim walczący." *Naprzód,* 24 June 1945.

Czech, Danuta. "Kalendarium der Ereignisse im Konzentrationslager Auschwitz-Birkenau." *Hefte von Auschwitz* 8 (1964): 47–109.

———. *Kalendarium der Ereignisse im Konzentrationslager Auschwitz-Birkenau, 1939–1945.* Reinbeck bei Hamburg: Rowohlt, 1989.

———. *Kalendarz wydarzeń w KL Auschwitz.* Oświęcim: Wydawnictwo Państwowego Muzeum w Oświęcimiu-Brzezince, 1992.

Davies, Norman. *God's Playground: A History of Poland.* 2 vols. New York: Columbia University Press, 1982.

———. *Heart of Europe: A Short History of Poland.* Oxford: Oxford University Press, 1986.

Dawidowicz, Lucy. *The Holocaust and the Historians.* Cambridge: Harvard University Press, 1982.

De Weydenthal, Jan B. *The Communists of Poland: An Historical Outline.* Stanford, Calif.: Hoover Institution Press, 1986.

Detlefsen, Wilhelm. "Nie wieder Auschwitz! Eine ungewöhnliche Reise durch Polen." *Die Kirche der Heimat. Evangelisch-lutherisches Gemeindeblatt in Schleswig-Holstein, Hamburg und Nordschleswig* 31, nr. 10 (2 May 1955).

Deutscher, Isaac. "Remnants of a Race," *Economist* (London), 12 January 1946, 15–16.

Dewar, Diana. *The Saint of Auschwitz: The Story of Maximilian Kolbe.* San Francisco: Harper and Row, 1982.

Długoborski, Wacław. "Obóz koncentracyjny Oświęcim-Brzezinka 1940–1945: fakty, problemy, kontrowersje." *Collectanea Theologica* 62, no. 2 (1992): 9–35.

Długoborski, Wacław and Franciszek Piper, eds. *Auschwitz, 1940–1945: Central Issues in the History of the Camp.* 5 vols. Oświęcim: Auschwitz-Birkenau State Museum, 2000.

———. *Auschwitz 1940–1945: Węzłowe zagadnienia z dziejów obozu.* 5 vols. Oświęcim: Wydawnictwo Państwowego Muzeum w Oświęcim-Brzezinka, 1995.

Długocki, Władysław. "Dyskutujemy dalej na temat: Czym ma być Oświęcim?" *Dziennik Polski,* 27 August 1947.

Dobroszycki, Lucjan. "Polska historiografia na temat Zagłady: Przegląd literatury i próba syntezy." In *Holocaust z perspektywy półwiecza: Pięćdziesiąta rocznica powstania w getcie Warszawskim* (materiały z konferencji zorganizowanej przez Żydowski Instytut Historiczny w dniach 29–31 marca 1993), edited by Daniel Grinberg and Paweł Szapiro, 177–87. Warszawa: Żydowski Instytut Historyczny, n.d.

———. "Restoring Jewish Life in Post-War Poland." *Soviet Jewish Affairs* 3, no. 2 (1973): 58–72.

Dohrmann, Rudolf. "Schritte der Versöhnung." *Zeichen* 12, no. 4 (December 1984): 4–5.

Doosry, Yasmin, ed. *Representations of Auschwitz: 50 Years of Photographs, Paintings, and Graphics/50 lat w fotografii, marlarstwie i grafice/50 Jahre Fotografie, Malerei und Grafik.* Oświęcim: Auschwitz-Birkenau State Museum, 1995.

Dunn, Dennis. "The Vatican's Ostpolitik: Past and Present." *Journal of International Affairs* 36, no. 2 (fall/winter 1982/1983): 247–55.

Dwork, Debórah and Robert Jan van Pelt. *Auschwitz 1270 to the Present.* New York: W. W. Norton, 1996.

———. "Reclaiming Auschwitz." In *Holocaust Remembrance: The Shapes of Memory,* edited by Geoffrey H. Hartman, 232–51. Oxford: Basil Blackwell, 1994.

Dybowski, Stefan. *Problemy rewolucji kulturalnej w Polsce Ludowej.* Warszawa: Ludowa Spółdzielnia Wydawnicza, 1953.

Dziękoński, Tadeusz. "Dymy nad Birkenau" *Życie Warszawy,* 6 January 1946.

Eisler, Jerzy. *Marzec 1968: Geneza, przebieg, konsekwencje.* Warszawa: Państwowe Wydawnictwo Naukowe, 1991.

Engel, David. "The Reconstruction of Jewish Communal Institutions in Postwar Poland: The Origins of the Central Committee of Polish Jews, 1944–1945." *Eastern European Politics and Societies* 10, no. 1 (1996): 85–107.

Ezrahi, Sidra DeKoven. "The Holocaust and the Shifting Boundaries of Art and History." *History and Memory* 1, no. 2 (fall/winter 1989): 77–97.

Feron, James. "150,000 at Auschwitz Pay Homage to Polish Martyr." *New York Times,* 16 November 1972.

Frank, Hans. *Das Diensttagebuch des deutschen Generalgouverners in Polen 1939–1945,* edited by Werner Präg and Wolfgang Jacobmeyer. Vol. 20, *Quellen und Darstellungen zur Zeitgeschichte.* Stuttgart: Deutsche Verlags-Anstalt, 1975.

Friedländer, Saul. Introduction to *Probing the Limits of Representation: Nazism and the "Final Solution,"* edited by Saul Friedländer, 1–21. Cambridge: Harvard University Press, 1992.

———. "Trauma, Memory, and Transference." In *Holocaust Remembrance: The Shapes of Memory,* edited by Geoffrey H. Hartman, 252–63. Oxford: Basil Blackwell, 1994.

———, ed. *Probing the Limits of Representation: Nazism and the "Final Solution."* Cambridge: Harvard University Press, 1992.

Friedman, Filip. *To jest Oświęcim!* Warszawa: Państwowe Wydawnictwo Literatury Politycznej, 1945.

Funkenstein, Amos. "Collective Memory and Historical Consciousness." *History and Memory* 1, no. 1 (spring/summer 1989): 5–26.

———. "History, Counterhistory, and Narrative." In *Probing the Limits of Representation: Nazism and the "Final Solution,"* edited by Saul Friedländer, 66–81. Cambridge: Harvard University Press, 1992.

Garliński, Józef. *Oświęcim walczący.* Warszawa: Volumen, 1992.

Gawalewicz, Adolf. "Czym ma być Oświęcim?" *Dziennik Polski,* 11 August 1947.

Gierek, Edward. *Edward Gierek: Przerwana dekada.* Warszawa: Wydawnictwo Fakt, 1990.

Gilbert, Martin. *The Holocaust: The Jewish Tragedy.* London: Collins, 1986.

Główna Komisja Badania Zbrodni Niemieckich w Polsce. *German Crimes in Poland.* Warszawa: Wydawnictwo Głównej Komisji Badania Zbrodni Niemieckich w Polsce, 1946.

Goban-Klas, Tomasz. "Pamięć podzielona—pamięć urażona: Oświęcim i Auschwitz w polskiej i żydowskiej pamięci zbiorowej." In *Europa po Auschwitz,* edited by Zdzisława Macha, 71–91. Kraków: Universitas, 1995.

Grinberg, Daniel and Paweł Szapiro, eds. *Holocaust z perspektywy półwiecza: Pięćdziesiąta rocznica powstania w getcie Warszawskim* (materiały z konferencji zorganizowanej przez Żydowski Instytut Historyczny w dniach 29–31 marca 1993). Warszawa: Żydowski Instytut Historyczny, n.d.

Gross, Jan T. *Neighbors: The Destruction of the Jewish Community in Jedwabne, Poland.* Princeton: Princeton University Press, 2001.

———. *Polish Society under German Occupation: The Generalgouvernement, 1939–1944.* Princeton: Princeton University Press, 1979.

———. *Sąsiedzi: Historia zagłady żydowskiego miasteczka.* Sejny: Pogranicze, 2000.

———. "A Tangled Web: Confronting Stereotypes Concerning Relations Between Poles, Germans, Jews, and Communists." In *The Politics of Retribution in Europe: World War II and its Aftermath,* edited by István Deák, Jan T. Gross, and Tony Judt, 74–129. Princeton: Princeton University Press, 2000.

Gutman, Yisrael. "Auschwitz—An Overview." In *Anatomy of the Auschwitz Death Camp,* edited by Yisrael Gutman and Michael Berenbaum, 5–33. Bloomington: Indiana University Press, 1994.

Gutman, Yisrael and Michael Berenbaum, eds. *Anatomy of the Auschwitz Death Camp.* Bloomington: Indiana University Press, 1994.

Gutman, Yisrael and Shmuel Krakowski. *Unequal Victims: Poles and Jews during World War II.* New York: Holocaust Library, 1986.

Halbwachs, Maurice. *Les Cadres sociaux de la mémoire.* Paris: Presses Universitaires de France, 1952.

———. *The Collective Memory.* Trans. Francis J. Ditter, Jr. and Vida Yazdi Ditter. New York: Harper and Row, 1980.

———. *On Collective Memory.* Chicago: University of Chicago Press, 1992.

Hartman, Geoffrey H. Introduction to *Holocaust Remembrance: The Shapes of Memory,* edited by Geoffrey H. Hartman, 1–22. Oxford: Basil Blackwell, 1994.

———, ed. *Holocaust Remembrance: The Shapes of Memory.* Oxford: Basil Blackwell, 1994.

———. *The Longest Shadow: In the Aftermath of the Holocaust.* Bloomington: Indiana University Press, 1996.

Hebblethwaite, Peter. "The Awakening of Poland." *Spectator* 242, no. 7874 (9 June 1979): 7.

Hebblethwaite, Peter and Ludwig Kaufmann. *John Paul II: A Pictorial Biography.* New York: McGraw-Hill, 1979.

Heimrich, Bernhard. "Block 13 in Auschwitz blieb geschlossen." *Frankfurter allgemeine Zeitung,* 19 December 1972.

Hein, Wincenty. "Czym jest Muzeum Oświęcimskie." *Dziennik Polski,* 19 November 1948.

———. "I tu obowiązuje realizm polityczny." *Dziennik Polski,* 11 August 1947.

Hennelowa, Józefa. "Problem Oświęcimia." *Tygodnik Powszechny,* 8 March 1970.

Heubner, Christoph. "Eine Vision wurde Realität." *Zeichen* 14, no. 3 (Fall 1986): 4.

Hilberg, Raul. "Auschwitz and the 'Final Solution.'" In *Anatomy of the Auschwitz Death Camp,* edited by Yisrael Gutman and Michael Berenbaum, 81–92. Bloomington: Indiana University Press, 1994.

———. *The Destruction of the European Jews.* 3 vols. New York: Holmes & Meier, 1985.

———. *Perpetrators, Victims, Bystanders: The Jewish Catastrophe, 1933–1945.* New York: HarperCollins, 1992.

Hirszowicz, Łukasz. "The Jewish Issue in Post-War Communist Politics." In *The Jews in Poland,* edited by Chimen Abramsky, Maciej Jachimczyk and Antony Polonsky, 199–208. Oxford: Basil Blackwell, 1986.

Hobsbawm, Eric and Terence Ranger, eds. *The Invention of Tradition.* Cambridge: Cambridge University Press, 1983.

———. "Introduction: Inventing Traditions." In *The Invention of Tradition,* edited by Eric Hobsbawm and Terence Ranger, 1–13. Cambridge: Cambridge University Press, 1983.

Hoensch, Jörg K. "Gegen 'Revisionismus' und 'Zionismus.' Gomułka, die 'Partisanen' und die Intellektuellen, 1964–1968." In *Zwischen Tauwetter und neuem Frost. Ostmitteleuropa 1956–1970,* edited by Hans Lemberg. Vol. 2 of *Reihe historischer und landeskundlicher Ostmitteleuropastudien.* Marburg: Herder, 1993.

———. *Geschichte Polens.* Stuttgart: Verlag Eugen Ulmer, 1983.

Hoensch, Jörg K. and Gerlind Nasarski. *Polen: 30 Jahre Volksdemokratie.* Hannover: Fackelträger-Verlag Schmidt-Küster, 1975.

Hoffman, Charles. *Gray Dawn: The Jews of Eastern Europe in the Post-Communist Era.* New York: HarperCollins Publishers, 1992.

Hołuj, Tadeusz. "Sprawa wiecznej pamięci." *Życie Literackie* 5, no. 44 (197) (30 October 1955): 3.

————. "Wielki konkurs." *Przegląd Kulturalny* 20 (15 May 1958): 1, 7.

Höss, Rudolf. *Commandant of Auschwitz: The Autobiography of Rudolf Hoess.* Cleveland: World Publishing, 1959.

Hruby, Suzanne. "The Church in Poland and Its Political Influence." *Journal of International Affairs* 36, no. 2 (fall/winter 1982/1983): 317–28.

Huener, Jonathan. "Antifascist Pilgrimage and Rehabilitation at Auschwitz: The Political Tourism of *Aktion Sühnezeichen* and *Sozialistische Jugend.*" *German Studies Review* 24, no. 3 (October 2001): 513–32.

————. "Geneza Państwowego Muzeum w Oświęcim-Brzezinka i jego koncepcja, 1945–1947." *Zeszyty Oświęcimskie* 23 (2002): 7–28.

————. "Pain, Prejudice, and the Legacy of the Shoah: On the Vexing Issue of Polish-Jewish Relations." In *Reflections on the Holocaust: Festschrift for Raul Hilberg on His Seventy-Fifth Birthday,* edited by Wolfgang Mieder and David Scrase, 39–62. Burlington: The Center for Holocaust Studies at the University of Vermont, 2001.

Hutton, Patrick. "Collective Memory and Collective Mentalities: The Halbwachs-Aries Connection." *Historical Reflections/Réflexions historiques* 15 (1988): 311–22.

————. *History as an Art of Memory.* Hanover, N.H.: University of Vermont/University Press of New England, 1993.

Institute of Jewish Affairs. *The Anti-Jewish Campaign in Present-Day Poland.* London: Institute of Jewish Affairs, 1968.

Irwin-Zarecka, Iwona. *Neutralizing Memory: The Jew in Contemporary Poland.* New Brunswick, N.J.: Transaction Publishers, 1989.

Iwaszko, Emeryka. "Wystawy Państwowego Muzeum w Oświęcimiu w latach 1945–1973." *Muzea Walki* 8 (1975): 215–19.

Iwaszko, Tadeusz. "Zakwaterowanie, odzież i wyżywienie więźniów." In *Auschwitz 1940–1945: Węzłowe zagadnienia z dziejów obozu,* edited by Wacław Długoborski and Franciszek Piper. Vol. 2. Oświęcim: Państwowe Muzeum Oświęcim-Brzezinka, 1995.

Jäckel, Eberhard. "Die elende Praxis der Untersteller: Das Einmalige der nationalsozialistische Verbrechen läßt sich nicht leugnen." *Die Zeit,* 12 September 1986.

Jagorski, Jerzy. "Żydzi, Polacy i zaminowane dusze." *Tygodnik Powszechny,* no. 26, 1945.

Jarnuszkiewiczowa, Jadwiga. "Z zgadnień rzeźby pomnikowej (po konkursie oświęcimskim)." *Przegląd Artystyczny* 7, no. 4 (April 1952): 24–26.

Jaworska, Janina. *"Nie wszystek umrę . . .": Twórczość plastyczna Polaków w hitlerowskich więzieniach i obozach koncentracyjnych, 1939–1945.* Warszawa: Książka i Wiedza, 1975.

Jay, Martin. "Of Plots, Witnesses, and Judgments." In *Probing the Limits of Repre-*

sentation: Nazism and the "Final Solution," edited by Saul Friedländer, 97–107. Cambridge: Harvard University Press, 1992.

John Paul II, Pope (Jan Paweł II, Papież). *Pielgrzymka do ojczyzny: Przemówienia i homilie Ojca Świętego Jana Pawła II.* Warszawa: Instytut Wydawniczy Pax, 1979.

———. *The Redeemer of Man—Redemptor Hominis.* Boston: Daughters of St. Paul, n.d.

———. *Return to Poland: The Collected Speeches of John Paul II.* London: Collins, 1979.

———. *Spiritual Pilgrimage: On Jews and Judaism, 1979–1995. Pope John Paul II.* New York: Crossroad, 1995.

Johnson, Paul. *John Paul II and the Catholic Restoration.* New York: St. Martin's Press, 1981.

Kamm, Henry. "Monument Unveiled for 4 Million Killed at Auschwitz Camp." *New York Times,* 17 April 1967.

Karpiński, Jakub. *Countdown: The Polish Upheavals of 1956, 1968, 1970, 1976, 1980. . . .* New York: Karz-Cohl Publishing, 1982.

———. "The Events of March 1968 and Their Historical Background." In *Proceedings of the Conference on Poles and Jews—Myth and Reality in the Historical Context,* edited by John S. Micgiel, Robert Scott, and Harold B. Segel, 508–14. New York: Columbia University Institute on East Central Europe, 1986.

———. *Poland since 1944: A Portrait of Years.* Boulder: Westview Press, 1995.

Kąkol, Kazimierz. *Spowiedź pogromcy kościoła.* Olsztyn: Ethos, 1994.

Keller, Stanisław. "Muzeum czasu nieluczkiego." In *Przewodnictwo turystyczne w Polsce,* 237–43. Warszawa-Kraków: Wydawnictwo PTTK Kraj, 1986.

Kenney, Padraic. *Rebuilding Poland: Workers and Communists, 1945–1950.* Ithaca: Cornell University Press, 1997.

Kersten, Krystyna. *The Establishment of Communist Rule in Poland, 1943–1948.* Berkeley: University of California Press, 1991.

———. *Między wyzwoleniem a zniewoleniem: Polska 1944–1956.* London: Aneks, 1993.

———. *Polacy. Żydzi. Komunizm. Anatomia Półprawd, 1939–68.* Warszawa: Niezależna Oficyna Wydawnicza, 1992.

———. "The Terror, 1949–1954." In *Stalinism in Poland, 1944–1956: Selected Papers from the Fifth World Congress of Central and East European Studies, Warsaw, 1995,* edited by A. Kemp-Welch, 78–94. New York: St. Martin's Press, 1999.

Kielar, Wieslaw. *Anus Mundi: 1,500 Days in Auschwitz/Birkenau.* New York: Times Books, 1980.

Kieta, Mieczysław. "Oświęcim 1959." *Wieści* 3, no. 4 (25 January 1959): 4.

Klukowski, Zygmunt. "How the Eviction of the Poles by the Germans from the Area of Zamość Was Carried Out." In *German Crimes in Poland,* edited by Główna Komisja Badania Zbrodni Niemickich w Polsce. Vol. 2. Warszawa: Wydawnictwo Głównej Komisji Badania Zbrodni Niemickich w Polsce, 1947.

Kłodziński, Stanisław. "Wytyczne dla Państwowego Muzeum w Oświęcimiu." *Wolni Ludzie,* May 1948.

Konopnicka, Maria. *Wybór Poezji.* Warszawa: n.p., 1953.

Korboński, Andrzej. "October 1956: Crisis of Legitimacy or Palace Revolution?" In *Poland's Permanent Revolution: People vs. Elites, 1956 to the Present,* edited by Jane Leftwich Curry and Luba Fajfer, 17–53. Washington, D.C.: American University Press, 1996.

Korboński, Stefan. *The Jews and the Poles in World War II.* New York: Hippocrene Books, 1989.

Kossak, Zofia. *Z otchlani: Wspomnienia z lagru.* Częstochowa: Wydawnictwo Księgarni Wł. Nagłowskiego, 1946.

Koźniewski, Kazimierz. "Drażliwy problem." *Przekrój,* no. 179 (12–18 September 1948): 3–4.

Krajewski, Stanisław. "The Controversy over Carmel at Auschwitz: A Personal Polish-Jewish Chronology." In *Memory Offended: The Auschwitz Convent Controversy,* edited by Carol Rittner and John K. Roth, 117–33. New York: Praeger, 1991.

Krzemiński, Adam. *Polen im 20. Jahrhundert: Ein historischer Essay.* München: Beck, 1993.

Kuby, Erich. "Zoppot, Weltbad ohne Welt." *Stern* 23, no. 35 (1970): 42–49.

Kulicz, Krzysztof. "Fałsz w encyklopedii." *Stolica,* 13 August 1967.

Kuncewicz, Piotr. *Leksykon polskich pisarzy współczesnych.* Warszawa: Graf-Punkt, 1995.

Kurek, Jalu. "Muzeum ludobójstwa." *Dziennik Polski,* 14 June 1947.

Lane, Arthur Bliss. *I Saw Poland Betrayed: An American Ambassador Reports to the American People.* Indianapolis: Bobbs-Merrill, 1948.

Laqueur, Walter, ed. *The Holocaust Encyclopedia.* New Haven: Yale University Press, 2001.

Lasota, Irena, ed. *40 Lat Władzy Komunistycznej w Polsce.* London: Polonia, 1986.

Le Corre, Dominique and Mark Sobotka, eds. *John Paul II in Poland—Jan Paweł II na Polskiej Ziemi.* Bagnolet: Le Corre, 1979.

Le Goff, Jacques. *History and Memory.* Trans. Steven Rendall and Elizabeth Clamen. New York: Columbia University Press, 1992.

Lechowicz, Włodzimierz. "Międzynarodowa współpraca organizacji kombatanckich." In *Zbowidowcy. Tradycje i zadania,* edited by Mikołaj Łomacki and

Jadwiga Szulc-Łyskowa, 366–71. Warszawa: Wydawnictwo ZG ZBoWiD/ Książka i Wiedza, 1969.

Lendvai, Paul. *Antisemitism without Jews.* New York: Doubleday, 1971.

Lepak, Keith John. *Prelude to Solidarity: Poland and the Politics of the Gierek Regime.* New York: Columbia University Press, 1988.

Leslie, R. F. *The History of Poland since 1863.* Cambridge: Cambridge University Press, 1980.

Levi, Primo. *The Drowned and the Saved.* New York: Simon & Schuster, 1988.

————. *If This Is a Man: Remembering Auschwitz.* New York: Simon & Schuster, 1986.

————. *Survival in Auschwitz.* New York: Simon & Schuster, 1996.

Lindsay, J. L. "It wasn't like this. . . ." *New Statesman and Nation* 36 (1948): 458–59.

Lipski, Jan Józef. *KOR: A History of the Workers' Defense Committee in Poland, 1976–1981.* Berkeley: University of California Press, 1985.

Lukas, Richard. *Forgotten Holocaust: The Poles under German Occupation, 1939– 1945.* New York: Hippocrene, 1997.

Lukowski, Jerzy. *Bibliografia obozu koncentracyjnego Oswięcim-Brzezinka 1945– 1969.* Warszawa: Międzynarodowy Komitet Oświęcimski, Sekretariat Generalny, 1968–1970.

Lukowski, Jerzy and Hubert Zawadzki. *A Concise History of Poland.* Cambridge: Cambridge University Press, 2001.

Luliński, Daniel. "Fałszowanie prawdy o Oświęcimiu w telewizji RFN." *Trybuna Ludu,* 28 January 1975.

Łeski, Czesław. "Jak pracuje nasz Związek." *Wolni Ludzie,* 1 May 1947.

Łomacki, Mikołaj and Jadwiga Szulc-Łyskowa, eds. *Zbowidowcy: Tradycje i zadania.* Warszawa: Wydawnictwo ZG ZBoWiD/Książka i Wiedza, 1969.

Łuczak, Czesław. "Szanse i trudności bilansu demograficznego Polski w latach 1939– 1945." *Dzieje Najnowsze* 26, no. 2 (1994): 9–14.

Madajczyk, Czesław. "Was *Generalplan Ost* Synchronous with the Final Solution?" In *The Shoah and the War,* edited by Asher Cohen, Yehoyakim Cochavi, and Yoav Gelber, 145–59. New York: Peter Lang, 1992.

Marcuse, Harold. *Legacies of Dachau: The Uses and Abuses of a Concentration Camp, 1933–2001.* Cambridge: Cambridge University Press, 2001.

Marguerite, Bernard. "Deux cent mille personnes ont assisté à l'inauguration du monument international élevé à la mémoire des victimes du fascisme." *Le Monde,* 18 April 1967.

Matz, Reinhard, ed. *Die unsichtbaren Lager: Das Verschwinden der Vergangenheit im Gedenken.* Reinbeck bei Hamburg: Rohwohlt, 1993.

Michlic-Coren, Joanna. "Anti-Jewish Violence in Poland, 1918–1939 and 1945–1947." *Polin* 13 (2000): 34–61.

Michnik, Adam. "Demonstration der Sehnsucht nach Freiheit." *Der Spiegel* 33, no. 23 (4 June 1979): 117.

———. *Letters from Prison and Other Essays.* Berkeley: University of California Press, 1985.

Middleton, David and Derek Edwards. Introduction to *Collective Remembering,* edited by David Middleton and Derek Edwards, 1–22. London: Sage, 1990.

Milton, Sybil and Ira Nowinski. In *Fitting Memory: The Art and Politics of Holocaust Memorials.* Detroit: Wayne State University Press, 1991.

Minerbi, Sergio I. "The Kidnapping of the Holocaust." *Jerusalem Post,* 25 August 1989.

Modras, Ronald. *The Catholic Church and Antisemitism: Poland, 1933–1939.* Amsterdam: Harwood Academic Publishers, 2000.

———. "Jews and Poles: Remembering at a Cemetery." In *Memory Offended: The Auschwitz Convent Controversy,* edited by Carol Rittner and John K. Roth, 53–61. New York: Praeger, 1991.

Myszkowski, Tadeusz. "Stare buty i okulary . . . w odpowiedzi na 'Drażliwy problem.'" *Wolni Ludzie,* 15 October 1948.

Naughton, James. "Ford, at Auschwitz, Cites 'Pursuit of Peace' for All." *New York Times,* 30 July 1975.

Nora, Pierre. "Between Memory and History: *Les Lieux de mémoire.*" Trans. Marc Roudebush. *Representations* 26 (1989): 7–25.

Novick, Peter. *The Holocaust in American Life.* Boston: Houghton Mifflin Company, 1999.

Nowak, Jan. "The Church in Poland." *Problems of Communism* 31, no. 1 (January–February 1982): 1–16.

Oberländer, Erwin, ed. *Polen nach dem Kommunismus.* Stuttgart: Fritz Steiner Verlag, 1993.

Obóz śmierci. Zbiór relacji z obozu w Oświęcimiu opublikowanych w kraju przez ruch mas pracujących Polski. London: n.p., 1943.

O'Brien, Darcy. *The Hidden Pope. The Untold Story of a Lifelong Friendship That Is Changing the Relationship between Catholics and Jews: The Personal Journey of John Paul II and Jerzy Kluger.* New York: Daybreak Books, 1998.

Ocalały (Anonymous Survivor). "Koniec Oświęcimia." *Życie Warszawy,* 1 March 1945.

Oleksy, Krystyna. "Historical Truth Comes First." *Pro Memoria* 7 (July 1997): 7–11.

Orth, Susanne, ed. *"Wie soll ich singen . . .": 10 Jahre Internationale Jugendbegegnungsstätte Auschwitz.* Berlin: Aktion Sühnezeichen Friedensdienste, 1996.

Ossowski, Stanisław. "Na tle wydarzeń Kieleckich." *Kuźnica* 38 (56) (1946): 1–4.

Ostańkowicz, Czesław. "Żeby ziemia nie parowała cyklonem." *Nowe Sygnały,* nr. 11 (23) (November 1957): 1, 3.

Pawełczyńska, Anna. *Values and Violence in Auschwitz: A Sociological Analysis.* Berkeley: University of California Press, 1979.

Pawlikowski, John T. "The Auschwitz Convent Controversy: Mutual Misperceptions." In *Memory Offended: The Auschwitz Convent Controversy,* edited by Carol Rittner and John K. Roth, 67–73. New York: Praeger, 1991.

"Pélerinage à Auschwitz." *Le Déporté* 80 (February-March 1955).

Penkower, Monty Noam. "Auschwitz, the Papacy, and Poland's 'Jewish Problem.'" *Midstream* 36, no. 6 (August/September 1990): 14–19.

Perkal, Jakub. "Polityczna historia prasy w Polsce w latach 1944–1984" In *40 lat władzy komunistycznej w Polsce,* edited by Irena Lasota, 151–85. London: Polonia, 1986.

Peters, Stanisław. "Oświęcim." *Dziennik Polski,* 4 April 1947.

Pilichowski, Czesław. "Pomóc i współnictwo." *Trybuna Ludu,* 25 May 1968.

———. "Straty i lokalizacja." *Trybuna Ludu,* 23 May 1968.

Piotrowski, Tadeusz. *Poland's Holocaust: Ethnic Strife, Collaboration with Occupying Forces, and Genocide in the Second Republic, 1918–1947.* Jefferson, N.C.: McFarland and Company, 1998.

Piórkowski, Jerzy. "Aus dem Notizbuch des Redakteurs." *Polen* 166 (June 1968): 2.

———. "Hoffnung." *Polen* 161 (January 1968): 14–18

Piper, Franciszek. *Auschwitz: How Many Perished? Jews, Poles, Gypsies. . . .* Kraków: n.p., 1992.

———. "Estimating the Number of Deportees to and Victims of the Auschwitz-Birkenau Camp." *Yad Vashem Studies* 21 (1991): 49–103.

———. "Gas Chambers and Crematoria." In *Anatomy of the Auschwitz Death Camp,* edited by Yisrael Gutman and Michael Berenbaum, 157–82. Bloomington: Indiana University Press, 1994.

———. "Liczba ofiar." In *Auschwitz 1940–1945: Węzłowe zagadnienia z dziejów obozu,* edited by Wacław Długoborski and Franciszek Piper. Vol. 3. Oświęcim: Wydawnictwo Państwowego Muzeum w Oświęcimiu, 1995.

———. "The Number of Victims." In *Anatomy of the Auschwitz Death Camp,* edited by Yisrael Gutman and Michael Berenbaum, 61–80. Bloomington: Indiana University Press, 1994.

———. "The Number of Victims at KL Auschwitz." In *Auschwitz: Nazi Death Camp,* edited by Franciszek Piper and Teresa Świebocka, 182–95. Oświęcim: Auschwitz-Birkenau State Museum, 1996.

———. "Zagłada." In *Auschwitz 1940–1945: Węzłowe zagadnienia z dziejów obozu,* edited by Wacław Długoborski and Franciszek Piper. Vol. 3. Oświęcim: Wydawnictwo Państwowego Muzeum w Oświęcimiu, 1995.

———. *Die Zahl der Opfer von Auschwitz aufgrund der Quellen und der Erträge der Forschung 1945 bis 1990.* Oświęcim: Verlag Staatliches Museum in Oświęcim, 1993.

Piper, Franciszek and Teresa Świebocka, eds. *Auschwitz: Nazi Death Camp.* Oświęcim: Auschwitz-Birkenau State Museum in Oświęcim, 1996.

Płuszka, Henryk. "Działalność Państwowego Muzeum w Oświęcimiu w XXX-leciu (1947–1977)." Master's thesis, Wyższa Szkoła Pedagogiczna im. Komisji Edukacji Narodowej, 1978.

Polonsky, Antony. "Beyond Condemnation, Apologetics, and Apologies: On the Complexity of Polish Behavior toward the Jews during the Second World War." In *The Fate of the European Jews, 1939–1945: Continuity or Contingency?* edited by Jonathan Frankel. Vol. 13, *Studies in Contemporary Jewry.* New York: Oxford University Press, 1997.

———, ed. *'My Brother's Keeper?': Recent Polish Debates on the Holocaust.* London: Routledge, 1990.

Polski Związek byłych Więźniów Politycznych. "14.VI.1947 R." In *Kalendarz b. więźnia politycznego na rok 1948,* edited by Polski Związek byłych Więźniów Politycznych, 120–23. Śl.-Dąbrowski: n.p., 1947.

Porter, Brian. *When Nationalism Began to Hate: Imagining Modern Politics in Nineteenth-Century Poland.* New York: Oxford University Press, 2000.

Pörzgen, Hermann. "Auschwitz, wie es heute ist: In dem ehemaligen Konzentrationslager." *Frankfurter allgemeine Zeitung,* 20 October 1956.

Przybysławski, Konstanty. "Jeszcze raz 'Drażliwy problem.'" *Tygodnik Powszechny,* 12 December 1948.

Ptakowski, Jerzy. *Oświęcim bez cenzury i bez legend.* London: Myśl Polska, 1985.

Putrament, Jerzy. "Notatki o Oświęcimiu." *Odrodzenie* 23 (6 June 1948): 3.

Radio Free Europe, Research and Analysis Department. *The Pope in Poland.* Munich: Radio Free Europe Research, 1979.

Raina, Peter. *Political Opposition in Poland, 1954–1977.* London: Poets and Painters Press, 1978.

Rajewski, Ludwik. "'Drażliwy problem' po raz czwarty." *Wolni Ludzie,* 15–30 November 1948.

———. "Oświęcim 14.6.1940–14.6.1947." *Wolni Ludzie,* 15 June 1947.

———. *Oświęcim w systemie RSHA.* Warszawa: E. Kuthan, 1946.

Rakowski, Mieczysław. "Interes nadrzędny." *Polityka* 33, no. 10 (10 March 1979): 1–2.

Randal, Jonathan. "Pavilion Honors Auschwitz Dead." *New York Times,* 22 April 1968.

Rawicz, Jerzy. "Oświęcim mobilizuje do walki." *Za Wolność i Lud,* 2 February 1952.

———. "W Oświęcimiu." *Trybuna Ludu,* 19 April 1955.

Rittner, Carol and John K. Roth, eds. *Memory Offended: The Auschwitz Convent Controversy.* New York: Praeger, 1991.

Ros, Jerzy. "Wyznanie wiary. Trzy razy Oświęcim." *Kurier Codzienny,* 19 June 1950.

Rousso, Henry. *The Vichy Syndrome: History and Memory in France since 1944.* Cambridge: Harvard University Press, 1991.

Rusinek, Kazimierz. "Hitlerowskie obozy koncentracyjne." *Polityka,* 11 November 1967.

Ryback, Timothy W. "Evidence of Evil." *New Yorker,* 15 November 1993, 68–81.

Santner, Eric. "History Beyond the Pleasure Principle: Some Thoughts on the Representation of Trauma." In *Probing the Limits of Representation: Nazism and the "Final Solution,"* edited by Saul Friedländer, 143–54. Cambridge: Harvard University Press, 1992.

Schatz, Jaff. *The Generation: The Rise and Fall of the Jewish Communists of Poland.* Berkeley: University of California Press, 1991.

Schmidt, Michael. *Die Falken in Berlin, Antifaschismus und Völkerverständigung: Jugendbegegnung durch Gedenkstättenfahrten, 1954–1959.* Berlin: Elefanten Press, 1987.

Segev, Tom. *The Seventh Million: The Israelis and the Holocaust.* Trans. Haim Watzman. New York: Hill and Wang, 1993.

Sehn, Jan. *Concentration Camp Oświęcim-Brzezinka.* Warszawa: Wydawnictwo Prawnicze, 1957, 1961.

Shneiderman, S. L. *Between Fear and Hope.* New York: Arco, 1947.

Siła-Nowicki, Władysław. "A Reply to Jan Błoński," in *'My Brother's Keeper?': Recent Polish Debates on the Holocaust,* edited by Antony Polonsky, 59–68. London: Routledge, 1990.

Skwarnicki, Marek. n.t. *Tygodnik Powszechny,* 17 June 1979.

Smolar, Alexander. "Jews as a Polish Problem." *Daedalus* 116, no. 2 (spring 1987): 41.

Smoleń, Kazimierz. "Blizko 4 miliony zwiedziło Muzeum." *Za Wolność i Lud,* January 1963, 15–16.

―――. "Działalność upowszechnieniowa Państwowego Muzeum w Oświęcimiu." *Biuletyn Towarzystwa Opieki nad Oświęcimiem* 1–2 (1987): 17–31.

―――. "Wystawy narodowe w Oświęcimiu." *Muzea Walki* 13 (1980): 53–59.

―――, ed. *From the History of KL Auschwitz.* Oświęcim: Państwowe Muzeum, 1976.

Sokorski, Włodzimierz. *Wspomnienie.* Warszawa: Krajowa Agencja Wydawnicza, 1990.

Spielmann, Jochen. "Entwürfe zur Sinngebung des Sinnlosen. Zu einer Theorie des Denkmals als Manifestation des 'kulturellen Gedächtnises': Der Wettbewerb für ein Denkmal für Auschwitz." Ph.D. diss., Freie Universität Berlin, 1990.

―――. "Museen, Orte, Eintrittszeiten." In *Die Unsichtbare Lager: Das Verschwinden der Vergangenheit im Gedenken,* edited by Reinhard Matz. Reinbeck bei Hamburg: Rowohlt, 1993.

Stachura, Peter. *Poland in the Twentieth Century.* New York: St. Martin's Press, 1999.

Stanisławski, Czesław and Wojciech Rawicz. "Podniosłe dni Oświęcimia: Otwarcie muzeum martyrologii polskiej." *Wolni Ludzi*, 1 July 1947.

Starr, Richard F. *Poland 1944–1962: The Sovietization of a Captive People.* New Orleans: Louisiana State University Press, 1962.

Steinlauf, Michael. *Bondage to the Dead: Poland and the Memory of the Holocaust.* Syracuse: Syracuse University Press, 1997.

Stola, Dariusz. *Kampania antysyjonistyczna w Polsce, 1967–1968.* Warszawa: Instytut Studiów Politycznych Polskiej Akademii Nauk, 2000.

Stowarzyszenie "Opieka nad Oświęcimiem." *Oświęcim-Brzezinka: KL Auschwitz-Birkenau.* Kraków: Stowarzyszenie "Opieka nad Oświęcimiem," 1948.

Strzelecka, Irena. "Budowa, rozbudowa oraz rozwój obozu i jego filii." In *Auschwitz 1940–1945: Węzłowe zagadnienia z dziejów obozu,* edited by Wacław Długoborski and Franciszek Piper. Vol. 1. Oświęcim: Wydawnictwo Państwowego Muzeum Oświęcim-Brzezinka, 1995.

Strzelecki, Andrzej. *Ewakuacja, likwidacja i wyzwolenie KL Auschwitz.* Oświęcim: Państwowe Muzeum w Oświęcimiu, 1982.

———. *Ostatnie dni obozu Auschwitz.* Oświęcim: Państwowe Muzeum Oświęcim-Brzezinka, 1995.

Symonowicz, Antoni. "Nazi Kampaign Polish Culture." In *1939–1945 War Losses in Poland,* edited by Roman Nurowski, 73–105. Poznań: Wydawnictwo Zachodnie, 1960.

Syrop, Konrad. *Spring in October: The Story of the Polish Revolution of 1956.* Westport, Conn.: Greenwood Press, 1976.

Szafar, Tadeusz. "Anti-Semitism: A Trusty Weapon." In *Poland: Genesis of a Revolution,* edited by Abraham Brumberg, 109–22. New York: Random House, 1983.

Szaynok, Bożena. *Pogrom Żydów w Kielcach 4 lipca 1946.* Warszawa: Wydawnictwo Bellona, 1992.

Szczepański, J. A. "Prawo narodu żydowskiego." *Dziennik Polski,* 19 April 1947.

Szczypiorski, Andrzej. "The Limits of Political Realism." *Survey* 24, no. 4 (109) (autumn 1979): 21–32.

———. *The Polish Ordeal: The View from Within.* London: Croom Helm, 1982.

Szmaglewska, Seweryna. *Dymy nad Birkenau.* Warszawa: Czytelnik, 1946.

———. *Smoke over Birkenau.* New York: Henry Holt, 1947.

Szulc, Tad. *Pope John Paul II: The Biography.* New York: Scribner, 1995.

Szurek, Jean-Charles. "Le Camp-musée d'Auschwitz." In *A l'Est, la mémoire retrouvée,* edited by Alain Brossat, et al., 535–65. Paris: Editions la Découverte, 1990

Szymański, Tadeusz. "Erfahrungen mit Jugendgruppen in der Gedenkstätte Auschwitz." *Internationale Schulbuchforschung. Zeitschrift des Georg-Eckert-Instituts* 6, no. 2 (1984): 159–63.

Świebocka, Teresa. "The Auschwitz-Birkenau Memorial and Museum: From Commemoration to Education." *Polin* 13 (2000): 290–99.

———. "Historia i współczesność dyskusji wokół strefy ochronnej byłego obozu." *Pro Memoria* 9 (June 1998): 115–19.

Świebocki, Henryk. "Ruch oporu." In *Auschwitz 1940–1945: Węzłowe zagadnienia z dziejów obozu,* edited by Wacław Długoborski and Franciszek Piper. Vol. 4. Oświęcim: Wydawnictwo Państwowego Muzeum w Oświęcimiu, 1995.

T. R. "Schemat organizacyjny Związku Bojowników." In *Zbowidowcy. Tradycje i zadania,* edited by Mikołaj Łomacki and Jadwiga Szulc-Łyskowa, 391–94. Warszawa: Wydawnictwo ZG ZBoWiD/Książka i Wiedza, 1969.

Tanay, Emanuel. "Auschwitz and Oświęcim: One Location, Two Memories." In *Memory Offended: The Auschwitz Convent Controversy,* edited by Carol Rittner and John K. Roth, 99–111. New York: Praeger, 1991.

Tomsky, Alexander. "John Paul II in Poland: Pilgrim of the Holy Spirit." *Religion in Communist Lands* 7, no. 3 (August 1979): 160–65.

Torańska, Teresa. *Them: Stalin's Polish Puppets.* New York: Harper and Row, 1987.

Turowicz, Jerzy. "Polish Reasons and Jewish Reasons." *Yad Vashem Studies* 19 (1988): 379–88.

"Ustawa z dnia 2 lipca 1947 r. o upamiętcieniu męczeństwa narodu polskiego i innych narodów w Oświęcimiu." *Dziennik Ustaw Rzeczypospolitej Polskiej* 52: 826–27.

Vinocur, John. "Pope Prays at Auschwitz: 'Only Peace!'" *New York Times,* 8 June 1979.

Walichnowski, Czesław. "Die Rolle der zionistischen Bewegung in der antikommunistischen Kampagne und der Rehabilitation der Bundesrepublik." *Polen* 6 (166) (June 1968): 17–22, 39–44.

Walicki, Andrzej. *Philosophy and Romantic Nationalism: The Case of Poland.* Oxford: Clarendon Press, 1982.

Wandycz, Piotr. "Historiography of the Countries of Eastern Europe: Poland." *American Historical Review* 97, no. 4 (October 1992): 1011–25.

Webber, Jonathan. *The Future of Auschwitz: Some Personal Reflections.* Oxford: Oxford Centre for Postgraduate Hebrew Studies, 1992.

Weeks, Theodore R. "Poles, Jews, and Russians, 1863–1914: The Death of the Ideal of Assimilation in the Kingdom of Poland." *Polin* 12 (1999): 242–56.

Weigel, George. *The Final Revolution: The Resistance Church and the Collapse of Communism.* New York: Oxford University Press, 1992.

Wellers, Georges. "Quelques impressions du pélerinage d'Auschwitz." *Le Déporté,* no. 5 (May 1967): 7.

White, Hayden. *The Content of the Form: Narrative Discourse and Historical Representation.* Baltimore: Johns Hopkins University Press, 1987.

———. "Historical Emplotment and the Problem of Truth." In *Probing the Limits* of Representation: Nazism and the "Final Solution," edited by Saul Friedländer, 37–53. Cambridge: Harvard University Press, 1992.

Wielka encyklopedia powszechna, 1966 ed. S.v. "Obozy koncentracyjne hitlerowskie."

Wieviorka, Annette. "On Testimony." In *Holocaust Remembrance: The Shapes of Memory,* edited by Geoffrey H. Hartman, 23–32. Oxford: Basil Blackwell, 1994.

Wilczur, Jacek. "Prawda obowiązek konieczność." *Za Wolność i Lud,* 1–15 September 1967.

Wilkanowicz, Stefan, et al. "Auschwitz po 50 latach. Czym był? Jakie ma dziś znaczenie?" *Znak* 42, no. 419–420 (April-May 1990).

Williams, George Huntston. *The Mind of John Paul II: Origins of His Thought and Action.* New York: The Seabury Press, 1981.

Wistrich, Robert S. *Antisemitism: The Longest Hatred.* New York: Pantheon, 1991.

———. "John Paul II on Jews and Judaism." *Partisan Review* 67, no. 1 (winter 2000): 100–111.

Wolanowski, Lucjan. "Ajschylos niczego nie widział—świeczka, która by zgasła ze wstydu. Dwa reportaże oświęcimskie, których wolałbym nigdy nie pisać." *Świat* 13 (1957): 8–9, 18.

Woycicki, Alfred. "Oświęcim, 14.VI.1940–14.VI.1947." *Dziennik Polski,* 11 June 1947.

Wożniakowska, Irena. "Tam było więcej śmierci niż chleba." *Dziennik Polski,* 4 March 1947.

Woźniczka, Zygmunt. "Z działalności polskiego i radzieckiego aparatu represji na Górnym Śląsku w 1945 roku." In *Obozy pracy przymusowej na Górnym Śląsku,* edited by Andrzej Topola, 51–76. Katowice: Wydawnictwo Uniwersytetu Śląskiego, 1994.

Wyka, Kazimierz. "Potęga ciemnoty potwierdzona." *Odrodzenie,* 23 September 1945, n.p.

Young, James E. "Jewish Memory in Poland." In *Holocaust Remembrance: The Shapes of Memory,* edited by Geoffrey H. Hartman, 215–31. Oxford: Basil Blackwell, 1994.

———. "Memory and Monument." In *Bitburg in Moral and Political Perspective,* edited by Geoffrey H. Hartman, 103–13. Bloomington: Indiana University Press, 1986.

———. *The Texture of Memory: Holocaust Memorials and Meaning.* New Haven: Yale University Press, 1993.

———. *Writing and Rewriting the Holocaust: Narrative and the Consequence of Interpretation.* Bloomington: Indiana University Press, 1980.

Zamoyski, Adam. *The Polish Way: A Thousand-Year History of the Poles and Their Culture.* New York: Hippocrene Books, 1994.

Zawodny, Janusz K. *Death in the Forest: The Story of the Katyn Forest Massacre.* Notre Dame, Ind.: Notre Dame University Press, 1962.

Zvielli, Alexander. "Jewish Pavilion Re-opens on Site of Auschwitz." *Jerusalem Post,* 18 April 1978.

———. "Poland Seen Warming to Israel." *Jerusalem Post,* 20 April 1978.

Żarski-Zajder, Władysław. *Martyrologia ludności Żydowskiej i pomoc społeczeństwa polskiego.* Warszawa: Związek Bojowników o Wolność i Demokrację, 1968.

Żaryn, Jan. "'Księża Patrioci'—geneza powstawania formacji duchownych katolickich." In *Polska 1944/45–1989: Studia i materiały,* edited by Krystyna Kersten, et al. Vol. 1, 123–49. Warszawa: Instytut Historii PAN, 1995.

Żółkiewski, Stefan. "O aktualnych dyskusjach literackich." *Nowe Drogi,* June 1955.

Żywulska, Krystyna. *Przeżyłam Oświęcim.* Warszawa: Wiedza, 1946.

Index

Page references in italics refer to numbered plates of illustrations appearing in the text after page 144 (e.g., *pl. 1*).

Acherson, Neil, 221

AK. *See* Home Army (AK)

Aktion Höss, 8

Aktion Sühnezeichen (Action Reconciliation), 189, 230–31, 241

All Saints' Day commemorations, 77, 91, 201, 204

American Joint Distribution Committee for the Aid of Jews, 43

anniversaries. *See* commemorative rituals/events

anti-Semitism, 3, 26, 39–41, 58, 76–77, 96, 102, 200, 202, 225, 237. *See also* "anti-Zionist campaign"

"anti-Zionist campaign," xix, 55, 146, 150, 169–84, 187, 189, 199, 232

archives. *See* documentary sources

Armia Krajowa (AK), 35–36

artistic representations, 51, 129–30

Ash, Timothy Garton, 287n83

Aufnahmegebäude (reception building/ hotel), 119, 191–92, 235

Auschwitz camp complex, xvi–xvii, 1, 45; administration of, 8; extent of, 4–8, 65, 136–37; housing/living conditions in, 11–12; killing operations at, 13, 15–20, 123–24; lands confiscated by Germans for, 5, 141; liberation of, viii, 18, 42–43, 60–61; origins of, 4–8; popular knowledge of, 42; prisoner experiences and, 8–14; survivors of, 20–21; victim statistics and, 19–20, 26, 42–45

Auschwitz I (postwar site), xv, xviii, 123–24, 136, 237, *pls. 1–2*; alternative uses for, 66; carnivalesque atmosphere of, 87–88, 138, 188–89, 192, 194; extent of, 118–19, *pl.*

34; as POW camp/internment center, 61; preservation/restoration/renovation of, 59–68, 70–71, 89, 119–20; thematic role of, 47, 71, 77–78, 80, 119, 123–24, 127, 132, 140, 242–44. *See also* commemorative rituals/events; State Museum Auschwitz-Birkenau

Baer, Richard, 8

Bakema, J. B., 156

Balicki, Zygmunt, 32, 86, 94

Bartoszewski, Władysław, 39–40, 188, 232

Bartoszewski, Władysław T., 47

Bełżec, 20, 23, 45, 180, 244

Benedicta of the Cross, Sister. *See* Stein, Edith

Benjamin, Walter, xxi

Berman, Jakub, 96, 275n14

Bierut, Bolesław, 83, 98, 110, 223, 275n14

Birkenau (Brzezinka) camp complex, 5–8; administration of, 11; killing operations at, 16–17, 123–24; Sector BII, 12, 139; women's camp and, 6, 72–73, 138–39, *pl. 23*

Birkenau (postwar site), 137–40, 192–93, *pls. 3, 11–12*; alternative uses for, 66; dismantling of, 61, 64–65, 71; extent of, 119, *pl. 35*; monuments in, xix, 117, 139–40, 145–47, 150–69, 192, 243, *pls. 20, 27–28*; neglect of, xv, xviii, 72–73, 77, 140, 186, 192–93, *pl. 12*; as POW camp/internment center, 61; preservation of, 61, 63, 120, 158; thematic role of, 123–24, 140, 193–94, 237, 242–44. *See also* commemorative rituals/events; State Museum Auschwitz-Birkenau

Blobel, Paul, 17

Błoński, Jan, 233
Boer War, 102
Bohr, Niels, 159
Borwicz, Michal, 168
Brandhuber, Jerzy, 67, 129, 150–52
Buna-Werke (IG Farben), 5–6, 61, 130
Buzek, Jerzy, 291n39

Camp Military Council, 134
Carmelite Convent controversy, xx, 30,
    217, 225, 234–39, *pl. 33*
Carter, Jimmy, 229
Casals, Pablo, 159
Casanova, Danielle, 135
Catholic Church. *See* Roman Catholic
    Church
cemeteries, xv, 34, 90
censorship, xviii, 85, 111, 122–23, 188, 236,
    264n67, 278n59
Central Commission for the Investigation
    of German [Hitlerite] Crimes in Po-
    land, 43, 45–47, 53–54, 71, 142
Central Committee of Jews in Poland
    (CKŻP), 43, 75, 102, *pl. 15*
Centre de Documentation Juive Contem-
    poraine (France), 196, 282n106
Chełmno/Kulmhof, 20, 45
Chlebowski, Jan, 80
Chowaniec, Tadeusz, xiii
Christian symbolism, xx, 30; cross, 33–34,
    70, 214–15, 241, *pl. 7*; crown of thorns, *pl.
    16*; "golgotha," 57, 186, 201, 217, 224–25,
    228; stations of the cross, 197
Churchill, Winston, 35
Ciecwierz, Mieczysław, 264n67
CKŻP. *See* Central Committee of Jews in
    Poland (CKŻP)
collaborationist activities, 41, 49–50, 174
Cominform, 82
commemorative rituals/events, xvi, xviii, 4,
    23, 27, 30, 37, 185, 191, 227–28, *pl. 25*; All
    Saints' Day as, 77, 91, 201, 204; Bolshe-
    vik Revolution as, 101; dedication of
    State Museum as, 32–34, 50, 57, 255n7,
    pls. 8–10; liberation anniversaries as, 79–
    81, 109, 112, 114–17, 143, 148, 153, 163–69,

191, 241, *pls. 20, 26*; March of the Living
    as, 241; political prisoner transportation
    and, 77; Roman Catholic Church and,
    98–99, 186, 200–25, *pls. 10, 32*; Warsaw
    Ghetto Uprising and, 54, 175, 196, 199;
    World War II anniversaries as, 230. *See
    also* demonstrations
Commission for the Investigation of Ger-
    man Crimes at Auschwitz, 43, 45, *pls. 4–5*
Committee of Antifascist Resistance
    Fighters (KdAW), 149, 176
communism: fall of, 25–26, 30, 187, 206–7,
    239; as Jewish conspiracy, 39–40, 76, 172
Communist Party of the Soviet Union
    (CPSU), 25, 82
Council for the Protection of Monuments
    of Struggle and Martyrdom, 32, 86, 160,
    265n4
Courthion, Pierre, 156
CPSU. *See* Communist Party of the Soviet
    Union (CPSU)
Crematorium I, 16, 70, 119, 123, 273n46, *pl. 6*
Crematorium II, 17–18, 127, *pl. 21*
Crematorium III, 153
Culture and Art, Ministry of: administra-
    tion of site and, 2, 60, 72, 80–81, 84–85,
    95, 106, 108, 112, 122, 141–42, 190–91, 194–
    95; Birkenau monument and, 146, 152,
    157–58; censorship and, 85; closing of
    site and, 91; conferences/commissions
    of, 71–76, 93–94, 196; "illegal" former
    prisoners' gathering and, 106; as official
    carrier of memory, 28; preservation/
    restoration/renovation of site and, 63–
    64, 71, 106, 109, 112, 143
Cyprian, Tadeusz, 46
Cyrankiewicz, Józef: administration of
    site and, 95, 142; Birkenau monument
    dedication and, 165; dedication of State
    Museum and, 32–33, 50, 255n7, *pls. 8–10*;
    1955 exhibition opening and, 116–17,
    272n18; Höss trial testimony of, 54;
    ouster of, 187; preservation of site and,
    62; Priests' Commission demonstration
    and, 98; PZbWP and, 263n52; as resis-
    tance hero, 135

Cywiński, Bohdan, 223
Czechoslovakia, 83, 177

Dachau, 42
Davies, Norman, 210
demonstrations, 25, 227; over Carmelite
    Convent, 236; Jewish victims, inclusion
    in, 216; participation in, 202; peace cam-
    paign (1950) and, 96–97; Priests' Com-
    mission and, 98–99; state sponsorship
    of, 30, 81, 83, 201, 241. *See also* commemo-
    rative rituals/events
Denmark, 195
departments, state. *See specific departments
    (e.g., Museums and Monuments of Pol-
    ish Martyrology, Department of)*
deportees, 18–19, 57, 90, 125–26, 251n13,
    252n28
Deutsche Reichsbahn (German Railway),
    130
De Weydenthal, Jan B., 111
documentary sources, 1–2, 20–21, 45–47, 51,
    112, 121, 141–43, 282n106
Dürrmeyer, Heinz, 135
Dybowski, Stanisław, 32

East Germany. *See* German Democratic
    Republic
Education, Ministry of, 43
Eichmann, Adolf, 16
Elina, Odette, 156
exhibitions, 4, 25, 30, 37, 227–28, 240, *pls. 13–
    15;* Block 4 (4a), 69–70, 75, 93, 101–2, 123–
    28, 138, 180, *pls. 7, 16, 21–22;* Block 5, 127–
    28; Block 6, 128–31; Block 7, 130–31, *pl. 23;*
    Block 11 (Block of Death), 16, 69, 75, 131–
    36, 273n46, *pl. 26;* Block 15, 71, 94, 101–2,
    121–23; Blocks 16–18, 71; Block 21, 92–93,
    101–3; Block 27/Martyrology and Strug-
    gle of the Jews, xix, 146, 170, 172, 176–83,
    186, 195–200, *pls. 29–31;* crimes against
    children, 164; 1955 installation, xix, 108–
    9, 113–14, 118–43, 185–86, 192, 284n22, *pls.
    21–24;* national, 71–72, 93, 147–48, 177,
    185, 196, 284n22; "New Laundry," 136–
    37, *pl. 24;* opening, 71–76, *pl. 7;* Polish

Nation's struggle and martyrdom, 190,
    192; POW labor and, 61; "Sauna," 240

fascists/fascism, xviii, 36, 55, 81, 86, 90–91,
    93–96, 100–101
Federal Republic of Germany. *See* Ger-
    many, Federal Republic of
Fédération Internationale des Anciens Pris-
    onniers Politiques (FIAPP), 32, 72, 97
Fiderkiewicz, Alfred, 61
Ford, Gerald, 190
former prisoners, 26, 42, 62, 66–68, 87, 105–
    6, 124
France, 38, 43, 82, 241
Frank, Hans, 54, 250n9, 259n70
freedom of religion, 37
freedom of the press, 37, 140, 236
Friedländer, Saul, 27, 289n5
Fritzsch, Karl, 16, 203
functionary prisoners, 4, 11, 13

Gajowniczck, Franciszek, 203, 213, 286n58
General Government, 4, 54, 250n9
Geneva Agreement (on Carmelite Con-
    vent), 236–37
German Democratic Republic: IAC and,
    149; "national exhibitions" of, 177, 196;
    relations with Poland, 95, 100, 137, 165,
    258n39
Germany: crimes of, 33, 43, 45, 51–52, 55–57,
    90, 100, 123; visitors to museum from re-
    united, 241. *See also* German Demo-
    cratic Republic; Germany, Federal
    Republic of; Hitlerites/Hitlerism
Germany, Federal Republic of, *pl. 19;* im-
    perialism and, 94–95, 100, 121–22; Inter-
    national Youth Meeting Center and,
    231; NATO and, 116, 149; *Ostpolitik* and,
    189, 286n69; relations with Poland, 121,
    137, 165; visitors to museum from, 189–
    90, 230–31
Gesing, Roman, 189
Gierek, Edward, 187–88, 205–6, 210, 222–23
Gilbert, Martin, 20
Giscard d'Estaing, Valéry, 190
Glemp, Józef, 237

Główna Komisja Badania Zbrodni Nie-mieckich [Hitlerowskich] w Polsce. *See* Central Commission for the Investigation of German [Hitlerite] Crimes in Poland
Gomułka, Władysław, 82–83, 95, 110, 143, 170–72, 187, 273n52
Great Britain, 38, 82, 100, 102, 241
Greiser, Artur, 54
Gross, Jan T., 2, 242, 256nn16, 18, 259n67, 285n49
Gumkowski, Janusz, 173
Gutman, Yisrael, 11
Gutt, Romuald, 156
Gypsies (Sinti and Roma), xiv, 6, 10, 13, 19, 94, 173, 193, 236, 239, 241, 251nn13, 24

Hagen, Wilhelm, 54
Halbwachs, Maurice, xviii, 24–25, 253n36
Hansen, Oskar, 157
Hartjenstein, Fritz, 8
Hein, Wincenty, 64, 69, 72, 85, 91, 104–5
Hermann-Göring-Werke, 8
heroes/heroism, Polish, 29, 59, 66–67, 85–86, 100, 109, 119, 162, 198. *See also* resistance movements; socialist heroes/heroism
Hilberg, Raul, 15, 54
Himmler, Heinrich, 4–5, 7, 15, 18, 53, 122
Hirszowicz, Łukasz, 171
history and historical narratives, xvi–xvii, 22–23, 26–28, 81, 89, 108, 223, 228–29
Hitler, Adolf, 15, 122, 179
Hitlerites/Hitlerism, xviii, 32, 34, 46, 52, 55–56, 93–94, 99–100, 120, 122, 162
Hoffman, Paweł, 104
Holocaust. *See* Shoah
Holocaust (television miniseries), 231
Holocaust Martyrs' and Heroes' Remembrance Authority. *See* Yad Vashem
Holocaust Memorial Council (U.S.), 229–31
Hołuj, Tadeusz: "illegal" former prisoners' gathering and, 105; Jewish exhibitions and, 124, 178, 196; museum management and, 112–13, 121–22, 140–41, 188, 191; resistance exhibit and, 92–94

Home Army (AK), 35–36
Höss, Rudolf, 4–5, 8, 15–18, 43, 46–47, 126
human rights and dignity, 208–9, 212–13, 220–22
Hungary, 8, 18, 83, 177
Hutton, Patrick, 24, 250n8

IAC. *See* International Auschwitz Committee (IAC)
identity, Polish national, 47, 52, 56, 58, 86, 197, 201, 213, 225, 228, 235. *See also* nationalism, Polish
IG Farben-Industrie, 5, 8, 101–2, 130
imperialism, xviii, 81, 100, 102, 116–17, 121–22, 137, 180
institutionalization of memory, xviii, 22, 28
instrumentalization of memory, xiv, xviii, 29–30, 80–81, 92, 108, 113, 228
International Auschwitz Committee (IAC), 145–50; "anti-Zionist campaign" and, 26, 150, 170, 174–76; Birkenau monument and, xix, 147, 150–64; funding and, 114, 143, 158–60; Jewish exhibition and, 177, 196; liberation anniversaries and, 112, 114, 148; museum management and, xix, 2, 145–50, 183, 189; ZBoWiD and, 149–50, 174–75, 275n10
International Auschwitz Council, 291n39
International Council of the Auschwitz-Birkenau State Museum, 239
International Federation of Former Political Prisoners. *See* Fédération Internationale des Anciens Prisonniers Politiques (FIAPP)
internationalization of memory, xix, 48, 72, 93, 114, 116–17, 145–46, 185, 195, 221–22
International Youth Meeting Center, Oświęcim, 231
Israel, xix, 171–72, 177–78, 178, 199–200, 230–31, 241
Italy, 241
Iwaszko, Emeryka, 196

Jäckel, Eberhard, 252n24
Jagiełło, Kostek, 135
Jay, Martin, 228

Jedwabne, 2, 242, 285n49
Jewish Historical Documentary Commission, 43
Jewish Historical Institute (Warsaw), 71, 142, 196
Jews: anti-Semitism and, 3, 26, 39–41, 58, 76–77, 96, 102, 200, 202, 225, 237; "anti-Zionist campaign" and, xix, 55, 146, 150, 169–84, 187, 189, 199, 232; as collaborators, 174; as deportees, 16, 20, 57, 251n13, 251n24; exhibition on "Martyrology and Struggle of the," xix, 146, 170, 172, 176–83, 186, 195–200, *pls. 29–31;* extermination of, at Auschwitz, xiv, xvi, 13–20, 26–27, 43–45, 95–96, 123, 125–26, 173, 182, 251n13; food parcels and, 251n20; Hungarian, 8, 18; pope's visit and, 216–19; as prisoners, 9–10, 13, 20; relations with Poles, 39, 47, 146, 231–39; resistance efforts of, 96; *Sonderkommando* and, 17, 261n17; terminology for, 5; as visitors to museum, 15, 230–31, 241; Western indifference to plight of, 180, 198. *See also* Shoah
John XXIII, pope, 221, 286n69
John Paul II, pope, xx, 202; election of, impact in Poland, 205–6; Jewish suffering and, 205, 216–19; *Redemptor Hominis,* 208–9, 220; visit to Poland by (1979), 26, 30, 186–87, 209–25, 232, 238, *pls. 32*

Kąkol, Kazimierz, 213
Kania, Stanisław, 219
Katyn Massacre, 90
KdAW. *See* Committee of Antifascist Resistance Fighters (KdAW)
Kenney, Padraic, 37
Kersten, Krystyna, 37, 255n13
Kieta, Mieczysław, 142, 175
Kłodziński, Stanisław, 113, 142
Kolbe, Maksymilian, 132, 186, 202–5, 208, 213–16, 220, 224–25, 241
Komitee der antifaschistischen Widerstandskämpfer in der DDR (KdAW), 149, 176
Kommandatur (camp command headquarters), 235, 238

Korczak, Janusz, 199
Korea, 103, 121
Korzycki, Antoni, 97
Kossak, Zofia, 73
Kościelniak, Mieczysław, 130
Koźniewski, Kazimierz, 88–91
Kraków Club of Catholic Intelligentsia, 188
Kramer, Joseph, 46
Król, John, 203, 213
Kruger, Friedrich Wilhelm, 259n70
Krupp, 8
Kuby, Erich, 189

labor camps, 7–8, 84, 90
Lafuente, Julio, 157
Lagererweiterung (housing/barracks), 65, 119, 235
lands, confiscation/reclamation of, 5, 40, 64, 143
Langbein, Hermann, 149–150
Lanzmann, Claude, 232
Le Goff, Jacques, 23
Lendvai, Paul, 275n10
Levi, Primo, 10–12, 174
Liebehenschel, Arthur, 8
Lipski, Jan Józef, 206, 210, 232
looters, 61, 63–64, 67–68, 71
Lublin Committee, 35–36

Macharski, Franciszek, 235, 237
Maidanck, 45
Mały Dziennik (newspaper), 202
March of the Living commemorations, 241
Marshall Plan, 82
martyrdom/martyrology, Polish, xiv, xvii, 2–3, 29, 34–35, 38–39, 42, 47–58, 82, 130, 195, 228; anti-Semitism and, 76; "base camp" as symbol of, 71; Birkenau monument and, 162; Christian symbolism and, 33–34, 70, 214–15, *pls. 7, 16;* criticisms of, 85; pope's visit and, 213–25
Matysiak, Henryk, 99
Mauriac, François, 159
Mazowiecki, Tadeusz, 239
media, 42; censorship and, 111, 236, 264n67; as cultural carrier of memory, 27–28;

media (*cont.*)
  freedom of the press and, 37, 140; Hit-
    lerism and, 55–56; internationalization
    and, 48, 114, 189, 221–22; looting of site
    in, 63; war crimes trials and, 46–47
memorial narratives. *See* history and historical narratives
memory, xiv, xvi, 21–31, 81, 228–29; carriers/
  vectors of, 27–29, 42, 110, 146, 183–84,
  227–28, 241; institutionalization of, xviii,
  22, 28; instrumentalization of, xiv, xviii,
  29–30, 80–81, 92, 108, 113, 228; internationalization of, xix, 48, 72, 93, 114, 116–
  17, 145–46, 185, 195, 221–22; social frameworks of, xiv, 24–26, 108, 110, 205, 225,
  228–29, 232, 238, 241, 243
Michnik, Adam, 211
Mickiewicz, Adam, 49
Mikołajczyk, Stanisław, 35–36
ministries, state. *See specific ministries (e.g.,
  Education, Ministry of)*
Moczar, Mieczysław, 150, 170–72, 187
Monowitz, 6–8, 10, 12, 61, 67, 119, 130
monuments, 3–4, 23, 25, 27, 51, 152–53, *pl. 20;*
  Monument of the Fallen, 117, 139, 153;
  Monument to the Victims of Fascism
  (1967 Birkenau Monument), xix, 145–47,
  150–69, 192, 243, *pls. 27–28*
Moore, Henry, 156–57
Motyka, Lucjan, 76–77, 90, 182
Muselmänner, 14
Museums and Monuments of Polish Martyr-
  ology, Department of, 50–52, 55, 265n4

national communism, 110, 143
National Defense, Ministry of, 61
nationalism, Polish, 48–49, 83, 99–100, 146,
  197, 212, 219–20. *See also* identity, Polish
  national
National Socialism/Socialists, 55, 93–94, 116;
  racist ideology of, 5, 11, 13, 58, 77, 122
NATO. *See* North Atlantic Treaty Orga-
  nization (NATO)
Nazis. *See* National Socialism/Socialists
Neuengamme, 23
"New Laundry," 136–37, *pl. 24*

Nora, Pierre, 22–23
Normand, Marie, 115–16
North Atlantic Treaty Organization
  (NATO), 95, 116, 121, 149
Nowak, Jan, 210
Nürnberg Tribunal, 42, 46, 125

Office for the Liquidation of German
  Property, 65–66
Ostańkowicz, Czesław, 141
Ostpolitik, 189, 286n69
Oświęcim (Auschwitz), 4, 32
Oświęcim zaorać initiative (plowing-
  under of Auschwitz), 81–82, 86–92, 104,
  109

Pacem in terris (papal encyclical), 221
Patriot Priests, 97–98, 201
Paul VI, pope, 286n69
Penderecki, Krzysztof, 164
Perugini, Giuseppe, 156
Pilichowski, Czesław, 173–74
Piper, Franciszek, 13, 19, 258n41
PKWN. *See* Polish Committee of National Liberation (PKWN)
Poland: church-state relations in, 110, 170,
  188, 200–201, 207–12; collaborationist
  government, lack of, in, 41, 49–50; collectivization in, 83–84; cultural policy
  in, 109–11, 187–88; destalinization in,
  108–17; East German relations with,
  258n39; economic/social conditions of,
  35–42, 38, 49–50, 82–84, 110–11, 169–72,
  187–88, 193, 206–8; nationalism in, 48–49,
  83, 99–100, 146, 197, 212, 219–20; Oder-
  Neisse issue and, 56–57, 190; politics in,
  35–37, 82–86, 187–88, 206–7; security apparatus of, 36, 39–40
Poles: extermination of, 19, 29, 43, 44, 53–55,
  57, 173, 239; heroism of, 29, 59, 66–67, 85–
  86, 100, 109, 119, 162, 198; martyrdom/
  martyrology of, xiv, xvii, 2–3, 29, 34–35,
  38–39, 42, 47–58, 70–71, 76, 82, 85, 130, 146,
  162, 195, 228; national identity of, 47, 52,
  56, 58, 86, 197, 201, 213, 225, 228, 235; as
  prisoners, 10, 13; relations with Jews, 39,

47, 146, 231–39; Shoah, complicity in, 2, 199–200, 233–34; terminology for, 5

Polish Committee of National Liberation (PKWN), 35–36

Polish Institute of National Remembrance, 43

Polish-Jewish relations. *See* Poles: relations with Jews

"Polish October" (1956), 110, 169–70, 273n52

Polish People's Party (PSL), 35

Polish Socialist Party (PPS), 83

Polish Union of Former Political Prisoners (PZbWP), 62, 71, 75, 96

Polish United Workers' Party (PZPR): administration of site and, 2, 25, 84, 92, 95, 99–101, 103–6, 111–13, 122–24, 141–42, 189–94; anti-Semitism and, 96, 170–71; censorship and, 122–23; liberation anniversaries and, 79, 115; Roman Catholic Church and, 201, 207

Polish Workers' Party (PPR), 35–37, 82–83, 88, 90–91

political oppression, 36, 83, 84, 110

political prisoners, xiv, 4, 45, 47, 77

Polska Partia Robotnicza. *See* Polish Workers' Party (PPR)

Polska Partia Socjalistyczna (PPS). *See* Polish Socialist party (PPS)

Polska Zjednoczona Partia Robotnicza. *See* Polish United Workers' Party (PZPR)

Polski Komitet Wyzwolenia Narodowego (PKWN), 35–36

Polski Związek byłych Więźniów Politycznych. *See* Polish Union of Former Political Prisoners (PZbWP)

Porter, Brian, 49

Pöragen, Hermann, 118, 119

Potsdam Conference, 38, 136, 255n13

PPR. *See* Polish Workers' Party (PPR)

PPS. *See* Polish Socialist Party (PPS)

President's Commission on the Holocaust (U.S.), 229

Priests' Commission (ZBoWiD), 98–99

prisoners: former, 26, 42, 62, 66–68, 87, 105–6, 124; functionary, 4, 11, 13; registered, 9,

13, 18–19, 124, 155, 193, 251n20; solidarity among, 11, 14, 32, 67, 134, 146, 155, 180; of war, xiv, 5–6, 10, 13, 19, 43, 45, 47, 61, 124, 219, 251n20

prisoners of war: German, 61; Soviet, xiv, 5–6, 10, 13, 19, 43, 45, 47, 124, 219, 251n20

propaganda, xiv, 25, 30, 81, 174

property, confiscation/reclamation of, 5, 40, 64–65, 127–28, 143

Provisional Government of National Unity (Poland), 35–36

PSL. *See* Polish People's Party (PSL)

Public Security, Ministry of, 84

Putrament, Jerzy, 86–88, 90–91

PZbWP. *See* Polish Union of Former Political Prisoners (PZbWP)

PZPR. *See* Polish United Workers' Party (PZPR)

racist ideology, Nazi, 5, 11, 13, 58, 77, 122

Rajewski, Ludwik, 73–74, 263n52

Rajk, László, 83

Rakowski, Mieczysław, 209

Ratzinger, Joseph, 213

Red Army. *See* Soviet Army

Redemptor Hominis (papal encyclical), 208–9, 220

registered prisoners, 9, 13, 18–19, 124, 155, 193, 251n20

Reich Security Main Office (RSHA), xvii, 17

Rek, Tadeusz, 263n52

religious symbolism. *See* Christian symbolism

resistance movements, xiv, 42, 50, 93, 124, 133–36, 228; among prisoners, 14, 92, 101, 115–16, 155; Jewish, 96; "national exhibitions" on, 177

Rijksinstitut Voor Oorlags Documentatie (Netherlands), 196

Rokossovsky, Konstanty, 83, 95

Roman Catholic Church: All Saints' Day commemorations and, 77, 91, 201, 204; Carmelite Convent controversy and, xx, 30, 217, 225, 234–39, *pl. 33;* church-state relations and, 110, 170, 188, 200–201,

Roman Catholic Church (*cont.*)
207–12; commemorative events and, 98–
99, 186, 200–25, *pls. 10, 32;* human rights/
dignity and, 208–9, 212–13, 220–22;
Kolbe and, 132, 186, 202–5, 208, 213–16,
220, 224–25, 241; Patriot Priests and, 97–
98, 201; PZPR and, 207; ZBoWiD and,
97–99. *See also* John Paul II, pope
Roosevelt, Franklin D., 35
Rosenberg, Alfred, 77
Rousso, Henry, 27–28, 183, 253n36
Rusinek, Kazimierz, 166, 173, 175, 177–78

Sachsenhausen, 4
"Sauna," 139–40, 240
Scheel, Walter, 190
Schütz, Klaus, 190
Schwarz, Heinrich, 8
Sector BI. *See* Women's Camp (Sector BI)
Sector BII, 12, 139
security apparatus, Polish, 36, 39–40, 84.
See also political oppression
Security Service (UB), 110–11
SED. *See* Socialist Unity Party of Ger-
many (SED)
Sehn, Jan, 113, 142, *pl. 5*
Shamir, Yitzhak, 237
Shneiderman, S. L., 40
Shoah, xviii–xix, 3, 239; Auschwitz as sym-
bol of, 15, 47, 53, 80, 230–31, 238; Car-
melite Convent controversy and, 235–
36; marginalization of, xiv, xvi, xviii–
xix, 29, 31, 35, 44–45, 53, 58, 74–78, 95–96,
102, 123–24, 126, 146, 155, 161–62, 166–70,
172–74, 177–83, 193, 216–17, 228, 243; Pol-
ish complicity in, 2, 199–200, 233–34
Shoah (film), 232–33
Siemens (firm), 8, 130
Siła-Nowicki, Władysław, 234
Siqueiros, Alfaro, 275n14
Siwek, Władysław, 129–30
Six-Day War (1967), xix, 171–72, 177, 199,
279n71
Skwarnicki, Marek, 210, 215–16
Slánsky, Rudolf, 83
Smoleń, Kazimierz: Birkenau monument

and, 153; closing of site and, 88, 90,
270n75; 1955 exhibition opening and,
272n18; "illegal" former prisoners' gathering and, 105; marginalization of Jewish experience and, 76; museum
management and, 69, 107, 122, 141–43,
190, 271n13; pope's visit and, 213; preser-
vation/renovation of site and, 59, 113
Sobibór, 20, 45, 180
socialism, 52, 55, 83
socialist heroes/heroism, xiv, 81, 132, 243
Socialist Unity Party of Germany (SED),
94
Sokorski, Włodzimierz, 275n14
solidarity, prisoner, 11, 14, 32, 67, 134, 146,
155, 180
Solidarity movement, 207, 210, 223, 232
Sonderkommando, 17–18, 261n17
Sonderkommando revolt (1944), 96, 101
Soviet Army, 20, 36, 43, 60–61, 83, 136, 212,
219, *pl. 6*
Soviet Union, 29–30, 38, 42–43, 82, 90, 177,
196. *See also* prisoners of war: Soviet;
Stalinism
Sozialistische Einheitspartei Deutschlands
(SED), 94
Sozialistische Jugend (Socialist Youth), 189
Spielmann, Jochen, 154–55, 163
Stalin, Joseph, 35, 37, 83, 96, 121
Stalinism, xviii, 26, 37, 80–86, 95, 96, 105–6,
108, 172, *pls. 17–19*
Stanisław, Saint, 209
State Museum Auschwitz-Birkenau, xv–
xvi, 21, 60, 69–78; alternative uses for,
xx, 30, 66, 81–82, 90–92, 104, 148, 241; archives of, 1–2, 141–43; censorship and,
xviii, 85, 122–23, 278n59; commissions
on, 42–43, 45–47, 53–54, 85–86, 99–101,
122, 124, 142, 153, 191–93, 196, 239; dedication of, 32–34, 50, 57, 60, 255n7, *pls. 8–10;*
extent of, 23, 118–19, 262n27, *pls. 34–35;*
former prisoners and, 62, 67–68, 87, 105–
6, 124, 142; funding of, 66, 107, 114, 141,
143, 148, 190; naming of, 247n2; as official
carrier of memory, 28–29; organizational plans for, 62, 71–76, 85–86, 93–94,

99–101, 107, 191–93, 239; pedagogical role of, xv, 27, 85, 100, 143, 188, 193–94; political role of, xviii–xx, 84–86, 88, 99–106, 150, 220–25, *pls. 17–19;* preservation/restoration/renovation of, 89, 101, 106, 109, 112, 114, 142–43, 148, 158, 193; proprietorship of, xx, 25, 30, 225; tour guides for, 62, 68, 87; visitors to, 15, 77, 91, 104–5, 114, 127, 140, 143, 164, 177, 185, 189–90, 192, 195–96, 200, 202, 214, 230–31, 241, 283n9; as UNESCO World Heritage site, 148, 230. *See also* commemorative rituals/events; exhibitions
Stein, Edith, 216–17, 220, 225
Steinlauf, Michael, 3, 40, 187, 232, 236, 289n113, 290n10
Stockholm Appeal, 96–97
Strzelecki, Andrzej, 44
Stutthof, 45
Światkowski, Henryk, 263n52
Światło, Józef, 111
Świerczyny, Benka, 150
Szczypiorski, Andrzej, 171, 178, 181, 210, 271n6
Szmaglewska, Seweryna, 73
Szymańska, Krystyna, 65–66
Szymański, Tadeusz, 68

Targosz, Franciszek, 67, 105–6
terror. *See* political oppression
Theatergebäude (theater/warehouse/convent), 235, *pl. 33*
Theresienstadt, 6
Towiański, Andrzej, 222
Treblinka, 20, 45, 180
Truman Doctrine, 82
Trybuna Ludu (PZPR organ), 174, 194

UB. *See* Security Service (UB)
UNESCO, 148, 230, 235
Union of Fighters for Freedom and Democracy (ZBoWiD), 2, 96–99, 103, 106, 109, 149–50, 174–75, 177–78
Union of Polish Patriots (ZPP), 35
United States: imperialism of, 81, 100, 102, 116–17, 121, 137; indifference to Jewish

plight in, 180, 198; Soviet Union relations with, 82; visitors to museum from, 230–31, 241
Universal Declaration of Human Rights (United Nations), 221
Urząd Bezpieczeństwa (UB), 110–11
Urząd Likwidacyjny, 65–66

Vitale, Maurizio, 157
Volksdeutsche, 61

Waitz, Robert, 162, 166–67, 175–76, 277n48, 278n59, 282n106
Waldheim, Kurt, 190
Walichnowski, Tadeusz, 171
Wall of Death, 15, 135–36, 214, *pl. 26*
war crimes, prosecution of, 42, 45–47, 56, 125, 165
Warsaw Ghetto Uprising (1943), 54, 175, 196, 199
Warsaw Uprising (1944), 36, 49
Wąsowicz, Tadeusz, 62, 66–68, 100, 135
Webber, Jonathan, 58, 290n15
Wehner, Herbert, 190
Weiss, Avraham, 236, 291n36
West Germany. *See* Germany, Federal Republic of
Wieczorek, Janusz, 197–98
Wielka Encyklopedia Powszechna, 173
Wiernik, Stefan, 104, 141
Wiesel, Elie, 229
Wieviorka, Annette, 253n35
Wistrich, Robert, 218
Włodkowic, Paweł, 221
Wojtyła, Karol, 203, 207. *See also* John Paul II, pope
Wolken, Otto, *pl. 5*
Wolni Ludzie (PZbWP organ), 71, 75
Women's Camp (Sector BI), 6, 72–73, 138–39, *pl. 23*
World Heritage List (UNESCO), 148, 230
World Jewish Congress, 180, 196
World Organization of Jewish Fighters, Partisans, and Camp Prisoners, 196
Woycicki, Alfred, 72–73
Wright, John Joseph, 203

Wroński, Stanisław, 213
Wyka, Kazimierz, 41
Wyszyński, Stefan, 203–4, 208

Yad Vashem, 196, 198–99, 282n106
Yalta Conference, 35, 38
Young, James, 3, 156, 162–63, 235
Yugoslavia, 43, 82, 97

Zaborowski, Jan, 178
Zamoyski, August, 156
ZBoWiD. *See* Union of Fighters for Free-
dom and Democracy (ZBoWiD)

Zeszyty Oświęcimskie (Auschwitz Note-
books), 143
Zionism, 180
ZPP. *See* Union of Polish Patriots (ZPP)
Związek Bojowników o Wolność i
Demokrację. *See* Union of Fighters for
Freedom and Democracy (ZBoWiD)
Związek Patriotów Polskich (ZPP), 35
Zyklon-B, 16, 101, 130, 181, 235
Złobnicki, Ałdam, 65
Żółkiewski, Stefan, 111
"żydokomuna," 39–40, 76, 172
Żywulska, Krystyna, 73